Elvis Presley's Twin, Jesse Garon

**THE RECORDS SHOW HE DIED...
BUT DID HE?**

Stan Knight

PublishAmerica
Baltimore

© 2002 by Stan Knight.
All rights reserved. No part of this book may be reproduced, stored in a retrieval system or transmitted in any form or by any means without the prior written permission of the publishers, except by a reviewer who may quote brief passages in a review to be printed in a newspaper, magazine or journal.

First printing

ISBN: 1-4137-3715-3
PUBLISHED BY PUBLISHAMERICA, LLLP
www.publishamerica.com
Baltimore

Printed in the United States of America

In loving memory of Annie Tompkins and Gene Goe.

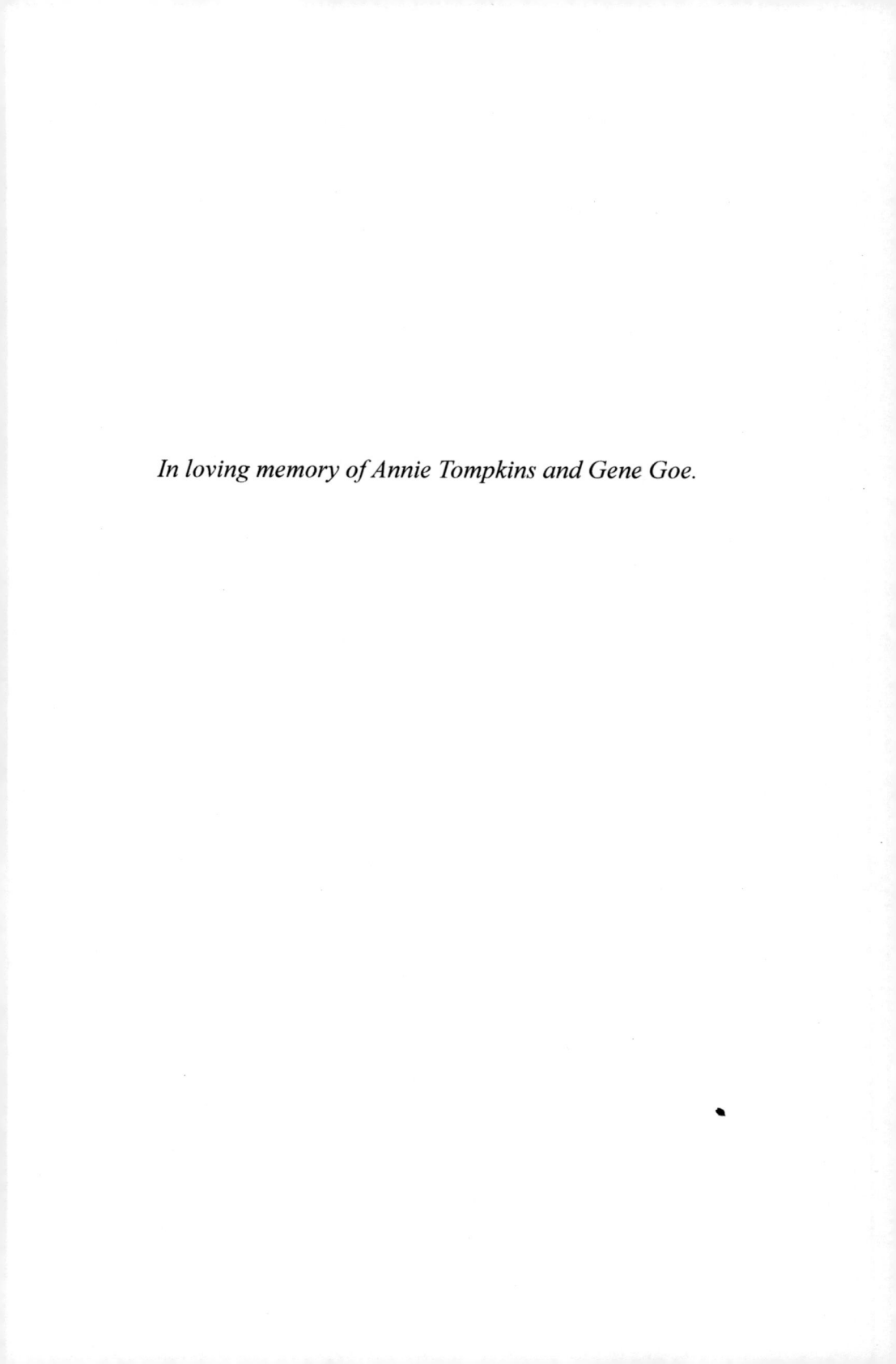

Many thanks to my friends Jerry Kennedy and Jimmy Spencer for their support during my trying times with my story. Many thanks to my neighbor Sherry Simpson for all her typing, and a special word of appreciation to the lovely Lynn Lawson, without whom I would have had great difficulty finishing my project.

Last, but certainly not least, I want thank my great friends Tom and Terri Eckert from "up at the ranch" for their unwavering help and moral support. Without them, the road would have been much longer.

Prologue

The early morning hours of January 8th, 1935 seemed to the rest of the post-Depression United States as just another difficult step on the road to the nation's recovery. Some wounds were healed, some stomachs were filled, some were better off, and some were not. None of the world's greatest minds could have forecast the importance of this day. The events of this day would change the world. However, most realizations of these events would come much later.

That morning, a dark-green Packard touring sedan crept along an unlit, foggy two-lane road just minutes from the little town of Tupelo, Mississippi. An impeccably dressed lady put her doeskin glove on her husband's shoulder. "T. D., how much farther?"

"I can't really say, my dear. The fog is so thick I can't see the road signs. I can barely see the hood ornament."

"Are the fog lights on?" asked the lady.

"Yes, dear," T. D. answered wearily.

The grim driver ran his hand through his beginning gray crop of thick hair and uttered, "Lillian, my dear, I know you're anxious, and you have waited a long time, but I don't dare go any faster."

The lady in the passenger seat nervously tugged at her curls with her right hand, and, at that moment, the syrup-thick fog miraculously lifted. The lights of a "meat plus three" restaurant showed on a sign saying, "Entering Tupelo." Delphia Hansen's directions now became clear.

The weary couple saw the lights from the sign advertising the small hotel they had been requested to stay at until they had been notified about the next step of the plan. The DeLongpres wanted a child, no matter what the cost or whatever it took to fulfill their dreams.

When the driver had picked up the room key and parked the car in the space provided next to the door with the matching number, he said, "I know it doesn't look like much, Lill, I'm just doing what she asked me to do."

The tall man's hand shook slightly as he turned the door key and looked into the room. It was a combination of the driving conditions and the anticipation of what was to come. They breathed simultaneous sighs of relief when they discovered that the inside was a vast improvement over the exterior. He dropped the two small bags on the floor, removed his coat, and sat on the end of the double bed. All they could do at this point was to make themselves as comfortable as possible...and wait.

A few blocks away in a dimly lit, smoke-filled bar, a slender, handsome, but shabbily dressed man in his early thirties removed his hat and laid it on a chair next to the pool table. A stout man wearing a printed shirt that made him appear even larger said, "Looks like it's your shot, Vernon."

Vernon Presley stooped and placed his left hand on the edge of the table. He lined up the shot, inhaled deeply, and exhaled slowly. He rejoiced momentarily when the eight ball rolled slowly across the seemingly vast expanse of green and dropped into the corner pocket, then held up his hands in dismay when the cue ball followed it in.

The fat man chuckled, and said loudly, "Hey, Vernon! Maybe you should stick to sharecroppin'! Either that or go home to your pregnant old lady. Whatever you decide, you got no money left to pay me, so get the fuck outta here!"

The Presleys were in love and, at first, like most couples, wanted a child from that union. They were not educated people, but realized the added financial burdens trying to raise a child would bring. As Gladys' pregnancy progressed, they discussed the possibilities of putting their baby up for adoption. They asked Delphia Hansen, the church lady whom had been aiding them during their recent struggles, one day when she brought them extra groceries what she thought of the idea. Gladys was a Christian and was never comfortable with the plan, but finally went along with it. They could certainly use the money, and, maybe when things got better, they could try and have another. Vernon became more used to the idea as the days and weeks went by. He had said many times since, "Yeah, we'll have another one. You bet!"

Vernon had enough money in his sock for another beer or two, so he told the fat man he'd pay him later. He went to another bar where he didn't owe anybody and spent the last of his meager funds. He knew Gladys was getting close to dropping that baby, but he didn't want to be there. He loved her when she was slim and pretty, but now she was fat with child and did nothing but bitch all day. Besides, Delphia was there, and, in that tiny shotgun shack, all he could do was be in the way.

Stumbling out of the bar in his drunkenness, he recognized a buddy's truck in the parking lot, and he knew it would be there all night. He opened the unlocked door, crawled in, and passed out on the seat.

Chapter One

If one were traveling in northern post-war Mississippi and should happen to experience wagon trouble, he would most likely be referred to Andrew Hansen "up in Tupelo."

Upon entering what could possibly qualify as a main street, there would be no way to miss Felder's General Store. Not because it was the largest building on the street, or had a white sign with faded-red letters, or had a slightly sagging roof that covered the porch. Most likely it would be the gathering of the town's leading senior citizens that met there on a daily basis to fix all the problems in Lee County. Sadly, these great intentions never left that sagging porch.

If a person was lucky enough to have his wagon make it that far or had to arrive on foot, he would be noticed by all on the porch the minute he came into view. By the time he set foot on the creaky boards, each would have formed an opinion. The weary traveler would usually ask, "Could anybody tell me if the Hansens, the family that owns the smithy, still live here?"

The one with the most tattered hat would brush his tobacco-stained whiskers with a hand tanned golden brown from many summer's labors and say, "Hansens, huh? I can't remember when they didn't live here. Matter of fact, they been here since the place was Gum Pond. Nice folks, too, taking them Ramsey kids in and all. Got a little wagon trouble, do ya? Well, you go that way 'til ya run out of buildings, and, another half-a-holler, you'll see a stand of trees on a rise and smoke coming out of Andy's chimney. Looks like you got here just in time by the looks of things."

Yes, Andrew and Wilomenia Hansen were nice people. They had been blessed with four boys, the oldest being Aubrey. Aubrey had been born big (11 lbs., 3 oz.), and showed no signs of slowing down. At a young age, he was able to help grow the family's food and later help his father in the smithy.

There were little signs of wealth in a land where it used to be abundant.

The Hansens were by no means well-to-do, but by late 1800s Mississippi's standards, they did all right. Being one of the best smithies in Lee County didn't hurt. They grew most of their food and had a few cows and pigs, some of which made their way to the family table from time to time.

Besides working hard, they were God-fearing folks, and, no matter how tired Andrew was, he always made it to church with his family. The First Baptist Church is where they met the Ramseys. That's where Aubrey met Delphia.

Andrew and Wilomenia had been in love since they met at a church social. She was sipping a cup of fruit punch as Andrew approached the big glass bowl. As he was trying to scoop a cupful without getting any of those horrid slices of lime, he looked up to see the bottom of another cup framed by a crop of curly auburn hair and two huge brown eyes that looked right into his heart.

Their romance began at that very spot. If there was a case of love at first sight, it certainly happened that night at the church social. As they say, "Right in front of God and everybody. There would never be anyone for either of them for the rest of their lives."

They were married the year they both became nineteen, and their first son, Aubrey, made his entrance nine months to the day from the wedding.

Andrew had worked for his Uncle Zeke part-time in his smithy to help support the family, so when he and Wilomenia married, he wanted to own his own business. With the help of his father and uncle, he was able to start his smithy, and, with the help of a few neighbors, they built a house that would hold a big family. The entire countryside would know about this fine family's deeds for years to come. The old men on the porch would often comment about it being worth walking by the smell of the smithy because the wonderful aroma of Mrs. Hansen's bread and pies were right down the walk. Aubrey and his brothers knew right where those pies were cooling, too. When one turned up missing, she would fake anger. Next time she'd allow for these four most-wanted thieves by baking an extra pie.

In the fall following Aubrey's ninth summer, the family gathered for the evening meal. This would not be a pleasant time. Wilomenia came to the table with the final dish of vegetables and announced that Mr. And Mrs. Ramsey had been in a fatal accident. She continued telling how a wheel had come off their carriage, plunging them off the Dry Creek Bridge. After saying the blessing, Andrew put his head in his big hands and lamented.

"I told Sam many times to bring that rig in and let me re-iron it. He said as soon as he got some extra money he'd see me. I told him! I told him! Don't worry; we'll work it out! Now, it's in pieces at the bottom of that bridge and we'll never see..." Wilomenia sat quietly for a moment. Aubrey and the boys were struck dumb, so Mom broke the silence.

"Andrew, we've got to figure what to do with those poor little girls. Delphia's the same age as our Aubrey, and I don't know the other two's ages, but I know they're much younger. I'll talk to the ladies at church tomorrow and see if we can't solve this terrible problem. The food's getting cold, boys."

The meeting with the ladies was not very successful. Some of the ladies said they could take one of the sisters, but none volunteered to take all three sisters.

Wilomenia parked her buggy in its usual place, which was closer to the house than the smithy, and called one of the boys to tend to the horse, "Rub him down and give him extra oats, Donald."

Instead of going to the house, she entered the smithy and asked Andrew to shut down for a few minutes if he could. He grabbed a cloth that he kept in cool water by his bench and began wiping his face and neck, "What is it, my love?"

That night at dinner, Wilomenia announced to the brothers they would have to double up and make room for three sisters.

The following months were not easy, but then nobody expected them to be. If children are not used to sharing, even the best-behaved and best-raised kids will experience little tiffs now and then. But this was a combination of two Christian families and, who knows, maybe the man up in the sky lent a helping hand now and then.

As the sorrow began to fade over time, life in general seemed to be smoothing out all around. Delphia was close to ten and had already been trained to help her mother care for her little sisters and tend to lighter chores around the kitchen. Wilomenia noticed this and began showing the young lady little tips on cooking. Delphia showed a lot of desire to help, and, with three extra mouths to cook for, the lady of the house didn't mind this a bit. The *future* Mrs. Hansen's favorite kitchen duty seemed to be baking.

Wilomenia also noticed how attentive Delphia was to her sisters and made a remark—one that would never come to pass, "You'll make a good mother someday, honey."

Aubrey had liked Delphia way back when he first saw her sitting in front of them at church. He would edge up to the back of her bench when he thought no one was looking and slowly lean closer to hear her sing.

After she came to live with them and the period of adjustment had passed, they became closer and closer friends. They would go on walks from time to time, now and then go fishing, and study together. Being close to the same age would explain a lot of that no doubt.

One day at school, a troublemaker named Martin made a remark that made Delphia cry, then laughed about it. This infuriated Aubrey, and he demanded an apology. Martin put his hands to Aubrey's chest and gave him a shove. What was he thinking? Aubrey was at least six inches taller and many pounds heavier. He sent Mr. Longley home with a large shiner and a piece of advice for the future, "Don't ever make my sister cry again!"

As the two were walking home, Delphia was silent but she kept looking at Aubrey funny.

"What's the matter?" he asked.

"Don't you know?" she queried.

"Know what?" the bewildered young man questioned.

"You just called me your sister!"

Aubrey looked at her for a stunned minute and chuckled. "I sure did, didn't I?"

They gave each other the first of what would be thousands of hugs and went home for dinner. This gave Delphia a chance to brag a little about her hero to her family.

As time will, it marched on, and the brother-sister relationship was working quite well. But Mother Nature always has to go changing things. Things like little boys becoming men and little girls start showing outward changes that can't be overlooked. Feelings come alive from something as innocent as holding hands. Questions come up that are more difficult to answer than they were a mere two or three years before.

Mr. And Mrs. Hansen had several conversations concerning the changes that were slowly arriving and would in no way disappear. They would have to talk to the blossoming young adults and see what they were thinking. One thing was for certain, it was time to bid farewell to the brother and sister business.

After supper one evening, Andrew sent the younger kids to bed and told

Delphia and Aubrey that their mother had some important things to discuss.

It seemed to go quite well and it was time to get the kids' reaction. Wilomenia asked Delphia what she thought about everything they had discussed, but the slightly embarrassed young woman gestured in Aubrey's direction. Aubrey was caught up between looking at his father, then to his mother, and across to Delphia several times before anything would come out. He was finally able to mutter, "Uh, wuh, well, Delphia, I really like you a lot! Maybe I love you. I don't know. I guess so."

They heard slight sobbing sounds, turned their gazes to Delphia, and saw her auburn head bowed.

"What is it, child?" Wilomenia implored.

She dried her eyes with her table napkin and half-spoke, half-cried, "I'm so grateful for everything this family has done for me and my sisters, and I didn't want to get anyone mad at me, but...."

"But what, child?" she asked again.

"That's all I've been thinking about for the past two years!" Delphia cried out.

They courted just long enough for Delphia to be able to show everyone her engagement ring that bore a modest diamond. Within the month they were married only sixty feet from where they first met.

"Delphia Hansen...Delphia Hansen...Delphia Hansen!" The bride of less than a year was sitting by a window replacing buttons on a very large shirt. The sun coming through the multi-paned French-style windows warmed her already happy soul even more. She loved repeating her new name.

The newlyweds had given a lot of thought to their parents' suggestion to stay home and add on to the bulging house. Wilomenia and her daughter-in-law grew closer every day. Delphia would dry a tear and admit that Wilomenia and she were closer than she and her real mom. The elder Mrs. Hansen, at supper one evening, told her husband in no uncertain terms, "I won't hear of the kids moving anywhere else, Andrew! We've got all this land, well, Lordy, where would they go anyway?"

The family structure was extremely important during this period in history. They were all they had, and sticking together gave them strength. Financial status didn't seem to matter.

Delphia looked down the hill toward the site of the new smithy, hoping to see the guy whose big shirt she was mending. She was happy about her husband's decision to accept his mother's offer to stay and add on to the house. After the addition to the house was completed, it was decided to move the shop down closer to the main street. This would settle a few things. It would eliminate a lot of noise, not just in the shop, but also of customers coming and going. Lastly, but very important for keeping peace, it would help keep the dust off the seats of Wilomenia's carriage. As a bonus, it made it easier access to the men from Felder's porch.

Delphia finished the shirt and placed it on a hanger for tomorrow, walked to the mirror gently patting her auburn locks, and went to the other side of the house where the big new kitchen was. Wilomenia must have felt like she was running a cooking school. The little sisters weren't so little anymore, and they wanted to be like their big sister, so it's a good thing while remodeling that Andrew and Aubrey had made the kitchen bigger. She saw her mother-in-law getting her sisters started kneading bread dough. She took her apron off the cupboard door hook, tied it neatly in back, and said cheerfully, "Good morning, Mom!"

Wilomenia was much more than a housewife. She was very busy in church and civic activities, such as they were. And, being the good Christian woman she was, she wanted to get her daughter-in-law involved also. Since the sisters were now old enough to assist around the house, this freed her to begin this new phase of Delphia's development outside the home. She was delighted that the younger lady took to it like a natural. There was so much to do, so many to help, and so little time.

A typical day would begin with the two Mrs. Hansens gathering veggies from their garden outside the large kitchen window. Breakfast had to be cooked, served, and then the mid-day meal prepared. After lunch, Wilomenia would give the sisters instructions for cleaning and supper prep and summon one of the brothers to hitch up her carriage. If they were in school or busy doing chores their father requested, she and Delphia were more than capable of handling the job. All the years of watching her husband work with the big animals was no doubt helpful. They would then be off to spread comfort and joy over the countryside.

One afternoon, she and her mother-in-law were taking some groceries to a family whose head of the house had been run over by a plow disc when the lead line from the horses broke. The Brysons lived a little over two miles from town. When they arrived, they found Richard Bryson and his wife, Mona, in a helpless situation. He was badly injured and couldn't move and she was about to give birth. Wilomenia told Delphia to go into town and find Doc Palmer. Upon arriving at his office over the hardware store, there was no doc and none of the old men over at Felder's knew of his whereabouts. "Probably out tendin' to a calf or new colt," said the brown-bearded owner in his signature tattered hat.

When Delphia returned without the doc, Wilomenia was disappointed, but rebounded boldly yelling, "Get those kids out of here, and boil me some water!"

Delphia was never allowed in the room when her little sisters were being born. This was a terrifying time for the young bride. Little did she know then how useful this experience would be later in her life.

Chapter Two

Moving the smithy made a lot of people happy. It wasn't just the modernization and better facilities, it was no longer "half-a-holler" away. Now, Brown Beard and his counsel had a new place to solve the world's problems, and the philosophies just poured out.

"Good God, I thought Andy was big, whew! Would you just take a look at that boy of hisn'. I don't think no ones gonna forget to pay his bill!"

Yes, it was working out rather well. The old-timers could sit on Felder's porch and sun themselves. When the sun decided not to show that day, they could warm their hands by Andrew's fire and warm their innards on Wilomenia's hot bread and cookies. And, if they wanted, Andrew could find them odd jobs around the place where they could earn that all-so-important tobacco money.

There was one young man who just kind of showed up one day and began hanging around. He offered to help out just for some food and maybe a place to stay. Aubrey liked the boy and asked his father if the newcomer could be his assistant. Andrew thought it over and told his son to make up a bed in the supply room. The large man boomed, "By the way, what's your name, son?"

"C. J. Clarkson, sir," replied the timid lad of fourteen summers.

C. J. remained with the Hansen's until he left town seeking an education.

Long, humid summer days would eventually give way to mild fall weather, stepping aside for howling winds and seemingly endless rain. This cycle faithfully repeated itself year after year.

Tupelo was growing, not at such a rapid pace that couldn't be kept up with, but nevertheless changing. The demands on Andrew to be a leader were also growing. People looked to him for advice on almost a daily basis. People would sometimes tire of their daily grind to make a living in this tough country and would look to sell out. Not too many had the wherewithal to accommodate the ones who'd had enough, so they would quite often turn to Mr. Hansen.

At yet another family dinner, he announced to all present his plan to turn over most of the business to Aubrey and pursue other ventures. "I'm not going anywhere, and I'll be home every day. I'm getting a bit tired of the smithy's demands, and, besides, my son can work circles around me. He knows all the customers and is good with people. He's also got C. J. to help him along with some of the old-timers when he needs them. I'm going to try my hand in the banking business. So, that's how it's going to be. Any questions?"

There were a few comments about this sudden change, but nothing that bothered anyone. The only big question left was, "what's for dessert?"

Aubrey had no trouble adjusting to his new responsibility. That is because nothing changed a whole lot. Now, he just moved at his own pace. He enjoyed making the parts for all the services. He liked controlling the fire, the heat of the fire, and being able to shape things with his hands. He enjoyed working with the animals more than his father did and was quite a sight to observe while working with the horses. He liked feeling their muscles and power, and liked the resistance when he had to bend their legs to install a shoe. These animals that stood between fifteen and seventeen hands somehow didn't look all that big next to Aubrey Hansen.

One day, something he (and no one close to him) would never have ever imagined, happened. He liked horses so much that he began collecting and studying all the books and literature he could obtain. He never went to school for this but, after some time, became a self-taught veterinarian. The townspeople had always and still did look up to his father, but now Aubrey was building his own identity. He would need to draw on this new image in the very near future.

For some time, Andrew and Wilomenia had been talking about doing a little traveling. It really didn't matter where, just so the two of them could, after all these years of working, business building, and family-raising, finally spend some time alone together. Things were going smoothly. The kids, although not fully grown, could now take care of themselves, and Andrew's little farmer's bank was mildly flourishing, so, why not?

Andrew kissed his wife good-bye, and he left to take care of travel plans and fix things at the bank so work would continue during his absence. Wilomenia would never kiss him hello or good-bye again. All those years of toil on the farm and smithy had taken their toll. They found him with his hands still on the reins and sitting straight up in the carriage seat, but he was no longer driving in this world.

All Tupelo, and especially the old men, were in a complete state of shock. All they could do was sit on the porch at Felder's and look to their new leader. Tupelo was facing the major issue of entering the twentieth century.

Their old friend and pillar of the community had left them. Their new leader was his son, Aubrey. The old men of Felder's porch were also leaving the rolling hills of Tupelo and the rest of Lee County for the life hereafter. Younger men replaced the old men. There were no more Jessie Jameses, no more Black Barts, and no more Overland stagecoach robberies. Wyatt Earp moved to the city and turned in his badge. Those noisy, horseless carriages were coming through Tupelo at the alarming rate of two or three a week. The young Mr. Felder kicked the senior citizens counsel off the porch while he was replacing the sagging roof and creaky boards. Wilomenia's hot bread and cookies didn't taste the same. Aubrey was digging holes to prepare for something called gasoline tanks. The smithy wasn't the same anymore.

The adage that says "behind every successful man, there's a woman," may have started in this part of the U.S.A. and maybe right here in Lee County, Mississippi.

Everyone liked this giant of a man whom everyone referred to as Andrew's boy. They looked to him for guidance up to a point, but the reputation of Wilomenia's love and kindness made most of the town and the rest of the county seek her out with their problems. Who said that cakes and pies couldn't rule the world?

Aubrey and his wife were not offended by this, for they, too, had listened to her counsel at the dinner table for years. But Aubrey and Delphia sensed that their mother was losing her lust and reason for living. This strong lady no longer presided at family meetings. Like so many couples, she followed her husband to the grave two years after his death.

Aubrey's younger brothers left Tupelo and struck out for the opportunities in other parts of the country. They moved to the big cities they'd read about. Delphia's sisters, like their older sister, had met and married their Prince Charmings.

Just like Andrew and Wilomenia, Aubrey and Delphia were left alone to start a whole new life. That was okay, because the promise they made to each other at the little First Baptist Church would never die.

It is inevitable that all things must come to an end. Nobody lives forever, and no country or civilization exists forever. Life is like the seasons. In the spring, there is birth. In the summer months, there is growth. When autumn moves in, we reap the summer's harvest and prepare for winter. Winter is cold and unrelenting. Only a few survive and see the new life spring has to offer.

Dr. Thaddeus Palmer had been around for a long time. He was a wealthy man. To prove this, he would open his closet and admire bushels of winter apples and spring potatoes as they would tumble out and cover his office floor. He always sported a dusty black suit and starched white shirt his assistant had lovingly pressed with a heated iron from the primitive black stove the owner of the downstairs hardware store provided.

In those days if a man lived to be fifty, he was considered old. But a year or so before his seventieth birthday, he hired a young doctor from South Carolina to be his assistant. Dr. Ezra Bartholomew left his hometown against his mother and father's advice and wishes and headed west. When Doc Palmer was unable to handle the demands for his services, he would politely say to his apple- and potato-paying clients, "Dr. Bartholemew will be there if I can't. If he can't be there, Delphia Hansen can."

Like many others before him, Dr. Palmer left all of Tupelo and other towns in Lee County with his blessing and told them good-bye.

The new century brought many changes to the country and, although not as noticeable, even to Tupelo. Tupelo had a new doctor in Ezra Bartholomew. Aubrey's former assistant had returned from "some big preacher school" up north, and now had to be called "The Reverend C. J. Clarkson."

Delphia's mentor and adopted mother had prepared her well. The lady of cakes and pies had left a legacy more valuable than money. Her legacy was her beautiful soul that always found some time between running her home and raising her family to help *other* families back on their feet. Especially Delphia would always remember Wilomenia Hansen.

Delphia had plenty of time to work in her garden, that is, if she started around sunup. Since the return of C. J. Clarkson, it seemed that her time was even more in demand. The Reverend would drop by the smithy-gas station, like returning for a class reunion and chat with Aubrey about meaningless topics. But the real reason would inevitably pop up, "What's Delphia up to today?"

Aubrey would shake his head and point in the general direction of the church. "Main Street ain't that crowded, C. J., how could you have missed her?"

Aubrey had liked C. J. since that day he first stumbled into the smithy, before he was a preacher. He never forgot about his father allowing him to make room in the supply shed for the future minister to sleep. He was proud of the young man for what he had accomplished, coming from nothing, so to speak, and he also could appreciate the good work his wife and the preacher were doing. He just wished C. J. wouldn't be so damned obvious when he knew the main reason the little man was there.

Aubrey didn't mind sharing his wife as long as it was for church work and the good of the community. They had no children, so in spite of her busy schedule, she always put him and taking care of the homefront first. They remained very much in love.

Despite the progress stemming from the railroads and the T.V.A., there remained much poverty in the south. Some families had trouble sustaining themselves and one child. With the lack of birth control devices, moments of passion could result in extra mouths to feed. This could break a family's back, and, many times, it did.

Although Delphia and her sisters' situation was much different, they were indeed orphans and were adopted, or better, taken in by the Hansens. She would never forget this, and it actually drove her to find a home for every child in the world if she could. The results of this special lady's work, along with her preacher sidekick, began to spread over Lee and surrounding counties. As the first line of communication was "word of mouth," it spread as far away as Hattiesburg and other cities in the state.

Aubrey wasn't exactly sitting around whittling while his wife's fame spread. His father had sold a good part of their land to the railroads, and then there was the success of the bank. Following Andrew's death, he bought property in nearby Pontotoc and Union Counties. His first love was the smithy-gas station, and, although he didn't work there much anymore, he still maintained an office while two Indians from the former Choctaw tribe did the physical tasks. He still enjoyed "the old folks," as Delphia called them, coming around and doing their best to keep the old days alive. Their tales grew longer as did their teeth, but they were a part of his childhood and his memories of his beloved father. They were indeed imbedded in his soul.

The years that followed were good to the Hansens. They were very active in the community, but would quite often step back and take personal inventory. This meant a hop on the train to New Orleans or any destination of their choice. On some holidays, their brothers and sisters would show up with their families and reminisce about their wonderful days growing up on the top of the hill, a "half-a-holler or so" from town.

It had been storming in most of the county for a few days, although the annual rainfall in the area only averages about four to five inches per year. This early summer storm was trying to get ahead of its prior visits to this part of the country.

About the third night, the rain began to cease and a damp, muggy silence was everywhere. Aubrey closed the smithy-gas station, bid goodnight to his "old folks," and went home to dinner. As their custom following dinner, they would go to the front porch and enjoy sun tea and some kind of special cookie recipe Delphia had dreamed up. She patted her damp forehead and cheeks with the tip of her apron and sighed, "The air is very heavy tonight, feels real close, like a tight shirt."

"Yep, sure does, honey, maybe the worst of it's over."

"I hope so."

They retired, and, since the rain had stopped, at least for now, they left the window open. The eerie quiet still persisted. Somewhere in the neighborhood of 1:00 a.m., they were awakened by a ferocious crack of thunder, and the entire room lit up from the following flash of lightning…and then the explosion. Aubrey leapt toward the window with Delphia inches behind and watched their beloved smithy being engulfed in flames. They ran outside clad only in their sleepers and watched, dumbfounded. The normally coolheaded Aubrey broke away and headed toward the inferno; his wife screamed, "Aubrey, stop!"

He ignored her plea and yelled back, "Phia, call the fire department! I'll get started while they're coming."

"Aubrey, please!"

"Don't worry, darlin', I'll be fine. It's only a fire!"

She paused for a moment and turned to go to the house, but not halfway up the walk came the second explosion. She couldn't turn around for what seemed an eternity, but, when she finally turned her rigid body to the blaze, there was no Aubrey, and never would be again, at least not on this earth.

In a few dreadful seconds, her world was cruelly jerked away. Never would those huge arms hold her again. Never would the big man who seemed like a little boy around her say, "I love you, Phia."

Chapter Three

Delphia kept busy for a few days after the funeral. The relatives stayed on for a while, so there was noise in the house. Kids were fighting, women were cooking, and the men were full of "do you remember when's...." Soon though, she was wandering around the big house; first to the front porch, no one to sit with; then to the kitchen, no one to cook for; then to the window, no more smithy, no more big shirts to put buttons on...no more Aubrey.

But this was a strong woman with a whole lot of life in her body. She was a woman who was born to change the world, or at least the part of it she could touch. And touch it she did. Before she only wanted to do her best to help children, now she was driven by this desire. She felt Aubrey's presence with her, and this gave her strength. Every now and then, when she would get almost too tired to walk, she'd look up and ask, "How am I doing?"

Maybe she got an answer, who's to say? But whether she did or not, suddenly, new energy poured in throughout her being, and she was at it again.

She mostly liked to help children. But by no means were her efforts confined to just children. Many of her visits to the poor were to couples that had no kids, but might in the future. She wanted to make sure the environment was healthy before the baby would arrive.

Most of the funds for the "care packages" were a result of donations from business people or generated by bake sales at church socials. Andrew Hansen had invested wisely and left a little for his family, so did his son. Delphia was not wealthy, but Aubrey's passing in no way left her destitute. When there weren't enough donations to go around, and indeed there were those times, she would take it upon herself to make up the difference.

Another way funds were generated was a form of adoption. A few times, a couple couldn't afford to have the baby, to say nothing about keeping it, so she and Reverend Clarkson would draw on the list of well-to-do families who couldn't have children and were willing to pay. It wasn't completely legal, but it made a lot of people happy and cut through a ton of red tape.

Usually, they had someone to help with the births, but many times there were no warnings, and since Dr. Ezra had more work than he could handle, Delphia became a midwife. This was something she would become quite proficient at.

This practice went on for several years and was always conducted in extreme privacy. The monies received were distributed in many different areas. Some was used to help the original parents and part went into a general fund. The cost to the foster parents was determined by their financial status. This could vary hundreds of dollars. One day this would lead to one of the nation's most important births…and also one if its biggest secrets.

Thurston Davis DeLongpre was born on Christmas Day, 1890. He would be the fourth and last child of Thurston and Isabella.

Isabella, for some reason, hated the "Junior" tag, and she was never comfortable calling her new son Thurston, II, so one day, out of frustration, she snapped, "T. D.!" This made the little boy smile and even giggle a bit. T. D. stuck, and that was the end of that problem. His three sisters would run around the house yelling, "T. D., T. D.," and they could hear him giggle. They'd pick him up and carry the little bundle around like a new toy, showing him off to their friends. Since they took him everywhere they went, Isabella never had to worry about a baby-sitter.

As the young boy grew, he loved being spoiled by his older sisters, but he idolized his father and wanted to spend more time with him. He imitated his father's every gesture and move, and even asked his mother to make him clothes "like Daddy's." His mother turned this matter over to Kathleen, Hannah, and Ruth, T. D.'s older sisters

To casual friends and guests it would appear the DeLongpre's were the ideal family. All occasions like birthdays, and all holidays including Christmas and Thanksgiving, were very festive. The family dressed for these parties, expected their guests to do likewise, and gave the impression of being well-to-do.

On one of his early birthdays, T. D.'s sisters presented him with a magnificent custom-tailored velvet suit. A labor of love they just knew he'd appreciate. Instead of the customary big smile he would flash upon receiving their prior gifts, he began to cry. "What's wrong, honey, don't you like it?"

"Well, I kinda do, but daddy doesn't wear this stuff, and he'll think I'm a sissy!"

The well-meaning sisters convinced him he looked fine and that his dad would think so, too.

The boy's fears were well-warranted. His father was late for the party and had made a few stops on his way home. When he saw T. D. in his bronze velvet suit and fluffy shirt, the drunken man exploded, "I bust my butt to come home for my son's birthday and see him dressed like Little Lord Fauntleroy. You're all a bunch of nincompoops and fools!" He staggered to the front door, slammed it, and went back to what he was doing earlier.

No matter how hard the sad little boy tried to please his father, he never came close. It seemed that following this horrible birthday; the abuse was on the increase. He was called a dreamer and a dummy and even made reference to his masculinity. The lad began retreating from this abuse and stayed in the background whenever his father was present. From this reclusive position, he barely spoke, but made mental notes of everything he saw and heard.

This infuriated the DeLongpre patriarch even more, especially when he had had a couple libations. He would call his only son stupid, and, in one display of anger, he demanded his wife to take the boy to be tested. The tests proved the elder DeLongpre wrong and just fueled the fire to ridicule the little man at every turn.

His sisters felt all they could do was give him more love, but nothing could heal the wounds suffered from his father's rage. For the next few years, the only time his loving nature surfaced was when he was in their company.

This man that he'd grown to fear and gradually lost respect for showed up for his high school graduation with what appeared to be a gift for this special day. Instead, it was a choice. If the graduate were to stay in Pennsylvania and live off his father, he would have to go to college. If he chose not to do this, the alternative was to go to Mississippi and manage his late Uncle Jarrod's farm, a man he'd heard about but never met.

The young man had no idea why his father offered him this opportunity. Even though he didn't know anything about farming, he did know that this would allow him to get away from his father for the first time in his eighteen years. It took him one minute to make his choice.

All T. D. knew about his father's older brother was the berating the younger brother gave him on a frequent basis. How he'd betrayed the family by going south to speculate on land and how he was nothing but a dreamer and a loser. He was never called any other name but "The Farmer."

This was nothing new to T. D. His father had treated him this way for what seemed like forever. He wondered on the train ride to Mississippi what was waiting at the end of the track. His father hadn't told him anything of what his duties were or what was expected of him. He didn't know who was on the farm, if anyone, or what anyone did. His usual warm smile was now a sneer as he spoke inside himself, *The S.O.B. probably knows less than I do anyway!* The sneer turned into a frown. A frown that said he would prove his father wrong, *I must not fail! I cannot fail! I will not fail!*

T. D. arrived in Hattiesburg a little after dawn. He'd been thinking so hard that he forgot to eat on the train. He went into the depot and found that the one car at the station was busy, so he inquired of the man standing next to a carriage if he knew where The Willows was located. The driver pointed due north. "'Bout twenty miles, I reckon."

"Do you go that far?"

The driver nodded, and, when T. D. had heard how long it would take, he decided to get a bite. He secured the carriage and went inside the depot to eat.

It was a long, but beautiful ride. When they had to rest the horses, the young Pennsylvanian stood in one spot and marveled at the beautiful trees and hills. He'd expected flat land and cotton fields. They were there too, but he was so busy looking out the sides of the carriage, he wasn't aware the driver had slowed down. The carriage came to a stop, and the black man, wearing a top hat and close-fitting coat, said briskly, "This is it, sir."

He asked the driver to wait before turning into the lane. He was very nervous and, as was his habit, needed to pause and prepare himself for any situation he faced.

He got out of the carriage, stretched, and began rehearsing his introductory speech. The young traveler looked up to see two massive pillars connected by an ornate wrought-iron archway, marking the entrance to the "little farm" which bore the name The Willows.

On the journey to and through Mississippi, he'd seen lush and fertile land through the train windows and later from the carriage, but this vision topped it all. He now realized how terribly his father had underestimated his Uncle Jarrod's accomplishments. For a moment he thought his father had deliberately misled him, but it made no difference now, so he just as quickly let that thought go.

He instructed the driver to proceed down the lane. Huge elegant willow trees bordered the drive. The last morning mist still clung to the leaves, blurring the edges softly. He was certain he could hear some magical song as the wind whispered through the graceful branches. They moved languidly in some unknown dance, and this tableau was immediately and indelibly etched in his heart.

As the trees parted, the lane ended and turned into a big circle. At the far side of the circle was a magnificent house. It looked a bit worn, but he could tell that at one time it had to be awesome. The driver unloaded his bags, bowed smartly, and smiled as T. D. paid him and threw in a little extra. He watched the carriage disappear down the road, turned, and stared at the grand old mansion. He allowed his imagination to take over and saw buggies carrying finely dressed gentlemen accompanied by beautiful ladies.

He was awakened from his trance by the pounding of hooves. The mount came to a stop with a noisy snort and whinny, and the rider dismounted and walked toward him. The tall man wore a wide brimmed hat that rested low on his forehead, partially hiding his face. As he drew closer, he pushed his hat back with a gloved finger. T. D. hid his surprise as he took the handsome black man's extended hand. Although T. D. stood six feet two, he looked level into the other man's eyes. Benjamin Hampton and T. D. DeLongpre shook hands in greeting.

Ben Hampton knew that he and his family were more than just farm workers. The many employees of The Willows did not live in squalor like others he'd heard about on other farms, but they didn't live as good as his family.

Ben considered it an honor to know the man who deeded the property to his father many years ago. But now they were both gone, and he had only memories of his heroes. He recalled sitting by the fire after a barbecue, hearing Jarrod speak, and his father quietly taking in every word and putting in his "two cents" worth whenever the time was right.

On this particular night, Jarrod told his friend, "Isaiah, you and your family have meant a lot to me, and, as you know, I have made sure of your future as best I can. And you also know, I do not communicate with my brother. But I have a nephew whom I have never seen, and one day I hope that he will be able to take my place and continue all we've accomplished here."

Isaiah casually put his hand over part of his face to hide the smile he was trying to keep his son and Jarrod from seeing. He and Jarrod had worked hard, and, yes, he was grateful that this Yankee rewarded him and his family for their labors. He couldn't help recalling a few times when his friend had strayed a bit after indulging in some homemade whiskey.

One evening the usually well-behaved Jarrod, aided by a few sips of courage, wandered into town seeking some female companionship. He found what he was looking for, but there was one small problem—the lady, even though she was alone, belonged to another man.

Later that night, Isaiah was awakened by gunshots and the sound of many horses near the entrance to the property. He looked outside to see Jarrod jumping from his horse and scampering for the cover of the barn. Isaiah grabbed his shotgun, fired in front of the angry mob, and reloaded. This was something none of them had counted on, and they froze in their tracks. The figure of the large black man with the shotgun aimed at their chests caused the leader of the horde to yell out, "Get out of the way, black boy. This ain't none of your concern!"

Another shot in front of them changed their collective minds, and they were on their way back to where they had first assembled.

There were a few more times when the man from Pennsylvania imbibed more than usual and decided he wanted to play with one of the young black women that lived and worked at The Willows. No harm was done, and, when reminded by Isaiah of his previous night's escapades, Jarrod was totally embarrassed. He would walk the straight and narrow for quite sometime afterward.

All of this was taken in stride and overlooked by Isaiah. He knew if it hadn't been for Jarrod, they all might be looking for work somewhere in the cold and cruel north.

Jarrod picked up a clod of dirt and tossed it in the direction of Isaiah. He reached out and caught it, bringing him back from his reminiscences.

Ben knew the terms of Jarrod's Last Will and Testament, but decided not to discuss it, because he saw that there seemed to be no real separation of property. He thought he'd just get to know "the nephew" and just let things happen.

As it turned out, this was a good choice. Their first meeting went as smooth and as amiable as the breeze that sang through the branches and leaves of the great willows.

This took most of the pressure from the young DeLongpre, and, though it surprised him some, he would just listen and watch like he'd done around his father for years.

Cotton was king for over one hundred years before the advent of the logging boom. During this time, forests were raped and deserted, leaving an ugly scar where these despicable fortune hunters had been. The Willows had not been subjected to this greed, largely due to the intelligence and foresight of Jarrod and Isaiah. However, the timber *was* used to supplement the income of the farm. In fact, it was probably its savior.

The logging from the once ample forests was slowing to a minimum. Jarrod had been a whole lot more than a speculating, lucky farmer. He and Isaiah were way ahead of their time. After cutting, they began replanting trees for future generations.

But this current planting season was in full swing. Since he was still, and would be for a while, learning, he asked Benjamin to show him the ropes by letting him work side by side. Now it was Ben's turn to be surprised. Ben got the newcomer some overalls, boots, and gloves, and smiled as he watched the young man almost enjoying getting dirty. A sigh of relief spread over The Willows.

The following three years went by rather quickly, maybe because they were filled with the daily development of T. D. DeLongpre. He would reflect back to his childhood, and, instead of sadness, a cool, confidant smile would find its way over his countenance. The things that brought ridicule from his father were now becoming his biggest assets. Being quiet, watching, listening, asking questions if necessary, and making the decision.

He also learned a valuable lesson from all the stories he'd heard about the triumphs and woes endured over the years by his uncle and Ben's father. "Work hard, be honest, and when the labors get to be too much, get the best man for the job." This would be one of the secrets of his success.

A boy chronologically becomes a man on his twenty-first birthday. He can now vote, drink legally, become liable for lawsuits, and even more significant, he can be tried in the courts as an adult.

But in T. D.'s case, he had all these privileges plus. He, like his Uncle Jarrod, had never returned to Pennsylvania for a visit. In the young Mr. DeLongpre's case, it had only been three years. Now, yet another surprise was in store for him.

A couple weeks before Christmas, he was on his way out the back door when he and Ben had two different ideas. One was going out and the other coming in, only problem was it was at the same precise moment. After almost knocking each other down, Ben handed him an envelope.

"The guy knew me, so he let me sign for it. You must have been in the shower or whatever."

The contents of the telegram informed the birthday boy of his family's plan to visit. They would be coming by train, and "we love you." It was signed by his mother, which made him force a mild snicker.

He had mixed emotions about this, but he loved his mother in spite of all the times he had looked to her for support and she wouldn't stand up to his father. And there was Kathleen, Hannah, and Ruth. This brought on a big smile. Now he could show his father how wrong he was about him *and* his Uncle Jarrod.

The end of the week brought another telegram. The carelessness of a train engineer made him the only surviving DeLongpre. He was obviously devastated by the loss of his mother and sisters, but being the last DeLongpre gave him the unhappy chore of returning to Pennsylvania to say good-bye to his family and settle their affairs. "Being twenty-one isn't all that great for me," he muttered.

He left the cemetery and made his way sadly to the house he hadn't seen for three years, one that held many mixed memories. It was a house that was never a home. Now, it was nothing.

He turned the key of the archway-rounded door and heard the loud click of his boots as he walked the forty feet to his father's office. The various smells were still there and they changed as he passed the kitchen's aroma of bread and things, to the stale odor of pipe tobacco as he entered the office. It was like the spotless old house was just waiting patiently for its family who would never return.

He stared for a moment at the huge desk and the chair he once got yelled at for sitting in. He rounded the desk and sat heavily on the chair, put his feet up, and clasped his hands behind his head. He thought about The Willows and said out loud, "What the hell am I going to do with all this?"

He wouldn't have long to find out what to do with the house and business. As if he hadn't been through enough the past few days, fate threw him another curve. His braggadocios and abusing father, this man who had ridiculed and terrified him all these years, was nothing but a blowhard, a goddamn blowhard and a liar. After criticizing his uncle and everyone else, he knew this monster of a man was also a failure!

The family fortune was not only depleted, it was gone. The estate was hopelessly in debt. He was, however, only about two-thirds into the sloppily kept records when he could see no other choice but to give up what should have been a nice inheritance for him.

As he neared the end of this arduous task, he came upon a document that was not a bill or lawsuit. His father had sent him to Mississippi never divulging any of the terms of Uncle Jarrod's will.

He was now seventy-five percent owner of The Willows. Why hadn't his father told him? Why hadn't Ben Hampton told him?

The trip back home gave T. D. a long time to think about his journey of the past twenty-one years. He was sad and harboring a certain amount of guilt for the tragedy that had befallen his family. If they hadn't tried to be with him on his birthday, they'd still be alive. He would deeply miss his mother and especially his beloved sisters, but, as he struggled to find some love for his father, all he could come up with was his regret of non-resolution. He only wanted the old man's approval on something, and now he'd never get it. This would leave him with a permanent scar. Not a deep scar, but one that would influence his life forever.

Another regret was that he'd never met the uncle who'd left him his fortune in trust. But he could see after the three years he'd spent at The Willows that he was more like Uncle Jarrod than his father, and that gave him great satisfaction. He finally saw a positive side to this tragedy. A warm feeling of freedom began to fill his soul. He would now face the future feeling very confident and secure. However, this would be the last birthday he would acknowledge for many years to come.

Chapter Four

It was good to be home, and this time he could really call it home. It was home before, but T. D. didn't know just how much of a home it really was. Knowing this also helped to ease the pain of the tragedy—and the disgust of his father's blatant dishonesty.

One thing that really stood out above most of the other pleasures of being home was Jennie's cooking. T. D. had enjoyed this treat the entire time he'd been there. After resting a day or two, the fragrance that floated on The Willow's breezes made its way from Jennie's kitchen window to his nostrils and called him to the Hamptons for dinner. After a generous portion of upside-down cake, and between his first and second cup of coffee, he reached in his pocket, pulled out a copy of Jarrod's will and handed it to Ben. Ben looked at it briefly and grinned. "Let's have a cigar."

The two went out on the front porch, lit up, and began walking nowhere in particular. A few steps and a couple puffs later, Ben broke the silence.

"You know, T. D., our families friendships are not only a bit unusual, they are also very real. Now, I've heard your uncle talk to my pa, and I've spoken with him once or twice myself. He wasn't very fond of your father, as you well know, and, from what I've heard, it worked both ways.

"You see, T. D., he made that will up when you were knee-high. And the reason he did it the way he did was because he didn't know if you'd like it down here, being a Yankee and all, so he just wanted to play it by ear."

T. D. took another puff, thought for a moment, reached down and picked up a handful of dirt. He gestured to Ben and said, "You and I worked hard for this, and I know you and your pa did before me." He said with a big smile, "Ben, I feel like I owe you money!"

Ben reached for his hat that wasn't there, and this drew a hearty laugh. The big man who had seen many planting seasons come and go said in a low, easy drawl, "Well, I know there may be a dollar or two in the pot for me and my family, but, from what I can see, you ain't goin' nowhere, and neither am I!"

This new knowledge of his uncle's and the Hamptons' history started the wheels turning in T. D.'s head. It also strengthened the bond that had been established many years earlier. The Hampton's had accepted T. D. as the plantation's manager and had never questioned his decisions, although these same decisions were greatly influenced by Ben's patience and the knowledge behind his suggestions. The people living on this "island" in South-Central Mississippi knew about this racially torn part of the country. Of course, they knew of it, but, at The Willows, it just didn't exist. The employees felt safe there and seldom ventured outside its boundaries.

Hampton could see the wheels turning in his friend's head. He could see that this ambitious young man he had tutored and loved was not going to stop here. All he wanted was security for his family, which would soon have a new addition. He would not stand in the way of T. D.'s dreams. All he wanted was what was rightfully his, and that was something he knew he'd never have to worry about.

He dutifully listened to T. D.'s plans and ultimate goals. They were big, and they would look bigger in the coming years.

T. D. wanted Ben to be a part of everything, from planting the seeds to the shipping and building gins, and taking their profits to diversify into other ventures. Again, Mr. Hampton would say, "You go ahead, and I'll be here if you need me. Just take care of my children and their children."

This was the last assurance T. D. needed to go out and conquer the world.

The first decision he would make was to continue his Uncle Jarrod and Isaiah's traditions. He cemented his vow with a handshake, but he wasn't finished. He decided to build his new family a new home. At yet another of Jennie's wonderful dinners, he presented them with carefully thought out architect's plans. The looks of appreciation on their faces would be as satisfying as any fortune he would make in the coming years.

Isaiah Hampton had never seen the inside of a classroom, so, obviously, he couldn't read or write. While Jarrod was learning the basic fundamentals of running a farm from Isaiah, he did his best to acquire books and other reading materials so he could teach him to read or at least recognize some important words and symbols. This way, Isaiah could keep up with new trends and machinery if Jarrod wasn't there. The *Agriculture Monthly* was always available for mail order or just learning. These books and publications added up over the years and became a pretty fair county library.

When T. D. learned of his new status, he decided to convert the library into an office. But after spending some time skimming through the contents, he found many books he liked and some very interesting papers and documents that gave him some insight into his own personal history. Since he had more than ample room to work with, he just expanded the library, rather than change it.

This library/office would be his private domain until some sixty years later when he took his last breath. Over the years, he would add to the contents of the room he simply called "Jarrod's Place." From Jarrod's Place, he could hear the music—the music that came in the late afternoons when the breeze ruffled the limbs and leaves of the ageless trees bordering the lane leading from the outside world to his paradise.

To T. D., like his Uncle Jarrod, The Willows meant everything. He deeply appreciated the fact that this land had given him his start in business. He would use this business to always protect it. No matter how far he traveled or how long he was gone, each time he passed beneath the wrought-iron sign into the arbor, his thrill was as strong as the very first time.

The young master of The Willows heard of a small cotton brokerage in eastern Mississippi owned by a shrewd old gent with the last name of Patterson. He made the trip and, upon seeing the business from the outside, thought, *Well, I gotta start somewhere.*

Ezekial Patterson heard the bell to the front door of his office. As he yelled, "Door's open. Come in," the silhouette of a large man shut out the late morning sun that had briefly blinded him. As the sun left his eyes and the tall man came closer, Ezekial could see this prospect was serious. He looked at the stranger's face and steel gray eyes. As his gaze lowered, his loose spectacles slid down his razor-thin nose, and he asked in a squeaky southern drawl, "And you are?"

"I'm T. D. DeLongpre. I understand you're interested in retiring."

"That so?"

T. D. could see that the little man wanted to dicker, but he got right to the point. He knew before he got there the amount of business Mr. Patterson did and what he was worth. He also knew that he had a wife twice his size and that she wanted to get out of there and back to her home in St. Louis.

T. D. was not one to throw money around, well, not in business anyway. However, he wanted this transaction to happen quickly, so he took Mr. Patterson's first numbers, added to these, and the Patterson's were on their way to St. Louis.

Time was of the essence when he was getting started. After this purchase, he bought a cotton gin, then a mill and refinery, all in quick succession. He finally slowed down but only just a bit.

This was the beginning of a new era for the last surviving DeLongpre. He would make some gains, suffer some losses, and make some friends. For the most part, the scales would tip in his favor.

Seasoned businessmen thought he was no more than a rich young gambler and that his streak wouldn't last. But, as always, he never exposed his hold card. His security was based on carefully planned research, and, because of this, his losses were minimal. Soon, the same skeptics realized his Midas touch wasn't based on luck. His reputation as an astute and honest businessman grew rapidly.

He would call Ben from various cities and towns to keep him appraised and see how things were at the ranch. Sometimes the calls were out of just plain loneliness. One of these phone calls would change everything at The Willows. "My friend we've got to prepare for something big on the horizon!"

"And what would that be?"

"The Great War, Benjamin!" the young rancher said emphatically.

The men began discussing plans for growing more cotton so they could prepare for military contracts that T. D. was beginning to negotiate. T. D. asked Ben about some acreage down below where the new trees had been planted. Ben informed him that it was close to three thousand acres, and they agreed this would be adequate for now. Ben's job was to find extra workers and pay more if necessary to get the best people he could find. Mr. DeLongpre ended the conversation by saying, "I have some more meetings, but I'll be home in two weeks."

T. D. went to his meetings full of confidence, knowing he had the facilities to provide what was needed for the war effort. After hearing his pitch, the clothing department for the Army invited him to make bids. Though he was young, they found him to be a tough but extremely fair negotiator.

During a particularly difficult contract negotiation, the liaison from the Department of Defense made an observation. He said he didn't know who was harder to please, the colonels he had to deal with, or T. D. He jokingly called him "The Colonel."

This story was repeated many times, and the title stuck from that day on. Mr. DeLongpre was now known as "Colonel DeLongpre." That, however, was only in the business world. He remained T. D. at home.

On one of his many trips before the war, while he was trying to secure his position in the cotton industry, he went to Meridian, Mississippi to meet with Harold J. Fontaine with the intention to acquire his refinery. This was one of the few offers he'd made that was not accepted, so he put the Fontaine project on the back burner. After the war, he was a very rich man, but now the demands for his product were even greater, so he needed to expand. He awoke one morning and told Ben he was off to Meridian.

The Fontaines' plantation was one that survived the Civil War, but had not been modernized like The Willows and others that had endured, so it was barely self-sustaining. They had recently been selling their land piece by piece in order to live. The house, refinery, and a few of the old manicured gardens were sadly all that remained of a once grand lifestyle.

This time The Colonel was not denied. He worked out a deal where Harold would receive a small percentage of the profits, and would still own the house. As the two men shook hands, The Colonel said softly, but firmly, "We have to think of your family, Harold."

Mr. Fontaine was elated with this prospect and invited The Colonel to his home for dinner that same evening. Elaine and Harold were gracious hosts. The old house was still beautiful, and dinner was delicious, but certain little situations during the meal told T. D. he was being set up for something. The business was completed, so what could it be? He wouldn't have long to wait, because Harold was being obvious when he seemed to go out of the context of the conversation and make it clear that his daughter was single. Several times during the course of the evening he would repeat, "She's my oldest daughter, Lillian."

He made it a rule not to mix business with other things, but, being the southern gentleman he was, albeit transplanted and keeping in mind the successful business deal he and Fontaine had completed, he decided to just lay back and enjoy the rest of the evening. At the conclusion of this carefully planned dinner, as Fontaine invited him to have a brandy and cigar, Lillian interrupted her father. "Would you like to join me for a stroll through the gardens, Colonel DeLongpre?" she drawled velvetly.

"That would be most pleasant, Miss Fontaine." He turned to face her father, bowed slightly, and requested, "Sir, with your permission?"

Harold nodded and grinned triumphantly to his wife. "Of course, of course. You two enjoy yourselves this balmy evening."

The Colonel hadn't paid a whole lot of attention to her during dinner, but, as she carried on a monologue, pointing out the various flowers, shrubs, and trees, he realized how very beautiful this petite, fine-figured southern belle was.

Eventually they came to a bench by a small stream that ambled through the still lovely gardens. Here they sat down upon the weathered wood bench.

Up until then, she'd done most of the talking and that was good. All he had to do was nod and drink in her beauty. He finally turned to face her and said, "Miss Fontaine, please forgive me. I planned my trip here to Meridian to finalize some business with your father. This is unusual for me, but I'm surely glad to have made your acquaintance. By the way, would you do me the honor of calling me T. D.?"

She looked in his handsome face, as she tugged gently on a curl for a second before replying, "I don't know about my father's business, Colonel…T. D., but I do know it'd be my pleasure if you'd call on me again."

She smiled, taking his hand in hers and squeezing slightly said, "I think you should take me back to the house now."

The next three years were productive ones for the residents of The Willows. T. D. was building outside businesses, and Ben Hampton was building on to an already successful farm.

T. D. was always on the lookout for any advances in the business world and in farming methods whenever he was away from The Willows. Any of these advances and farming techniques that warranted their attention would be tried and tested by Ben and T. D. If they worked or someway fitted into their scheme of things, they were kept. If not, they were discarded to make room for more.

Even though he had been extremely dedicated to his plan, when he had free moments, his mind would drift back to a gentle hand squeeze in a moonlit garden in Meridian, Mississippi. The picture of her pretty fingers twisting the one lock of her hair kept fading in and out like in a dream. From some magic imaginary place, he could hear an echoing, soft, velvety drawl, saying, *"Call on me sometime…" "Call on me sometime…" "Call on me sometime…"*

He mentioned this meeting with the Fontaines and their daughter to Ben and Jennie. This was the first they could remember him saying anything about his social life. They were a bit surprised. They had visions of him being a bachelor like his Uncle Jarrod. Not that that was bad, but they were hoping someday soon to bring some new life to their beloved Willows.

There was a reason for concern. No babies had been born here for years.

Ben and Jennie had been trying for quite some time now, but to no avail.

One morning, a tired Jennie was trying her best to fix her husband's breakfast when she became nauseous. While she was in the bathroom, it suddenly occurred to her that the monthly punishment God had given to all women hadn't happened. She consulted her physician and guess what?

Everyone from T. D. to the stable boys was overjoyed.

The Hamptons had waited a long while for this, and not even the doctor's strict orders about Jennie's activities could mar their happiness. Jennie made it clear that no matter what, she'd never allow anyone else in her kitchen. Well, those were pretty strong words for a lady who had never experienced pregnancy. Anyway, she compromised with the doctor. She'd rest a little more each day and cook a little less as her pregnancy progressed.

As the big day loomed nearer, they became increasingly anxious. At night, Ben would crawl in bed, put one arm around Jennie and place his big weathered hand on her tummy, waiting for their baby to move. They would cuddle and giggle, suggesting dozens of boy and girl names out loud, over and over, until one or two would roll off the tongue and sound good with Hampton.

As sure as day loses to night, months turn in to years, and seasons change and start all over again. Once a baby is ready to make its debut, not much is going to change its mind.

Jennie woke up and realized her labor was beginning. She hit Ben in the ribs with a well-aimed elbow, but all he did after many years was roll over and continue snoring. Another elbow would do the trick, if a bit more force were used. He was no longer snoring now and something inside told him exactly why he was being attacked.

Ben looked at her worriedly. She was at least a couple weeks early, and he was frightened. Jennie cried out for him to call the doctor. By the time he found the number and made his shaky fingers dial, he returned to her side and almost caught his first-born son.

After all their hopes, all their efforts, and all the time that they'd waited, their dream had come true in the form of a beautiful little boy with a great set of lungs.

The doctor arrived thirty minutes later and ran in the house, expecting the worst. What he saw was a beaming Ben Hampton sitting on a very messy bed next to his wife with his son in his arms. He took a deep breath, and, after examining mother and child, he found them both to be in good health. He looked upward and a silent "thank you" left his lips. No matter how many times he'd done this, the miracle of birth brought tears to the old country doctor's eyes.

There was but one thing left to do, and Jennie reminded her husband, "You'd better call T. D., honey, as I remember, he made that very clear!"

The man with the new title was in the process of checking out of the hotel he had called home the previous two nights. The phone rang and the man at the desk excused himself, then returned seconds later and said, "It's for you, Colonel DeLongpre. The man says it's urgent!"

The first thing that passed through his mind was *Jennie! Oh no, something's gone wrong!*

He tried to remain calm as he walked to the desk phone. He picked it up slowly and the look of concern that had enveloped his usually stolid face transformed into a huge smile. The man at the desk saw this transformation and asked, "Good news?"

"You bet!" said a beaming Colonel Delongpre.

This time when T. D. passed through the entrance to his home, he felt differently. The arrival of the Hamptons' child was the first birth at The Willows in all the years he'd been there. From what Ben and Jennie said, it had been a while before. More than anything, he was very anxious to hold his godson.

He burst through the back door into the kitchen of his friend's home. Jennie put her fingers to her lips and said, "Shush, the baby's asleep."

This normally even-tempered, easy-mannered man had trouble containing his feelings. Jennie and Ben stifled a chuckle. As he tiptoed to the doorway, they giggled quietly. This is the first time they'd seen T. D. "burst" anywhere.

He came out of the sleeping baby's room and joined the proud parents at the famous kitchen table. Jennie had already poured him a cup of coffee and, per his demand, began a detailed description of everything that happened.

During her attempts to tell the story, Jennie was interrupted dozens of times by both men. She actually got through it three times, but they still asked her to repeat it, until the new mother couldn't hold her head up or make her mouth work.

As the tired mother excused herself, a whimper was heard by all present, and the new daddy jumped up to fetch the baby. He returned with the baby in his arms and announced to the mother and new godfather, "Ladies, and gentlemen, I give you William Jarrod Hampton!"

T. D. loved his role as a godfather, but they all agreed that uncle sounded a bit cozier, so the formal-sounding title changed to "Uncle T. D."

The times he spent with Willie were very precious indeed. And seeing Ben and Jennie with their baby boy underlined his feelings of wanting a wife and family. He realized that all he had and would accomplish, meant nothing unless he was working for something…or someone.

He had met many women during the course of doing business in so many places, and they all knew he was eligible. He had enjoyed their willingness to fulfill his needs, but, when they tried to get closer, his mind would take him back to the little lady who tugged at her curls.

T. D. invented several "business trips" back to Meridian, and, while he was there, he might as well call on the young lady who had invited him to do so.

Everyone knew that the refinery in Meridian was well-staffed. The Colonel would not leave there unless it was. And Harold J. still had a small piece of the action, so everything was almost guaranteed to run smoothly.

On any given evening, Jennie would tell Ben to call Uncle T. D. for dinner.

"Oh, honey, he won't be joining us this evening."

"Another emergency trip to Meridian?"

"Yeah, looks that way."

The Hamptons enjoyed this little joke, and they liked these unexpected trips to Meridian because, when T. D. returned, you could ask him any question and the answer would always be yes.

After several of these invented trips, he first proposed, and, as the custom called for, he asked Mr. Fontaine for his daughter Lillian's hand.

It was 1922, while the rest of the world was full tilt in to the jazz age, the last DeLongpre brought his bride home to begin their life at The Willows.

In this era, couples rarely got a chance to know each other before they were married. Lillian was happy about the way she and T. D. had met and knew it could have gone the other way due to her father's loveable but clumsy attempt to introduce them. She was also grateful they'd had a chance to court; only she wished it hadn't taken so long.

She'd liked him that first night, in spite of the uneasy atmosphere created by her father. She knew Papa had good intentions, that he loved her, and that he'd been concerned about the whole family's future. He only wanted to make sure his little girl had a good life. She was glad the evening turned out as well as it did, but why did it take so long for him to call on her again? Life holds many surprises, and here she was, next to the most wonderful man in the whole world. She was on the way to her new home and hoping with all her heart that she could make him as happy as he'd made her, by asking her to spend the rest of their lives together.

He was giving her a running commentary on the trip from Meridian to The Willows. He went on about Ben and Jennie and how much he enjoyed little Willie. She liked the way his eyes glistened as he talked about the wonderful place he called home.

She listened intently. When she didn't catch all of some particular sentence, she would look out the corner of her eye to see if he was through, then clear her throat and ask him to repeat it please.

He was quiet for a moment, and she seized the chance to ask him something she'd been giving quite a bit of thought to. She slid across the leather seat, and began gently caressing the nape of his neck. She asked sweetly, "T. D., why don't you tell me a little history of my new home?"

"History?" he asked as he enjoyed the pleasure of her soft touch.

"Yes, tell me about how the wonderful place began. You see that little lake with the trees and park benches over there? Let's go have a picnic and you can tell me all about it. Look! I packed a little lunch." She picked the basket out of the back seat, peeked around the end of it, and teasingly batted her eyes. "Okay?" she asked, already knowing he would agree.

He thought that was a fine idea, and now he knew what was in that odd-looking container.

The newly married Colonel took a blanket out of the touring box that contained things like flares and tools for emergencies and spread it out on the cool grass. As Lillian began to unwrap the carefully packed items, he thought of what a joy she was just to watch. The cold chicken was delicious, but he'd tell her at a later date to leave the crust on his sandwiches.

"Well, are you going to tell me?" she asked again.

"On an empty stomach?" he answered.

They enjoyed a quick kiss and a hug and he began, "Well, my Uncle Jarrod named the place 'The Willows' after he bought it for back taxes. I don't know what it was before, but Ben told me that his relatives had been there over one hundred years. Anyway, Ben's father, Isaiah, and his family along with a group of ex-slaves were there when my uncle bought the place."

"You mean they owned it?"

"Oh no, after or during the war, I don't know which, the people that owned it just up and left. I guess they couldn't make it when they had to pay somebody. Anyway, Uncle Jarrod saw what these ex-slaves had done with little or nothing. The part they were living on was very productive, while the rest had more or less gone to hell. He talked Isaiah into staying. That actually wasn't too difficult because he thought Jarrod was going to kick them out."

"How did Jarrod hear about the place when he was up in Pennsylvania?"

"I'm sorry, Lill, I was getting a little ahead of myself. When my grandfather died, he left a goodly amount of money to my father and Uncle Jarrod. The brothers never really got along that well, so my dad decided to stay in the mining business, or at least that's what we thought he was doing. Jarrod wanted to travel, speculate, and see different parts of the country."

"How or why did he pick this part of Mississippi?"

"There were these two other brothers who belonged to the same hunting club as Uncle Jarrod did. I think their family name was Benton or something like that. Anyway, I guess they took a trip through the south, just for the hell of it, and, when they returned, they told Uncle Jarrod about some parts of the territory that could be bought real cheap. So, Uncle Jarrod took off and kept looking around until he found this place. From what I've been told, he planned to come in and work it, then turn it over for a quick profit. I guess he fell in love with it, just like I did. Is there any more chicken?"

Lillian pulled back the pink cotton tablecloth that covered the picnic basket, and cooed, "Thigh or breast?"

He gave her an "it's all good" gesture and polished off the breast. After wiping his hands and taking a sip of lemonade, he stood up, stretched, and held out his hands to her. As they walked hand in hand by the lake, she urged him to continue.

"The idea of turning the place over kind of went by the wayside, and, not only that, Uncle Jarrod and Isaiah worked the place side by side. Slowly, it got going really well, and they became real good friends. Sorta like Ben and me, I guess."

Lillian smiled as she watched him enjoy telling the tale of The Willows' history and asked, "Uncle Jarrod must have been real nice. What was he like?"

The Colonel laughed softly, and this caused his wife of only hours to look at him questioningly.

"I never met him, Lill. If I did, I was real young. Some of his philanderings were sort of like folklore around The Willows. It's told that every so often he would tire of the routine and enjoy a cocktail or two. Ben told me of his father saying that after a few drinks, no woman was safe in most of southern Mississippi. I'm sure that was an exaggeration, but it made for a good story. No, I never did meet him, because he never came back home again."

Lillian was amused by the tale, feigned embarrassment, and asked. "How'd you get the place then?"

"Uncle Jarrod never married, and, since he wasn't real fond of my dad, I was next in line. I sure would like to have met him though. I never was very close to my dad, so it would've been nice to have someone to look up to when I was growing up."

He bent down, picked up a flat rock, and flung it over the lake. They watched it skip five or six times as they giggled with satisfaction. Sometimes boys never grow up, they only get taller.

"T. D., I've heard a lot of different names from different nationalities. I know the French were around here for awhile, but you're not from here, so where do the DeLongpres come from?"

"From my grandfather, Joseph. He came over in the early 1800s. I don't know if it's true or not, but my father told me he had some kind of dealings with Napoleon."

"Wow, I'm impressed!"

"Well, don't get too impressed. Like I said, my father told me that. Anyway, on my eighteenth birthday, or my graduation, my father gave me an option to go to college there or go down and manage Uncle Jarrod's farm. I didn't really have to think that long. I'd have done almost anything to get away from him."

"That's sad."

The DeLongpre's packed up the car and began the rest of the trip home. He warned her about the condition of the mansion, but told his bride that she could have carte blanche and fix it up anyway that pleased her. He told her not to worry about the money because they'd be there for a long time.

"I'm sure I'll love it just the way it is!"

The Colonel looked over at her sweet, trusting face and decided to leave well enough alone.

Chapter Five

There was a serenity and peaceful feeling to the estate. Bachelors had occupied the house for almost sixty years, and Lillian was taken aback by the condition of the thirty-room mansion—even though she'd been warned. All the furniture she could see was covered and a dark gloom penetrated everything. She couldn't understand, with all the rooms available, why her husband used only two rooms on the ground floor. He had a bedroom and a library/office and that was it, with the exception of a kitchen that looked like it hadn't been used much. She was *extremely* glad to see they had indoor plumbing, at least.

But right now, she was anxious to meet the legendary Hamptons, and when he began to explain the unused kitchen, she interrupted him in mid-sentence, asking when they would meet his partner. He took her by the hand, said they were expected at the Hamptons for dinner, and began the short walk.

Earlier, Jennie had seen the car through the kitchen window as it pulled up when the DeLongpres first arrived. The Colonel didn't have to knock because the door burst open just as they stepped on the porch. They were immediately engulfed in the open arms of Ben and Jennie. Lillian was caught off guard for a split second. T. D. never mentioned they were "colored." She heard him say ex-slaves, but she just assumed that they were a bunch of people that worked there. *Isaiah was a slave, too. I must have missed that.* She was sure no one had noticed her slight gasp. As she was recovering, she was nearly knocked over by a little two-year-old running at full speed and grabbing her knees.

Lillian tried to keep up with the dinner conversation, but was just lost with so many questions flying around. The three knew each other so well that they almost talked in shorthand. So, she ate slowly and tried to handle all the questions about the wedding and trip home.

As she looked at the Hamptons and their lovely home, it wasn't anything she was prepared for. None of her family or friends ever had any relationships with the "colored," and she had never imagined sitting down to dinner with them. They certainly lived better than any coloreds she'd seen in Meridian and, as far as that went, better than a lot of "whites."

She excused herself to use the powder room and took a second to peak at the rest of the house. Jennie certainly had lovely taste. Yes, they were not like any she'd ever met before. They were clearly very nice, and that little boy with the huge brown eyes was an absolute treasure. When he demanded, in the most serious manner a two-year-old can, to sit next to "Tilly" (it was easier to say than Lillian) at dinner, she was hooked. She was glad he liked her so much.

She had a lot more to learn about her man and the way he lived. What other surprises were in store for her? No matter, she loved him with her whole being and knew all would be well at The Willows.

For several years, there had been a smooth rhythm at the estate. Ben and his staff kept everything going in the right direction while The Colonel was off building an empire. Jennie was busy making a nice home for them, hoping and praying they would someday be blessed with a little Ben or little Jennie. The three of them became closer every day. The Hamptons had many reasons to be happy. They were blessed with the birth of Willie, and, two years later, The Colonel would be blessed with Lillian. Now there were five.

Being friends with the Hamptons was a perfect way for the young bride to ease into the estate's routine. When T. D. was gone, she had lunch and dinner or both at Ben and Jennie's every day. There was also her new little pal, Willie. When The Colonel was home, they would go out to eat quite often. Lillian announced to her husband that she wanted to make the kitchen and dining room her first project and take a little of the load off of Jennie. She also had Willie to take care of when he wasn't in her apron pockets.

"Then we can have them over here once in awhile. Walking up the path to our house would be almost like going out to dinner for the poor dear!" And a dear she was to Lillian. Jennie's warmth and straight-from-the-hip look at things charmed the new mistress of The Willows. Lillian was surprised they had as much in common as they did. They were both educated, liked to read, and, from what Lillian had seen from Jennie's home, she knew she could learn a few things to incorporate into her project. And there was Willie. He was simply a bonus.

Lillian's cup was full to the brim. Of course, she missed her husband, but she grew not to mind that. Now and then, she would accompany him when he had to go to some special place like New Orleans or Boston, and that kind of made up for them not yet having a real honeymoon. She was always eager though to get back to Willie, The Willows, and her project.

T. D. had given her a no limits sign for her redecorating, and she was anxious to begin. She asked him if he had any recommendations for architects or contractors. Yes, he did, *and* she could have her pick. They began arriving in a few days, as if a great leader at a summit meeting had called them.

The gentleman she chose could see the young lady was inexperienced, but sat very patiently through many glasses of iced tea. There were reasons for his patience. One was, The Colonel asked him to be there, and, two, even considering her inexperience, the woman was bright and knew what she wanted. He also marveled at her long-range scheme.

After getting the better part of her dream in his head, he told her he needed a couple of days to check out how close he could come to fulfilling it.

Following his tour of the old mansion, he sat down with her and another pitcher of tea. "Mrs. DeLongpre, I can do what you want in the long run, but I can't do it one room at a time. The house is surprisingly stable after many years of neglect. It's going to take at least a year, maybe longer. I can do your kitchen immediately, however, because it was added on after the initial construction."

This was not exactly what she wanted to hear, but she knew he was telling the truth, or he wouldn't be there. At least she'd have her kitchen soon.

On a shopping trip into Hattiesburg, she discovered a beautiful park with the most magnificent array of roses she'd ever seen. This solved two problems. Now she knew what to do with that vacant expanse between the back door and stone-bordered path leading to the Hamptons and the old barn and corral. This would also keep her busy until she could begin her big project. The lady was very pleased with herself and her life in general.

Lillian returned to the park in Hattiesburg several times and to the city library. She got all the literature available on every variety of rose she saw. She had considered going to Jarrod's place for this information, but, on the way home from their wedding, the image painted of Jarrod by his nephew did not identify him as a man who cared about flora and fauna.

During that year, she had rose plants shipped from Portland, Oregon; Pasadena and San Francisco, California; and places that she had never *heard* of. Somehow, between sore muscles and fifty questions an hour from Willie, she was able to fashion a garden of which she was very proud.

Time, as it always seems to, did pass, and the moment Lillian had waited for was upon her. The contractor had finished the task of solidifying the mansion. Now the fun part could start. She had her kitchen, and, as the saying goes, "the way to a man's heart is through his stomach," could be proven once again. She had all of his heart and wanted a place for all his love. So, they began building the master bedroom.

A few weeks later, the newlyweds slept in the elegant four-poster bed between the lovely silken sheets that she'd been saving in her trousseau. Her husband's response was very gratifying. He teased her a little about not using these sheets before, and she chastised him, "T. D., these aren't sheets used for camping out!"

He looked rather startled for a second before they both broke out laughing. During the remodeling, they'd indeed roughed it a bit. But they were happy now, so it was worth it!

T. D. never believed in luck. He did believe that success was the product of careful planning and minimal risks, never chance. Meeting Lillian was not luck. Though that had been planned, he would always say he was lucky as hell to have her love him. And he *loved* his beautiful wife! Needless to say, he was more than a little proud of her. Yes, she'd been groomed to be the wife of a successful southern gentleman, but her lessons never included a task the scope of remodeling The Willows mansion. He would say to the Hamptons or anyone else in earshot, "My God, look what she's done!"

And just look what she's done! No, she didn't carry around an apron full of nails and a hammer, but, for the time it took, she sure as hell kept the contractor and workers on their toes. The main thing The Colonel liked—granted there were many things—but the one he enjoyed the most was when he returned home. His suitcases had hardly hit the floor when she'd grab his hand and lead him off to a special showing of her handiwork. Then she'd let him relax, and, after a sumptuous meal, they'd go to the kitchen table. Cigars weren't allowed in the dining room yet, so in order for her to give him a financial report, they would have to use the kitchen or the veranda. The Colonel could have cared less about the report, but he marveled at her grasp of the smallest details and once again enjoyed her combination of beauty and brains.

Now, it was time for retrospect. The Colonel was away, somewhere up in Louisville she thought. She enjoyed a light breakfast and went to the window overlooking her multicolored garden. Another color flashed in the corner of her eye. It was Jennie in her bright yellow dress helping herself to some roses for her dining room table centerpiece. This was okay because she had set apart a special section just for this purpose. Roses always needed trimming anyway.

She waved to Jennie and wondered where "Wondrous Willie" was. She was usually busy, but there was always time for her little treasure. She smiled as she caught herself still referring to him as a baby. *My God, he's almost six.* She might have had her garden and house finished months earlier if it wasn't for him, but she wouldn't have minded had it taken longer. Now, Willie was getting taller and so were his questions.

He'd followed her around since the first day she'd arrived, bombarding her with questions by the millions, and, though it was almost impossible, she did her best to answer them all. Jennie always laughed, saying that if she ever wanted to find her boy, all she needed to do was look out the window where Lillian was toiling in her garden. Willie'd be right at her heels, talking a blue streak. One might think that Jennie would mind this, but she somehow didn't. Later on, her unselfish attitude would loom very large.

As Lillian continued her lookin'-at-nothing-in-particular gaze through the kitchen window, she was reminiscing about all of those wonderful days. Those wonderful days, days when he asked questions she couldn't answer. Days when big brown eyes would look up at her and melt her heart. Those days were fewer now, but they still made up for her not having her own child…almost…but not quite.

She came out of her little daydream and began working on the room she had saved for the last. That would be the nursery. She thought about the word nursery for a moment. It sounded too much like a place to buy plants. So, from this day forth, it would be "the children's wing." As she was doodling a few sketches, the thought of T. D. and her not having their own kids by now would drift in and out. *Well, we've just been too busy* or *he's gone away so much.* She convinced herself that when she became an older married woman, having kids would just happen. That seemed to satisfy her drifting thoughts and bring them back to the sketchpad.

When the basic work on the children's wing was nearing completion, Lillian made an executive decision. She asked her husband on his way out one day to take an extra week or so when he returned next time. No, she wouldn't explain why right now, but it was extremely important to both of them. *No, don't worry!* T. D. was a man of his word and proved it one more time.

This time when he arrived home, he opened the door, dropped his suitcases, threw up both arms, and shouted, "I'm yours, your majesty, for a whole month!"

His open arms were soon filled with several "thank yous" coming from the occupant filling those arms. He was a bit surprised when he wasn't drug off for yet another private showing. He waited patiently through dinner, but the woman of mystery still did not utter a single word. Finally, when he'd lit his after-dinner cigar, she led him upstairs.

If he was surprised that he had not been dragged upstairs immediately upon his arrival, he was in for a bigger surprise. She had come up with an elaborate plan for them. They would decorate this together. When he saw the old paint clothes laid out, he started laughing.

"Now, I'm serious, T. D., you and me. That means no contractors or painters, no Ben and Jennie. You and me! Got it!"

"Now, darlin', you really don't trust me with a paint brush, do you?"

"You bet I do, T. D. I won't accept anything but a good day's work out of you and with a smile on your face, Colonel, sir! This is going to be for our kids, and I want it perfect!"

"I'm ready and willing, my dear." He rubbed his full tummy, and said inwardly, *she's done it again.*

Later that year, Lillian was putting the finishing touches on the children's wing. She had gone through a month in very close quarters with her husband. This man was efficient at most everything he attempted, and he certainly was a love for taking time off to help her with the final project at the mansion. She looked at the pictures she had taken of his clothes and hair with nearly as much paint on them as the walls, and chuckled out loud to no one. "There's lots of things that go together in this world, but T. D. DeLongpre and a paint brush are not one of them!"

She was putting little knick-knacks on some corner shelves when she looked at the time, "My Lord, Willie's going to be here in an hour, and I have to clean up!"

It was Ben and Jennie's anniversary, and she'd promised to entertain her Willie for the evening, or until whenever. This was never a chore. She always looked forward to their adventures.

The Hamptons drove into Hattiesburg for dinner and dancing. They never worried about Willie. He was as much at home in the big house as he was in his own. In fact, one would be pressed to figure where between the two he spent the most time. This night, they had a grand rug picnic and sort of a camp-out inside. They always stuffed themselves. Lillian told him spooky stories or went through reams of paper drawing farm animals—well, they were intended to be farm animals anyway. They always did this or something equally as decadent when Willie slept over.

The anniversary couple enjoyed a wonderful evening. Dinner was excellent and Ben the Charmer told his lovely wife that the food was almost as good as hers. That and the flowers were all a girl could handle for one evening. But just in case it didn't fill her heart to capacity, he took her to a place where they met some well-wishing friends and danced into the late hours.

When they began the drive home, Jennie, for some reason, felt very young and impetuous. She slid across the seat, put her arm around her man's shoulder, and rested her head against his neck. After she began to feel all cozy and loving, she looked up at him and just gazed without speaking for a long minute. She decided she'd make an effort, or maybe dream up an occasion to get him in a suit more often. She told him how much she loved him, and she softly started crooning one of his favorite ballads. He smiled down at her in enjoyment. When he looked back at the road, the last thing he would see were the taillights of a stalled truck.

Dr. Scanton Lane could see that Ben had been killed instantly. He told an aide that he would get to the death certificate later. All his energy would be needed to save Jennie. Her body was severely crushed from the impact. It looked like she'd been stomped on like a child would do to a doll she no longer wanted. Her chest and upper body suffered multiple fractures, and her left lung had collapsed. From what he could tell, the worst injury had been sustained around her collarbone, which had lacerated her vocal cords and crushed her voice box. He beckoned a nurse, "You better find a next of kin."

The nurse found Jennie's purse on the table at the entrance to the emergency room. She found an address and two phone numbers. The first number didn't answer, but the second did.

A sleepy voice said, "Hello, this is Mrs. DeLongpre." Lillian sat straight up in bed, shocked and confused. "What? Oh my God! No!" she cried.

With the nurse still on the line, Lillian woke The Colonel. The nurse told of the horrible tragedy and all that was being done. They had to go to the hospital, but what about the sleeping Willie? There was nothing they could do about the situation. Ben was dead, and Jennie was in intensive care. There were many employees at The Willows, but no one they could think of who Willie would be comfortable with should he awake. The decision was difficult, but they had to take Willie with them. Lillian took a blanket and wrapped it around the sleeping boy. The Colonel gently picked him up and carried him to the car. Lillian sat in the back seat with Willie cradled in her arms. The twenty miles seemed like one hundred as The Colonel tried to miss all the bumps, so as not to wake him.

By the time the DeLongpre's arrived at the hospital, Dr. Lane had finished with Jennie and signed the necessary papers for Ben. He told them her life had been saved, but, after setting all the bones that he could and medicating her, the rest would be up to the head surgeon. Now all they could do was wait. Jennie didn't regain consciousness after surgery and lapsed into a coma.

The Colonel finished a quiet private conversation with Dr. Lane and walked down the bleak, colorless hall on the way to Jennie's intensive care unit. He saw his wife gently holding her friend's hand, but there were no tears, just a sad stare. He laid his hand on the distraught Lillian's shoulder and whispered, "Let's go, Lillian…. The boy…."

Lillian looked up at her husband. He saw deadness in her eyes and an emptiness he had never seen before. "Lill, honey, there is nothing we can do. Dr. Lane and his staff are doing all they can. Let's take Willie home and try to get some rest."

Lillian couldn't speak, but acknowledged her husband's request with a nod. He gently took her hand that was holding Jennie's and led her to where Willie was sleeping.

The gray skies matched the mood of the DeLongpres as they motored back to The Willows. They had to somehow break the terrible news to little Willie. None of the news would be good—just a part of it would be easier to take.

The six-year-old was told that his momma was hurt very badly, but would be okay in time. His daddy, however, had gone to be with Jesus. His mother being hurt upset him greatly, but somehow his father going away more confused than upset him. Maybe he thought "Daddy" would return in time.

In the days leading up to Ben's funeral, there wasn't a whole lot of time for grieving. There was too much going on with Jennie, who was still in critical condition. The Colonel took care of all the details, just as calmly as he handled all his business, but at the funeral he wept openly. Oddly enough, Lillian, who would weep when The Colonel would bring her little gifts from abroad, was like a rock. She had both her men to see to, so it would be some time before she could grieve Ben's passing.

Until Jennie's condition could be resolved one way or another, The Colonel stayed at home and handled everything to do with his outside interests from "Jarrod's Place." With Ben's passing, he also had to run The Willows. He was very troubled and thought many hours about who could replace Ben. He could only hope to find someone suitable to fill Ben's big, big shoes.

Except for the funeral, Lillian had never known her husband to be very demonstrative, and, during this trying period, he became even more introverted. She knew he would heal in time but had no idea, even with her upbringing, how to help or soothe him.

Lillian also had a problem. She could keep Willie out of school for a while, but she couldn't take him with her to the hospital, at least for now. So she decided to ask Ben's old-maid sister, Odetta, to move in from her cabin across the way and take care of him.

Now, when Lillian was home, Willie would stay with her, there was no discussion there, but he should sleep and be around his own things as much as possible. Odetta was a kind and even-tempered lady and knew her way around a kitchen. This freed Lillian's time to sit with Jennie, which she did many hours every day.

Willie went back to school a couple weeks later, but Lillian learned after the first day or so that she needed to be there when the boy got home and came to the big house. He would be close to panic-stricken if she wasn't there. She'd have milk and cake or cookies and hold him in her arms for long periods at a time. This would reassure him that the doctors were doing everything possible to make his momma well again and that nothing was going to happen to Aunt Odetta, Uncle T. D., or her. They'd be there for him. When he would ask for his momma, Lillian would kiss his forehead and promise, "Your mommy will be home soon."

This reassurance seemed to dry his tears and lift his sadness a bit. At night, the DeLongpres would take solace in each other's arms. It had seemed like forever since that horrible evening. It had been very painful for all concerned, but these last few days were filled with joy and anticipation…Jennie was finally coming home!

The scars on the outside were barely visible. The bones had properly mended, but it wouldn't be the same around The Willows for a while yet. Not only were they deprived of hearing that lovely, happy singing, she didn't even utter a sound. The delicate surgeries were successful. The doctors were sure she could speak, but the injuries to her soul remained, and Jennie Hampton remained silent. The first Sunday morning after Jennie got home, Aunt Odetta brought her breakfast in bed, just as she had done for all these weeks. On the tray were roses from Lillian and funny papers. Jennie took one look at the roses, smiled, looked at the comics, and placed the tray back in Odetta's hands. She got dressed and went to her kitchen where she began frying potatoes, bacon, and eggs, just like she'd done forever.

She wouldn't talk, communicating in gestures to everyone. She seemed all right in every other way, and the doctors would throw up their hands and say, "Just be patient and ignore her silence."

Almost a year passed since the accident. Jennie had been home for several months, and, though she appeared quite jovial to those around her, when the bedroom door closed at night, she would lay and stare at the empty pillow next to hers, and softly cry herself to sleep. Willie now became the center of her universe. If she knew her boy was over at Lillian's, that was all right. Beyond that and school, she didn't like him out of her sight.

The end to her months of silence came suddenly and unexpectedly. She couldn't find Willie and she panicked. Willie had been around the house a little too much for his liking. Somewhere out there, there were sticks to break, rocks to throw in the lake, birds to scare out of the thickets, and, more importantly, he got a new puppy that had never seen him perform all these marvelous acts.

Willie started out on his adventure with his new best friend. He had gone quite a ways when he realized the only way he could see the sun was through the trees, and the light jacket he was wearing wasn't keeping him warm anymore. He gave his trooper the command to retreat and headed for home.

Jennie, however, was frantic. She went to find the old triangle that had been used for many years to call in the field hands, but she couldn't find it in the dark. Without thinking, she let out a scream, "Willie!" She did this a few times, but there was no response. Finally, somebody heard her. Odetta and Lillian heard her scream and went to see what the commotion was all about. As they began running down the great hall, Jennie burst through the door.

She shocked them both when she huskily yelled out that her son was missing. By the time the women got to Jennie's, Willie was sitting on the porch putting food out for his puppy. He had no idea why these three crazy women that ran his seven-year-old life were jumping up and down and dancing in circles. Then he realized his mommy was singing with them. "What a day," he yawned and went in to wash up for dinner.

Chapter Six

Ben had been gone for over a year. It was time for The Colonel to get back on the road. He had all his businesses set up to function without his presence, but another of the major reasons for his success was knowing people and their capabilities, coupled with a frequent show of his face at any given moment. This kept them on their toes. It also assured them that he really cared. Everyone was impressed with him remembering and calling each by their first name.

After many hours contemplating who to replace Ben with and the miraculous final healing of Jennie, it was time to contact Amos and Laurie Ann Hubbard.

Lillian had sent her car to the train station to pick up the Hubbards. Willie and Lillian, along with Jennie and Odetta, were sitting on the veranda enjoying iced tea and various baked delights while waiting for them.

The impossibility of totally replacing Ben was never mentioned or probably never even thought about. But everyone agreed that the running of The Willows demanded a wise and strong overseer.

From what The Colonel had told them about how the Hubbards' son had turned out, there were no better teachers for Willie to assume his "heritage."

Willie is going to be fine. This thought passed through Lillian's brain as she reached for a curl and just as quickly dropped her hand away.

From the moment the car door opened and the Hubbards stepped out, Lillian liked them. They looked tall, lean, and fit, reminding Lillian of an ad she'd seen in a magazine promoting a dude ranch somewhere in Texas. As introductions went around, she loved the northeastern accent and firm handshakes.

A "how does he always know?" grin flashed silently between Jennie and Lillian.

Willie stood silently looking up at these newcomers for a moment, and, like any fine young southern gentleman, he extended his hand and said, "Welcome to The Willows, Mr. Hubbard and you, too, ma'am!"

As the group sat down, Willie suddenly bounded down the stairs and said over his shoulder, "But my daddy was taller!"

"Well, I guess the hardest part is over." Jennie smiled.

It was not known, even by all of the world's tobacco experts, but a certain part of the Connecticut valley produced some of the world's best tobacco. The Hubbards were from right in the heart of it. The Colonel had met them on a trip to the region a few years prior. He wasn't necessarily looking to invest in tobacco, but he'd heard of several good opportunities in the valley, if one was patient and ferreted them out. He offered to buy them out, but was politely turned down, explaining that their land had been in the family for over a hundred years and it would go to their sons.

The Colonel liked the rugged but refined couple. In spite of the rejection, he began stopping by to visit with them whenever he was in the area or on the way through. It wasn't the physical resemblance, but Amos reminded him a lot of Ben and he enjoyed their many conversations about advanced agriculture and planting rotation. Amos sent valuable information about northern technology down to Ben, and The Colonel and Ben would try it out and send back a report with an idea or two of Ben's for possibly improving it. After this exchange had happened several times, The Colonel suggested Ben take a few days to visit with Amos face to face because, as he joked, "I'm the most expensive messenger on the planet."

Timing is everything, and, now that Ben was gone, this was the time. If anybody could take Ben's place, it would be Amos Hubbard. And if not, he was still The Colonel's choice.

On the last visit The Colonel had with the Hubbards, Amos was going through the first horrible months of retirement blues. He went through periods of feeling he'd outlived his usefulness to being just plain bored. He'd moved aside and let his sons take over. But he thought maybe he should've waited. Not that the boys weren't doing a good job. They were doing an excellent job, but after half a century of getting up with the roosters, he could not sleep in, as hard as he tried. When one has to work to relax, another approach may be needed.

They had considered a long vacation. But Laurie Ann confided to The Colonel she wouldn't take a trip to Europe or anywhere again with Amos.

She said sarcastically, "That man gets out of the car, or climbs off the train and can't get past the first patch of dirt that he sees!"

Amos was greatly saddened by Ben's death, and, when presented with The Colonel's offer said he wouldn't mind taking over for Ben, fine gentleman that he was, but he was a tobacco farmer. On top of that, he didn't think his wife would go for the move. Upon hearing this, Laurie Ann chastised her husband, "Don't you put this on me, Amos Hubbard! If I can get you out of the house and find you another patch of dirt to play in…."

After The Colonel went over the fact that Amos would still be growing things, with complete authority beyond the borders of Lillian's rose garden to run the farm in any manner they chose, the Hubbards were convinced. The new home, handsome salary, any other benefits within reason, and travel vouchers to return to Connecticut twice a year, if they chose, was enticing. There was, however, one last item on The Colonel's list. He wanted Amos to do his best to groom Willie for the eventuality of him running the place. This was not an option. Being in tune with nature and the understanding of how to use the land, not abuse it, is a talent you inherit. It is a gift that the Hamptons and Hubbards both possessed. The Colonel was positive that Willie was blessed with this, but if no one nurtured the boy, what would happen? What if nothing happened?

But the Hubbards relished a chance to have a little boy on the premises and such a polite one, too. Willie's "and welcome to you, too, ma'am" won Laurie Ann over. Amos saw the chance to raise another planter.

Amos agreed to all The Colonel's terms with one request of his own. He knew his youngest son, John, was staying on working with his brothers only to please his father. So, Amos wanted to make a trade. He'd teach Willie everything he knew about the land, if The Colonel would give John a position and training in his importing and exporting business with opportunity for advancement. The Colonel and Amos shook hands and the deal was done.

John was soon working his way up the corporate ladder in The Colonel's New England Company. His performance was outstanding, and it wasn't long before he'd worked his way into management.

The Hubbards decided that for their first official tasks, Laurie would furnish their new home, and Amos would be buying horses and other livestock needed to carry out his duties. Even though they had the latest farming equipment and techniques at their disposal, he still preferred the dying form of transportation, the horse, as he'd always supervised his fields and employees from the back of a horse.

Amos wasn't the only Hubbard who liked the equines. Laurie Ann, when she had time, enjoyed a good ride as much as anyone. Even though Amos may have spent most of the day in the saddle, he would enjoy a hearty supper prepared by Laurie Ann. She would make some sort of tasty dessert, a thermos of fresh coffee, and package up a special blend of favorite tobaccos. Amos would pick out a fresh mount and they'd ride to a secluded place and just smoke, eat, and relax. They'd done this for as long as they'd been married.

During these rides at their new address, Amos was educating himself on the different parts of the large estate. He'd dismount, pick up a handful of dirt, and, to Laurie Ann's dismay, sometimes even taste it. The geography was different, but it was still land, and it didn't take long for him to feel right at home.

The Colonel's plan was falling smoothly into place. The Hubbards had been there about three months, give or take a few days when Willie's school term ended and he started hanging around the stables. As Amos taught the young man to ride and handle various horses, the bond The Colonel had hoped for was coming together.

During the Hubbards' vacation over Christmas and New Year's, The Colonel and Willie decided to do something nice for Amos and Laurie Ann. They built a little gazebo-like structure out near their favorite smoking corner. It was rugged but adequate, with a roof and a couple of benches. A hitching post was provided, and water was diverted from a nearby creek.

The DeLongpre family demanded a lot, but always gave more than a fair amount back in return. The Hubbards would always remain part of The Willows rich history.

When birthday cards began arriving from Lillian's friends in the ladies club celebrating her thirty-fourth birthday, they drilled home the fact that she still had no children of her own. Loving Willie was wonderful, but she wanted her own baby to hold in her arms. The many awards she'd received for her rose garden were great, but you can't hug and kiss roses. She wanted a baby.

Lillian had her annual physical. As he had said every year previous, she was in excellent health. The doctor blamed her inability to have children down to being too anxious...*another Southern belle with the vapors*. That wasn't what he told her, it was his own little private joke he'd come up with from treating many women over the years with similar symptoms. However, he decided to have a conversation with his lovely patient. He asked her to have a seat while he reviewed his notes. He removed his glasses, wiped them with his handkerchief, put them back on, and looked across at a mildly nervous Lillian. He tried not to stare, but he found her to be extremely attractive. He got back to business by asking, "Mrs. DeLongpre, does your husband still travel a lot?"

"Why, yes he does. Are you inferring that this could be one of the reasons?"

" I'm not 'inferring,' as you put it, anything. I'm only trying to explore all the possibilities of why you are not having any success. Now, if you don't mind me asking, do you try on a regular basis?"

She started to reach for her ringlets, but quickly placed her hand back on her lap and squeezed her hanky. She trusted Dr. Fisher, but he was the only man she had ever discussed this subject with…other than her husband, of course. "I guess so," she considered, "but it's just that he's away so much, well, maybe when he gets home, I'm a little too anxious."

The doctor raised his hands and eyebrows simultaneously and smiled warmly. They talked a few minutes longer and he prescribed a mild sedative for her to take a few minutes before they tried the next time. He handed her the paperwork and scheduled an appointment in sixty days. He also asked her to have her husband contact him at his earliest convenience. As he watched her turn and walk through the door, he realized once again how much he missed his wife who had passed away two years previous. He shook his head slowly, exhaled, and thought, *if I were fortunate enough to have a mate who looked like that, I would try and find another way to make a living, and stay home.*

The Colonel came home the following week. He touched bases with the Hamptons, in fact, they all had dinner together that very evening. After everyone had dined and gone home, Lillian told him about her visit to the doctor. He agreed with what his wife and Dr. Fisher had discussed, but he had some bad news. He had to leave again the next day.

They made love that night, if one could call it that. It was more like "trying" one more time. She asked her husband how long he would be away this time, he answered, "Gosh, Lill, I really don't know for sure, but I'll try to cut my trip as short as possible."

This wasn't even close to what the lady wanted to hear. She was very stoic and gave him a hug and kiss good-bye, but her heart was very heavy.

Several days went by without the Hamptons seeing her. Jennie was accustomed to talking with her friend on a daily basis and couldn't hold off any longer. She went through the back door, which was always open, with Willie right on her heels. She stood in the hall and yelled for the lady of the house. Lillian heard Jennie's powerful voice and came down to the kitchen. Jennie put her hand to her mouth, and gasped, "Lill, you look horrible! Now, I want you to take a bath and let me put some makeup on you. After that, we will get you something to eat."

   This brought her around a little. The next day she actually worked in her garden. She liked the way the sedatives made her feel, even though she didn't use them for the purpose they were prescribed for. So, when she ran out, what else was there to do but make another appointment with Dr. Leland Fisher?

   The doctor was surprised when his nurse told him of Mrs. DeLongpre's call. At first he thought his advice had been heeded and something good had come of it. He realized, after gloating in his success, that it hadn't been nearly long enough for anything to develop. He could only think to himself, *I wonder what she wants. Maybe she just wants someone to talk to. I wouldn't mind that.* He scheduled her appointment for 5:00 p.m. the following evening. She would be the last patient on the schedule. As Lillian's custom, she arrived on time. He told his nurse that she was free to go and to have a nice evening.

   Lillian was a bit curious as to why the nurse was leaving, and asked Dr. Fisher why. He responded by saying, "She puts in a lot of hours, and I thought she would like to go home and spend some time with her family. I don't have one, so it doesn't matter to me how many hours I work. What can I do for you this evening?"

   Lillian was almost sorry she came. She had to ask him to refill her prescription, and it was embarrassing. She looked up and saw the doctor staring at her, and it made her feel naked. *That's silly, he's a doctor for goodness sake.* She finally got up the nerve to ask. "Dr. Fisher, I need more of those pills you gave me last time. I know I shouldn't have taken them all, but when T. D. didn't have time...."

   She couldn't finish and began weeping. The doctor stood and walked over to where she was sitting on his couch. He sat down beside her, put his arm around her shoulder and said, "There, there now, calm down. Just take a deep breath and, when you feel up to it, tell me the story."

   She felt his hand on her shoulder and looked him in the eye. There was tenderness that seemed genuine, and it drew her to him. She fell into his arms and began crying even more. He let her get it out. When she had calmed a bit, he leaned closer and kissed her gently...on the mouth. She didn't resist or even say anything, but her eyes were wide with shock. He tried to kiss her again, yet, when his lips were just centimeters away, she slapped him. This caught his full attention and caused her to sit up straight up and cry, "Oh! I'm so sorry. That wasn't nice of me at all! But why did you do that? I mean, I don't understand!"

"Lillian, I've wanted to do that from the first time you came in. It may not be right, but I just had to."

She relaxed a little and sat back on the couch. He started to kiss her again, and this time she didn't try to stop him.

The patient chauffer, Daniel, had been waiting in the car for a long time. When he saw his boss lady's face, he knew something wasn't quite right. He didn't say anything, however, he only asked if she was okay. She didn't look him in the face but assured him that she was. He was still worried. When one exits a doctor's office with a countenance such as hers, it could be bad news.

The bad news was how she felt inside now that this was over with. The satisfaction she'd experienced was at war with her other emotions and was producing a large measure of guilt. She smiled dryly. *And I forgot the pills.*

Dr. Fisher watched through his office window as Lillian's car drove away. He had always had a feeling for her, but the idea of actually having this lady, had been no more than a fantasy...up until now. He sat down at his desk and realized this feeling that overrode good sense could be fatal. Of course, that would only happen if The Colonel ever found out.

He and the man had already discussed another possibility concerning the DeLongpres having a baby. He had heard of some folks up in Tupelo who had been successful in making connections with unwanted babies and couples that wanted but, for some reason or another, couldn't have children. There was a church worker, a preacher, and a doctor. The Colonel didn't seem to mind bending the rules a little. Without Lillian's knowledge, they began making arrangements.

Since he and Lillian's early evening encounter, he was losing interest in the "baby" project. He figured if he were to drop it the man might get suspicious, so he decided to follow through and hope that Lillian didn't say anything. Besides that, there was money involved.

There were a couple weeks to go before The Colonel would be home, and Lillian was miserable. She had done something she swore never to do. She felt weak, sinful, and ashamed. She had let the depression get to her and hadn't used the good training she'd received while becoming a woman. She wanted to tell her husband but didn't know how. She wondered what the doctor was thinking and if he was entertaining any further plans as far as they were concerned.

All these things weighed on her mind, but still she really, with all her heart, wanted a baby. She only hoped God, and eventually her husband, could forgive her. As the days went by, she began to feel a little better and decided to continue with her plan.

She promised herself that when he got home this time, she'd demand that he find a way to do his business from his office downstairs, like he had when Jennie was sick. She was sure that the only reason they hadn't had a baby yet was because he was gone so much. They were both healthy, and the doctor had never found anything wrong, so it had to be timing. And that year after Ben died didn't count. The pressure and worry were just way too much.

Lillian felt that she was completely justified with her "demand." She'd never questioned a single thing her husband did. When she presented her idea, she knew he had to agree.

Like a brand new bride rather than a wife of many years, she counted the minutes until her husband arrived home. She made sure everything was perfect before she made her case.

Their life together, for the most part, had been more beautiful than seemingly possible. Lillian hoped she wouldn't have to pay for this near perfect marriage by having no children of her own.

She enjoyed a leisurely bath while rehearsing her plan. T. D. would be home this evening. She'd asked the cook to take special care and prepare the menu with all of his favorites. All she had to do was light the candles and decant the wine. She emerged from the bath and began toweling off. Looking at herself in the full-length mirror, she was pleased that she didn't look more than twenty-five.

The windows in her bedroom were open to catch the evening breeze. The fragrance of the magnolias blending with the roses from her garden filled the air. The gentle warm winds caressed her face and teased her hair. She inhaled and said aloud, "What a perfect place to have children."

The beautiful dress she'd chosen for this evening was in her favorite shade of green. She finished doing her hair and checked herself in the mirror one final time as she heard her husband's car come up the driveway. "He's home."

By the time he entered the foyer, she was halfway down the staircase, "Welcome home, T. D."

He was almost rude as he cut her off. "I want you to pack your trunks, and we're leaving for Gulfport in the morning."

"But, T.D...."

"Lillian, we'll have plenty of time to talk later. We're going on a cruise. You know what you need to bring. And by the way, dear, you look most lovely tonight." He spun on his heel, leaving an open-mouthed Lillian and headed for his office. He still had a lot of details to finish. The timing had to be just perfect; he would leave *nothing* to chance.

Dr. Bartholomew confirmed Mrs. Gladys Love Presley's pregnancy. A bittersweet aura descended on the little shotgun house in Tupelo, Mississippi. At first they were excited by the news, but as the days and weeks passed by, reality began to set in.

Vernon and Gladys Presley could barely provide for themselves. How would they handle the additional financial burden a child would bring? This realization was causing a strain on an already shaky situation. They argued and fought constantly. Vernon started drinking and carousing. It got to the point where Gladys couldn't work any longer, which made things worse. After much soul-searching and prayer, she decided that the only solution was to ask Delphia Hansen to find a good home for their baby. Vernon gave her no argument.

Lillian stood on the upper deck of the *U.S.S. Baton Rouge*, as the majestic vessel passed the Florida Keys, its course set south toward the Caribbean.

The purpose of this sudden voyage was very mysterious. She twirled her hair round and round her finger, pondering her husband's statement: "My dear, I have a very special surprise for you."

Somehow, this lifelong habit of tugging at her curls made it easier to "figure things out." She'd always say this when someone teased her about it.

Since they'd never had an official honeymoon, she concluded that this must be what he had in mind.

It had been two days since they left Gulfport and her husband had joined the men after dinner for cards and cigars, as was the tradition. She spent this time with the ladies in the salon.

The trip had been nice so far, yet she was on pins and needles waiting for her "surprise."

The third day out, when the evening meal was over, the couple made their way to the private deck instead of joining their shipboard companions. As Lillian sat down, The Colonel pulled her lap robe up and placed a small box in her hand. She looked up at him, and he nodded for her to open it. It contained an exquisite broach fashioned in the shape of a tiny golden carriage set with diamonds, rubies, and sapphires. When she started to speak, he silenced her.

"You've been very patient with me for the past few days. I want to thank you for that. I've taken some unusual steps concerning our future and I needed to be sure we didn't have any acquaintances aboard."

The Colonel continued, "I have a plan, but I couldn't tell you about it until I knew it was feasible. We both want to have a family. I think I've found a way to make it possible, but I'm going to need your complete trust. We'll be at sea for about six months, and, during our cruise, you must pretend you've become pregnant." If he hadn't had her attention before, he most certainly had it now. She put her hand over her mouth as he continued, "At the end of this voyage, we'll return to The Willows as a family, my dearest Lillian. When we get home, we'll just explain to everyone that the doctor felt the sea voyage would be a good, relaxing, environment to assure you'd have a safe delivery." He almost said this whole thing in one breath and stopped to see how his wife took his news.

Lillian's face had opened into an ear-to-ear smile. She tugged her husband's arm to join her on her chair, "T. D., this is probably the second best day of my whole life."

"Second?"

"Yes, the first was my wedding day. The second will be our 'delivery' day. Thank you so much, my darling."

"And you don't mind that you'll have to masquerade a bit?"

Lillian DeLongpre shook her head and put on her little broach. She would wear it every day for the rest of her life.

Chapter Seven

The cover-up cruise was over. The petite Lillian had to do something she'd never done before in her life. Before the cruise, The Colonel consulted with a friend he could trust in the medical business to construct a series of special padding for his wife to wear so it would appear she was pregnant. If that wasn't enough, during their cruise, she was asked to gorge herself at every meal and in between meals. This chapter was never in the manual of her training to marry well.

She and her husband crept closer through the dense fog to this town called Tupelo, at a time of day when all civilized folks should be sleeping. There wasn't a plethora of choice hotels in this town in January of 1935, but they were told the one at which to wait, so that is how it would have to be.

Lillian looked at the sparsely decorated room and back at her fatigued husband. He returned her gaze without a word or an explaining gesture. She knew that look. She'd seen it many times before. It was his "trust me" look.

The Colonel's lady looked at the modestly covered bed, took off the doeskin glove from her right hand, and gently pressed the center. She removed her shoes, the left one first, and placed them neatly by the off-white one-drawer nightstand.

The great man took in his bride's every move, saying to himself, *Thank you, Lord, for sending me one of your angels.*

It had been a long and exhausting six and one half months. Not only had this man who had built his business and most of his life with integrity gone a step further, he had asked his wife and eternal mate to go along with this subterfuge.

The deal had been made. There was no turning back. All that was left was a phone call that would keep alive the DeLongpre legacy. Little did they, Delphia Hansen, the rest of Mississippi, and the upcoming generations know about the importance of this hour.

Colonel DeLongpre asked his wife if she needed anything, or could he get her anything. She smiled with appreciation and added, "No, let's just wait."

A little before 2:00 a.m., they were awakened by a tapping on the door. They were full of anticipation, only snoozing, not really in a deep sleep.

The Colonel looked at his wife, and she returned his questionable glance. He opened the door to a breathless young boy. "Sorry, sir, there was no phone. Miss Delphia said you should come now!"

It was a bleak winter morning that day in east Tupelo, January 8, 1935. Gladys Presley began her labor shortly after Delphia Hansen arrived. Vernon Presley was not there. He was out drinking and playing pool. He had been doing this ever since they'd learned of Gladys' pregnancy.

The Colonel pulled the dark green Packard as close as he could to the darkened side of the shotgun shack. He turned off the lights and settled back in the seat. Lillian leaned her head on his shoulder, placed her petite hand on his, and gave it an anxious squeeze.

A little after 4:00 a.m., a tiny baby was delivered in a bundle of one sheet and a blanket to the waiting occupants of the big car. The dark and fog swallowed the car and all three people in it. Had they ever been there?

The Packard disappeared into the morning fog and drizzle; the midwife began the necessary clean up. As Delphia moved about the room, Gladys suddenly gasped. The midwife rushed to her side.

"My God, Gladys, there's another one!"

Delphia looked at Elvis Aaron Presley. He was a beautiful child as babies go, but long and underweight. The lady with the golden heart shook her head in dismay thinking, *The poor dear just didn't get the proper nourishment since day one!*

Delphia had visited the Presley's home, as many times as she could, but even with God's help, she couldn't be spread any thinner. She told Gladys she'd try and hunt down Vernon and have Doc Ezra somehow get the mother and future King of Rock to a hospital.

The tired but happy midwife tucked the large envelope the tall graying man had given her in her pocket. She couldn't help thinking how distinguished he was and what a bright future this lucky young man would have.

She drove home, had two oatmeal raisin cookies with a glass of milk, and laid her clothes out while she was deciding whether to take a bath. She donned her old comfy brown robe and lay down on top of the comforter. Exhausted, she went into a deathlike sleep.

The next thing she heard was a loud ringing that seemed to come from another world, and it grew louder and louder. She fought to run away, but it kept following her. At last, she woke up. She picked up the irritating instrument and said groggily, "Hello?"

"Delphia, darlin', we're waiting for you at the restaurant. The ladies are all here!"

"Count me out today, Agnes." She sat up in bed, stretched, yawned, and looked for the robe she was still wearing from last night. She felt a bit foolish, but arose and padded her way to the bathroom. She took a slight detour to the kitchen and plugged in the coffeepot.

She felt the wonderful warm water gushing out of the showerhead. It began to restore her. She stood there for several minutes, then toweled off. She took her favorite cup from the hook on the cup rack, filled it with the hot rich brew, dropped in two lumps of sugar, a thimble full of cream, and sat down to read the rest of yesterday's paper. She took a sip, put the cup down rather suddenly, and said loudly, "Delphia, you're growing senile!"

She went to her bedroom, picked up the DeLongpre envelope, and returned to her coffee, pausing for a moment. She enjoyed how good it felt every time she could fatten up the church fund.

Picking up her bone-handle letter opener, she cut through the top, and gently shook the contents onto the table. The usually calm Mrs. Hansen let out a squeal that sounded like an excited young schoolgirl. She quickly counted the money. "Ten thousand dollars!"

She counted it three more times for no reason that could be explained, jumped up, and dialed The Reverend Clarkson. "C. J., drop everything and get over here as fast as you can!"

The Reverend finished signing the necessary papers from the previous day's events, took one more sip of his lukewarm coffee, grabbed his coat, dress straw, and was Delphia-bound. As the slightly built preacher began the short drive to the Hansen residence, he wondered why there was this sense of urgency in Delphia's voice. They had successfully repeated the adoption procedure many times without a hitch. Could something have gone wrong? There was always that chance, but, with Delphia running the show, it was highly unlikely.

Reverend Clarkson had been in love with Delphia for as long as he could remember. He'd first laid eyes on her when Andrew Hansen had hired him to be Aubrey's assistant and nothing had changed over the years. There *was* one time several years following Aubrey's death from that horrible fire when Delphia allowed him to share her bed.

About the only thing Delphia ever drank was eggnog around the holidays. Every now and then since Aubrey's passing, she became a tad melancholy, dusted off a bottle of brandy, and called a friend. More often than not, that friend would be The Reverend.

One balmy evening she and C. J. sat on the front porch and got absolutely sloshed. It had been a very long time for her, and she knew how he felt, so she thought, *Why not?* The amorous man of the cloth had finally realized his dream he had carried with him all those years. When he could love her no more, he laid sweating and breathing heavily, but managed to blurt out, "I love you, Delphia, with all my body and soul!" She looked at him, smiled tenderly, and patted him at the beginning of his receding hairline. That is when they became "best friends" for life.

C. J. guided his old Plymouth coupe into the driveway, past the remains of the place where he used to work, and where his good friend and mentor had perished that sad, sad night long ago. He liked the fact that Delphia had let the wildflowers grow right into it. It was soothing to him in a way. He parked his car and rapped on the front door.

"Come in, C. J."

After good mornings were hastily exchanged, The Reverend was asked to sit. "What's up, D?"

Shaky hands pulled back the tablecloth to reveal its hidden treasure. The Reverend, after catching his breath and pouring a badly needed cup of coffee, listened intently to his lady friend's unbelievable story. After much discussion, they agreed to change the modus operandi they usually followed. No one was to know of this until they had formulated a plan.

Dr. Ezra Bartholomew was having a bad morning. There were the patients he couldn't get to, and the ones that he got to, couldn't pay him. He looked tiredly at the stack of bills, wishing he could at least find a bigger place to keep them. He was understaffed, overcrowded, and overworked. Removing his glasses, he rubbed his eyes remembering he had an appointment with C. J. and Delphia. "Any day but today!" he groaned.

The doctor wondered what all the hush and mystery was about. He clasped his hands in back of his head and looked up to the heavens silently begging for help. Help can come in many forms, and at the least expected times. This form would be Delphia Hansen and The Reverend C. J. Clarkson—and the time would be now. He lowered his head as he heard the knocking. Delphia and C. J. both started talking at the same time.

The news was so overwhelming that, for a second, he forgot he wasn't really comfortable with the way some of these things came about. But they were such good friends, and he had asked the man in the sky for help so many times that he would get closer to believing that this being did, in fact, move in mysterious ways. This time when he looked up to the heavens, he smiled. "Oh, that Presley business, wow!"

Gladys Presley had plenty of time to get well and think in the hospital. Her frail son Elvis was also gaining strength. Their part of the DeLongpres money took care of the medical bills plus a little for the household. She thanked God for this very special gift. She knew in her heart that the Almighty had something for her to learn. She vowed not to fail. The rest of her life would center on her son and this promise.

The DeLongpres had a few hundred miles to cover and decided to take their time getting back home while getting used to being parents. They stayed at several private residences in towns where The Colonel's wish for discreetness was just part of the package.

The records show that Thurston Davis DeLongpre, III was "born" in Poplarville, Mississippi, January 12, 1935. C. J. Clarkson had made the arrangements through a friend in this town halfway between Gulfport and Hattiesburg. All they had to do was pick up the birth certificate or have it mailed.

In a week and a day or two, Lillian saw a road sign that read Hattiesburg, 13 miles, "How do I look, T. D.?"

She had gained about fifteen or sixteen pounds and she looked down at her little round belly. She had never been that heavy and wasn't at all thrilled with the situation, but one must now and then sacrifice. This was one time, it was well worth it.

The Colonel pulled the car off the road, put his large hand under her chin, and said softly, "Like you just had a baby, my love." The new family passed under the arch that read The Willows. Nothing had ever looked so good to the new mom and dad.

The plans they had for a nice quiet evening alone with their baby went by the wayside when they turned the corner to the parking area in back of the mansion. They now wished they hadn't called Willie and Jennie when they docked in Gulfport.

Everyone who lived and worked at the estate surrounded a huge banner. This may not have been what they wanted the first night, but how can anyone be upset with that much love? The banner said, "Welcome Home T. D., III."

His proud father held aloft this baby, who would be the DeLongpre heir. The child was an answer to all of their prayers. The great joy was evident on all their friends' and staff's faces. Lillian's only sad note on this occasion was that both her parents, Harold and Sylvia Fontaine, had passed. They would never see their grandson, at least not in this world.

The new parents took time to chat with each and every one in attendance. The entire Willows family was anxious to extend their best wishes. They finally got around to Willie, Jennie, and Odetta. The Colonel asked Willie if their baggage had arrived, and he answered, "No, but they called and said it would be delivered tomorrow."

Jennie looked Lillian up and down, "Lill, you look absolutely wonderful considering everything. Doesn't she look wonderful, Willie?"

Jennie finally took over and led Lillian to the big house. She made sure the happy parents made a polite and comfortable exit.

Lillian was happy to go inside with her precious bundle in her arms. She was tired, but she practically floated upstairs and down the hall to the room she and her husband had personally decorated.

Jennie ordered her friend, "Now, don't you go doing anything that I can easily do for you, just enjoy and get some rest. After all, you just had a baby!"

Lillian looked down at her precious little boy all snuggled in his crib. Tears spilled from her eyes and splashed on his tiny forehead. He moved ever so slightly as she took a hanky and blotted his damp face, "Your grandpa and grandma would have loved you, little one." She took the hanky, dried her own face, and looked up, "Momma and Daddy, I know you're up there somewhere. Do you see that I finally have my baby? I know you're both just as happy as I am, but I wish you could have waited a while longer so you could have held him like I can."

She kissed him gently and pulled the blanket up to where only his face was showing. She left the room to tend to her other children, her roses. There was another problem that needed tending to, one that wouldn't go away.

Dr. Fisher sat in his office with Mrs. DeLongpre on his mind. He figured he had given the new parents enough time to settle in. Finding out when The Colonel's next trip would take place shouldn't be too difficult. Now, all he had to do was convince Lillian that she should come visit him.

He told his nurse that he was taking the afternoon off and to reschedule his appointments. He took his hat off the rack, left the building, got into his '36 Ford coupe and began the half hour drive to The Willows.

Jennie saw the doctor's car arrive and park. She was curious but didn't give it too much thought. She had seen him at the house a time or two for parties and such. Anyway, she would find out why he came from her friend later. The only one who was surprised was Lillian, who was talking with one of the house's cleaning staff when she heard the rapping on the back door. This was strange, hardly anyone ever knocked, whoever it was just came in and yelled. When she opened the door and saw Dr. Fisher, she was taken aback to say the least. All she could say was the obvious, "Dr. Fisher, what in God's name are you doing here?"

"I just dropped by to see if we could have a little talk. It's been awhile, you know. Don't you agree, my dear?"

Lillian bristled at the "my dear" part, then asked him to come in. She dismissed the cook, and they sat down at the kitchen table. Many thoughts were racing through her mind, but one stood out from the rest. She said to herself, *I wonder how long I will be paying for my sin?*

Dr. Fisher sensed her inner conflict and decided to press the issue, "Well now, Mrs. DeLongpre, it seems like you've got most everything you dreamed about. It appears that you are in good health, and I assume that the child is also. I'm happy for you and your husband, and glad that I was able to be a small part of it. Now, I think you and I should discuss a few things."

Lillian was about to offer him some coffee, but changed her mind. She didn't want him around any longer than absolutely necessary. She looked at him with disdain and said, "Is that what this is all about? All you wanted was my body? What kind of doctor are you?"

This was not the reaction he'd expected from this vulnerable woman. He decided to change tactics by saying, "Now hold on, Lillian, I honestly do care for you. You're the one that's making this difficult! It would be just fine with me if we were to...."

She stood up and cut him off, "Dr. Fisher! I think you had better leave here before I forget I'm still a lady!"

The doctor smiled and slowly picked up his hat. It wasn't a friendly smile, more like a "we'll see about that" smile. She followed him to the door, and, as he neared the top step, he turned and said, "It's a shame. It didn't have to be this way. However, you will be seeing me later."

She watched him descend the stairs and walk to his car. She didn't know who she hated the most, him for the arrogant ass that he was or herself for what she had allowed to happen. One thing was for certain. She would have to put her marriage on the line and give it its first major test.

She would tell her husband the whole story when he came home. At this moment, however, she had something more important to do, and that was to go upstairs and see if her son was waking from his nap.

The Colonel arrived home the following week. His wife was holding their son while waiting for him at the top of the stairs; it was indeed a wonderful sight to behold. This is what life is all about. They all spent the remainder of the afternoon together. The Colonel was certainly enjoying himself but couldn't help noticing that his wife was more reserved than usual. Most of the time when he came home she was very glad to see him and behaved like a newlywed.

After putting the baby to bed, they had dinner, and it was as always very special. When they finished dessert he asked what was troubling his "pretty little wife" this evening. She knew now for certain that he would have to be told. She inhaled deeply, let it out slowly, and said, "T. D., there is something I have to tell you."

She was nervous and trembling as the awful story unfolded, but she looked him in the eye the entire time. She fought to keep from saying "I'm sorry" at least a dozen times. She explained her depression and how weak she was this time when he wasn't there for her. She blamed herself as much as she did Dr. Fisher.

After she had finished, her husband's face, which appeared at times on the verge of exploding, now became almost colorless. He excused himself by saying, "I need a drink!"

More than an hour had passed when she heard his heavy footsteps coming up the stairs. Her heartbeat increased and she began shaking again. He walked in the door, looked at her for a moment, and sat down heavily on the bed. She could smell the bourbon and cigar smoke. She feared the worst.

Instead, he spoke very calmly, pronouncing every word precisely, "Lill, I am very upset by this news. I'm not so much hurt by what has happened, I haven't exactly been a saint either. What scares me is the finding out of how fragile our family structure is at present. I want to forget that this happened between us, but Leland Fisher has to pay."

She wasn't quite ready for the last part of his statement. There was a tone to his voice that frightened her. She could only say, "T. D., what are you going to do? Please don't kill him or anything. I couldn't take it if you got in trouble."

"Don't worry, Lill. When the time is right, I *will* hurt him but only in his wallet." He reached over, picked her up like a doll, and brought her close to him. They stayed that way for a long time.

They would be together forever.

Chapter Eight

The arrival of T. D., III was like icing on their collective cakes. What better environment could a little boy ask to grow up in?

Thurston Davis DeLongpre was a happy and bright child. His parents doted on his every move, and so did all who lived and worked at The Willows. And why shouldn't they? This was their little prince who would lead them someday. His father has the job locked up for now. This little prince would lead their children when they themselves leave this world at peace. One and all know there would always be The Willows.

Although their son had everything wealth could possibly provide, they also instilled in him a strong sense of responsibility and respect for others, not just those at their Willows.

The boy was walking by the time he was one year old and could speak in whole sentences before he was two. Extremely inquisitive, he drove everybody nuts with his questions. Lillian one day said, "Willie, I swear, he is exactly like you were at two or three!"

The tall handsome black man looked down at the little white boy and smiled, "Yeah, Tilly, you're right. He's exactly like me!"

As the little boy got older, he was into everything—not in a meddlesome kind of way, just a curiosity that no one seemed to mind. He would talk to anyone who would listen. Whether it was his momma in her rose garden, Willie with the horses, or a worker climbing out of a truck.

In the beginning, Willie didn't like little T. D. following him around. In some ways, Willie was a big kid himself, and, as the relationship grew, he began to enjoy having this little bundle of energy looking up to him. As the months rolled by, this new responsibility actually caused him to mature, as well. And, anyway, his Tilly had said, "He's just like you." So Willie became a combination brother and friend who would be there for a lifetime.

The Colonel had promised Ben Hampton that no matter what happened, his boy would get an education. He could probably get all he needed at The Willows, but The Colonel said with the same convictions as always, "It's college for you, my boy." There were no arguments, except from The Colonel's own son.

No one, his father, mother, God, or Willie himself, could convince the young boy that this was a good idea. Didn't anybody care how he felt? How dare they take away his Willie, his pal! This seemed like the end of the world for the little prince.

Willie left for college, leaving his little pal alone to cry himself to sleep for about a week. But time heals all, and the spunk began to return. He finally accepted the explanation that Willie would only be gone for a little while, and he wouldn't have too long to wait for his pal to return. He'd have to find someone else to bother until then.

The Colonel, unlike most at The Willows, was aware of the problems outside the island. He knew that some colleges wouldn't accept Willie due to the ugly thing called prejudice. So he shopped around a bit and then remembered a small college in southwestern Pennsylvania, not too far from where he lived as a child. He visited Clearfield University and met with the members of the faculty. He saw many students from all walks of life, from China to Germany, that were in attendance. He told the faculty about Willie and that he'd be there for the next term. He took out his checkbook, left a sizeable donation, thanked all present, and headed home with good news.

Willie had lost his father at a very young age. He loved his mother dearly, but when it came to a father figure, there was no other choice but The Colonel, nor did he want to make one. As much as The Colonel was gone, his influence remained, and the sorrow that had invaded his island world when his father died was a mere shadow in his memory.

He was understandably a bit apprehensive about leaving the safety of his fortress, but, after a few days at the serene and beautiful campus, his fears quickly waned. He'd always worked hard and kept up his studies. Without the extra duties he was used to at home, now he had a lot of time on his hands. His *only* job was just to study, so he did.

Willie shared a dorm room with Danny O'Gwinn, a red-haired Irish boy from Boston via County Cork, Ireland. Danny was a bit more outgoing than Willie, at least in the beginning, but soon they began enjoying most of what the busy campus had to offer. Even Einstein took a break now and then.

One Friday night would change Willie's life forever. Danny was shaving and noticed Willie still at his desk buried in weekend homework. He smiled, shook his head, and yelled, "Now come on, Willie, we've got to get out of here. You've got Saturday and Sunday to hit those books. It's Friday night, man!"

Danny's vocal explosion startled Willie at first, but he recovered nicely and hollered back at his roomie, "Hang on, I'm almost done. You know I can't believe all this stuff old man Bunch laid on us. Does he think he's the only professor handing out assignments, or what?" Danny quickly agreed, and added, "He's got a little bit of a Napoleon complex, and he's not even as tall as the little general!"

"You nailed that one, Danny, and you're right. Let's get the hell outta here. There's a dance or something, isn't there?" After dousing themselves with enough cologne for the whole dorm, the twosome headed for the campus activities center for the Friday night dance.

The band was from somewhere like Pittsburgh, and they were really pretty good. Danny seemed to know everybody and always introduced his still-shy roommate. But the inevitable thing happened, Danny scored, and Willie was on his own. He decided to go to the refreshment table. He would remember for the rest of his life what a great idea this was.

He inhaled the first glass of punch and had dipped up another. While turning to see if he could spot Danny, he had an accident. He emptied most of his punch down the front of the blouse of a young lady. As his eyes rose past the red stains to her green eyes, his embarrassment was tripled. He was face to face with the most beautiful human being he'd ever seen. For the first time in a long while, he was completely speechless. His Tilly would never believe this. The pretty co-ed broke the silence. "Will you please get me a napkin?" He stood there like he was planted. Finally she grabbed the napkin herself and dabbed at her blouse and asked, "Would you like some more?"

Willie was still mute, so the young lady continued. "Well, I guess not. My name's Darcy."

Still, not a word could he utter, so she stuck out her hand and tried once more, "I'm Darcy Landis. What did you say your name was?"

After all this, Willie almost found his voice and managed a muffled reply. Darcy mockingly put her hand to her ear and asked, "I'm sorry, what was that, Mr. Hampton?"

He could now almost finish a sentence. "I said, I'm really sorry about your blouse. How did you know my name?"

Darcy stifled a laugh, and said, "It helps when you work at the registrar's office."

The couple danced until the band wouldn't play anymore. Willie walked Darcy to her dorm and managed a kiss on her cheek, then floated back to his room to compare guy stuff with Danny. No Danny. He grinned at the thought of what Danny was up to, took a quick look at his still-open homework and crawled into bed for a night of delicious honey-colored dreams. Before closing his eyes, he thought, *She's not the only black girl at Clearfield, but she's far and away the prettiest!* They began to see each other exclusively and would for a long, long time.

The DeLongpres were having a light and late breakfast that began with a couple Bloody Marys. They were not really drinkers, except for wine with dinner, but, every now and then, The Colonel would have a cognac. It was the morning after they'd thrown a New Year's Eve party for all the employees and a few select friends.

The Colonel was deciding on another portion of some tasty hash brown potatoes when he heard, "You hoo! T. D., Lillian?"

"Come in, Jennie," they said almost in unison.

"Now, y'all, it's none of my business, well, come to think of it, it is my business. I've changed that little boy's diapers and...."

"Jennie!"

"It's just that he's out there trying to get on that big old horse of Willie's. I'm just frightened silly he's going to hurt himself!" They all made a hasty exit in the direction of the main barn to see the picture Jennie was trying to paint.

The Colonel wanted to yell out to his son to be careful, but he thought better of it since it would probably scare the boy and spook the horse. The trio eased up slowly on the situation developing. They had to stifle a laugh, because, somehow, the determined little man had managed to get the bridle on the huge animal. He was precariously perched on the top rail of the corral fence, trying to get a blanket on the horse's back. His daddy was able to catch him just when the horse decided he had enough and stepped away from all this. His momma hugged him, half-crying and half-angry, while his daddy patted him on the head and said, "Nice try there, my boy, but I think we should consider getting one of these," as he gestured toward the retreating horse, "in your size." The week preceding his birthday, his folks gave a lot of thought about a special present for their young wrangler. After hours of discussion, they went out and got "one" in his size.

It was bitterly chilly as it usually is in January. It had rained slightly in the morning and felt cold enough to snow. Mother and father woke their sleeping son and led him to the stables. Miraculously, the sun broke through just as the colt exploded from the barn wearing a big red bow around his neck. The boy squealed with delight. He immediately named his pony Sunshine. Not even The Colonel could have staged this wonderful event. Not even *he* could predict the magnitude of this gift and how it would influence the remainder of his son's life.

A couple of months later, at his mother's birthday celebration, the little horse owner realized that birthdays were not just for kids. Jennie had baked a gorgeous multi-layered, technicolor cake with Lillian's name on it. There were quite a few more candles on it than his, and, needless to say, there were piles of gaily wrapped gifts.

Little Thurston viewed the festivities and found them very much to his liking, so he said gleefully, "Momma, this is fun. We should do this a whole bunch. We can have one for Willie and Aunt Jennie, and…when's Daddy's birthday?" Lillian smiled as her son's question reminded her of when she had posed the identical query to her new husband.

"Thurston, your Daddy's birthday is on Christmas Day. That's the baby Jesus' birthday, too. Remember all the lights and decorations we put up to celebrate that day?"

The lad's gleeful face of only seconds earlier now became pensive, but he snapped right back, "Yeah, but, Momma, those lights and things were there for a lot of days!"

"Well, honey, that's because it's a very significant day and your Daddy thinks that Jesus shouldn't have to share it with him. He wants us to only celebrate Jesus' birthday." The little man was a bit confused because his daddy was more important than Jesus and maybe even Willie, but he still wasn't quite satisfied, so he quietly asked, "Will we ever have a birthday for Daddy?"

"I don't think so, honey, only for the little baby from Bethlehem." This would be the only time this sad and confusing subject would be brought up by the youngest member of the family that called the big house at The Willows home.

When the young sweethearts first school term had ended and it was time to go home, Willie asked Darcy to please go with him and meet his folks. Darcy politely turned down the invitation. Even with Willie's objections, her decision was final.

When he returned home after his first term at school, a now more mature Willie was full of stories about his adventures, his roommate, and his new girlfriend. How exciting it was to be away for the first time, but how wonderful it was to be back home. He could hardly keep up with all the questions from everybody at the welcome dinner the DeLongpres threw for him, especially his little buddy Thurston. His mother wanted to know more about Darcy. Jennie had always been very patient, so she waited until they left and went home. He knew that his mom wasn't through with him. He learned this lesson *before* going to school.

They sat at the kitchen table. Jennie folded her hands and asked, "Well?" As anxious as she was to know more about Darcy, and as much as he wanted to tell her, he couldn't really come up with much at all.

"Well, son, at least I know she's pretty and you like her a lot. I guess that's a start."

He said it seemed like Darcy and he talked constantly and he'd told her everything he could think of about himself, but come to think of it, he had very little to pass on. Jennie thought maybe it would be different next time.

Willie returned to school eager to see Darcy. He shared every detail of his holidays at home, and then realized why he had little or nothing to tell his mom. It was because Darcy had very little to tell him. Finally, after pushing her, the pretty co-ed realized he wasn't going to leave her alone until he got the whole story.

They sat down; she took his hand and began, "The first thing I remember, Willie, was a bespectacled face bordered with black and white looking down on me. I never knew my folks, and I've heard three or four different stories of how I got there. It depended on what sister I asked that day. The Catholic school is where I grew up and learned to study. It was a very simple life. I never wanted for food and clothing, but, just to show you, I'd never heard a radio before I came to Clearfield on my scholarship. I love you, Willie, and, if you still want to take me with you next time, I'd love to go."

From then until graduation, Darcy was with Willie on every break at The Willows.

Beginning with her very first visit, the lovely young lady was considered family. It was like she'd always belonged there. Jennie would never question her son's judgment again—well, maybe just once in a while. Less than three years later, the DeLongpre's gave Willie and Darcy a wonderful graduation gift. It was a fully catered wedding and reception right next to Lillian's rose garden.

The only thing prettier than Lillian's roses was Mrs. William Jarrod Hampton.

"Little Thurston," as his folks called him, had just got his pal back, and, although he had to share his buddy with Darcy, he was still delighted to have him home so they could pal around from time to time.

Then another trial presented itself to the young man. It was time for *him* to start school. This did not please him at all. He never would even consider going against his parents, and he wouldn't start now. He did, however, attempt to show his independence by withdrawing to his new bedroom. The nursery where he'd spent his first few years was no longer acceptable. He was just too big for that now. Lillian understood and had another one of the rooms fixed up for her little man.

At first, his parents let him stay in his room, but he had to join the family for dinner, that was made very clear. After a few days, Lillian realized they had a problem. She decided to ask Willie for help.

On the fourth day she knocked on Thurston's door and asked to come in. When this didn't work, she raised her voice enough to penetrate the door, and simply said, "…Willie wants to see you at his place right away!" This opened the door as if by magic. He passed his mother in the hallway and announced that he and Willie had some important things to do. She smiled after him as he bounded down the stairway en route to the Hampton house. The door was open and he heard Willie say, "Come on in, buddy."

Willie and Darcy were sitting at the kitchen table and invited him to join them. "Now, little pard, we need to talk. You don't mind if Darcy sits with us do you?" In a short time, the charming Darcy had gained Thurston's confidence. He politely nodded his approval and Willie continued.

"I want you to listen to me. I know you're a little upset with your folks right now, but, believe me, they love you very, very much and only want the best for you. What they are trying to do is get you to know the world outside of our Willows. I was a lot older than you when I first left here, and it was really tough for me at first. I wish that your daddy had made me do what he's asking you to do now when I was your age. You see, when I was your age, I didn't have a daddy like you do now. Your daddy became sort of like my daddy after mine died. Believe me, little man, there are no two finer people in the world than your mom and dad."

Thurston felt a lot better after listening to Willie, but a burning question still remained. "Willie, you went far away, and I didn't see you very much for a big, long time. Now they want me to go far away, too."

Willie understood the boy's dilemma and responded, "See, buddy, that's where you're wrong, you're not going far away, you're only going down the street. Hattiesburg is real close, and I'll see you every day."

"You promise?" Thurston pleaded.

"Yes, I promise. I've talked to your folks, and I told them I need you here. I can't do all this work without your help!" Willie went on to explain to his little pal that when he got home from school, he'd have to work with him for a couple hours a day before dinner and then do his homework.

Thurston had listened to Willie, but he wasn't quite finished, so he put up his last line of resistance, "Darcy, you told me that you went to college to be a teacher. Why couldn't I stay and have you be my teacher?"

Darcy smiled and placed her hand on his and quickly announced she had some things to take care of. As she exited the room, she was thinking, *I'm too new around here to get in the middle of this!*

The two comrades talked for a few more minutes. Willie ended the conversation by asking a favor of his young friend. "Now I want you to do one more thing for me. I want you to go home and tell your mom and dad you're sorry!"

The future heir of the DeLongpre fortune walked slowly back to his house, sheepishly went to his mother's side, fell into her arms, and said, "I'm sorry, Momma."

Lillian felt herself tearing up and remembering when her tears fell on baby Thurston's forehead. This time she just held him close and said, "It's okay, sweetheart, it's okay."

The crisis ended, at least temporarily, and the dreaded school term began. It wasn't too bad after his talk with Willie, at least in the beginning. When his dad was in town, he would drive the boy to the academy, or, if Willie weren't too busy, he would be happy to do it. Most of the time though, the job was handed to Lillian's driver, Daniel. She still hadn't learned to drive.

At first, the academy was an adventure, however, he soon got tired of the drab walls, the uniforms they were forced to wear, and the way they were asked to not speak as they moved from room to room in the halls. It was the rules and the rigidity that constantly pressured this young man who'd been used to roaming around thousands of acres. To make matters worse, some of the boys made fun of his name.

He went along with this school out of respect for his parents. Only Willie knew he hated it. He thought it might get better in time, but he was wrong. In the middle of his second year, during Christmas vacation, he exercised the right given him much earlier by his parents to speak his mind. "Momma, I've got to tell you something. Promise you'll hear me out. I don't want to go back to that dumb school. You can't make me do it."

"Thurston, mind your manners...."

"And, Momma, I don't want to be called Thurston anymore, either!"

"What's the matter with you? You've never acted like this before."

"Momma, please! I hate that place and those boys aren't our kind of folks. They think they're better than everybody else. We're all supposed to be equal. That's what you and Daddy always tell me. Please, Momma, don't make me go back there, and *please* can't we call me Davis from now on?"

Lillian's first inclination was to reprimand her son, but the family had always solved their problems together, and it always seemed to work, so she thought, *Why change?* She gently placed her hand on his forehead, brushed his hair back, and said, "Well, son, I'll make sure we talk about it with your dad when he comes home."

The DeLongpres and the Hamptons got together and laid out a working plan to allow "Davis" to stay home and have Darcy tutor him. This way, he'd put time in with Willie and help his mother whenever she needed it. Darcy ended the meeting with an explanation of her rules, "Now, Davis, just because we're friends, don't you think I'm going to be easy on you. You're going to put in a certain amount of hours every day and do homework too!" Mr. and Mrs. DeLongpre nodded their approval. Life at The Willows began another run of smooth highway.

Davis held up his end rather well. He did his studies, chores, and seemed to adjust to the new regime. However, little boys have only so much of an attention span and, eventually, begin to seek out and experiment with various things. In other words, they get bored.

One afternoon, Willie told Lillian he had to go into town and asked if there was anything he could do for her while he was there. Lillian asked him to stop by Thompson's Hardware and Nursery and see if the new-fangled fertilizer for her roses had come in yet and to pick up some picket fencing to go along a new path at the far end of her garden.

Davis, still Thurston to his mom, overheard this and asked if he could go with Willie. He hadn't spent much time away from The Willows since he dropped out of school. His mother, aware of this, thought it might be a good idea and gave her approval.

Harley and Mary Louise Thompson had met and married in Jackson. When Harley's mother died (his father left them several years before), he sold the farm and moved himself and his bride to Hattiesburg. They bought a home with lake-front property and, shortly afterward, started "Thompson's Hardware and Nursery."

The following year they brought a little girl into the world and gave her a beautiful Biblical name, Rebecca. As Rebecca grew older, she was blessed with a total package of good looks along with a sometimes independent attitude. Her dark brown hair framed a delicate ivory face with large, almost black eyes. If she was happy about any situation, her eyes were full of love and compassion. If she wasn't happy, those same eyes could literally smolder.

She loved her father and didn't like it a bit when he had to go to work at the store. When she was older, he would sometimes come home for lunch and then take her back to the hardware store with him. When she started school, as soon as the three o'clock bell rang, she'd chat with her classmates and friends for a few minutes, and then it was off to Daddy's store. On weekends they'd often close early and go fishing or sailing on the small lake behind their property.

Rebecca was dusting some shelves on the particular Saturday afternoon when Willie and Davis went to Thompson's to pick up Lillian's supplies. She had told her friend that she worked for her daddy, but this wasn't really work to her. She liked cleaning things and knowing what things were for. Talking to people was something she enjoyed, too, and it came easily to her.

All of a sudden, the sound of something crashing interrupted the normally quiet little store. She dismounted the ladder and raced around the counter. There, surrounded by what used to be a display of empty gasoline cans, sprawled a young man, Thurston Davis DeLongpre, III, *himself.*

Davis looked up in the laughing face of Rebecca Thompson. If he ever wanted to disappear into thin air, this would be the perfect time. The pretty little ten-year-old giggled and made a hasty retreat back to the counter, and Willie helped his little pal back on his feet. They finished loading the supplies, climbed into the truck, and began the trip home. Willie finally got Davis to laugh about what had happened, and it looked like everything was going to be fine, but their joy would prove to be short-lived.

Willie heard the siren first, then saw the red light in the rear view mirror. He checked the speedometer and saw that he was going 45. He pulled to the shoulder, stopped, and reached in his right jacket pocket for his driver's license. A young cop dressed in a gray uniform bearing the Hattiesburg City patch, came to the window, billy club in hand. Willie asked him, "What's going on, Officer? I didn't think I was speeding!"

The cop placed his hand on the butt of his gun, tightened his grip on the billy club, and yelled adamantly, "Get out of the car, boy, and take it real slow!"

A wide-eyed Davis watched his pal get out of the car. His heart was racing, and he heard Willie say through the open window, "Officer, the speed limit reads 50 M.P.H., and I was going 45. What did I do wrong?"

"Put your hands on the hood and spread your legs! Now, what are you doing with this white kid?"

"I work with his father, and we all live together at The Willows. You know, the DeLongpre spread?"

"I don't know about no DeLong…whoever. Now, one more time, what are you doin' with the kid?"

"I just told you. I work with his father."

The outraged cop grabbed Willie, spun him around roughly, and shoved his face on the hood. Davis bounded out of the truck screaming at the top of his lungs, "You leave him alone! He's my friend!"

The cop had laid his club down while cuffing Willie. Davis picked up the club and swung wildly at the cop, hitting him solidly in the back. The startled officer released Willie momentarily, grabbed Davis, and lifted him off his feet. Davis screamed again, "Leave him alone! If you hurt him, my daddy will kill you!"

The young cop must have called for back up before he pulled Willie over, because another patrol car arrived on the scene. A stout older cop jumped out of his vehicle and walked quickly to the side of the truck. He glanced at the logo on the door, and began yelling, "You stupid fuck! Don't you see the writing on this here door? Everybody knows what that means around here! Now take off them cuffs, and give me your weapon, then get in my car! Now!"

Willie was rubbing his wrists and, at the same time, trying to console Davis. The older cop turned to them and said, "I'm sorry about this. Ah, what was your name?"

This was the first time Davis had ever seen his pal the least bit angry and wondered how he could be even as calm as he was. Willie said with controlled rage, "My name is William Hampton, and this young man is Colonel DeLongpre's son! As anyone can see, we're in town picking up supplies for the ranch!"

The stout officer took one step forward and said through clenched teeth, "Now, I said I was sorry, but I won't say it again. You're lucky that you work for DeLongpre!"

"No, Captain, *you're* lucky I work for The Colonel! I'm sure you'll be hearing from him soon."

It was a somber drive back to The Willows. This would be the first time both of these young men had been exposed to the cancer known as prejudice, and they didn't like it. Davis didn't understand it at all, but Willie did. It reminded him of what a wonderful place The Willows was to live.

This ugly event caused quite a stir around the ranch, as would be expected. Lillian and Darcy were devastated, but, in time, everyone present would survive what happened this day. City Hall, however, would feel The Colonel's wrath for a long time to come.

Another earth-shaking thing occurred that important day. Two ten-year-olds fell instantly in love, as only ten-year-olds can. After the crisis had subsided somewhat, Davis announced that he'd like to go to public school in town. This announcement was acknowledged, but put on the back burner temporarily by a call from downtown.

Captain Emile Perkins decided not to wait for the inevitable call from The Colonel. The veteran lawman tried to ease into the conversation by saying to the man, "Good afternoon, sir. And how are you and your family doing today?"

"As good as can be expected, Emile. I think we both know why you're calling, so why don't we cut to the chase!"

The captain knew the sound of that voice very well. He had heard it many times in town meetings and various other assemblies in the past. It had always come from this man with a solid opinion, and was most believable when he thought something wasn't exactly right. The captain cleared his throat and began his apology, "Well, Colonel, on behalf of the Hattiesburg Police Department, I'd like to extend to you our sincerest regrets for the actions of one of our patrolman the day before yesterday. As a courtesy to you, we have decided to relieve him of his duties, effective...."

"Now, hold on, Emile. It's not me you owe the apology to. My partner, Mr. Hampton, is the man you should be apologizing to."

"Excuse me, did you say your partner?"

"Yes, I did, Captain. If you like, I will be more than happy to call him to the phone."

The top dog in the H.P.D. was stunned. He really didn't want to do this. He felt that all people of color were beneath him. Grudgingly, he promised The Colonel he would comply with his wishes. The captain apologized and asked "Mr. Hampton" if he wanted the officer to be fired. Willie smiled with satisfaction into the phone's mouthpiece and said to the waiting captain, "Tell me, sir, does this man have a family?"

Chapter Nine

The Presley's never had it easy. Either one of them was working and the other one was not, or they were both unemployed. It seemed that no two good things ever happened at the same time. Even with help from Delphia Hansen and others, it was simply never enough. Things were desperate, and they had to make a decision. They knew they had to leave Tupelo because there wasn't any steady work. Every time the subject of moving was mentioned, Elvis would throw a tantrum. He had developed a morbid habit of visiting what he thought was his brother's grave, and he didn't want to live anywhere else. In the end though, poverty won out. They moved to Memphis where they heard Vernon could get work.

Colonel and Lillian DeLongpre had carefully given their son the best of everything. This was not in any way relegated to just material things. He also had to be prepared for life outside their fortress. They wanted him to be a part of and have something to say about decisions that were made. When he displayed his hate of the academy, his father was a bit disappointed. However, when he explained his reasons, The Colonel digested them and decided that the reasons had merit, so Davis was allowed to drop out and be tutored by Darcy. And believe it, nothing was lost there.

The announcement about wanting to go to public school in town didn't seem to have any foundation. Because of the ugly events that had transpired the same afternoon, his parents hadn't been told of the gasoline can caper, until they asked Willie if Davis had mentioned anything to him about school in town.

The dust had pretty much settled from the nasty events of the previous day, and Willie was beginning to be Willie again. He looked at The Colonel and Lillian and said with a sly smile, "Well, Tilly, Pop, I think a lot of it may have to do with Rebecca Thompson."

"Rebecca Thompson?" they chimed.

"Yeah, Harley Thompson's little girl—you know, Thompson's Hardware?"

Lillian had been there quite a few times. After a couple hair twirls, she inquired, "You mean that little brown-headed girl that's always dusting things and comes up and talks to me and everyone."

"The same, Tilly, the very same."

Lillian stood up, smoothed the front of her dress, and exclaimed, "Oooooh, T. D., I think we've found the heart of this."

They sat for a while putting this together and decided to call their son. The talk was held in Jarrod's place, where they agreed to go along with his wishes. However, he would have to give his most excellent promise to keep up good grades and take care of his chores at home. In addition, he would have to promise to see this choice out, which meant no more changing schools. This did last through high school, but it would not be the last time this young man would alter his life's path.

He not only kept his word to his parents, he excelled in school, and this was not confined to the classroom. He played baseball and football as hard as he studied. The only time his mind wasn't on studies or sports was when he passed Rebecca Thompson in the hall. As if seeing those flashing eyes and toasty smile wasn't enough, the scent of her perfume would stay in his nostrils for hours. He just never did anything about it. He was shy and frustrated when it came to her. One could only imagine how she must have felt.

When he was away from school and Rebecca, he loved his 4-H activities that involved exhibiting his animals at local and county fairs all over Mississippi and with excellent results. The only thing that bothered Willie and his folks was his attachment to them. He took wonderful care of all his charges, but even the greatest animal handlers experience some failure. Once in a great while, Davis would lose one to sickness or at birth. The boy was devastated by almost every incident.

The Hubbards had gone back to Connecticut soon after Willie had come home from college with his new bride. Their job was finished, but what a job they'd done. The education Willie received from them surpassed all The Colonel's expectations. He was totally prepared to run The Willows, and The Colonel and Lillian agreed that meeting the Hubbards ranked right up there with the happiest days of their lives. But this was down the list from their marriage, getting their baby, and Willie and Darcy's marriage.

The love of animals that Amos and Laurie Ann Hubbard had brought to The Willows was quite different from what the people who worked and lived there were accustomed to. The pre-Hubbard animals were never mistreated, only cared for, and well-fed. A vet was always summoned if one seemed to take seriously ill. The seeds of love and camaraderie were planted there for God's other creatures, and they, too, flourished. It took a little while for Willie to open up after the loss of his father, but it came much earlier than it might have, because of the support given him by his two families, and, yes, the Hubbards.

Amos never tried to force anything on Willie. He had learned this trait of patience raising three sons, so Willie benefited from this. At first he would ask gently, "Willie, we're going for a ride, want to go?"

"No, thanks, I'll just finish my chores." He would watch them disappear over the hill with that old hound Harpo trailing close behind. He wondered where they were going, but he knew they'd probably end up at that smoking place The Colonel had built for them. "Silly to ride all that way to smoke. Silly to smoke."

After a while, Willie decided to give this riding thing a try. It seemed like every time they returned, they were in such a good mood. So, he asked Amos for some lessons. Amos now had two shadows, Harpo and Willie. Willie learned from Amos on *some* rides, but when the conversation was over, Amos would ride on, but he kept on talking. This confused Willie at first, but he dared not say anything. He just let Amos talk to his dog or horse or to whomever it was he was talking. One evening, he pulled along Laurie Ann's mare and asked, "Does Amos do this all the time?"

Laurie Ann just smiled and said, "As long as someone is listening, my dear, as long as someone is listening."

Willie learned everything he needed from Amos, such as breeding methods, the importance of bloodlines, and how to match them successfully. Willie could now pass this gift to his little pal, Davis.

Davis was growing faster and faster. Each time The Colonel returned from his many business trips, he just marveled at the boy's physical changes and his increasing interest in his animals. He and his wife would spend a good deal of time, usually after Davis went to bed, discussing their son's activities and early maturity in some areas.

As Davis' birthday neared, they discussed what they should give him. It was agreed that an animal would be something they wouldn't have to return.

During one of these sessions, The Colonel suggested to his wife that their son still treats each one of his charges like pets. "Maybe if we give him an animal with significant commercial value, he'll recognize its business potential, and not become so attached."

They decided to give him a yearling Charlet calf from blue ribbon stock. This was a great idea. Davis fed and groomed him, and spent many hours preparing to show him at various fairs where he won many awards. With the bloodlines and trophies, Davis was able to use the bull for stud and began earning money from his hobby. The Colonel was elated that, for the first time, he didn't name the animal. Well, he did name it, but only for business purposes, but he didn't talk to it or ask it to come. Davis started breeding his other winners with the same results, and, naturally, the stud fees increased.

This had always been a working farm, growing and harvesting crops of many kinds since Jarrod and Isaiah first shook hands those many years ago. Now though, many prize animals called it home. As the budding breeder's business grew, Davis entered the next phase of his development. Who else better than his mother to seek this education from? The Colonel had given her the job of running the "house accounts" as he always referred to them. Needless to say, she had done a magnificent job. Lillian set up a business account for her boy entrepreneur and helped him manage his new enterprise. Willie didn't say much, but it did his heart good to see the progression of building this dream. Amos taught Willie, and, in turn, Willie passed his knowledge to Davis.

The summer before his senior year, Davis decided what he wanted to do for the rest of his life. He wanted to raise thoroughbred horses and go to college to become a veterinarian instead of majoring in business.

Davis, nor anyone else at The Willows, with the exception of his mother and father, had any idea whatsoever of his origin…nor ever would. As he matured, he never attained his father's physical stature but showed and possessed his strength. Many people, Rebecca being one of them, noticed the same habits and characteristics the boy had that were very close to his mother. All these things could possibly be accounted for by association, nevertheless, it was indeed there.

Like The Colonel, when Davis made up his mind to do something, there was no turning back. Another trait he learned from his father was to never reveal his entire plan at one time. No one knew about his financial worth except his mother. Not to say this worth was anything to stagger the mind, but it was indeed substantial, at least for a boy still in his teens.

Davis and his mother were not trying to hide anything from The Colonel. In fact, he knew and approved of what they were doing, and why not? He'd given Lillian carte blanche to refurbish the mansion years before. Not at any time did questions or audits ever come forth.

Davis did, however, ask his father how long he would be away on his upcoming trip. The answer, with no hesitation, was five or six weeks.

Before he'd made his plan for a new barn, he had surveyed the layout, from the entrance to The Willows, all the way to the parking area between the big house, the barns, the livestock area, and beyond. He didn't need a crew to do this. He'd played and worked with Willie to the point where he could just stand in one place and visualize his concept.

Without causing any questioning looks from anyone, he casually started from where his father and his Great-Uncle Jarrod before him began their plan. He walked down the three hundred yard lane from the arch to the half-circle driveway in front of the mansion that at one time many years before had been filled with expensive horse-drawn carriages for the extravagant gala parties in the middle 1800s. He'd heard of the feats of everyone from Isaiah, Jarrod, Ben, and, yes, even Amos Hubbard.

The old barn and corral that he'd known as a boy were still in tact and serviceable but would just not suffice for the vision in his head. He walked around the east end of the mansion and saw where the new barn should be. He stood in the parking area that he had watched being repaved recently by those big smelly machines and looked beyond his mother's fabulous rose garden. Willie's and Darcy's home stood one hundred yards to his right. The old barn and corral were situated on the end of a triangle to the farthest point away from the big house and the Hamptons home.

Again, the old barn still served a purpose, but the new one he had in mind should be a lot closer to the lake. This would be better for the temperamental thoroughbreds and their training. He didn't want to break horses, he wanted to train and pamper them. Now that he had formulated this in his mind, he had something to tell his mother and Willie.

Davis had hoped they would approve of the design and location. Willie told him that he would help as much as he could, but Davis knew he had plenty to do with running The Willows. Besides, there were enough skilled people at his disposal. He teasingly told his mother he wouldn't need her for any interior decorating.

About ninety miles to the north, in Memphis, Tennessee, a young man told his mother and father that his voice and his twelve-dollar guitar would make him the biggest star that this world has ever known.

Chapter Ten

Davis had always been a little shy around girls. Not so much in a group, like a students activity or a party, but, one on one, he hadn't quite overcome that, especially with Rebecca. They'd known each other for close to five years and had never been alone. This wasn't critical at their age. Rebecca wondered if it would *ever* happen.

That's kind of the way it went for this couple. Davis would go to class, and afterward the gym or athletic field, then home to his animals. If Rebecca hadn't been on the cheerleader squad, she wouldn't have seen him at all. Occasionally, however, fate does smile on the patient.

One afternoon, Davis had finished football practice and the girls were about to wrap up their rehearsals on the sidelines. The stadium was built facing east and west to make the best use of the wind that always seemed to be blowing in the fall.

The exit for the ballplayers was on the east end in the shade. Rebecca had forgotten her notebook and went back for it. They were both running, him going, her coming, and, because of the shade, they didn't see each other coming around the corner. Crash!! He almost knocked her over, but she too was athletic and remained upright. She just about caught all her books before they hit the ground.

He was tongue-tied again, and he was cursing his luck. *Why do I always make a fool of myself when she is around?* He'd discussed this ongoing problem with his parents, but it didn't help all that much. They just told him to use his sweet personality and talk to her. "You'll charm her to death," was their staple answer. He just chuckled at their advice, though not in front of them. They thought he was perfect and didn't understand that the rest of the world might not agree with them. No matter what Mom and Dad thought about him, he just couldn't make the words come out whenever she was present. *What an idiot!*

This God-sent collision was all the opportunity Rebecca needed. She'd waited for this chance for years, and, out of nowhere, here it was. *Damn!* She was all sweaty from cheerleader practice. *Why now?* She looked at Davis, who was also sweaty and covered with dirt and grass stains, which was okay because boys were expected to do that. It was a no-no for young girls of that era.

When he began to stammer slightly, she jumped in and took over. She'd been rehearsing what she would say if the chance ever presented itself. Just like an accomplished actress, her words flowed easily. She talked about his studies, her studies, his animals, their blue ribbons and trophies, and, of course, his brand new "old" red pickup.

From that day on, if Davis wasn't tending to his livestock, studying, practicing football, or washing his truck, he was holding "Becky's" hand. If Rebecca wasn't studying, sailing on their little lake, or helping her daddy, she was thinking about what to wear to look good the next time she was with "her guy." After their last class of the day, they would go to the local drive-in and split a cheeseburger and a cherry fizz with two straws. Two straws was a good excuse for getting close, like they needed one. After that, they would dance and laugh, and let off steam with their classmates and friends. When the after-school hour was done, he'd drop her off at her daddy's store, where she'd help her father close.

Rebecca had worked with her father at the hardware for as long as she'd been tall enough to climb a stepladder. But poor Dad had to start looking for part-time help now because Rebecca wasn't there every weekend. She was out at The Willows getting to know her prior competition, Davis' animals.

Harley Thompson would jokingly complain to his wife, "That DeLongpre boy, he just came in here and stole my best helper!" He knew his little girl had to grow up someday, and, besides that, he kind of liked that "clumsy kid." That's the way he liked to refer to the gasoline can caper.

Rebecca not only got to spend time with her guy, she liked his folks a lot too. She'd say to herself, *Mrs. DeLongpre is so pretty and so smart. I want to be just like her when I get to be her age.*

It's funny how one's goals change as Father Time marches on.

The Colonel also liked the charming little lady whom everyone assumed would become one of the family someday. He would see Davis and Rebecca holding hands strolling around or see them yell with glee when they would get into a water fight while washing one of the horses. He would push his hat back on his head, smile, and hope his son would be as lucky as he had been.

There were a few things The Colonel and all at the ranch didn't see. The Willows encompassed at least forty thousand acres, and there obviously were countless places for a couple seeking privacy to go and play. When Davis and Rebecca grew weary of tending to his various animals, they would walk or ride to one of these hideaways. One of their favorites was a small lake about twenty minutes ride from the main barn. Because of the surrounding trees, the water was not visible from the riding trail. If one wanted to wet a hook or enjoy a picnic, he or they would have to tie up the horses and hike about one hundred yards. After a short walk through a stand of cottonwoods, a small beach suddenly appeared that afforded its visitors complete privacy. The two young lovers made it one of their haunts.

The rides and the picnics started off rather innocently. The swims and basking in the sun that followed were no more than two kids enjoying nature and each other. But when two young, healthy, red-blooded people approaching adulthood (Davis and Rebecca certainly fit into that category) are alone in a setting such as this, any number of situations may occur.

One lazy Saturday afternoon, they finished washing and currying one of Davis' prize bulls that he intended on showing at a fair in an adjoining county. They decided at the last minute to go cool off in their lake, so no lunch was packed. As they rode along, several glances were exchanged, and, when the trail permitted, they rode close together and held hands.

When they arrived at the water's edge, Davis ripped off everything down to his underwear and dove in. He wiped the water from his eyes, turned around, and yelled for Rebecca to join him. She hesitated briefly, and then quickly shed her blouse and blue jeans. This was the first he had seen her in only her frilly things, and he felt a sensation down below, even in the cold water. The only thing that escaped his puckered lips was, "Wow!"

She dove in and surfaced within touching distance. Ever so slowly, they came together. She slipped her arms around his neck and they kissed, really kissed, for the first time. They got out of the water and Davis asked her to wait while he went to the horses where he kept a blanket rolled up behind his saddle. It was the one they always used for their picnics.

He returned, they unrolled the blanket, and spread it out under a tree in the shade. They lay down, embraced, and began kissing again. They carefully explored each other's private parts and soon the remainder of their clothes came off.

As he slowly and tenderly mounted and entered her, she cried out faintly, so he stopped for a second. She put her arms around his back and urged him to continue. In only a few minutes she felt his explosion coming on. She placed her hands on his shoulders and, with all of her strength, shoved him off of her. He landed clumsily on his side and cried out, "Becky, what the hell is going on? What's the matter with you?"

She didn't answer him immediately, but, after a few minutes, she sat up and said, "I'm sorry, I just don't want anything bad to happen, you know?"

"Oh yeah, I guess you're right. Sorry I yelled."

They dressed and were getting ready to go, when she took his hand and asked him to lay down with her on the blanket. They lay in each other's arms for quite awhile. Not a word was said, and, with the exception of an occasional bird's call, the water lapping at the shore, or the breeze rattling the leaves, all was silent. Rebecca wouldn't wonder anymore why it had taken so long for them to get together, and Davis lost almost all of his shyness around girls, at least one.

Sometimes after he'd dropped Rebecca off, Davis would drive along and absently twirl a piece of his shortish hair while thinking about his girl. She always teased him about pulling on his hair, so he was trying to break himself from doing it. He knew he'd picked up this trait from his mother—and she was still doing it.

He remembered the first time they'd met, and it still caused a little warm rush of embarrassment. Rebecca never brought it up. As much as she talked about almost everything, he thought she surely would have brought that up by now, but she didn't. He'd tell himself to quit worrying about it, and he would stop, until the next time. He uttered aloud, "I don't know exactly what she's got, but whatever it is, she takes my breath away! Now I understand why Willie used to go on about Darcy all the time."

The DeLongpre family had entered the fifties. The Colonel had been through two world wars and the Korean conflict. Each one of these had made his little empire and family even wealthier. He was not in favor of these horrible wars, but somebody had to be there, so why not him?

In the months following the end of the Korean War, he switched his plants from military to peacetime almost overnight. He realized that he had to get from point "A" to point "B" as quickly as possible. Knowing this, he purchased and refurbished a DC-4 transport. He had his engineers make it comfortable and fuel-efficient. He had experienced traveling by car, train, and now planes.

The Colonel stood up like a great orator finishing his message to the world and beckoned his wife and son to join him. Davis arose from his end of the eight-foot-long polished oak table and joined his mother and father in a huge heartfelt hug. The DeLongpres were stronger than ever.

Davis was taking inventory of his busy young life. He was fully aware of how fortunate he was to have the things he did. It wasn't just material things that surrounded him at The Willows, but also his parents and how they'd let him be a part of the decision-making. And then there was the camaraderie and good advice from Willie. This brought him back to what was bothering him right now.

All during his life, the importance of land had been stressed. The Willows was his parents' mainstay, particularly his father's. When The Colonel was establishing his various businesses around the world, he would always try to buy the property the plant or structure sat on. The acquisition of land had always been stressed to Davis, and, one of these days, it would be his. He would try to make the same wise decisions as his father, but now something was missing.

He didn't want to press his luck or offend his parents in any way. He'd been lucky so far on a couple occasions, but the love and respect he had for Willie and their partnership needed to be dignified. He wanted to share The Willows with Willie Hampton. He would bring that up the following evening at dinner.

The next night he could hardly swallow the food on his plate, not that it wasn't good as it always was, it just didn't want to go down his throat. He was anxious to get this over with, but, as he knew, these kinds of discussions had to wait until after dinner. He pushed the food around on his plate, waiting until his father leaned back in his chair and lit up. He choked out his words. He did an admirable job of explaining his wishes, and he waited for those piercing eyes to really stab him. The Colonel waited until the young man was finished. As he was wrapping it up, he noticed a slight smile cross the stern face. His mother daintily dabbed the corners of her mouth and looked down like she was trying to keep her smile from him. "Well, son, I've go to hand it to you. There is no doubt, you're a DeLongpre through and through." Davis didn't understand. His parents began to explain about his Great-Uncle Jarrod's will. They went a little further and explained how very proud of him they were, again. He'd revealed the true nature of his soul, and it was good.

The young man was totally knocked for a loop. He always thought he was pretty smart, but never had the slightest hint about the Hamptons position at The Willows. At first he was a bit angry, but that quickly subsided when he told his father what a great thing that was to do. The Colonel held up his hands and said, "Now, hold on there, son, I'd like to take credit for that, but it was Jarrod's idea. I just told you that."

"But, Dad, you and Momma kept it going. You didn't try to change anything!" There was no reply to that. It was just another one of the lessons that Davis had learned at his mother's dining room table. He may be bright and most of the time prepared, but nobody could possibly know everything.

The next day when he ran into Willie, he wasn't sure of what to say. He thought he should be angry with his friend for not saying anything previously, but since there was no confrontation with his parents, why should there be with his best friend. So, he just cuffed him on the shoulder and asked why he'd never mentioned any of this all these years. Willie feigned a punch back and said, "Thought you knew, pard. Sorry about that, but that's why I never brought it up. I just thought you knew. Anyway, would it have made any difference with us if you had?"

"I don't think so. No, I know it wouldn't have."

Willie put his hand on his friend's chest and tried saying with a straight face, "Uh, by the way, would you move over a couple of steps? You're standing on my part." They shared a laugh and walked to the barn. Everything was back to normal, if normal was possible between these two buddies.

Davis enrolled at University of Kentucky and was comfortably settled in. His routine was very simple. He rose at 5:00 a.m., turned on the light over his study desk and underlined the important words in his text. He would try to be quiet and not disturb his roommate. He would study for about an hour, then close the books, and go out and run full bore around the campus. Upon his return, he'd take off his sweats, shower, and go to the commissary for a light breakfast before for his classes.

One morning, around 6:00 a.m., he was walking from the cafeteria back to his room, and, as he passed the big water fountain, he felt a stabbing pain in his left leg that shot clear up to his shoulder. He'd never experienced this before, so he consulted the college physician.

Dr. Phillip Crowder couldn't find the source of his discomfort, but assured the freshman it was nothing serious. "Davis, you seem okay to me, but just to be sure, go see your family doctor during semester break."

Some distance from the university, down Memphis way, Elvis Presley was involved in an accident while driving his new Harley Davidson and injured his knee. This was the first of many unexplained physical and mental episodes Davis would encounter.

Davis had never been completely aware of his family's vast wealth while growing up, but he started putting things together when he was away from the paradise where he had grown up. The confusion he'd experienced when he found out that his buddy Willie was not just an employee of The Willows now made sense. He realized why Willie and Darcy had such a beautiful home, just footsteps away from the extravagant house where he lived. All the Willows' employees had a lot more than shacks to live in. Although their homes couldn't compare with Willie and Darcy's, they were fully piped and plumbed, pleasant to the eye and very comfortable.

When Davis entered college and saw the heavy load put on him, he was at first dismayed. He wanted to call his father and admit that he might've been wrong. But he now realized that times were changing, and, though his father had never gone to college, he would have to if he wanted to be a veterinarian.

He missed his life at The Willows, his mother and dad, Willie and Darcy, and, at times, he missed Becky. One day when he was sitting in the college library, he made a decision. The University of Kentucky he had chosen was indeed the best. It had to be a great state also. Well, if it wasn't, why were all the great horses from this area, all the winners and runners-up at the derby and other major events.

He decided that the four years needed to graduate were too many out of his life and his plan. So he skipped his weekend leaves and summer vacations, kept his room at the dormitory, and stayed there. His teachers lived on the campus and were readily available.

Instead of the four years required, Davis doubled up and completed his mission in less than three. He finished in the top five percent of the class and received his diploma from an unbelieving university faculty.

He had originally planned to return home with his credentials, marry Rebecca, raise horses and have some kids. This plan somehow dissolved into a rose haze in the young man's eyes.

For most young folks, any graduation is a monumental event to which relatives and friends are invited. Parents are almost always there. There wouldn't be any of this for the over-achiever from Mississippi. First of all, he didn't graduate with any particular class. He finished a year and one half ahead of the norm, so there were no festivities for anyone to attend. When he arrived back at The Willows, his folks wanted to have some sort of graduation celebration, but Davis wanted to keep it simple. He wanted to have a nice dinner with Mom and Dad and, of course, Willie and Darcy. He was impatient to get on with his plans for life.

It was great to see his family after being away for over two-and-a-half years. He marveled at how good his dad looked, even though he was nearing seventy. He still stood tall and had that wonderful mop of gray with just the right amount of subtle black streaks. His mother was still very beautiful, but most boys think their moms are beautiful.

While he was still at the University of Kentucky, Lillian had written about The Colonel's semi-retirement and how happy she was that Amos Hubbard's son, John, had worked out so well. The Colonel had begun to minimize his business trips during the last few months and had chosen John Hubbard to take over. John had transferred to headquarters over fifteen years earlier. Since he'd worked very closely with The Colonel, he was now ready.

Two-and-a-half years are a long time for a family as close as the DeLongpres. There was a lot to catch up on. Lillian finally brought up the subject of Rebecca, which now turned this into a two-bottle-of-wine dinner. She was more than a bit surprised that Davis hadn't included her in the homecoming dinner plans.

"You know, son, she was here yesterday and had tea with me when we thought you just might come home. On all her vacations, she would spend a little of them with me and your father."

The Colonel watched his wife, and, when she stopped, he began, "I don't know, son, maybe we failed in teaching you the intricacies of male-female relationships. I know things are different these days. Parents don't arrange their children's lives like they did in our day or tell them whom to wed. But I really believe you should think about Rebecca. If your intentions are to spend your life with her, you should make them a bit clearer. Your mother and I believe, from what you've said to us, that you love her. Son, I'm not sure if Rebecca understands."

Davis was tired from his trip, the big dinner, and maybe from the extra glass of wine. He wanted to comment on what his parents said but decided not to complicate his first night home. He thanked his mother for the dinner, his father for the conversation, and bid them good night. He laid his head down and wondered what it would be like to see Becky after all this time. Would he have trouble talking to her? Would she even want to talk to him? He mulled all this over a few times. As he drifted off to sleep, he was taken back and once again sitting in the middle of a pile of gasoline cans.

Chapter Eleven

Rebecca, like most children, was a very curious child. In her case, it wasn't just curiosity. She wanted to know why something was painted red instead of blue. She'd ask her father why one tool worked better for this than the other one worked for that. Being with him so much in the hardware store while meeting a lot of his customers, only added fuel to this already busy mind of hers. And she could talk, too! Harley used to say to his wife, "That little lady can talk you to death!"

In the late forties, America's love for the radio was challenged by a new medium—television. Although still in its infancy, it was available if you could afford it, but it wasn't in every household. The Thompsons could afford a TV.

Shortly following her graduation from high school, Rebecca announced to her folks and to Davis that she had been thinking about a career in communications for some time now. Both parties tried to discourage her, warning her about the trouble she'd have getting into a male-dominated business. But this only added to the fire behind those serious dark eyes. She looked Davis squarely in the face and exclaimed, "You're going to college for what you want, aren't you, Davis?" She'd sold her point to her parents. All that was left was to decide on one of the schools she'd been researching. She decided on Memphis College since it was the closest and best.

Rebecca had been crazy about Davis for half her life. She never understood why they never got close until way into high school, but it made no difference now. She was sure Davis loved her and would marry her someday.

She knew there was a chance that things might change if they didn't see each other every day, but they'd get together on weekends, Christmas, and summer vacations, right? Wrong! When Davis told her about his plan to go straight through school without coming home, she wasn't at all pleased. She was further confused, when just before they were ready to leave, he decided to stay out a year to get his horse business a little more off the ground. She often sat with an open text in front of her and thought, *What am I going to do with him?*

That first year wasn't too bad. Even though Davis was busy, they still found time to see a little of each other on Rebecca's leaves and vacations. If the weather permitted, they would sneak off to their little lakeside hide-away, but, after that, it became a lot harder for Rebecca. She was a beautiful girl, and, along with guys hitting on her, and the snide remarks from some about a woman having no place in this business, she was tested. She would wonder if Davis, as handsome as he was, was being bothered by some of those local belles, but she thought to herself, *All work and no play, I know him! At least I think I do!*

It was June of 1956. The weather was still pleasant and balmy this early in the summer. The muggy weather that accompanies southern summers had not yet arrived. The Thompsons' home was situated on a small lake with the shoreline consisting of five large lots where each residence's beach was completely private. The size of the lake was perfect for a little light sailing and, of course, in the south, fishing.

Rebecca awoke and opened her bedroom window. The breeze off the lake was cool and teased her hair like it was welcoming her home. She was glad to be home, *and* she was looking forward to breakfast. That was the thing she missed most of all being away at college—her mother's cooking...and of course, one certain fellow. She took a nice long bath. That was another thing she missed, there were no tubs at school. She never liked showers. As the warm water and the essence of the flowery smelling soap took over her body, she began to reminisce about the last eleven years and the love of her young life, Davis DeLongpre.

Davis finished wiping down his new Chevy pickup, a graduation present from his folks. It really didn't need washing, it was brand new, but he turned the hose on it anyway. He loved the way the cold water beaded up and slid off the shiny, slick surface. He dried the front and side windows, stepped back, admired his truck and his work, and went to check on a mare that Willie said was ready to drop her foal any minute. Willie saw his friend approaching and asked what he was up to.

"I've got a lunch date with Becky!" Davis announced.

The mare was still not quite ready, so he left her in Willie's good hands. Davis smiled at Willie, who smiled back knowingly. He went into the house to shower.

As he was toweling off and slipping into his briefs and T-shirt, he was looking forward to seeing Becky. He was telling himself he really hadn't missed her all that much. As he took ten minutes to pick out a shirt and slacks, he was thinking about not being ready for her to be in his life full-time yet. As he was putting on his shoes, he thought, *Well, maybe a couple of years down the line*. After all of that, as he checked himself out in the mirror, why was there a slight catch in his throat?

As he drove the fifteen minutes to her home, he wondered if she'd changed any since he'd last seen her. He was picturing that shiny brown hair, soft, nice-smelling skin, and those wonderful eyes. He missed the entrance to the Thompsons' circular driveway, backed up a bit, then turned in and parked. As he walked up the steps to the front door, he felt a warm sensation he hadn't experienced in a long time. He pressed the button on their huge brass doorbell and waited…and waited. *Well, at least that hasn't changed*, he thought.

Mrs. Thompson was closing the oven door on a roast for dinner and heard the doorbell. She wiped her hands on her apron and headed for the front of the house. Halfway into the hall, her daughter bounded past her. "I'll get it, Momma. It's Davis!" Rebecca stopped just short of her door, adjusted her blouse, patted her hair, and, just as the bell rang again, she flung the door open like Loretta Young. They stood looking at each other for a second before both began to speak at once.

"You first."

"No, you first."

Then, to hell with it, they fell into each other's arms.

As they had in high school, they drove to the Crystal Diner for lunch. Before ordering, Rebecca narrowed her eyes and said, "I shouldn't even be talking to you Davis DeLongpre! Two-and-a-half years! Boy, do you have some making up to do!" She had caught him off guard, but the waitress approaching their table to take their order saved him. When Davis ordered cheeseburgers, fries, and a cherry fizz with two straws, they both laughed and held each other's hands.

Now that they'd settled in a bit, Davis finally had a chance to look straight into the face of this girl who had become even more lovely than ever. Gone was the soft little-girl baby fat, (which wasn't all that bad) here was a beautiful, elegant lady. He regretted that he hadn't witnessed this girl becoming a woman.

While Davis was trying to make sense of his feelings, Rebecca was analyzing him also. She was fighting being angry with him for not making an effort to see her all this time. She had missed him terribly and tried not to be obvious as she looked back at him, but his pretty, boyish face had become more angular and there were signs of a beard. Now he was handsome, possessing a cool confidence that almost frightened her. He was only twenty-one but seemed older, much older.

Davis was explaining his future and the plans for his own path in life. Rebecca listened, but in all these things he spoke about, there was no mention of "us." This caused her mind to wander. She didn't hear him when he asked, "How about you, Becky? How's that communications thing you were so hot on working out?"

"Huh?"

"You haven't heard anything I've said, have you?"

"Of course, Davis, go on."

"Becky, I just asked you a question."

Rebecca wanted to reply but chose not to. There were many things troubling her about the "I, I, I," and no "us," from Davis. But she didn't want to ruin this first time back with him, so she decided to wait until tomorrow and just try to enjoy the day. Although she knew he loved her, or at least she thought he did, she still wondered if the last couple of years had caused them to grow apart. Instead of voicing her concerns, she just kept quiet, letting him ramble on, hoping that eventually the word "us" would come up in the one-sided conversation.

As they drove back to her home, the dialogue consisted of humorous little antidotes they'd shared over the years. Before he kissed her good-bye at her door, he asked if she'd like to have dinner the next evening at a new restaurant called the "Creole Castle." Of course, her answer was yes.

Davis walked back to his truck, started it up, and leaned toward the passenger window to blow Becky a kiss. She returned the gesture while watching the red pickup fade from sight. She stood for a moment looking at the neatly manicured front lawn and garden of mixed flower varieties. She was happy this particular aspect of her life hadn't changed while she had been away. The smell of her mother's roast cooking in the oven filled the hall on the way to her bedroom, triggering a smile. She went to her vanity table and began brushing her hair.

Suddenly she jumped up, changed into a pair of pink pedal pushers and walked down to the little pier where their boat was tied. When she was a little girl, her father had taught her to sail. Since then, she'd gone out on the lake when she needed to get her thoughts together. Right now, she had to figure out what Davis had been telling her. But, there was something else bothering her, too. Something she had seen while gazing at Davis during that nearly one-sided conversation was nagging at her. What was it she saw in that face? That little voice in the memory part of her brain was screaming. She couldn't put it together, so she raised her hands in an "I give up" gesture. Maybe the water would help. It always had before. She began untying the bowlines on the little blue and white sailboat.

The sail didn't provide any answers. But, as usual, it calmed her. She returned to her bedroom and sat on the edge of her bed. Something made her go to her closet and pull out a couple of boxes she still hadn't unpacked. At the bottom of the second box was the answer to one of her dilemmas.

There weren't a lot of girls at the communications college, but there were a few, and the way things were, they counted on the strength in numbers.

One weekend, during the final semester, she and the other girls attended a concert at the Overton Park Shell in Memphis. She had kept the program from that night, like she kept almost everything. She was glad she was a pack rat at this particular time. She quickly looked through the listing of entertainers who had performed that night. It showed their pictures and song selections. The fourth celebrity on the bill was Elvis Presley. She took the program over to her dresser, and picked up the photo of her and Davis at the senior prom. She looked from one picture to the other, back and forth. One had dark hair and sideburns and wore a gaudy pink sports coat with a black and white open-collared shirt. The other was clean cut with a flattop haircut, wearing a tuxedo with a boutonnière neatly stuck on his lapel.

But wait! Look at their faces. Yes, there were some differences, Elvis' nose was a little longer and his chin a trifle squarer, but, even with the difference in the hair and clothes, the two were eerily identical. She lay back on her bed and tried in vain to steady her heartbeat but couldn't. She went to the bathroom to get a glass of water to calm her. Halfway through the glass of water she exclaimed, "Wow. They look so much alike. I wonder what that means?" She knew The Colonel and Davis both had blue-gray eyes, and sometimes a father or son might be a little shorter than the other. His hands were larger, but looked more like his mother's, and they both had the same mannerisms. This in no way made him effeminate, at all.

Rebecca fought the urge to pick up the phone, call Davis, and ask him about the plans he'd mentioned earlier and why they didn't include her. If she did call him and question his plans, it would provide the opportune time to say to him, "And, by the way, I just discovered the strangest thing...."

Suddenly, she thought better of it. She didn't want him to think she was childish and immature. And, besides, they were having dinner tomorrow night. She'd have ample opportunity to bring it up at that time. She closed her eyes and drifted off into a troubled dreamland.

The new restaurant was interesting. The Creole food was quite spicy but good. Becky, though, needed some orange sherbet to cool it down. She had decided to ask Davis if he'd heard or knew anything about Elvis Presley before she tested the waters concerning their future together.

"Davis, have you ever heard of a singer by the name of Elvis Presley?"

Davis gave her a funny smile. "Becky, I was away at college. I wasn't living in a cave. Of course, I've *heard* of him, but I've never seen him. Why?"

"I don't know. I was just wondering."

Davis put his coffee cup back on the saucer, took the napkin off his lap, and absent-mindedly played with it while folding it in half. He tossed the napkin aside, looked up at her and said, "Now that I think of it, my roommate was complaining that this Elvis guy was all his girlfriend could talk about. He's got a couple big records out, I guess. Haven't heard them, though."

Rebecca decided to change the subject. "How's your father feeling these days?"

While Davis was answering, she remembered when they used to park on the hill over-looking town. All the kids laughingly referred to it as "Make-Out Mountain." When they weren't cuddling, they would play guessing games, like who sang this song or starred in that picture. Davis was almost unbeatable. He knew singers, stars, musicians, years, months, and whatever. Now, he hardly knew anything about the hottest singer in the country. Didn't know, didn't care, but Rebecca couldn't leave it alone. "Well, anyway, my girlfriend and I talked a little this afternoon and we thought you looked a lot like him."

"Yeah, how about that? You know, Becky, that's no big deal. Remember in Biology 501, they were talking about everybody having a double somewhere in the world?"

"Yeah, I guess so, Davis." Somehow, she couldn't bring up the subject of "us" again, not wanting to take a chance on spoiling the evening. She reminded herself, *We do have the rest of the summer.*

Chapter Twelve

During the summer months, they saw each other often. They dined at several different restaurants, enjoyed barbecues at The Willows, and went fishing with her father once. But the major part of their time was spent at the "ranch."

They managed to find time to visit their private little part of the plantation during this period. It was more enjoyable these days, probably because they were more relaxed with each other. Rebecca had taken time to go to the local pharmacy and pick up some protection for their encounters. Now, she wouldn't have to push him away when they were reaching the top of the mountain. Their lovemaking became more intense, and, after a few climaxes, Rebecca didn't concern herself with "us" factor, at least not for a few hours.

Even though Davis was still unable to bring up anything with "us" in a sentence, everything seemed pretty good otherwise. They would go on rides together, with Becky sometimes staying overnight (in her own room, of course), if they happened to get home late.

One day, Davis surprised her with a Lady Stetson. She loved it, and, these days, his mind strayed from his goals long enough to notice how well Becky filled out her riding pants.

On one of those magical evenings, Rebecca finally threw caution to the wind and asked Davis a question that would change their relationship, at least for several years to come. "Davis, what do you see in the future for us? I mean, have you ever thought or do you ever think about us getting married and having children?" Davis didn't reply immediately, so she continued, "Is there something wrong with me? Do I make you happy when we make love? I can't tell you how long it's been since you've said I love you, Becky!"

Davis held up his hands, which meant, "Hold on a second." He did that nervous napkin thing, took a sip of coffee, and sat back in his chair. Rebecca's heartbeat went from fast to almost sprinting, and it felt like it was leaving her body. Finally, he spoke, "Becky, I do have a lot of plans and goals that will require a lot of work and take up a major portion of my time for the next few years. I don't think it would be fair to either of us to divide my work with the task of raising a family. I want to give you the attention you deserve."

Rebecca interrupted him, "What are you saying, Davis? How much time are you talking about? Do you ever want to marry me at all?"

He took her hand and said, as tenderly as he knew how, "Becky, you know I love you. There will never be anyone but you for me. I promise you that. But I just can't think about us right now. As you know, my dad traveled a lot while I was growing up. It was very tough on my mother 'cause we missed him. He wasn't a bad father. He was a good father—when he was there. I don't want to do it that way. I want to get my business going first, and then I can be a proper husband and father."

This is not what Rebecca wanted to hear. She was exasperated but didn't feel like fighting, so she asked Davis to take her home.

Rebecca went back to Memphis to finish her final year in college. It was a troubled year, but the spunky young lady got through it, in spite of the unrest about her and Davis. When she came home on vacations, they still saw each other. After her graduation, she felt he would finally make up his mind about his plans for them, but their time together was spent more talking about horses than anything else. She didn't bring up the subject of "us" again. She just hoped her patience would be rewarded and left it at that.

One night during dinner, she told him about a job offer from K-JUN in Gulfport. Certainly, this would make him do something, but all he offered was his congratulations. They left the restaurant and drove home in silence. They looked at each other with the love they both had, but it just wasn't enough. A hand-squeeze replaced good-bye.

Things at the "ranch" were going quite well in the summer of '58. Since The Colonel had semi-retired and joined his son and Willie Hampton, a lot of changes had been made. New paddocks had been built, a workout track had been completed, and, thanks to Amos Hubbard, they had accumulated some quality stock. Yes, everything was going well—maybe a little too well.

Most of the farms and ranches in this rural area had big mailboxes by the entrance to their estates. The DeLongpres were no different, but their box was never used. The postman would drive down the tree-lined lane and deliver the mail to Lillian. The fact that there was always a refreshing snack waiting for him, along with the nice little envelope he received at Christmas, probably had nothing to do with it. This day was no different for the faithful man in the blue-gray uniform. He handed her the mail, enjoyed his snack, and bid her good-bye until tomorrow.

Lillian began sorting the delivery. There was usual stuff from her clubs and flower sources. There was more mail from all over for The Colonel and a strange-looking letter for her boy, with an official-looking return address. She didn't give it much thought, however, all kinds of mail was arriving these days.

She walked to the corral and handed The Colonel and Davis their mail. Davis, his dad, and Willie were watching a promising filly on her morning workout. Lillian returned to the big house to begin planning dinner for the evening. Rebecca was invited, so playing cupid was very important to her today.

Davis opened his envelope and saw the greeting, which simply said, "Uncle Sam wants you." He had not included this invitation in his plans. All he could say was, "DAMN!"

His father was startled by his outburst, and asked, "What is it, son?"

Davis handed his dad the letter, and said hurriedly, "Willie, I'll see ya. I'm going for a ride."

The Colonel and Willie both looked at the letter of bad tidings and couldn't believe it. Davis had a bout with asthma when he was very young, and his doctor told them it would heal in time, but he probably wouldn't have to worry about the service. The Colonel began to go after him, but Willie interceded, "Let him go, Pop. He'll be back when he's ready." They watched him disappear into the trees, turned around, and continued watching the filly. The Colonel, however, already had his mind in action. He knew that he could make some calls and change this if he wanted to badly enough, but he would wait for his son to return.

Lillian was determined to make Rebecca a member of the family. She knew Davis saw her for dinner or whatever when she was in town and thought maybe she would fuel the flame and hurry things up a bit. It was easier to play cupid if all involved were gathered about her and she could throw things in like grandchildren, etc. She arose from her desk and made her way from the study to the expansive country kitchen. She was about to confer with Loretta about the menu when she heard her husband's voice, "Lill, I think you'd better see this."

"What is it, T. D.?" She recognized the official-looking thing she'd taken to the corral only minutes before. She read it and was more upset than her son or husband. The Colonel reminded her there was no war on and he would do something about it.

Davis had been gone on his ride for about three hours, give or take a minute or two. Willie locked up the office, but he left the right half of the big barn door open so Davis could put his horse away. He waited a few moments longer and was headed up the path to his home when he heard hoof beats. He looked around and saw his friend ride in at a full gallop and dismount. Willie yelled out, "Are you all right, pard?"

"Oh! Yeah, man! I'm going to put up my horse and then meet me at the house. I've got something to tell you and Dad."

Willie noticed that Davis' mood sounded very upbeat as compared to when he left. He went home and asked Darcy to hold dinner because he had to meet Davis at the big house.

Davis washed up a bit and then went in to talk to everyone. He saw that Willie was talking to his dad and heard his mom and Rebecca from the kitchen. They were all glad to see him home safe.

The Colonel was the first to speak. "Are you okay, son?"

"Yeah, Daddy. I'm fine. We've got to talk."

They all gathered around the kitchen table. Davis first told his father that he knew he could probably fix it so he wouldn't have to go, but he didn't want that. What he wanted was to be stationed in Europe where he could do something for his country. When this was completed, he could see first-hand about these European horses he'd been reading and hearing about.

This plan was accepted as a good idea by half of those in attendance. The Colonel and Willie didn't want to see him go, but it *would* be good for their business.

Lillian wasn't too crazy about the idea, but she knew how her boy ate, slept, and breathed horses. The idea seemed to please her husband, so she didn't have any comment at the present time. Rebecca, however, was visibly unhappy. She wanted to say something, but she could tell from his excitement that it would do no good. She simply rose and kissed him on the cheek goodnight.

"Becky, let me walk you to the car."

"No, Davis. I can find my way."

Lillian witnessed Rebecca's exit, as did The Colonel and Willie. Each had a different interpretation of her actions. Davis watched her until she disappeared into the hallway. Any other time he would have gotten up and pursued her, but tonight he was too intent on discussing his plans with his family. They all had just assumed that Rebecca would be a part of their lives, and were all a little shocked at the events that took place on this evening. But The Willows family was very strong and had always taken care of its own.

The following morning, father, son, and the twenty-five percent partner got together for breakfast. Lillian was invited, but she chose not to be there. Many things were discussed, and most were agreed on and settled.

A few days later Davis reported to the draft board in Hattiesburg, took his physical, and he was told he'd have approximately two weeks before receiving his orders.

There were many young men in this decade of the fifties that came from poor roots and were making their names in the rock and roll music business. There was Eddie Cochran, Sanford Clark, Johnny and Dorsey Burnett, Charlie Feathers, Gene Vincent, Charlie Rich, and others. One of these young men that stood head and shoulders above all was Elvis Presley.

Elvis had many big record hits and, unlike the rest, got Hollywood's attention. In 1958, he had already starred in three movies, *Love Me Tender*, *Loving You* and *Jailhouse Rock*.

While starting his fourth movie, *King Creole*, he received his draft notice. He was terrified that this would put a halt to his meteoric career. His manager, Colonel Tom Parker, made a deal that would allow him to complete the movie. He finished the movie but never saw it when it was released in the theaters.

Before he had finished his basic training in Texas, he experienced a heartache that would forever leave a huge hole in his life. His beloved mother, Gladys, passed away, and he never totally recovered from this.

Rebecca had driven home that night and went straight to her room. She fought the urge to drive to Gulfport right away and decided against it because she was so upset. The next morning, after a fitful night of beating up her pillow, she joined her folks at breakfast and told them she was going back to work. Her mother noticed her puffy eyes and could see "tired" written all over her.

"Do you want to tell us what's wrong?" a concerned Mary Louise asked.

"Momma, I do not know *what* to do about Davis. I love him so much, but he's so damn...." She couldn't finish, so her mother took her hand and tried to calm her. When she had calmed down, she told her mother about Davis being drafted, the fact that he was actually excited about it, and also how none of his plans seemed to include her. Her mother's only advice was to hang in there, not push too hard, and if it were meant to be, Davis would come around.

She drove to Gulfport, checked in with the radio station, and told them she'd be there in the morning. The next two days she just went through the motions. The next evening, she came home and checked her messages. There was only one, but it was the one she'd hoped it would be. It simply said, "Becky, I'm sorry. Please call me." She mulled this over for a few minutes. She kept hearing the urgency in that one sentence. She watered her plants and washed the breakfast dishes that she hadn't felt like doing that morning. All the time, she kept glancing at the phone. Finally, she picked up the receiver and dialed "0."

"Person to person for Mr. Davis DeLongpre in Hattiesburg...please."

The operator made the necessary connections.

"Is that you, Becky? Thank God!"

They talked for a few minutes. He apologized for ignoring her, using his draft notice as his excuse. He had just over a week left and would sure like to see her. Should he come down there or could she come up here. She let him dangle for a few seconds and then, "I'll come up Friday night."

It was a different Davis that Rebecca saw sitting across from her at dinner. He wasn't preoccupied; instead, he seemed very relaxed and attentive. For once didn't bring up a thing, not *one* thing about those damn horses. But to her dismay, still nothing about them.

Rebecca had intended to have a discussion with him and get some things straight. She wanted him to know how much it hurt her when he never included her in his decision-making. Her intentions were good, but again, when they were close together and their eyes met, the spunky little go-getter turned into a bowl of mush. She hated that. Besides, she rationalized that this was their last night for quite some time and didn't want to spoil it.

They danced and drove out to "their place." They walked and hugged and kissed and she was waiting for him to break down and tell her how much he loved her. It didn't happen.

He took her home at first light and got back in time for family farewells before reporting for active duty.

Davis didn't really care much for boot camp. It kind of reminded him of that awful school he went to as a boy. He would later say, "Everybody's in a big hurry to go nowhere."

He did, however, experience something he could never explain. It really bothered him for quite some time. There had been several of these occasions where something happened suddenly, with no connection to what was going on at the present. After a rigorous, twenty-mile, full-pack maneuver, his entire company was completely exhausted. He choked down another lousy dinner at the mess hall, went to the barracks, put together his gear for the next day, and turned in.

He dreamed that his mother was calling him for help. The tone of her voice sounded like she was pleading for him to come to her. As hard as he tried, he couldn't get to her, but the haunting plea that seemed to be coming from some deep cavern, wouldn't stop. He was running full speed, going nowhere. Obstacles kept popping up and doors kept slamming in his face. He finally got to a door where he could hear her pleas the loudest, and, when he tried to open it, it wouldn't budge. He backed up, took a run at it, and knocked it down. There lay his mother on a bed with her eyes closed. She wasn't calling anymore. He begged her to wake up, but she wouldn't move. He shook her but, alas, with same results. She was dead.

The next thing he saw was the pissed-off face of the master sergeant, shaking him, and yelling for him to wake up. Davis' screaming had awakened his bunkmates and they in turn had beckoned the sergeant. He survived the threats from the man wearing the chevrons, the good-natured ribbing from the guys in the barracks, and made it through the remainder of the night. As soon as he got his first liberty, he phoned home to see if his mother was okay. She was in the kitchen planning the evening meal with Loretta when she heard the ringing. She picked the phone and said cheerfully, "Good morning this is Lillian."

"Momma, are you okay?"

"Thurston, what a pleasant surprise! Yes, I'm fine, how about you, darling?"

"I'm all right now, Momma. I just had a bad dream, that's all."

He made it through basic and went home for a few days before he received his orders. He was assigned a base in the heart of West Germany, which was perfect. The Colonel had pulled the right strings. He was only home for a short time, so he didn't see Rebecca or even call.

Chapter Thirteen

The arrival in Hamburg, Germany was quite an experience for Private DeLongpre. The base outside of town was a bit of a let down from the beautiful brochures he'd seen on the walls of the draft board. There was none of the rolling hills and tree-covered landscapes he'd expected. He'd grown up in better surroundings than this.

On Davis' first furlough, he and several service pals saw parts of Germany that he *had* seen in the brochures. Now, this was more like it. The country and towns were beautiful, along with the young women, who were quite plentiful. They were very different from the southern belles of his homeland. They were much more aggressive, and, even though they didn't speak a lot of English, the servicemen had no trouble whatsoever communicating with them.

Their English, compared to Davis' German, though, made them sound almost fluent. They were very warm and friendly and some of their attire didn't leave much to the imagination. He did notice a couple of times that they banded in small groups and pointed at him, giggling. When he would ask why, they'd say in broken English, "You look like American singer and movie star, Elvis, ah, ah, are you?"

He indeed did love Rebecca, but he was a long way from home and it had been some time since their last torrid encounter. There wasn't a bad-looking girl in any of these groups, and every one of them knew exactly how to make a boy away from his country forget his loneliness. He justified his actions by thinking that *It's not really cheating if I pay for it.*

Davis wanted to be a good American. He wanted to do his part. He'd just wished the timing had been better. He wondered why his father had even suggested that he could change his son's military status, but, when he'd had time to think about it, he realized it was only a test of his mettle. His father was also a good American, and Davis worked hard to be a good soldier. He was not impressed by nor had any desire to become an officer. He only wanted to do his job, finish it, and get on with his plans. This attitude eventually earned him the rank of sergeant.

His time off, however, was seldom spent with his buddies. He did join the guys on a few trips to town to visit the frauleins, but mainly he busied himself studying up on the many European horse breeders. He didn't want to waste any more time than necessary.

At night, when his day was finished, he'd lay back on his pillow and, before drifting off, would think about his home, his father and mother, and how Willie was doing with the stock they had, and ...Becky Thompson.

No more than a day's drive away, Elvis was adapting to his new home next to another Army base in Germany. Although the bases were both in Germany, the young men's paths never crossed.

These two years passed by very quickly for Davis but not for his family, Willie, and, of course, not Rebecca. He dutifully answered their many letters, filling them in on the little details of his life in the service. One particular evening, around Christmas time, he talked to almost everyone in attendance at a party given for all who lived or worked at The Willows.

"This is funny, Momma. About three or four times, some of the young ladies have mistaken me for that rock and roll guy, Elvis Presley. Isn't that crazy?"

Lillian stiffened a bit, then said, "Now, honey. That's silly! You don't look anything like that greasy-looking boy!" When the good-byes were done, Lillian hung up the phone and took another deep breath.

Davis actually called back to the states a few times a year—for Becky's birthday, his parents' birthdays, and their anniversaries. He corresponded with Willie, giving his partner detailed descriptions of all he'd been learning about the people he'd planned to see upon his completion of duty.

Another thing that kept alive his connection with home was the cakes and cookies that came on a regular basis. Davis loved and appreciated this little break from Army chow—so did all of his buddies.

When his hitch was over, Davis packed up his uniforms that sported his new sergeant stripes and sent them home. He was now ready to begin his quest.

His father and mother weren't surprised when they opened the package from Germany. Davis had told them he'd be staying in Europe for "however long" it would take. They'd just kept a glimmer of hope that he might miss them and change his mind and come home for at least a short visit. This, however, was not going to happen.

Rebecca had hoped he would come home, too. But she wanted him to miss *her* enough to change his plans. Davis had always been secure in himself as far as his decisions, but he didn't realize how much Rebecca needed to hear the words that included her in his future.

Thurston Davis DeLongpre, III, boarded the train that would take him out of Germany and on to his destination in northern France. He leaned back in his Pullman seat and began to review the past two years. He looked out the window at the passing countryside. The objects closest to the speeding train seemed to blur, but, as he lifted his eyes out away and toward the fields and foothills, everything seemed to clear. At that moment, he would try to run his life as close as he could to that sight outside the train window. If he focused on "right now," the view in the distance would probably be made clear. He listened to the hypnotic sound of the wheels clicking on the track and dozed off.

The DeLongpres had arranged to communicate through the American Express offices while Davis traveled in Europe. When he arrived in Amiens, France and collected his mail, there were several brief notes from home. His parent's greetings were per usual: "We love and miss you and so does Rebecca." However, Willie Hampton's and his father's message was more important, especially to the hurrying young man. Both of them told him, "Get on with it and send us some good horse flesh."

Willie added, "Good luck, pard."

Every so often Davis did get homesick. Most of this, however, was at night. During the waking hours, he kept his axe to the grindstone, rationalizing that the quicker this job was over, the quicker he'd be home raising horses with Willie and his father—and kids with Becky.

Lillian had transferred a large sum of money into a special account that her son could draw from during his stay in Europe. Armed with a fat bankroll and a vote of confidence from his partners, he set out to meet the first man on his list. He had chosen a very prominent rancher of wine and horses in the north of France, Jon-Pierre Genevive.

Genevive, as many Frenchmen, was not fond of Americans. He was known for saying, "Although we gave them the Statue of Liberty and they came to help drive the Germans out of our country and the same colors are in the flags, they are all basically heathens. And most of them are rich heathens with absolutely no trace of culture or breeding."

When the young American called to confirm his appointment, Jon-Pierre asked his wife to have Davis call back in a day or two. He used this time to make some inquiries about the DeLongpres. His sources informed him of the family's international prominence. He covered his embarrassment by saying, "at least their name is French."

The next day, when Davis called, Jon-Pierre himself invited Davis to his home. He simply said, "I will have my car at your hotel at 5:00 p.m. You will join me and my family for dinner. Is that convenient?" Davis assured him that it was.

He had allowed three days in his schedule to spend with this man. He was anxious to get on to the business at hand, because two of these days were almost gone. He had just learned from his first mistake. From now on, instead of only calling, he would send information about himself and his business intentions ahead of his arrival.

Jon-Pierre had kept him waiting two days, but the car was there exactly at 5:00 p.m. as promised. The driver opened the right rear door of the large black car and Davis saw an extremely large young man motioning him to slide in. Davis immediately thought he was much too young to be Jon-Pierre Genevive. He was right. The large man extended his hand and introduced himself as Robespiérre Montan, personal assistant to Jon-Pierre Genevive.

They drove for approximately thirty minutes through the beautiful French wine country and "Robey," as he preferred to be called, gave him a running commentary in a combination of French and English. Davis listened carefully, but all he saw were rows and rows of grapevines and couldn't really understand which ranch Robey was referring to. He didn't really try and just sort of muttered an acknowledgement. So as not to appear rude, he finally got up enough nerve to ask, "When do we get to the Genevive ranch?"

This amused the large Frenchman, and he said, "We've been driving through it for about ten minutes, monsieur."

Jon-Pierre Genevive was a pleasant-looking man in his early sixties. His slightly over six-foot frame wasn't heavy or thin, and medium wouldn't really describe him. Davis noticed his gray hair was like his father's, but not as thick, so he just left it there.

The two men shook hands and the impatient young Southerner got right to the point. "I'm eager to see your herd, Mr. Genevive. Do you have some special stock selected for me?"

As they walked up the steps towards the fifteen-foot high double doors, the older man put his hand on Davis' shoulder and then said, "Monsieur DeLongpre, there will be plenty of time for that. First, let me show you to your room. You can relax for a few moments and then prepare yourself for dinner." He beckoned to the driver to have his guest's bags brought up the stairs.

As he saw Davis move out of earshot, he muttered, "Americans! Always in such a terrible hurry."

The Colonel's words now came back to Davis, "A Frenchman will get your money, but he will be in no hurry to do it." This would not be the last time he would use something he'd learned from his father during one of the family discussions.

After taking a quick shower, Davis laid down on something resembling a chaise lounge. It reminded him a little of the fainting couch in his folk's bedroom. *What a silly name,* he thought. He looked around the room and, although it was decorated in a casual manner, he could see that there was considerable wealth here. He wondered how old the chateau was, and how long it had been in the Genevive family. From his lessons in school, he knew that most of the grand estates in Europe were much older than the century-old-plus mansion he called home. He didn't like this casual approach to business, but his father was right. This man will take my money in his own time. Tomorrow he would not be so over-anxious. This was the Frenchman's turf. He'd have to play it that way until *his* time came.

His thoughts were interrupted by a gentle knocking on the door. He put a towel around his naked torso and opened the door to see a smartly clad older man, who said in the most proper way, "Dinner will be served in twenty minutes, monsieur, and, tonight, we dress."

Now his *mother's* voice came from his memory bank. *'Son, always have a dark evening suit and several shirts and hankies ready at all times.'*

He went to his suitcase, pulled out a freshly laundered tux shirt and found the little box containing the cufflinks and studs. The starched shirt felt good and crisp, but he hated fighting to get those tiny little studs where they belonged. This completed, he went to the bathroom and ran a brush through his slightly longer-than-military length sandy-brown hair, donned his dinner jacket, gave the tie a final adjustment, and was off to face a room full of French people.

He took his last step from the winding staircase onto a highly polished marble floor and looked around for a dining room entrance. He turned to the right and was greeted by a stunning young woman. She was dressed in a honey-beige colored dress that flattered everything God had blessed her with and matched her hair. The voice that came forth was just as sweet. As she extended her hand, she said, "The dining room is this way, Monsieur DeLongpre. Please follow me."

Two things got Davis' attention immediately. Number one, the girl was exactly what every man dreamed of when they thought of a French maid, second, Jon-Pierre's staff dressed as well as his mother and Rebecca.

He followed this golden girl into a huge formal dining room that made Davis take a deep breath. The family was surrounded by multi-colored rays of light that caused him to look skyward to see a magnificent thirty-foot ceiling constructed of cathedral-like panes of stained glass. The disappearing sun was playing a symphony of lights for the dinner hour. As his host arose and approached him, his escort faded out of his eye line.

"Good evening, Monsieur DeLongpre. My family welcomes you to our home. I would like for you to meet my wife, Emma, my sons, Hubert, André, Robiérre, and my daughter, Céleste."

Davis shook hands with the family in the order they were introduced and gasped when he turned and saw Céleste. Boy, did he feel dumb. *How in the hell could I have mistaken this delectable creature for the maid? I wonder what else this Frenchman has in store.*

This evening would be the first of many new experiences for the eager but genteel young man from southern Mississippi. Dinner at the DeLongpres had always been special, but this was more like a celebration. Moreover, none of the DeLongpres' dinners, even with their discussions, ever lasted the better part of three hours.

Davis had learned quite a bit about wines. His father and mother had a large cellar and they owned a sizeable vineyard in central California, but, until now, Davis had never seen or tasted this much. There was a different wine for each course.

The conversation was enjoyable, and, since all the Genevives spoke surprisingly good English, it made it easy to cover many different subjects. They politely asked him about his background and schooling, and touched briefly on his time in the service. One thing they seemed a bit more interested in was his last name, DeLongpre. They were imagining all sorts of possibilities, including asking which part of their country his ancestors came from. He couldn't help them, as his parents had never discussed this with him at any length. Eventually, the conversation ended up on the subject of horses—the favorite subject of everyone at the table.

Following the grand presentation of the meal, Genevive served the best cognac Davis had ever tasted. Maybe that's why it was one of the best cigars, too. Davis figured he must have consumed at least two bottles of wine in addition to the cognac, but he didn't feel the least bit intoxicated. He was getting tired, though, and asked to be excused. He took one last look at Céleste. With the room bathed in candlelight, the golden halo around her deepened. He abruptly turned and went up to his room.

While he was carefully hanging his tux in the closet, his father's final advice kept ringing in his ears, *'Remember, son, you are a handsome young man and there will be many temptations while you are overseas. You will, no doubt, succumb once in a while. But never, I mean never, mix business with pleasure!'*

Davis was twenty-five years old, and, with the exception of Rebecca and a few of the girls in Germany, he lacked experience. There was his drive to succeed in college and to get through his obligation to his country. But now, for the first time, he was completely on his own. This was a bit frightening. He was alone and was indeed human.

During the three-hour dinner, he did his best to be the perfect guest. Even though he was busy answering all Genevive's questions, he couldn't ignore the glances from the daughter of his first business venture. He knew that her brothers noticed because he saw them smiling at each other while this was going on. If the brothers saw this, he was sure that her parents did also. He believed that he handled the situation very well but the next morning would surely tell.

He lay down on the soft, comfortable bed and thought of home and a lovely lady in Gulfport. Until the last few hours, he'd never met any girls as beautiful as his Becky. But, my God, this French beauty was in a class all by her self. Even if it wasn't for the business he wanted to conduct with her father, he shuddered at the ramifications of anyone making a move on this powerful man's only daughter. He didn't feel tired and was excited about the possibilities the next morning might bring. He pulled the cozy, feather-stuffed comforter up to his chin and fell into a delicious and deep sleep.

Chapter Fourteen

On this expansive ranch, nestled in the hills outside the town of Amiens, the morning was clear, cool, and very exhilarating. Jon-Pierre's house person woke him with a tray of hot, savory-smelling coffee and told him that Jon-Pierre would meet him in the foyer in fifteen minutes. He glanced at his watch and muttered, "Jesus, I'm still in the Army." It was 6:00 a.m. on the third day.

He descended the stairway, saw Jon-Pierre pacing, and heard the heels of his boots clacking on the hard surface. Again, it sounded like his Army days. His host saw him as he neared the bottom of the curving stairway and said in a gracious manner, "*Bon matin,* Monsieur DeLongpre."

The modern-day Napoleon was sporting a very English riding outfit. This was something to behold before breakfast and somehow this well-dressed man did not match the very common-looking pick-up they boarded for the short ride to the stables. However, the stables were quite impressive, but no more really than what he, his dad, and Willie had constructed just a couple years previous.

The Frenchman was ready to present his offerings, which included at least a dozen very fine specimens. One of these fine animals, though, just jumped out of the pack. Highlander Chief was sixteen-and-a half hands of pure excellence.

Jon-Pierre instructed one of his stable personnel to begin the show. Davis zoomed in on "The Chief," his mind made up. He pointed and exclaimed, "That one!"

The French rancher was a bit surprised by the eagerness displayed by his guest. *Is he on his own or simply representing his powerful father?* He decided to just play it by ear and see how much he could get, so he said, "Good choice, my young friend. How many others have caught your eye?"

Davis said calmly, "You have picked several horses, Monsieur Genevieve, and they are all very beautiful. But this is the only one I want at this time."

"Fine, but let's go to the house and have breakfast while you think over your decision."

"Well, sir, I *am* very hungry, but I don't need any more time."

"Then Highlander Chief is the only one of my beauties?"

"No disrespect, sir, but for now, yes. You see, I'm just getting started, but I'm sure I'll be seeing you again."

The Frenchman could now see that The Colonel's son had been well-schooled. He knew from running a check on the DeLongpre family that the son's decision was not based on any kind of a budget. He had gained respect for the young man and realized he wasn't dealing with an amateur.

Jon-Pierre and Davis enjoyed a ranch breakfast. After a serving of French-style coffee, he waited for the young man to make an offer. This didn't happen, so the wily European offered a price that was more than he had originally intended to ask. He was attempting to see if the young visitor from America knew what he was doing. Davis didn't react or even counter, and Jon-Pierre mistook this as a stall. In actuality, the young trader was in over his head, but the greedy Frenchman missed that.

After studying his eyes, an impatient Jon-Pierre threw in a bonus, "You are a formidable negotiator, so I'll tell you what I will do. The Chief has a beautiful son, which I will show you. If you accept the terms, he is yours as part of the package." Both men were satisfied that they had made a good deal. After seeing the colt, Davis paid him in full. However, Jon-Pierre insisted he stay another night.

There were more glances from Céleste at dinner, but Davis kept his head down, enjoyed another lengthy meal, and this night went to bed with nothing on his mind but planning to meet Vittorio Benevento.

Davis awoke early the next morning and remembered the promise he'd made to himself. He uttered a mild curse word, dressed, and went downstairs to ask Jon-Pierre if he could use the telephone for a long distance call. The Frenchman was obviously not concerned as to where, so he gave his approval and the privacy of his office.

He put in a call to the Benevento ranch in Torino, Italy. Mr. Benevento's son answered, asked who was calling, then handed the phone to his father. Davis introduced himself, but, before he could finish his request to meet with the Italian breeder, he was interrupted, "I know who you are, Davis DeLongpre. I have recently spoken to your father."

Davis bristled momentarily at his father's interference, then responded, "What did he tell you, sir?"

"It may appear to you that he was meddling, but he was not. You and I share a common bond which I'll discuss with you upon your arrival. Have a pleasant flight. I'll have Gianni meet you if you'll just tell me the flight number and time."

Davis finished his conversation with a "thank you" and went upstairs to pack. He thought about the family he'd just spent two days with and marveled at their interplay. He had no complaints. He couldn't help but wonder what it would've been like if he'd had brothers and sisters.

While he and Jon-Pierre were bidding each other good-bye, he wondered where the golden girl was. He hadn't long to wait because while they were still in their handshake, Céleste rode up from her morning gallop. With her hair flying in the wind and no make-up, the girl was still undeniably beautiful. The sun seemed to form a golden curtain behind her. Yes, she was in a class all by herself. She dismounted, walked over to them, and said, "We hope to see you again, Monsieur DeLongpre…Davis."

He nodded and wondered if her invitation would ever come true. *Will I ever lay eyes on this beautiful creature again?*

As Robey opened the door for her Prince Charming, Céleste turned, faced her father, and teased him. "He will be back, Papa. He will be back because he likes me."

"*Ma petite!*" her father scolded, "Every man does not only look at young girls. Forget about this one who only looks at horses. Why would you think such a thing? He is mentally sound, I admit, but one of us he never will be!"

"Papa, I don't care if he *is* American. I like him. I can tell he likes me too. As a matter of record, I think he will be my husband and give you many grandchildren."

She really hadn't taken her thoughts that far, but she loved seeing her father dance on this string she had around his heart. She could see the conflict in his eyes and, even though she loved him dearly, couldn't help adding, "Papa, he *will* return to me"

Delphia Hansen turned the key in the lock, opening the door to the clinic she and The Reverend C. J. Clarkson had established some twenty-five years earlier. It had been three years since Ezra Bartholomew, who also helped them establish the clinic, had passed away. His death left a big void in their lives, but she liked the young man who replaced him. It was the morning of her seventy-eighth birthday.

She was looking forward to the "surprise party" being held in her honor later that evening.

She busied herself making a pot of coffee for herself and C. J., like she had done for years. While thinking about the life she'd had, she smiled when she realized that she was still no more than "half-a-holler" from where it all began.

She said to a stack of mail that cluttered her desk, "I've had a pretty darn good life, all things tolled. I feel exhausted at times, but I guess that's the penalty of getting old. I'm sure glad I've had C. J. all these years. Don't know what I woulda' done. He ain't no Aubrey, but I love that ol' preacher to death."

She sat down and began to go through her mounting bills, waiting for that worn-out, old coffee maker to do its job. She used to wonder which would happen first: the coffee would finish perking, or C. J. would arrive.

Rev. Clarkson could smell the coffee as soon as he came through the front door. This was a smell that was almost as dear to his heart as the lady who made it. Yes, Delphia was the love of his life, and he would do anything she asked him to. He stuck a bouquet of mixed flowers through the door ahead of him and knocked gently to announce his presence. "Delphia?" He waited for a response and some feigned surprise as always. "Delphia?"

He eased around her desk and tenderly put his fingers on the inside of her wrist. His eyes filled with loving tears as he removed her glasses and gently closed her eyes with his other hand. The lady with the golden heart would never do another good deed for her fellow man. God would now take her into his arms and give her her just reward.

The Rev. Clarkson held himself in check as he conducted the funeral for his beloved. He was not surprised by the amount of people that showed up at the outdoor service. She'd helped a lot of folks and was very much loved. There were flowers from everywhere, but one arrangement stood out. It was a six-foot-tall red and white roses tribute. It was simply signed, "Love, Elvis Presley."

Willie Hampton liked his old comfortable office. He liked the smell of the hay, the leather oil, and everything associated with horses—everything except the part that Lillian used to make her flowers grow.

When The Colonel had semi-retired and joined Davis and Willie, they had to enlarge the office to accommodate three desks. Two were being used, while the other would have to wait a year or two. He looked at Davis' empty desk, picked up the "Paid-in-Full" invoice from the Genevive ranch in Amiens for maybe the ninety-ninth time and said out loud, "When I said send me some prime horse flesh, you obviously heard me."

The Colonel didn't rise as early as Willie did these days, but you could bet he'd be there. He saw his other son reading the bill of sale and the telegram from the steamship company. After they exchanged morning greetings, he asked, "What do you have there, son?"

"It's the bill of sale and the notice of Highlander Chief's arrival," Willie said as he handed both papers to The Colonel.

The senior partner looked at the invoice and raised his brows, "My Lord, Willie! What's this boy gone and done? This horse costs more than our entire stock."

"I know, Pop."

"Wait a minute. It says two horses are arriving. What's the story there?"

"One of the Chief's colts, I guess."

Willie stood up, grabbed his hat off the hook, and said, "Well, you want to go with me to Gulfport?"

"Yeah! You better believe I do!"

On the flight to Torino, Italy, Davis scanned the research he'd assembled about Vittorio Benevento. It had surprised him that Benevento and he had gone to the same college, although there had been many years in between.

From his research, Davis could see that Benevento was not a familiar name in the United States horse circles but highly regarded in most of Europe. Their bloodlines were mixed with many of the European champions.

Davis was anxious to acquire some of this stock. He was not always the cold, calculating person he appeared to be. Granted, he was career-driven and he was in a hurry, thus explaining again his getting through college much earlier than most. However, he was also a very emotional young man, which shows why he reacted as he did when he laid eyes on Highlander Chief. It was not the move of an experienced businessman. It was more like the move of a gambler. Truthfully, though, it was an over-anxious young man in a hurry. His father and Willie saw this and just crossed their fingers. Whether it was luck, or whatever, the future would prove the selection of "The Chief" to be a wonderful move.

As he finished going over the last of his notes, he heard the hostess inform all on board in Italian, French, and English that they would be landing in twelve minutes. He fastened his seatbelt, took a deep breath, and exhaled. "Take it slow. Take it slow. Take it...."

He was waiting in line for his turn at Customs when he heard a rapping.

He turned to see a young man with longish hair in a pale yellow sweater waving frantically and smiling broadly. Davis mouthed, "Gianni?" The young man nodded.

In about thirty minutes, they were dodging traffic and Davis was listening to Gianni talk faster than he was driving. He breathed a sigh of relief when they left the highway and turned onto the private road leading to the Benevento main house.

Unlike his previous stop, he was accepted and taken in immediately. Signore Benevento was exactly what Davis had expected. He had pictured a middle-aged Italian, well-fed but not fat, jolly gentleman, who enjoyed his success, loved his "vino" and his pasta.

His whole family was cut from the same cloth. They had wonderful wide smiles and quick laughs. The warmth and love among the family was very evident. Davis only hoped they didn't all drive the same way. He did expect them to look more Italian, but this was Northern Italy and Davis wasn't aware that the northerners were fair compared to their southern cousins.

During introductions, Vittorio noticed Davis' signet ring from the university, so Davis showed his host a newer version. This tie would set up the beginning of a solid, easy-going, working and social relationship.

Vittorio asked one of his sons to trade places with their guest so he could talk to Davis easier. This was done, and Vittorio began the conversation.

"My father was quite generous to me when I was a young man. I was so enamored with horses, he allowed me to forego the family furniture business to follow my heart. This was quite a departure from Italian traditions, but he said if I were serious about making these animals my life's work, I would have nothing but the best. And so, he sent me to Kentucky to gain my degree."

Davis listened to the grand gentleman's story and marveled at the parallels with his family. There wasn't the warmth and playfulness that the Benevento's displayed but, most certainly, a father that understood. He volunteered the story about how his own father had done the same for him.

"I've always loved horses. I can't remember when I didn't. And my father, with a little urging, sent me to Kentucky, too."

Again, as in Amiens, the business was put on hold. This time, however, the more experienced Davis didn't mind. This family was boisterous and loved to argue. They were quite a contrast to the patrician Genevives. Everyone talked at the same time and moved food around like a well-drilled army platoon. They laughed hilariously at his southern accent as he tried to pronounce the new words they taught him.

But all it took was the head of the house clearing his throat, and Mario, Carlito, Gianni, Ernesto, and Angelo turned the party into the quietness of a church. Sophia, his wife, didn't say much to Davis at first, but, by the second day, she talked him silly and wanted to know what his "mama" was like.

Dinner lasted a little longer than usual. It seemed like every time Davis thought it was over, a new story would begin. They weren't really trying to entertain him. It's just something that happened, and no one was complaining. Finally, Vittorio stood up and mentioned that it was going to be a big day tomorrow. Goodnights were exchanged and everyone was off to bed.

Davis looked at the ceiling and tried to picture the stock Vittorio would show him in the morning. He promised himself he would look every horse over very carefully since he needed a variety to balance out his stable. In addition to balancing it out, he needed some good mares for his beautiful French stallion. His eyelids grew heavy. As he drifted into the other world of dreams and fantasies, he saw another pair of eyes thousands of miles away and wondered what the owner of those eyes was doing, and was she thinking of him, as well.

Dawn brought a beautiful morning to Northern Italy. Gianni Benevento was instructed by his father to awaken their guest. The young man was used to this. Being the oldest, he always got the tough assignments. The empty place setting at the breakfast table was next to his, so he arose and went to the far end of the house to awaken the absent young American.

Davis was now used to people rapping on doors since his discharge from the service. It was somewhat annoying, but not nearly as much as that infernal bugle he'd heard those two years in the army. He stopped the rapping by yelling out, "Yeah, yeah, I'll be with you in a minute."

Gianni answered back, "Davis. It's Gianni. Mama is serving breakfast."

Davis yelled back and promised the oldest Benevento son he would be with them promptly. He threw back the quilt, and, when his feet hit the floor, he realized he was on the wrong side of the bed for easy access to the bathroom. He contemplated taking a shower but didn't want to keep the family waiting, so he sponged and shaved and headed for the table where he'd dined the previous evening.

As he walked to the dining area, he felt the tightness of the new boots that Jon-Pierre's son, Hubert, had given him. They were great-looking boots, even with the pointed toes he was not accustomed to, but he would get used to this in time.

The closer he got to the breakfast room, the wonderful aroma of coffee and fresh baked bread overwhelmed his nostrils. He didn't think he'd be hungry after that huge meal the night before, but, suddenly, when he saw the mounds of scrambled eggs, potatoes, and Italian sausage, hunger made its presence known.

He looked at his watch that told him it was 6:30 a.m. He glanced at Sophia Benevento and saw how composed she was. He wondered what time she had to wake up to put together this incredible feast. He thought about his mother, Lillian, and wondered if she could pull this off.

The five sons of Vittorio and Sophia made the mounds of food disappear while Davis was not even halfway through his coffee. When they asked for more, Davis now found out why Sophia appeared so composed. Two matronly women came through the swinging doors that separated the kitchen from the dining area with more eggs, more sausage, and more hot bread. He remembered his mother's cook, the chubby Loretta, and felt silly.

There was one major difference at the breakfast table, as compared to last night's dinner. There were no jokes, no stories, just pleasant conversations that were punctuated by the delegation of duties for the new day's business. The boys and their mother left the table. Davis now found himself alone with the other man with a degree in Animal Husbandry from the University of Kentucky.

Vittorio asked his client if he would care for another cup of coffee, which Davis declined. So he politely asked his guest would he mind if he did. He picked up the silver pot and poured himself another cup. Next, he picked a smaller vessel and topped off his cup with a generous portion of cream.

He stirred it gently and said to his young guest, "Davis DeLongpre, we share a common bond as I have already mentioned. However, the time I spent in your United States of America was very important and fulfilling. I not only learned to speak your language, I learned about the men who built that wonderful country. I don't have to name all the presidents and inventors because you are an educated young man who knows all of this. However, there are many men *and* women whose names are not in the history books but still were very important to all of us.

"Davis, I know that your family is brand new in the business of horses, but your father is certainly a man who is well-known to a lot of us in Europe and is to be respected. You are his son, his flesh and blood, and I promise you the full respect that I would give your father if it were he at my table."

Davis looked down at his empty coffee cup then looked Vittorio straight in his eyes. He wanted to reply but was overwhelmed and speechless. He knew his father was a powerful man in his homeland but had no idea about anywhere else. He now realized why his father was gone so much while he was growing up.

He finally regained his composure and softly said, "Thank you, Mr. Benevento."

"My pleasure, Davis. Let's saddle up."

There was no pick-up truck waiting for them at the back of the house as there was at the Genevives. Gianni needed it to "fly" into town for whatever, so the two men walked the two hundred yards to the stable where Vittorio asked one of his hands to saddle two horses. They mounted and rode a half a mile to a holding corral.

The DeLongpres and Mr. Hampton had accumulated a fair amount of fine domestic horses in the previous few years, but Davis had never seen this many quality animals all at once in his life.

Vittorio told Davis to stay where he was, leaned over, opened the gate, rode through and closed it behind him. He eased into the herd, picked one horse out, took his lariat, expertly lassoed it, and brought it back to the gate. He dismounted and motioned to Davis to do the same. Davis tied his horse to the rail and climbed over the fence. Vittorio held the rope in his left hand while he slipped on a halter. He motioned for Davis to join him.

Per Vittorio's instructions, Davis ran his hand over the horse's sturdy neck, down his forelegs and hindquarters, and then turned to Vittorio. This was all that was necessary. He knew that from now until they were finished, he would be looking at quality.

Davis picked out ten of the sixteen, and the two men rode back to the corral. He had spent most of his money on the French horse, but the American Express office was not that far away. To his surprise, his Italian host never mentioned money. He only said, "I will ship. You will get my bill."

The Italian and his client dismounted and walked to the house in time for the mid-day meal. The sons had completed their assigned tasks and were waiting for their father and their new American friend to return. Their new friend said "hello" to all and went to his room to wash up.

While cleaning up and changing clothes, he reviewed his business deal that had taken only the morning hours to complete. He was very confident in the choices he'd made. This time, instead of being impulsive, he'd slowed down and examined each horse thoroughly. He wanted his father and Willie to know this. After lunch, he asked Vittorio if he could call home. Of course, it was all right with his host.

Davis went to Vittorio's office and sat down at the decades-old desk. He began to compute the time difference and decided to wait for early morning. Davis knew that this time he had shared with the Beneventos would eventually come to an end. This bothered the ambitious young DeLongpre.

Willie Hampton was a man who wore many hats. He was Davis' buddy, best friend, partner, and sometimes even a father figure. The years that separated these two made no difference. But now, in Torino, Italy, Davis was in a position he was not familiar with. All of Vittorio's five sons were younger than him, and he was, for the very first time, looked up to. Vittorio and Sophia saw this and thought that it was good. Davis enjoyed this also, so he was almost reluctant to leave.

But, with the business being over, it was time for good-byes. Davis was an only child and wondered, once again, what it would've been like if he'd had brothers and sisters.

Gianni was the oldest, and next to him was Angelo. They had planned to go to a university in Madrid, Spain to further their education. Like Davis, their father was very wealthy and they could have stayed home and not worried about more education. But, unlike Davis, they wanted to go to a college just to get away from their father's everyday presence.

Davis' hurry-up plan had been altered somewhat during his stay with the Beneventos. Fall was approaching, so was the time for Gianni and Angelo to enroll at the university. But that was three weeks away. Davis' original plan was to finish business with the Beneventos and proceed to Rodolpho Montoya's spread outside Barcelona, Spain.

Vittorio Benevento was happy with the sale of his horses to The Colonel's son. He knew there was no chance of playing games with this powerful man from Mississippi and coming out ahead, nor did he want to. But he saw the friendship developing with The Colonel's son and his boys, so he was not surprised when Davis approached him with a plan. He wanted to spend more time with his little "brothers" and see some more of Italy. Where they were was just fine, but Davis wanted to see the parts of Italy he'd heard about and seen in pictures.

The boys hadn't traveled since they were kids and it would be good for them also. They could drop him off in Barcelona on their way to Madrid. Vittorio and Sophia thought this was a grand idea and a great adventure was in the works.

Davis made a call back to Mississippi to confirm the shipment with his father and Willie, and advise them of his trip to the Montoya ranch-estate in Barcelona, Spain.

Gianni rented a car in Torino and drove it out to the ranch. Davis asked him why he didn't use his car or any of the other cars at the ranch that were at his disposal. Gianni made it very simple when he said, "You see, my friend, *paisan*, we are going to take you to some wonderful places. We are going first to Milano for some fine food, fine wine, and pretty, pretty women. Then we take you to Plazenza, Reggio, and Bolonga. Then we take you over the mountains to Florence, then Roma, and finally Napoli. I think by the time we get to Napoli, we will be running out of time, so we leave the car there and fly to Barcelona. Then we tell you good-bye and get another car and drive to Madrid. Okay, my friend?"

What was Davis going to say? Of course it was okay. They loaded the car, said good-bye to Vittorio and Sophia, and the big adventure was under way.

The boys got in the car, and Davis, remembering Gianni's driving him to the ranch from the airport, hoped he wasn't driving again. He was in luck for at least the first leg of the trip. Angelo slid behind the wheel. He grimaced when he realized that Angelo couldn't drive for the entire trip.

They made the 130-kilometer trip to Milano in about three hours. Angelo was upset because it took so long. All of his Italian gestures and frantic dialogue translated to: "Roadwork, always Goddamn roadwork. Why can't they do that at night? Tell me Davis, do they always have roadwork in America?" he asked.

Davis was pretty sure he heard all of that right. So, he said to the younger Benevento, "You have no idea, Angelo. There is just as much or more in America."

Another Italian opinion sounded like, "That's too bad!" with an added expletive.

Giannni thought it would be a good idea to spend the night in Milano and get an early start the following morning. Angelo countered with an attack on his brother's suggestion. It would probably translate to: "Yeah, yeah, you bet. You just want to get plastered on your first night away from Papa. You drink and you chase the ladies. You do not believe what you say about an early start."

All this conversation was making *Davis* feel like drinking. They checked into the hotel, freshened up, and went to a restaurant called "The Corsico." It was nice weather, so they opted for an outside table.

It was about 7:00 pm when they sat down to eat. They enjoyed a glass of vino (what else?) while waiting for the first course. Halfway through the first glass, Gianni spotted a short skirt and he popped up like a "Jack-in-the-Box." He followed her half a city block. He walked by her side, walked in back of her, walked backwards in front of her, and all that time never lost a syllable. He came back to the table and took a bunch of crap from his little brother because he got shot down.

The salad and bread arrived and of course more wine. Now it was Angelo's turn to show off his girl-hunting prowess. He spotted two lovelies going down the opposite side of the narrow street and said to his big brother, "Hey, you watch this. Maybe you learn." He was back, and single, just as he'd left, before the next course arrived.

Davis watched this action with a mixture of admiration and hysteria. He appreciated both of the brothers' nerve and all out cockiness, but when they came back empty-handed, the real show began. That was, watching and listening to them harass each other.

The pasta arrived and Davis took a generous first bite. The satisfaction spread all over his face, and he said to his traveling companions, "What is this, or what do you call it?"

Gianni looked at him with surprise. "It's spaghetti, my friend. They don't have spaghetti in Mississippi, U.S.A?"

Davis finished chewing the second mouthful and said, "Well, it looks like spaghetti, but it sure isn't like what we have at home!" Davis would find that there would be many dishes he would enjoy on the trip with the same names, as he'd read on the menu at "Mama Gucchi's" in Hattiesburg. He knew one thing; they sure didn't taste the same.

They finished dinner and Davis had eaten so much that when the meal was over, bed sounded like a good idea but not for the Benevento brothers. When he mentioned how he felt, Gianni said excitedly, "Oh no, my friend! We have to go to this place with the music and the beautiful young women!"

Davis thought, *So much for an early start.*

They found a place that was blaring American rock 'n' roll, and the only thing that made him realize he wasn't in America was when the people he said hello to didn't answer back in English. Davis wasn't much of a dancer, but, with a few cocktails consumed by everyone there, no one seemed to notice, or at least mind. Gianni and Angelo were hustling girls all over the place, but after remembering where the hotel was, they went home with all their virtues in tack.

The morning brought with it a beautiful sight. The housekeeper knocked twice, once normally, and the second time to the level where any one should be able to hear, but not our guys. She opened the door to find Davis lying across the bed, Gianni reclining half on a stuffed chair and half on the floor, and Angelo, wrapped around the toilet looking rather green. They *did* get an early start though, early afternoon!

That night was probably the first time Davis had ever been "drunk." He had drunk beer with his buddies at college, and wine a few times at the family dinner table. He'd experienced a buzz now and then, but this was the day he finally understood what people meant by saying they had a "hangover." He was thinking about getting some food in his body but decided against it when they were leaving. The brothers wanted to go to a café. He saw and smelled the espresso in the tiny cups. Gianni downed three or four and asked Davis if he'd like to try one when Angelo piped in, "Yeah, Davis. Go ahead."

Davis took one swallow and wanted to spit it out, but his manners checked in. All he could say was, "How do you drink this shit?"

"It does the job," Gianni threw back.

They drove the 75 kilometers to Piacenza, and, because none of them felt like eating when they awoke, this is where they had "breakfast," close to dinnertime. After the food healed them somewhat, they piled into the car. The brothers were now well enough to start arguing again. Angelo started on Gianni first. "Oh yeah, you're a big Romeo. I saw them shoot you out of the tree like a bird! Hell, you couldn't even score on that big ugly one, and I saw you try!"

Gianni fired back, "And you were so successful? I had the sister in my pocket and you made her so mad they both went home!" This went on for a good hour. They stopped for fuel in Parma and decided to drive into Bolonga and spend the night. Davis kidded them, "I can hardly wait to try the night life in Bolonga. I get another chance to see you two experts at work!" This statement got them all laughing and they quit picking on each other, at least for the next 50 to 60 kilometers.

Bolonga was a town Davis would fondly remember always. They went out to eat and, on this night, the brothers ganged up on him. They talked this group of young girls into believing he was a movie star from America. "He's our American cousin, and he's on vacation." The girls came over to Davis and began firing questions at him. One even sat on his lap, and another took his hand and said, "I'm Appolonia. It's nice to meet you Davis Benevento!"

Davis responded, "Benevento? Gianni, Angelo, what did you tell these girls?" He looked around for the brothers and realized that he'd been ditched.

When the brothers came back to rescue him, he wasn't there. They looked up and down the street and still couldn't find him. They eventually did, back at the hotel with three of the girls. They couldn't understand how he pulled this off, but they certainly didn't complain. One thing for sure, they had plenty to talk about as they drove through the Appennino Mountains on their way to Florence. Gianni had to ask, "Davis, how did you do it? You don't speak the language."

Davis grinned and said with a laugh, "I watched you guys and learned!"

They ate, drank, and chased all the way down to Rome. The boys asked him if he'd like to visit the Vatican. He could only answer, "You guys go ahead. I'm a Southern Baptist!" They did stay in Rome for a few days. There was a lot to see, eat, drink, and touch.

Partying and dining wasn't all they did. Sometimes they were just too worn out. They did some sightseeing along the way. They took their time and stopped at several little towns on the 500-kilometer drive between Rome and Napoli. When they reached Napoli, the boys decided to relax, get some sun, and just take it easy for a change. If anything exciting happened to pop up, "Well maybe, we'll see."

Something, or better, someone, did "pop up"; Napoli is where he met Francina.

Davis arrived in Barcelona in the late summer of 1960. The three-week romp with Gianni and Angelo Benevento had been one of the highlights of his life. They'd eaten their way around Italy, introducing Davis to the various cuisine and wines from different regions. They'd laughed and danced with party girls, and were continually teasing Davis when people would stare at him. Davis enjoyed the trip and was sad when it came to an end. He knew that one day he would return to the north of Italy.

Vittorio Benevento was a very astute businessman. He had just sold Davis DeLongpre ten horses cut out of his prime stock. He had not gouged the young American as did Jon-Pierre Genevive, but he did realize a handsome profit. This is the way it should be. Both parties were satisfied.

He and his wife, Sophia, had been blessed with five wonderful sons. They had hoped for a daughter, but this had not happened. The arrival of the young man from Mississippi had given them a new prospective of dealing with Americans. During Davis' stay, another thing happened that he and his wife hadn't planned on. His boys had found a new friend. Not to say they hadn't any friends previously, but this son of Colonel DeLongpre had become somewhat of a " hero" to his five sons.

Vittorio knew all of the important horse breeders in Europe, including the next one Davis intended to see. Before his departure, he gave his new friend some advice.

"Davis. I'm all in favor of your and my sons' proposed gallop through our homeland. I feel, in my heart, it would be very good for you and them. I would suggest, however, that you not go directly to Montoya's upon your arrival in Barcelona. After you and my sons part company, I think you should check into a hotel for a day or two. Don't appear to be in a hurry like I know you are. Go to the Casa de Oro and call Rodolpho Montoya from there. It's a fine hotel, what you Americans rate as a five-star establishment. This is only my advice. Do what you think is best. God bless you, my friend."

Davis, Gianni, and Angelo said their good-byes at the entrance to the Casa de Oro. They hugged while the boys gave him a kiss on each cheek. Davis was not accustomed to this, but, *Ah, what the hell?* They were Italian, and nothing could change the wonderful three weeks they had all spent together.

The bellman picked up his many bags, instructing him to follow. Davis obeyed and walked behind the well-dressed young man up the steps and into the very impressive lobby. Davis was no stranger to beautiful designs; still, he couldn't help noticing the gleaming Spanish tiles on the floor. They appeared to him as a giant and very ornate jigsaw puzzle that started at the front door and blended into the artistry on the walls, all the way to the lushly carpeted stairs.

Halfway to the stairs on his left was the check-in area. The bellman sat his suitcases down and stood next to him at the counter. An attractive young lady who looked more like an airline hostess than a hotel person, greeted him, "Good afternoon, sir. What can we do for you today?"

"I'm Mr. DeLongpre. I have reservations. "

"Oh, yes, Señor DeLongpre. You are in Room 311."

She handed Davis his key and he headed toward the stairs. At the same time, he noticed a young lady sidestep the bellman and go behind the desk.

Davis stopped and turned to look at this striking creature. She was attired in a fitted skirt, olive green in color, that was business-like but, at the same time, very sensual. The light blue blouse was a foundation for her flaming red hair to flow over. It was all he could do to take his next step forward, especially when their eyes met and locked.

She had not been given a description of their arriving guest, but he did stand out from the rest of the people in the lobby, so it wasn't very difficult to figure out. She snapped to and said, "Mr. DeLongpre. You have a message. It's from a local rancher who calls himself 'Rodolpho Montoya.'"

Davis thanked her and, after taking a long breath, followed the bellman upstairs to his room. The young Spaniard placed Davis' luggage by the dresser to the right of the bed and extended his hand. Davis filled the extended hand with the appropriate amount for a tip, thanked him, and said good-bye.

The room was more than adequate. Davis looked at the view from his room, took another deep breath, lifted his main suitcase from the floor, and tossed it on the bed. Vittorio Benevento was right. This was indeed a fine hotel. Vittorio's advice was also ringing in his subconscience as he removed his coat and took his passport from its inside pocket. He also found the note left for him by Rodolpho Montoya. He unfolded the note and read the contents:

> Mr. DeLongpre,
> I am unavailable at this time. Please forgive me.
> However, I want you to come to my hacienda at your
> earliest convenience.
> My wife, Ireñe, will accommodate you.
>
> *Respectos de Sincerest,*
> Rodolpho Montoya

This was nice to read in this foreign land, but Davis couldn't help thinking about the lady that handed him the message. Also, how did Mr. Montoya know he was staying there?

Estrelita Bravo was twenty-three years old. The only child of Isabella and Alejañdro Bravo grew up in Casa de Oro and was all too familiar with the hotel business. Her mother died shortly after Estrelita's tenth birthday, leaving Alejañdro and their daughter to fend for themselves. In an effort to raise his daughter on his own, the Casa del Oro became their home as well as their business. This situation might have ruined any chance for a father and daughter to be close, but, in the case of Estrelita and her father, it only strengthened the bond between them. The downside was that after father and daughter said their final good-byes to Isabella, Alejañdro just gave up. There was a bond, but this once power-driven man lost his ambition and passion for the running the hotel once his wife was laid to rest.

Estrelita loved her father as much as anyone could. She was only a little girl who sat on her daddy's lap and tried to make him feel that there was still life to live. This worked for many years. But, as Estrelita grew older, her father's will to live and carry on grew weaker. The young lady had no other choice but to adapt and take charge. When she was only fifteen or sixteen years old, she knew quite a lot little about what it took to run a major hotel. Her father still signed the checks, but he was seldom present.

When she laid eyes on Mr. Davis DeLongpre, her life turned completely around. She had put up with many suitors who were not only boring but disgustingly immature. Davis was, without a doubt, lacking maturity, but there was something about him that separated him from the rest. He didn't "hit" on her, well, not right away. The fact that he was incredibly handsome had nothing to do with it. *Wrong,* she thought. *It has a lot to do with everything.*

After reading Rodolpho Montoya's message, Davis had a better idea of where he stood. He decided to stay overnight, well, maybe two nights. He lay down and closed his eyes for a second, then sat up and looked at his watch. *I'd better call home,* he thought. He buzzed the front desk and asked them to put in an overseas call. A few minutes later he heard a familiar voice.

"Willow Wind Stables. This is Willie Hampton. What can I do for you today?"

"You can tell me if you received any horses in the mail."

"Davis! Where in the hell are ya? How are ya? Or whatever…yeah we got 'em."

"I'm in Barcelona. I just checked into this great hotel and I'll be seeing Montoya in a day or two. So, they got there okay, huh?"

"They did and in fine shape. You did good, pard. Want to talk to your dad?"

"You bet, put him on!" Willie told him to take care and called to The Colonel.

He was obviously glad to hear from his son. He answered joyfully, "How ya doin', son?"

"Pretty good, Daddy, how's Momma?"

"She's fine, but she's not here now. She'll be sorry she missed you. Son, from what I can see, you took your time choosing from the Benevento stock. I'm really proud of you."

They talked for a few minutes. The Colonel teased him good naturedly about his million-dollar stud, filled him in on some of the local happenings, and gave the phone back to Willie.

That call felt good, he really missed them. Now he could relax and think about dinner...and Estrelita. He felt a touch of hunger pangs. His stomach was sending him a message, but his body was telling him to take a nap, so he lay down once again. It seemed that every time he climbed into bed for a nap or for the night, his thoughts included Rebecca as he drifted off.

After a couple hours of delicious rest, he woke up famished. He showered, dressed, and decided to try the Casa de Oro's cuisine. He walked by the desk, hoping to catch a glimpse of the lovely hotel manager. She was not there, so he went directly to the dining room. The seating captain led him to a table for one and signaled a waiter.

Before his waiter arrived, he felt a hand on his shoulder. He looked up and saw the striking young lady he had been looking for only minutes ago. She flashed a million-dollar smile, and said, "Señor DeLongpre, it seems we are both dining alone this evening. I don't know about you, but I hate eating by myself. Would you do me the honor of joining me for dinner?"

He nodded, arose from his seat, and followed her to a booth just off the main dining room. The private booth was by a floor-to-ceiling window with a breathtaking view of the city. It was now late evening. Though he could not see the Mediterranean, he could see where the city lights stopped and formed a border around the bay.

Estrelita asked if he was hungry, and he gave her an affirmative nod. "Are you familiar with Spanish food?"

"No, not really. I've eaten Mexican a few times."

"No comparison. May I order for us?"

"Please do."

Diners in any country are used to waiting for service, but, if they should happen to be guests of the chef or owner, these annoyances do not apply. Within a few minutes, the waiter came to the table with two bowls of albondigas soup. (A combination of miniature meatballs with onions, chunks of fresh tomatoes, and green peppers in a spicy chicken broth.) After placing the bowls of the steaming soup in front of each, he took a plate of white corn tortillas covered with a cloth to keep them warm off the serving cart.

Davis dove into this like a man who had just been released from prison. In the middle of taking the spoon from the bowl to his mouth, he raised his eyes to see a smiling Estrelita. Suddenly, he felt like an ignorant hillbilly. He was so embarrassed but had no idea of how to recover.

Estrelita sensed this and decided to step in and save the young man from further discomfort. She laughed pleasantly, "I see that you like the soup. Have another tortilla. The main course will be here very soon."

Davis finished his soup and the torn-off half of his tortilla, settled back, and played with his napkin.

They finished the wonderful meal, enjoyed the desert, and creamy after-dinner Spanish coffee. It was very apparent that these two young people were attracted to each other. Things could have gone a lot further that evening, but somehow the combination of good upbringing and common sense prevailed…or maybe just fatigue.

Estrelita took Davis' hand, squeezed it gently, and said, "I have to leave now. Thank you for a beautiful evening. I'll see you *mañana en la mañana*" (tomorrow in the morning).

Chapter Fifteen

Rebecca Thompson had been in love with Davis DeLongpre since the day he had ruined the gasoline can display in her father's hardware-nursery. That magical Saturday afternoon years ago seemed rather distant and not quite as precious given her current state of mind.

"You'd think he'd at least drop me a postcard more than once a year. Doesn't he think about anything but his God damn career? He can be the most wonderful man in the world, and, while I'm sure he loves me, what does he expect me to do? After all, I should have the opportunity to do what I want, too." Then in finality, she said at the top of her voice, "Davis, you just make me crazy!"

This stimulating conversation took place in the privacy of her bathroom. The two principles were Rebecca talking with Rebecca. She was soaking in a hot bubble bath. She still believed that being in or around water made it easier for her to work out her problems. She hadn't had any contact with Davis since her birthday, which, of course, he always remembered. She leaned forward to reach the hot water knob, picked up the soap, leaned back, and lamented, "I'm going to be an old maid sitting around waiting for you. Do you expect me to spend my life talking to myself while you're out conquering the world?"

She squeezed the bar of soap so hard that it flew from her grasp and disappeared beneath a mountain of suds. This did not improve her disposition one iota, and she realized how odd all this would have sounded had someone been eavesdropping.

Rebecca didn't live at home in Hattiesburg these days and was hardly just sitting around. After graduating from college in Memphis, she was offered a job at the Gulfport/Bay Saint Louis TV station. She wore several hats at the fledgling but promising K-JUN radio and TV station.

Memphis College had prepared her well. She had taken an elective,

Meteorology, so she could forecast a little weather along with everything else. Rebecca was a pioneer as far as women being on the TV news. She was a bright star in this medium, but she was still a woman. A beautiful, bright, and talented woman, but that's how medieval the owners' thought processes were in that era. Another test she had to endure was the constant onslaught of propositions from the male co-workers, big shot visitors, and guests. She turned them all down one by one because she was waiting for Davis.

She was a busy young lady with most of her thoughts centered on her work. But tonight, as she luxuriated in the hot sudsy tub with a glass or two of wine, she was feeling a tad sorry for herself, and missed him something awful. She had fears of becoming an old maid, even though by the standards of the south, she already was.

Mark Lewis had attended a school for up-coming radio and TV personalities. "Career Academy" prepared their students for every job in the business. The school was located in Houston, Texas, where the hub of the McDaniel radio-TV chain made its headquarters.

Since most of the newsmen up to this time had begun their careers as journalists, Mark couldn't really compete with them. He'd wanted to be taken seriously, but his good looks seemed to get him further than his brains, so he opted to take the easier road. He had no trouble landing an on-the-air position since the camera loved his good looks. He wasn't much more than a talking head, but he did that extremely well.

The McDaniel chain of sixty radio and television stations moved people up through the ranks as they became better at their jobs. Mark was ready for another step up when the anchor slot for the evening news became available. He was sent to the Gulfport/Bay Saint Louis station where Rebecca was.

It was the program Rebecca had been working on for over a year. She knew as much about how the show was put together as the program director did, who, as fate would have it, brought her the bad news. Although she knew in her heart that the position wouldn't be hers, it was still disappointing.

"Rebecca, I know you're qualified for this, but the company is looking for a handsome young male face to attract the interest our female audience."

She nodded her understanding, but, as she walked away, she uttered, "No Shit!" Adding insult to injury, her job was to take him under her wing and show him the ropes.

When he met the movie-star-beautiful Rebecca, the handsome Mr. Lewis didn't even bat an eye. Instead, he shook her hand firmly and said, "It's a pleasure to meet you, ma'am."

That did it! Now the bathroom conversation intensified. One more glass of wine should do the trick. She took a sip and lamented, "All of the slobs that hit on me, why doesn't the first guy I think is halfway decent even notice that I'm in the same room!" As her mood changed, the boisterous bathroom became quiet. A few moments later, some feel-sorry tears left her cheeks and made their way down her body to drown in the tub water. "Why can't Davis just get on with it?"

She and Mark worked together on a daily basis. He continued to be very mannerly and professional towards her. It began to get to Rebecca. He seldom called her by name. It was always "ma'am this" and "yes, ma'am that." Finally, she said to herself, *If I hear one more ma'am...ma'am, huh? I'll show you ma'am!*

After this had gone on for a couple months, with still no word from Davis, she decided to use the aggressive side of her nature and test the waters. She planned a barbecue at her home and asked a few of her friends and those from work to please help her welcome Mr. Lewis.

Mark had been working to justify his position that many people had been passed over for. He was very aware again of how he got there. This would be a chance to show a few folks that he was a regular guy, so he gracefully accepted the invitation and actually enjoyed the party.

They began seeing each other once or twice a week, dining in the best restaurants the area had to offer. He was always the gentleman, maybe overly so, and seemed to enjoy being with his pretty co-worker. To Rebecca, these dates took on significance. Mark was no Davis, but he was so charming and attentive. He wasn't like the guys she tried to enjoy being with. There was no grabbing or mauling. This she interpreted as respect. She had a feeling that it was the beginning of a love affair.

However, along with this new feeling came mixed emotions. She'd been in love with Davis over half her life but really resented the way he took her for granted. He seldom ever wrote or called, and she missed him. The fact was, she was very lonely and had been for some time. She felt guilty. She was cheating on Davis by seeing another man. She also thought that Mark's intentions were long-ranged regarding their future, so she made a surprising decision. She composed a letter to Davis breaking off their relationship. The letter said:

My Dearest Davis,
I've loved you from the first day I saw you in my father's hardware store and thought no one could ever take your place. I have waited patiently for you all my life and even though you never made a commitment to me; I've been faithful to you, always. Though many gentlemen have desired my company, I have always said no because I was waiting for you.
Now, after all this time, I've found someone I love and want to be with. I only hope that you understand.
I will never forget you, my dear Davis.
       Love,
       Becky

She called Lillian and asked for an address where she could send a letter to Davis. Lillian gave her the Montoya's address in Spain. After some light chitchat, they said good-bye. Rebecca mailed the letter she would regret…for many years to come.

Davis thought very well on his feet but did most of his planning on his back. If he rested during the day, he would stare at different designs that a painter's brush or a plasterer's trowl had made on the ceiling and pretended they formed different countries he had been to or planned on visiting. If it were nighttime, he would just stare into the infinite blackness and see images. This somehow freed his mind to plan or create.

This beautiful Spanish morning, he awoke and lay there staring at the ceiling. Not intently, however, mostly remembering the wonderful dinner he shared with Estrelita the previous evening. He was thinking if it wasn't for Becky, he just might be interested. *But enough of that. Big day today.* He decided that although he was enjoying the Casa de Oro and the company of its manager, it was time to get back to work.

He called the Montoya Ranch and asked to be picked up. He was told he had an hour.

Hearing this, he showered and packed his suitcase, then nibbled at the light breakfast delivered by room service while he had been bathing. It was time to say good-bye to Estrelita.

He called down to have his baggage picked up and went to find her. This would not take very long at all. She was in the entrance of the lobby giving one of the workers "Holy Hell" for missing some black heel marks. She looked up and saw Davis walking toward her. The stern looks of just seconds earlier changed to a broad, warm, good-morning smile. "Bueños Dias, Señor DeLongpre. I can see that you are leaving us."

Davis replied almost sheepishly that he would like to stay longer, but his business would not permit it.

Estrelita looked a bit sad but forced a smile, saying sweetly, "Well, we can only hope to see you again soon, Señor...Davis."

He nodded good-bye and went outside to the waiting truck. The driver was securing his luggage in the back. Davis opened the passenger door and was about half-way in when he stopped. A thousand things were speeding through his mind. It may be wrong, but he had to see this Spanish beauty again.

He jumped out, and, as he headed for the front entrance, he yelled over his shoulder, "I'll be right back."

Estrelita was just going up the grand staircase in the lobby when she heard a breathless, "Estrelita! Wait!"

She turned to the source of this outburst and saw Davis come to a halt at the bottom of the stairs. She went three steps down to meet him. "Señor DeLongpre, what is it?"

"I'm really happy I got to meet you! I'd like very much to see you again!"

Estrelita smiled and nodded at the breathless foreigner, took his hand, and gave it a gentle squeeze.

The impatient but cordial driver sat in the truck until Davis got back. After he opened the door for him, Davis apologized and looked at his luggage in the back as they drove off. The ride was a quiet one. Although the driver tried to converse with his passenger, the language barrier did exist.

As the road climbed gradually, they entered a pass and came upon a most beautiful scene. Maybe it was the foggy steam that seemed to hover over the valley below, almost kissing the green carpet of the thick grass, but, whatever it was, that picture was etched in stone in his memory.

Ireñe Montoya met the young man at the door when he arrived. She was a full-figured yet very attractive woman with a wonderful smile, and her English was exceptionally good. "Welcome to our home. I must apologize to you, Señor DeLongpre. My husband Rodolpho has been called away on urgent business but will be home for dinner this evening."

"Thank you, Señora Montoya. I'm happy to be here."

"I will have your luggage taken to your room. Enjoy our custom of an afternoon *siesta*. We will dine at 7:30 this evening. It will not be formal. We live very simply here. Is there anything I can do to make you comfortable until then?"

"Not that I can think of. You sure have a beautiful home, señora. Has it always been in your family?"

"Sí, Señor DeLongpre. The Montoya's have owned this land for over two centuries. Come now, Yolanda will show you your room."

"Thank you."

"Oh, Señor DeLongpre, one thousand pardons. We have mail for you. I will get it."

The Montoya's spread was not as grand as the last two ranches he had visited, but every bit as vast. Davis knew the reputation of their excellent stock and looked forward to seeing if his research was accurate once again.

Standing at the window of his room was like looking at a wide-screen western epic. There were small herds of horses grazing randomly on lush green hills that ended at the horizon.

He sat down and opened the letter from Becky, "His" Becky, as she had been for over ten years now. He smiled as he thought of her, and then a slight twinge of guilt warmed his face, as he felt badly for thinking of Estrelita.

My Dearest Davis....

This is not how Becky talked. He thought about that for a second then continued reading. When he realized what he was reading, his smile left. He stared at the page until the letters became blurry. He was in shock, and that was an understatement. He dropped the letter and returned to the window. This time he did not see the beautiful scenery. He couldn't believe Becky had found somebody else. She had always been his girl. In his heart, he couldn't blame her for getting tired of waiting for him, but still.... Suddenly, a deep black awful void filled his soul. He continued to stare out the window for more than an hour. Staring at nothing, nothing to stare at, everything was gone.

His thoughts were interrupted by a knock at the door. It was Yolanda asking Davis through the door if he would like to join the señora for refreshments.

The view from the veranda overlooking the Montoya's ranch was like coming in on another reel of the same western epic. It was quite different, but every bit as magnificent. Davis was devastated, but he wanted to maintain his composure and show respect to his hosts. Besides, it wasn't their problem. He said as cheerfully as his soul would permit, "What I've seen of your ranch so far is beautiful. You must love it very much. How many acres do you have?"

"Oh, *gracias*, señor. We are very happy here, but only my husband can fill you in on details of that nature."

Their conversation continued for some time, as any conversations between strangers do, during which Ireñe was able to see that the young visitor had undergone a transformation. He had been exuberant and eager when he arrived. She thought, *Mí Dios, what a mannerly young man and so handsome. My husband may never let him leave this place. But just look at him now!*

She and Rodolpho had been blessed with three lovely daughters, but no sons. She knew how much he had wanted a son but had never mentioned it. She also thought about Davis and her oldest daughter but, when considering the age difference, dismissed the idea entirely.

She thought when he came down from the *siesta* that something was wrong, and now she could see the sorrow emanating from his eyes. She said to herself, *I wonder what sadness that letter brought to this young man. Whatever the news was, it was of large proportions.* The first lady of the Ranchero de Montoya wanted to find what was really bothering their guest. Unfortunately, this was interrupted by the sounds of her husband coming home.

Rodolpho didn't travel much because his business was well-established. Clients usually came to him, but, every now and then, he would have to do business out of town. However, he was usually only gone for a week or less. Wherever he went, he would somehow find some odd or special gift for his Ireñe and three teenage daughters. He would come in like Santa Claus, minus the reindeer and sleigh, to squeals of delight from the girls.

Ireñe heard the car pull up, the door shut, and the sound of her husband's Spanish-heeled boots coming up the stairs and across the front porch. "Señor DeLongpre, I believe my husband has returned home."

And at that moment Rodolpho entered the room—or rather, he *entered* the room. He removed his tan sombrero, put several packages on a leather couch by the window, and walked toward them.

"I see you have not wasted any time bothering our young guest with your chattering, Ireñe."

"No, I have not, my love. I can tell you he is most courteous and charming, unlike some of the other guests you've invited here."

He gathered her up in a bear hug and gave her a kiss. She ran her fingers through his hair. She hated the fact that he never tidied his hair after removing his hat, but she'd straighten that out in another twenty or thirty years.

Rodolpho released his wife from the hug and extended his hand to Davis. "It is nice we finally have a chance to meet, Señor DeLongpre. I must apologize for not being here to welcome you personally. Please forgive me. I see you have tried some of our wine. Let me freshen up, and I'll join you." With that, he patted his wife's cheek and excused himself.

Davis was amazed at the affection this couple exhibited and wondered if this was a show for him or if they always behaved like this. He had never seen his parents carry on like this. They always kissed and were loving but *nothing* this exuberant.

His research had told him nothing about the personality of the Spaniard and certainly nothing about his family. While Rodolpho was cleaning up, his three daughters arrived home from some after-school activity. They were a bit boisterous while entering the front door asking for their father, but when they saw Davis with their mother, they calmed down and let her introduce them to the American guest.

Rodolpho came back and hugged his girls, then pointed to the couch where the gifts were. The quietness the young ladies showed while being introduced to Davis now ceased as they saw what their father had brought them. Rodolpho sat down, had a glass of wine, and then asked if dinner would be on time. He looked at his watch, arose, and beckoned Davis to come with him.

"Let's go for a walk before our dinner. We can get acquainted and work up a good appetite."

As they walked around the grounds, Rodolpho pointed out various buildings and explained what they were. He also talked about his horses and probed Davis about what he was looking for. As they were strolling the grounds, Rodolpho did most of the talking. Davis was able to listen and observe.

He looked at his host, noticing what an impressive man he was. He wasn't quite as tall as Davis but had a barrel-chest. He looked like someone to reckon with, *even* at his age. His rugged appearance contrasted with his soft voice and permanently etched smile. With his outdoor, sun-bathed complexion, Davis could tell this was no gentleman rancher. He thought, *This, is what a real horse rancher should look like.*

Montoya began calling Davis by his first name and invited the American to do the same. It was hard for Davis to pronounce Rodolpho with his southern accent and when Rodolpho pronounced Davis, it came out like "Davy." It actually worked out okay and made them both laugh. It was like having a nickname to Davis. Since he'd never had one of those, he decided just to enjoy that along with the rancher's friendship.

Their walk had taken them almost in a full circle. When they were nearing the house, Rodolpho came up with a plan for the next day.

"Tomorrow, I will drive us around and give you a complete tour. Now, it is time for us to sit and eat."

Davis hadn't eaten since his light breakfast at the hotel, so this sounded like a fine idea. He responded to Rodolpho's statement with enthusiasm; "I'd like to do that."

The young rancher from Hattiesburg had a good feeling about all this. After the letter from Becky, he needed a *lot* of good feelings.

The Montoya's three daughters were all mannerly and quite pretty. They said very little at the dinner table. Davis wondered if it was because their father was so outgoing. It was very amusing to him that, while they were eating or in his company, they were so shy and quiet, but as soon as they left the room or went out the front door, there was a joyous teenage explosion heard by all. Ireñe pretended it annoyed her, but it really didn't.

Later, after retiring, Rodolpho and Ireñe discussed their visitor. Their custom for years had been to go over recent events or whatever before going to sleep. Rodolpho respected and depended on his wife's input and counsel. She began with the transformation she had witnessed.

"He received a letter from America today. When he arrived here, he had the look of eagles, but, later when he came down to join me, there was great sorrow in his eyes. He covered his pain very well, but I could feel it. The change in his demeanor was obvious."

Rodolfo mulled this information for a moment. "I wonder what it was all about, Ireñe? But, as always, you have the gift of the third eye. I will see if

I'm able to discover the source of his sadness."

While Rodolpho and Ireñe were having their nightly discussion, there was a monologue going on at the other end of the *casa* on the second floor. Davis was lying on the top of his unturned bed, trying to make sense of Rebecca's letter.

The dinner was wonderful. Even with his sadness, he couldn't recall when he had eaten so much. There was a ton of food at the Benevento's table, and he had been served many helpings, but, with all the laughter from the many stories, he really hadn't eaten all the food on his plate. Tonight, the combination of food and wine had taken its toll. He drifted off in to a fitful, dream-filled sleep.

Rodolpho had discussed their guest's problem with his wife and decided to let their troubled guest sleep in. About 8:00 a.m., Rodolpho knocked on Davis' door and got no answer. He carefully opened the door and saw Davis still wearing his clothes from the evening before. With the blanket pulled only halfway up to his shoulders, revealing his feet and lower legs, he was quite a sight. He smiled and said softly, "At least he took his boots off."

The family's cook had been dismissed until lunch; the girls had finished their breakfast and gone off to tidy their rooms and do their daily chores. Ireñe prepared a special breakfast for the three of them. Rodolpho had made sure that Davis was awake then went downstairs to kiss his wife good morning. "Our boy will be joining us in a few minutes, my love."

Ireñe noticed the tenderness in her husband's voice when he said "our boy," and, though it made her swallow, she said nothing. The lady with the third eye knew that many changes in all their lives were imminent.

Davis pulled on the pointed-toe boots, tucked his shirt in, and went to the window. The horses were grazing again. He fumbled in the side pockets of his suitcase for his toothbrush and remembered it was in the bathroom. Traveling can be so confusing. As he walked downstairs on his way to join his hosts, the tiredness he had felt from his tossing and turning began to disappear. His heavy heart now seemed a bit lighter. The sight of Rodolpho and Ireñe's smiling faces gave his tortured soul new life. In his best Spanish he said, "*Bueños Dias, mí amigos!*" This drew laughter from them and set the stage for what promised to be a wonderful day.

Davis finished his second plate of eggs and homemade sausage with potatoes that had some red and green things mixed in. He didn't ask (and really didn't care) what the ingredients were. One thing he knew for a fact, they were indeed delectable.

Rodolfo waited until he had relished the last morsel, stood up, and said, "Let's get on with the business, Davy."

The two men thanked the lady of the house for breakfast and headed for the great outdoors. At the bottom of the stairs was a vehicle that took Davis back a few years. It was a red Chevy pickup much like the one he had been given on his graduation from college.

Rodolpho saw the surprise in his client's eyes and said, "Do you like my truck?"

"Oh, yes, I do, Rodolpho. I really do."

Rodolpho wasn't aware of its significance, only that he was pleased.

They drove for what seemed like a hundred miles. Of course, it wasn't, but the rutted roads and the bouncing truck made it seem that way. The herds of horses Davis had seen through his window were now up close. Davis saw his host hit the brake, bringing the Chevy to a stop. He took this as a sign to get out of the truck, but, when he reached for the door handle, he felt his driver's hand on his chest.

"Not yet, my friend, not yet." They continued up another one of the rolling knolls and stopped once more. Davis looked out his window to see another group of beautiful equines. This time he made no effort to reach for the door handle.

This went on for what seemed like hours, and, actually, it was close to three. He had experienced the pushy Jon-Pierre Genevive, and the gracious Vittorio Benevento, so what was this amiable Spaniard up to?

Finally, his patience ran out. "Rodolpho, I know we had a big breakfast, and I don't want to sound like a complainer, but we've been riding for a long time. We're miles from home...and I'm hungry."

The robust rancher with the built-in smile grinned even larger. "No problem, my friend."

He watched with curiosity as the thickly built Spanish gentleman got out of the pickup, climbed in the bed of the truck, and opened a wall-to-wall box behind the cab. He picked up a basket and showed it to Davis through the back window, saying so Davis could hear through the glass, "Let's eat!" They enjoyed the lunch that Ireñe had packed for them. They lay back on the grass and took what might be considered a short *siesta*.

This completed, Rodolpho put the empty basket back in the chest and started the truck. They drove by several small herds of horses. Rodolpho asked Davis to look out his window. Davis did and saw what appeared to be hundreds of cattle. "Horses are my love and life, my friend, but my other job is to feed some of the people of Europe." It was another surprise for the stranger, in this wonderful but still foreign land.

Except for lunch, the pickup never stopped until the hacienda and barns he had seen the evening before came into view. As close as Davis could count, he'd seen around seven hundred plus horses, of varied types or species. His indoctrination had only just begun. The jovial Spaniard stopped in front of a large barn that they'd walked by before dinner the night before. "This is the center of my whole operation, my friend." They entered through the two large double doors, and Davis saw something that dwarfed not just his set-up, but also the French and Italian horse breeders he had seen thus far on his journey.

Under the one roof were washing stalls, a blacksmith shop, and saddlery, and, if that wasn't enough, a complete veterinary clinic. He changed his mind about his first observation. Rodolpho's operation was not at all that flashy from the outside, but far superior than he could ever have imagined.

Rodolpho didn't brag or make any demands on Davis for an opinion, he just watched his young friend's reaction.

"Señor Montoya, you have the most beautiful and complete operation I have ever seen or read about!"

"You are most kind, Davy. I was hoping you would like what I've shown you. I have many horses, and, whether in the fields or in my barns, they receive the best of care. They are only second in importance to my wife and children. I cannot buy them jewels or send them to college, but I would if I were able."

Davis had never met anyone in his life, male or female, who showed this kind of compassion for anyone or anything. He wished that someday his father and his best friend, Willie Hampton, could meet this extraordinary man. Little did he know, at this time, that his wish would someday become a reality.

His thoughts were interrupted by Rodolpho's hand on this shoulder. "Come, my friend. I have something very special to show you."

They walked past many stalls with the occupant's name on the gates, all the way to the end of the straw-covered pathway. Here, he took his hand from Davis' shoulder and proudly pointed to a stall that resembled a hotel room. "Davy, this is where it all began. This beauty, and his father, and fathers before him is the reason I am who I am."

Highlander Chief was a beautiful and magnificent animal. Davis had every right to be proud of his first acquisition. But this horse was breathtaking. He was seventeen hands tall and looked as though somebody had sprayed black lacquer all over him, manicured his hooves, and styled his mane and tail. Rodolpho gestured to his prize and proudly said, "Señor DeLongpre, meet El Negro Grande."

Davis knew enough Spanish to know that this meant "the Big Black."

He watched as Rodolpho caressed the animal's neck and talked softly to him. He saw El Negro Grande's eyes follow his master's every move. He motioned to Davis to take his place as he went to a corner and brought back a three-step stool. Davis backed off and watched as the Spaniard left the last step and eased his way on to this splendid animal's back. Rodolpho sat there like a magnificent conquering soldier and looked down at his impressed young guest. "This is *my* horse, *mí amigo!*"

Davis knew that this animal was not for sale at any price.

This was the end of the second day that Davis spent at the Montoya ranch. He had arrived there in the absence of Rodolpho, and now it was Ireñe's turn to make her apologies.

At dinner, Ireñe announced that she was leaving the next day for Madrid and taking the girls with her. Rodolpho was not surprised because he'd asked his wife to hold off this trip until he had returned from his. He didn't want to chance missing Davis.

"I have some shopping to do to prepare our daughters for school. I am also going to visit my sister whom the girls and I haven't seen in almost two years."

Rodolpho nudged Davis as if to say "watch this."

"Is it necessary for you to go and take my daughters to teach them to spend all my money, Ireñe? You do a good job all by yourself. If they follow *your* example, they will soon bankrupt me!"

Ireñe feigned anger at this statement from Rodolpho in front of their guest.

"It will be *good* for them to learn to do this. It will prepare them for when they are married and have much time to kill before our grandchildren arrive. We'll be back within the month."

The girls giggled and were joined by their parents and Davis. After the laughter subsided, Rodolpho said to Davis, "You will stay with me while they are gone? It would be good."

"Well, I don't, Rodolpho, maybe…."

"Please, no maybe, Davy. You must stay. I will not accept your refusal."

"Yes, yes, you must stay and keep my husband company," said Irene passionately. "He does not care to be alone."

"I'll have to call my folks and Willie Hampton. They're expecting some horses...and me. I'll call them right away."

Davis had wondered what he could do to keep from going back to *Beckyland.* Now he had an excuse, but how would he explain his extra stay to his folks and Willie. Granted, he was a man who could make his own decisions, but a couple of people were depending on him. He would have to give this some thought before picking up the phone.

He excused himself from dinner and went to his room to think it over. He looked at his watch and subtracted six hours, which told him that his dad and Willie had finished lunch. He dialed the office they had built on to the barn.

The Colonel and Willie had lunch at the Hamptons. Lillian had gone to one of her club meetings and wasn't expected back until early afternoon. They thanked Darcy for the delicious meal and went back to the office.

The patriarch of The Willows removed his Stetson and began toying with the sterling silver hatband his "boys" had made him a gift of when he joined them in the business two years before. He made sure the raised letters spelling "the boss," were facing perfectly to the front.

"I wonder how our wandering horse buyer is doing?" he said to Willie.

"Well, Pop, we heard from him a few days ago when he called us from that Casa de something hotel in Barcelona. He's probably just getting started with Montoya."

"Yeah, okay. I know we'll be hearing from him soon. I'm not really worried, Willie. I guess I just miss him."

"Me too, Pop. Me too."

They chatted for a few minutes about their plans for the remainder of the day and decided to work out one of their charges. The Colonel picked up his hat and stood up. Willie put a folder in its right place in the cabinet next to his desk and followed suit. They were halfway to the door when the phone rang. Willie was walking behind The Colonel. Since he was closest to it, he picked up the receiver. "This is Willie Hampton, can I...? Davis!"

The Colonel heard this, pivoted, then walked back to where Willie was standing. He heard Willie say, "How's it going, pard...Uh huh, well...uh huh...So he's got a nice operation? It's okay with me, but maybe you should talk to your dad."

Willie handed the phone to The Colonel, went to his desk and sat down.
"Hi, Son. What's going on with you, is everything okay?"

Davis went on to describe the ranch and all of the wonderful facilities. He told his father that he wanted to spend another few weeks with Rodolpho Montoya because he figured he could learn some valuable things from him that would be beneficial to the operation at The Willows. The Colonel let his son talk, but, while this was going on, he thought he heard a car pull up. He knew it must be his wife, so he handed the phone back to Willie.

Lillian's club meeting was finished. She had decided to do some shopping in Hattiesburg before returning home. This completed, she instructed her driver to head for home. The driver obeyed and began to leave the main street and turn onto the highway, but Lillian changed her mind. "Daniel, I'm sorry. I need a few things from Thompson's Hardware." She could have had anything delivered, as had been the case for years, but there was something she wanted to do.

Harley Thompson was surprised to see Lillian walk into his establishment, but nonetheless happy to see her. It had been a while, to say the least.

"Lillian, my goodness! This is a pleasure!"

They made some friendly small talk that included her fabulous rose garden. Lillian began easing into the real reason she was there.

"Harley, I haven't talked to Rebecca in a while, how's she doing?"

"It's funny you should ask, Lillian. Rebecca usually calls us at least once a week, but I was talking to my wife only this morning. We just plain haven't heard from her. I know she's alive cause we've seen her on the TV doing the weather report."

They parted with the usual good intentions that they'd get together for dinner in the near future.

The Colonel was right. He went out the front of the barn and saw Daniel unloading some packages from the big black car. He yelled for his wife to stop, which she did about half-way to the back door.

"Lill, come running, your son is on the phone!"

She asked Daniel to take the packages to the potting shed and the house and rushed to join her husband. Willie was still talking to Davis when he saw Lillian coming through the office door with The Colonel right behind. He handed her the phone.

"Honey, I'm so glad you called. I've been worried about you!"

Davis told his mother the same story he'd relayed to his father only minutes earlier. Mrs. DeLongpre was not a bit happy with this news, but there was not much she could say or do to change this. They exchanged good-byes. Lillian took the receiver from her ear and slowly hung it up. She blotted the tears that were threatening to spoil her make-up and turned to the two men who'd been listening.

"T. D., Willie, I don't know exactly why, but I have a feeling that something is not quite right here. Like I said, I don't know what it is, but, believe me, I intend to find out!"

Davis put the receiver back on its base and took a big breath of relief. He wanted so badly to tell his mother about the letter, but he just couldn't do it at this time. At least he had cleared the way to grant Rodolpho's request. He went downstairs and made his way to the dining room. He was hoping that Mr. and Mrs. Montoya would still be there, and they were. They saw Davis approaching and waited for him to speak.

"If you still want me to stay here, Rodolpho, I'm yours."

This was grand news, especially for Señor Rodolpho Esteban Montoya.

Chapter Sixteen

The following weeks would turn out to be a milestone for both men. Davis would learn more from Rodolpho about the raising and breeding of horses than he could have ever learned from his stint at the university or from his brief association with Jon-Pierre and Vittorio Benevento...or even the hand-me-downs from Amos Hubbard to Willie.

On Rodolpho's side of the equation, he had now found the son he had always longed for. His wife cautioned him about becoming too attached to the young man from America, and he agreed, but it was extremely difficult. No matter how long Davis would be with them, it would break Rodolpho's heart when their time together was over. He loved his three daughters with all his heart, but here was the answer to his prayers. He had so many emotions that he had to keep in check. His businessman's ethics that had made him so successful were being tested to the max. He was in heaven, so to speak, so a month would pass by very quickly. What was going to happen when his young friend's time to leave finally came about?

Davis knew little or nothing of his mentor's history. He could see the sincerity in this great man and saw the love he had for his family and his horses. He was always so cheerful and very talkative. He not only wore *him* out, he talked to all the ranch hands, the horses, and himself. At times, he seemed to talk to the winds that were always buffeting the rolling landscape.

At first, this amused Davis, but, as the days rolled on, he began to compare the Spaniard to his father and Willie. They were as different as a plow horse to a thoroughbred, yet there was a definite similarity. They all possessed some of the same honorable traits: honesty, integrity, and just plain faithfulness to all they cared for.

They worked very hard every day. At the end of each day, they would enjoy dinner, wine, and the brandy afterwards. The big table seemed to be a waste without Ireñe and the girls, but the void was filled with many discussions about their mutual love of horses and the land. There were no alarms set for them to wake up and go to work, just a really nice feeling that their tasks would be completed before the Spanish sun bid them "*bueños noches.*"

One morning Davis said to his host, "We've been working very hard, and I think that much of this has been more for my benefit than anything pertaining to your daily routine. If I'm wrong in this assumption, please correct me, but I have a favor to ask you."
Rodolpho saw the seriousness in the young man's face and voice and responded with, "I'm listening, Davy. Just tell me what you have inside your soul."
"Rodolpho, could we just go riding today and maybe just talk?"

He'd gone all over the ranch with his host in the red Chevy pick-up, but it had been some time since he'd felt a horse between his legs. Rodolpho thought this was a grand idea, and responded to his "boy," "This is something I think we should do. I can see that your heart wants your mouth to say something. We'll go to the special stalls and spend our day as men who should talk." They mounted two horses that Rodolpho had selected and began a slow gallop.
They followed the rutty road that they'd ridden on the initial tour that first day. Rodolpho motioned Davis to follow him. They left the road, turned right, and climbed up a steep path to the top of a grassy knoll. Davis was riding behind and saw Rodolpho raise his hand and yell "whoah!"
In the middle of a grove of stubby trees was a bench about five feet in length. A few feet away was a trough to water the horses. They dismounted and walked to this old but sturdy-looking structure.
"This is where we will talk," Rodolfo said as he pointed to the tree-shaded bench. "I've been coming to this place for more than forty years. When I want to be alone, this is where I come. It is very special to me for a few reasons. I not only come here to think. It is where I have made many good decisions—the best one being; this was the place where I asked Ireñe to be my wife."
They tied the horses and let them drink from the trough and graze. Davis was so overwhelmed by this that he almost forgot the problem he wanted to discuss. He began by thanking his host for all they had done for him. Rodolpho put his fingers to his friend's mouth, telling him this was not necessary. He apologized for interrupting and got right to the point. "Davy, you're a man whose heart is filled with sorrow. I may be wrong, but I sense that the letter

my wife gave you when you arrived is a part of your sadness."

Davis marveled at this man's intuition. Suddenly, he felt he could confide in Rodolpho with anything and everything that was in his heart. He went on to explain the contents of the letter…and why in his mind it had happened. He also explained the situations that had led up to it.

Rodolpho listened to him and did not interrupt, except for the times the English terms were beyond his comprehension. He had his own thoughts about the situation but kept silent, speaking to himself, *As usual, Ireñe, your sensitivities are correct.* Davis was deeply wounded by the letter from this "girl." After a few minutes, Rodolpho removed his hat and with his bandana, wiped the sweat from his forehead, ran it around the leather strip inside the brim, and said, "My young friend, one must be capable of dealing with chance if one is to make his way in this world successfully. Nothing is what is seems and one must be flexible."

They sat silently for a long time. Rodolpho was bothered by one small limb from a tree growing next to the bench. It was protruding into the sitting area, so he snapped it off. He idly scrapped it back and forth on the dirt in front of them, like it was some sort of broom. He then broke the silence.

"Davy, if this girl is very special to you, perhaps you should attempt to persuade her to change her mind. Are you friends for long?"

Davis managed a slight smile and answered, "Long is right. I think I fell in love with her when I was about ten years old, and I just thought we would always be together. I guess I should have made it clearer how I felt. It just didn't seem important since I assumed she felt like I did."

"Ah, Davy, women are a curious lot. They are like the wind, here one moment and gone the next, but, once you have won their hearts, they are as constant as the tides. This is what I think you should do. Either make up with this girl or go on to something else. It is not good for a man to fret or pine."

Estrelita Bravo sat at her desk in the hotel office. She was making final preparations for a large banquet that would take place on the weekend. Her father made one of his rare appearances at the Casa de Oro. He had a small house a little way from the hotel where he had been living since his wife died. He moved out of the hotel, hoping to run away from her memory. He would help with the hotel's management if his daughter asked him, but otherwise he didn't show much interest.

Her father looked pretty good for a man who had given up. His spirits were better than she had seen in quite some time. She smiled as she had a funny thought. *Maybe he's got a girlfriend.*

She decided to take a break for lunch. After telling the desk clerk where she would be, she went to the private table where not long ago she and Davis had enjoyed dinner. While she was waiting for her salad, the sight of the breathless young American kissing her hand went though her mind. *I wonder if I'll ever see him again. Hmmm.*

The talk on the hilltop with Rodolpho had been comforting to a point. Rodolpho's advice—to do something about Rebecca or move on, stuck with him. *Should he call her? Was this letter some sort of an ultimatum? Was there really someone else in her life? No, Becky wouldn't lie about that, would she? Whatever it was, he didn't want to pursue it at this time, especially not long distance. Maybe he should try other things before he committed to anyone. Maybe he should try seeing the lady hotel manager?*

He did indeed think of Estrelita quite often during the following couple of weeks. Still, he elected to hang with Rodolpho for a few reasons. He was truly fascinated with this man's over-all knowledge of the facets of the horse business and wanted to learn all he could. To be very honest, he just plain liked being with him.

They saw all or, at least, most of the spread during the morning hours, then after their *siesta*, they usually ended up in the veterinary section of the big barn. Evenings found the two men taking up only a small part of the big dining table. Most of the time they retired early, but once or twice a week they would refill their brandy snifters and Rodolpho would talk of those days when he was young and chasing dreams, his ideals…and Ireñe. Davis enjoyed these nostalgic trips with his friend but could tell him far fewer stories being a young man.

September made it's way to the Spanish countryside and with it brought a slight change of weather. The leaves began to turn, marking the return of the ranchero's first lady. Femininity would once more abound. The dining room would no longer be empty.

Davis and Rodolpho had certainly enjoyed their time as bachelors, but, for the older of the two men, it was nice to have his lifelong love back in the house…especially in a certain room. Davis liked to hear the daughters squealing about daily new teenage discoveries and again see the playfulness between his host and hostess.

Ireñe was glad to be home. The shopping with her daughters was always an experience. For the most part, it was fun, but, as they grew and their tastes changed, it could be a real project. The pain of not giving Rodolpho sons had subsided over the years, becoming a source of dry humor for Señora Montoya. In the middle of some of their shopping afternoons, she would look to the heavens and say *Mí Dios, I'll trade two of these for only one boy!*

The spending spree came to an end, but the tough part still loomed. Ireñe loved her sister, but going to see her was more of an obligation. Ramoña had not married as well as Ireñe. She was jealous of her sister's happiness and wealth. She wasn't poor by any means, but after the hellos and nice-to-see-you hugs, the little snide and envious remarks would begin. That's why Ireñe saved seeing her for the last day, so she wouldn't ruin the entire trip.

Yes, it was nice to be home. It was nice to see her husband after almost a month and especially in such a great frame of mind. *What a great idea, having the young man stay!* she thought. Not only was her husband in good spirits, she noticed their guest had improved considerably. There was still some sorrow in his eyes, but also a bit of some kind of anticipation. She adopted a "let's wait and see" attitude. Sometimes she cursed the "third eye" gift God had bestowed on her.

Another week or so went by. The lady of the house had sent the girls off to school. With her days free, it didn't take her long to restore order. Rodolpho and Ireñe were happy once again, but Davis had Estrelita on his mind. He had promised to see her again, but it had been going on two months. He couldn't help but wonder if she would still be available. He decided to test the waters.

One night at dinner he told his hosts that he would like to go into town the next evening, just to check things out, you know, see more of the of the city of Barcelona. Rodolpho thought this to be a grand idea, so with enthusiasm he said, "Of course, I think we should show you some of the notable things in our city, it would be good for all of us…." He stopped as he picked up this wife's stare and quickly went on to something else. "However, maybe you would enjoy getting away by yourself. We can always go another time."

Davis didn't want to appear rude so he said carefully, "Yeah, I mean no disrespect, but if it's okay…. Oh, by the way, do you mind if I use the truck?"

Davis had called Estrelita the day before. He was happy that she remembered him and equally as happy that she said yes.

The next afternoon after Rodolpho and his protégé finished their tasks, Davis went to his quarters and began to prepare for the big evening. He wanted to be flexible as far as his attire for this night. He didn't want to overdress or go the other direction. All he had to go on was that they were going to dinner. He picked out a pair of brown slacks and a beige sport coat, a pale yellow shirt, and brown loafers. It was getting chilly at night, so he threw a topcoat over his arm. He took one more look in the mirror and went to the living room area to say goodnight to the Montoyas. He walked to where they were sitting and asked, "Rodolpho, I'm ready to go, can I get the keys to the truck?"

"Of course, my friend, they are on the little bar between the dining room and the kitchen."

Ireñe looked at the handsome young man and arose to find her purse. She came right back and said to Davis, "My, my, don't you look handsome! Doesn't he look handsome, Rodolpho? I'm sure you're welcome to use my husband's means of transportation, but, as nice as you look, I don't think you should drive that dirty old truck. I think these would be much more appropriate."

Ireñe took a set of keys from her purse. As she dangled them, they could see the glitter of the Cadillac crest halfway across the room. At that moment, one could have knocked the robust Rodolpho over with the touch of one finger.

He said with surprise, "Ireñe! I don't believe it! Your baby!"

"Oh, hush, old man!"

As she handed the keys to Davis, she began a short story. "I saw the car in a New York magazine. It was on the page opposite from a display of jewelry. I asked my husband, as a joke, if I could make my choice of the page I preferred. When he nodded, I decided on the car. My love, please take Davis to where we keep it."

Rodolpho threw up his hands and they began walking to the one building Davis hadn't been in. He hadn't been there and never asked why. Rodolpho opened the big double doors and asked Davis to help him remove the cover. This exposed a beautiful coffee-colored Sedan Deville, which was surprisingly without a coat of dust. Rodolpho looked at a smiling Davis and sighed, "And I was giving *you* advice about women!"

This brought a chuckle from Davis. He was glad to see another man who had experienced the same dilemma. He slid in to the front seat, checked the tilt of the steering wheel, and found the button to press for adjusting the seat backward so his legs would fit. He gave Rodolpho a big smile, and he was off to the Casa de Oro.

Davis's parents always had nice cars, but, when he was a boy, all he did was ride. If his father was in town, he drove, if not, it was his mother's driver, Daniel.

When he became old enough to drive, his first car was an older truck. His folks bought him a new Chevy pick-up for graduation, and he loved that truck. Besides that, no respectable young rancher would be seen driving something with white walls and spoke wheels. This car was special for a few reasons. It was beautiful, a pleasure to drive, and it handled and rode so well that it gave him time to think. It also made him feel good about Ireñe's trust in him. Lastly, it gave him a connection with his homeland, something he hadn't had for over two years.

He drove on and, when his homeland came into focus, so did Becky. He felt justified in his actions but still had a strange pang of guilt somewhere in the outer boundary of his heart. Well, at least this unsure heart would arrive in style. He was only about seven or eight minutes away from Estrelita.

Davis told the parking attendant that he was there to meet the owner and would he please leave the car in front since they would be out directly. That being assured, he ascended the stairs, entered the lobby, and walked over to the front desk to inquire of his date's whereabouts.

The lady with a big greeter's smile told him she was changing and would be down shortly. He thanked her and sat down in one of the plush chairs that were neatly placed at the other side of the lobby. That didn't last long. He was a bit antsy, so he began exploring the paintings and sculptures. Something made him look in the direction of the stairway. Suddenly the wait was worth it.

His date for the evening was descending the stairs, looking like an auburn-haired angel floating on a cloud. He gulped and then went to meet her. At least this time he wasn't out of breath. His heart was running at top speed, but, so far, he was managing to stay under control. He bowed slightly and kissed her hand. In his best southern gentlemanly drawl said, "It is so nice to see you again."

"Well...it's nice to see *you*, Señor DeLongpre. It has been much too long."

She sounded good, she looked good, she smelled good...and that made him feel good. For the moment, there was no loneliness or guilt...and no Becky. All he could think of was losing himself in this delicious creature. No matter how nervous he was, he knew that this was going to be a good night.

As they began walking from the hotel to the car, he said, "You know I haven't been out for a while due to my business with the Montoyas. I know nothing about your city, but I'd like to take you someplace nice. I was hoping you could give me some suggestions."

"I would be more that happy to, Señor DeLongpre."

"One more thing, Estrelita, could we stop with the Señor DeLongpre and Miss Bravo?"

Her warm laugh removed the bit of tension that had been hanging around, and she slid over closer to him. She was wearing some perfume that was driving him nuts. It wasn't overwhelming, just the right amount, but it was certainly doing the job. Davis was not yet a man of the world in some ways. He didn't even hear her when she told him to turn right at the stop sign.

"I think you missed the turn, Davis. It's okay. Go up one more street, and we can go around the block."

They finally arrived at the "La Sierra del Brisas" restaurant. It was a very unique and intimate eatery that combined the traditions of old Spain with all the modern conveniences the public demands in these times. It was considered one of Barcelona's finest.

When the handsome couple pulled into the entrance, the smartly clad parking attendants practically fell over themselves at the sight of the awesome Sedan Deville. There weren't many American cars in their town at that time, especially one this beautiful. They both laughed at this and walked through the stained glass doors that were opened for them by two additional well-dressed young men.

It was Saturday night, and the place was very busy. Davis saw quite a few parties sitting in the waiting area and wondered if they could even get a table. Estrelita squeezed his arm and pointed to the seating captain's podium. The snobbish looking man in his fifties recognized Estrelita and gave her a casual smile. She used her eyes to give him a high sign. She was curious to see just how international her date for the evening was.

The seating captain asked Davis, "Have you reservations, señor?"

Davis had spent two years in the military service in Europe, and, granted, since his discharge, he mainly dined at his client's homes. He had been brought up well, needless to say, and knew what it took to get attention in any country. He reached in his pocket and pulled out a substantial roll of bills. Then, so the captain and Estrelita could both see, he pealed off a few bills and politely said to the rigid-looking man, "I'm sorry, no reservations. Just see what you can do for us. We're *very* hungry!"

As the couple turned to go to the waiting area, they heard a voice over their shoulder. "Señor, señorita, I seem to have a cancellation that I somehow did not see." As they turned back toward him, the stuffy little man snapped to like Davis was some kind of three-star Spanish general and smartly said, "Follow me, please."

He led them to a semi-circular booth with its back to the rest of the room that offered a panoramic view of the city at night. The captain looked over at the two busboys, gave his hands a firm clap, and, within seconds, they were buzzing around bringing water, salsa, and warm tortillas in a napkin- covered basket. Finally, a waiter was standing by their table with a wine list.

Davis looked at his beautiful date and said, "Wow! I haven't had this much attention since my Charlet bull won first prize at the Mississippi State Fair!"

Estrelita waited until things calmed a bit and then began laughing softly. She saw the confusion on her date's face and explained, "Davis, my love, you just gave the captain a whole lot of money, probably as much or more than our meal will cost. In fact, we could keep this place open all night if we so desired."

"Oh? I thought I only gave about twenty dollars."

She put her hand on his. The feel of the long, soft fingers felt divine, and he couldn't help but think that the rest of her must feel just as good. He barely heard her say, "If you don't mind, I'd like to show you something. You see I'm used to handling all kinds of currency at the hotel. Why don't you give me a few of those bills and let me explain their value."

Davis smiled and complied. She went on and explained the different denominations while he pretended to be attentive. He knew them almost as well as she did. She finally finished all that and then touched his hand again.

"I'm sorry you gave him all that money. It won't happen again, well, at least not if you're with me."

"Ah, it's okay. It's only money, and everybody's got to live."

She looked at him and only could say, "Oh?"

They enjoyed a superb meal followed by a yummy Spanish dessert. Davis didn't know what it was or even try to pronounce its name. The service remained great, and, he didn't have to tip anymore.

They sat and talked while sipping some special coffee peculiar to the area.

"Do you like to dance?" Estrelita asked softly when they seemed to be running out of topics.

"Well, I don't do that very well. I don't know this music, but I'm sure you could teach me a little."

Estrelita went to the bandleader and asked him to play some romantic ballads.

As they were dancing, she was studying her date, and, in between bits of conversation, she was thinking, *He didn't seem to mind all that money. Doesn't know how to dance, huh? What have I got here? Maybe there's something behind that pretty face that doesn't show. Well, I'm going to find out some way or another.*

Davis felt her gaze and the slight bit of her warm breath on his neck; he could only say inside, *It's working.* They danced until it was almost dawn.

On the way back to the hotel she sat close and put her hand on his shoulder. When they weren't talking, she gazed at him fondly. It had been a beautiful evening and morning. She only hoped that he wouldn't do anything to ruin it.

As he walked her to the door, she asked if he was all right. He was. A great wave of relief swept over her being when he gave her a hug and kissed her gently, adding a promise to call her soon. She watched him walk away and said out loud, "I'll bet my hotel that someday I will marry him."

Davis DeLongpre was drunk. Not from the alcohol he had consumed. They had danced that off. He was 5-feet-4-inches-120-pound-auburn-haired-Estrelita drunk. Her perfume was still in his nostrils as he put his foot to the accelerator of the powerful Cadillac. He literally flew back to the ranchero.

He put Ireñe's baby back in its house, covered it up, and then put his jacket back on. The sun was out and it hurt his eyes, but the air was a little chilly. He turned up his collar and walked to the main house. It was about 6:30 a.m. when he walked through the front door. Normally the kitchen and dining area would be buzzing, but this was Sunday, so Davis kept on walking to his quarters at the far end of the expansive house. He had no trouble falling asleep. For the first time since "the letter," he didn't think about the little lady from Mississippi who'd been his first love.

Chapter Seventeen

Ireñe's maternal ears heard Davis come home. He didn't really make any noise, but she somehow knew and woke up. She watched Rodolpho's chest rising and falling, listened to his mild snoring for a moment, and then arose to put on her robe. It was time to make coffee.

Rodolpho adjusted his pillow and rolled on his side, putting his big arm out where his wife was a half-hour or so before. He listened for sounds in the bathroom but hearing none, knew where she was and what she was up to. He lay there groggily for a few minutes, then sat up, stretched and yawned, and put on his robe. After washing his face and performing other necessities, he went to join his wife.

"*Bueños Diás, mí amor.*"

"*Bueños Dias, y tu usted.*"

He stooped and kissed her cheek, then sat down heavily and watched Ireñe pour him a cup of the savory-smelling brew. He enjoyed a satisfying whiff and topped it off with a touch of cream. Irene looked her sleepy husband in the eye and said, "I wonder who the *señorita* is?"

"Señorita?"

"Yes, Rodolpho, a señorita. No young man greets the sunrise without a señorita being involved."

"Ireñe, I swear to...."

Davis awoke and looked at his watch. It was late afternoon. The first thing he thought of, after reliving the previous magical evening, was to go and apologize to Rodolpho and Ireñe about staying out all night with the car. He didn't consider it a problem. He wanted to do it out of courtesy, not only out of respect for his hosts. He just might want to do this again soon. Ireñe had been right. The Cadillac was much more suitable than the "dirty truck."

He rolled out of bed, went to the window, and pulled back the curtain. The Spanish sun blinded him again on the same day. He didn't close the curtains. He just turned away, rubbing his eyes while heading for that delicious oasis known as the shower. He stayed under the healing water until he was fully awake, then shaved, dressed, and went downstairs to seek his hosts.

He knew that Ireñe gave the cook Sundays off but went to the kitchen area just to see if any bread or fruit was lying around. He was famished. There were a couple pieces of fruit in a bowl, but just to the left of the bowl was a note:

> Dear Davis,
> I took the girls into town to see a movie.
> Rodolpho is where he usually is, and he wants you to join him if you feel like it when you awake.
> There is chicken in the refrigerator and rolls in the breadbox by the sink. We hope you had a nice evening!
>   Love,
>   Ireñe

Just like my momma, he thought as he gratefully devoured the chicken and the strange-looking vegetable dish, grabbed a piece of bread, and headed for the barn. He was glad to feel that the cowboy boots had formed to his feet a lot better. He would write and tell Hubert about that some day soon.

He found Rodolpho in El Negro Grande's stall, caressing and talking to the magnificent horse. He stood and listened to the one-sided conversation for a moment or two, then surprised his mentor.

"*Bueños tardes, Padre del Negro Grande.*"

Rodolpho looked up while laughing at Davis' attempt at the Spanish language.

"*Bueños tardes* yourself, my young wandering friend. By the way, your Spanish is getting better. One day you will speak Spanish as bad as I still do English."

That brought a hearty laugh from both. Davis figured he had a long way to go even to accomplish that.

Rodolpho continued, "Well, now, how was your adventure? Did you enjoy my wife's baby?"

Davis reached up, stroked the forelock of Big Black and said, "I don't see how it could have gone any better."

The Spaniard smiled broadly, patted the haunches of his charge, and sat down on a bale of hay. After motioning Davis to grab a bale of his own, he said, "Come sit and tell me of your evening, my young friend, if you don't mind my curiosity. As you know, I haven't any sons to talk with about the things that men do."

Davis realized that Rodolpho was not trying to pry, only to share. He decided to indulge his friend with the details of his venture. He saw Rodolpho's eyes light up as he sat on a bale close to his.

"Rodolpho, I had dinner with a beautiful girl last night. My date and her father own a hotel close to the airport called the Casa de Oro. Have you heard of it?" Suddenly, he felt very silly. Rodolpho had left him a note there that he had received upon his arrival from Spain.

"Oh, yes, Alejañdro Bravo is an acquaintance of mine. His wife passed away several years ago. They had a little girl, her name was...."

"Estrelita."

"Yes, that's right, Estrelita. We haven't seen them in years. My heavens, she has to be at least...."

"Twenty-three."

Davis went on to tell him the highlights of the evening and early morning. Rodolpho was glad to hear the young man had a good time. He'd been a little concerned for a while, but it looked as though his friend was starting to come around. He thanked God for blessing him with Davis' company for the last two months. He didn't want to pass judgment on the girl who had sent the letter, but, if she'd hurt him, he didn't think he would be able to like her.

"Is this daughter of Alejañdro of any importance to you?" he asked.

"I really don't know, Rodolpho. She's special, but at this time it's really impossible for me to say anything for sure."

The Spaniard was happy with Davis' answer. The young man was showing maturity by not jumping in to a new situation right away. He wondered what Ireñe would think of this. After Davis told his friend that he would probably see Estrelita again soon, Rodolpho arose, walked over to Black, and gave him a farewell pat on the neck.

"Come, let us walk for a while, Davy. There is one thing I've learned about women. They all like flowers. Those fragrant, fragile petals can melt the hearts of the coldest woman. I give my Ireñe flowers on a regular basis, and, no matter how many times we disagree, those beautiful things seem to cure all problems. If you like this young señorita, send her flowers. Depending on her response, you will find if she cares for you."

Estrelita worked very hard in her father's absence to keep the family's mainstay operating at the highest possible level. As a reward for her efforts, she demanded a certain amount of luxury. She often worked late and rarely arose early. About 8:00 a.m. each morning, her breakfast was delivered to her suite. She would eat and maybe read the paper, then luxuriate in a steaming hot bath before going down to face the day's business.

She had an absolutely wonderful time with Davis Saturday night. It started well, went well, and ended well. She could still feel the hug and the warmth of the kiss that he had given her close to sunrise. She hadn't expected to hear from him for a few days, but on her Monday morning breakfast tray was a beautiful surprise. A dozen long-stemmed roses with a card that simply read:

> Beautiful flowers for the most beautiful lady in all of Spain.
> From the world's greatest dancer and biggest tipper.

Estrelita read the card and giggled like a schoolgirl. She took the flowers, put them in a vase, carried them to the bathroom, and sat them by the tub. She took one of the large flowers in her hand, smelled it, and kissed it before sliding into the steamy sudsy water. She leaned back and said aloud, "Davis, you are the greatest *anything* you want to be!"

Davis and Rodolpho spent the next few days picking out horses to ship to Mississippi. It was rather like trying to pick a beautiful girl from a Broadway chorus line. Any one of them chosen would be a winner. Out of the seven hundred plus head, he started with a dozen and made notes of several others.

Rodolpho suggested they ship only three or four at a time. He said the caretakers on the boat would pay more attention to a smaller number. If shipped one or two days in between, they would arrive close to the same time and be held in destination pens until they could all be picked up together. It was a little more expensive this way, but that didn't really bother the DeLongpres.

All in all, it was the best way to go. Rodolpho was right. Each horse they shipped arrived in Gulfport healthy and quickly adjusted to the new environment.

Having accomplished this, Davis now had to think up another excuse to stay in Spain a while longer. He had not only become comfortable with the Montoyas and their casual approach to life, he also had the auburn-haired lady on his mind. He would summon up the courage and just make the call.

Lillian DeLongpre asked one of the ranch hands to load the wheelbarrow with the Portland bare roots she had recently picked up from the Thompsons' nursery. To her husband, it was the hardware store, but, to her, it was always the nursery. He followed her to the section of the rose garden she'd picked out for her new arrivals. She thanked him and began easing the gloves on her manicured fingers a little at a time.

She was not a happy woman this day. Her son had called and informed them of his extended stay. This and the evasive phone conversation with Rebecca were starting to eat at her. She looked at the 50'x25' patch of "Albas," better known as the "White Rose of York," and decided to plant her "Portlands" just this side of the Alba section.

The Albas were a sturdy five feet high and gave off a strong perfumed scent. This was good because when the breeze brought the stable smells toward the house, the perfumy Albas blocked a lot of that odor the refined lady really didn't like. As she picked up the shovel, she said angrily, "What is going on with my boy? Those damn Albas have been here since Edward V brought them here in the fifteen hundreds. It seems at least that long since I've seen Thurston!"

She kneeled down and dug a hole about six inches wide and elbow deep and put some bone meal on the bottom. "His father was gone a lot, but never for two-and-half years!" She picked up the bare root, removed the protective cover, and felt the damp, mossy dirt. The roses had traveled well. She took her shears and trimmed the longer fibrous roots to match the others, then took a mixture of the original dirt blended with cocoa bean shells and filled the hole. As she went for another plant, she thought, *I don't understand why his father and Willie aren't upset. All they do is nod, grunt, and tell me not to worry. Well, I'm worried. So there!*

Rebecca had apologized to Lillian for not keeping in touch with her and her folks. She said she'd been too busy training the new anchorman from Houston. Maybe not training him, per se, but getting him acclimated to the K-JUN system. Lillian finished another planting and went to the wheelbarrow for one more. She stopped and brushed back her ringlets with her forearm and mused, *Mark Lewis. Who the hell is Mark Lewis? Hmmm....*

She had had enough for the day and asked the man who had brought the bare roots for her earlier if he had been watching. He said that he had, so she asked him to finish the remaining planting they had with them. She would start again in the morning. "Oh, could you also dig me four rows of holes before you leave? Thank you."

Lillian was not really all that tired, but being upset probably made her feel like she was.

Before she removed her gloves, she looked to her left to see her "Bourbons" were into their autumn bloom. She had gotten these beauties from Harley Thompson, but they originally came from the Ile de Bourbon in the Indian Ocean and were good for the Mississippi climate. She decided to cut a few for her centerpiece. She was still upset, but the roses always seemed to heal her soul.

In the short time since Davis and the U.S. Army split company, he had seen quite a variety of family life. His first encounter, Jon-Pierre Genevive was a tough way to start, but it worked out okay. Going to the happy and robust Beneventos was somewhat of an adjustment, but that worked out even better. He saw a non-family situation with Estrelita, that was strange, but he really didn't have any thoughts on that. Ah, then the Montoyas. If he were to write a memoir of his travels, they would surely take up half the book.

One thing these different families had in common was the evidence of a strong woman. Each lady had her unique personality but seemed to share one bond. They were indeed the foundation of the family structure.

Davis loved his mother. He had spent most of his life with her. Part of that was because his father was out conquering the world. When The Colonel was home, he never saw his mother go against him. The many hours he spent with Willie and Darcy were pretty close to the same thing. These two women showed their husbands all the respect in the world and ended up doing more or less what they wanted in the end.

He had only spent a few days with the Genevives but could see that Emma had things pretty much under control.

Sophia Benevento was very quiet at first, but he later found that this was more out of respect to him being their guest. After a day or so, she loosened up a lot and almost talked him to death. She wanted to know all about his mother. He also got a kick out of the way she carried on with her sons. Davis figured that she had her boys when she was very young, because it looked like she had grown up along with them. However, when she was finished tussling and cutting up with them, she was quite a lady.

Estrelita? She certainly wasn't shy or quiet.

Ireñe Montoya had been outgoing from the beginning but in a very classy way. She was hovering around the half-century mark but, like his mother, still extremely stunning. Rodolpho ran everything beyond the front porch at the "Casa de Montoya" and Ireñe *never* interfered. Within their walls, there wasn't one shadow of a doubt that she was in charge. If Davis were to have a family some day, he would like it to be like theirs.

There is no way that Davis could or would ever want to complain about the way he was brought up. There was just something about how Rodolpho and Ireñe and the way they got along with their three lively daughters. They were just something really special, that's all. They had been married over twenty years and still acted like newlyweds. They hugged, kissed, and playfully batted each other around almost all the time. Even when they were arguing, it sounded funny to him. That carried right through to their daughters…and to Davis.

Yes, Davis was getting real comfortable at the ranchero. He was no longer a guest. Actually, he never really was one as far as Rodolpho was concerned, and he could tell that Ireñe had accepted him as well. One of his first clues was that she would tell him to wipe his shoes off just as quickly as she would her husband. How much more at home could he feel than that?

When first Davis had asked his host if they could go riding that day instead of taking the truck, he hadn't ridden a horse in quite some time, and it was a bit painful at best. *Now*, he'd been there a couple of months and his buttock muscles had built back up, so the two men rode on a regular basis. As big as the ranchero was, there were still new places to go.

One afternoon, they were riding out on the east boundary when Rodolpho, whether intentional or not, put the proverbial bug in his riding partner's ear as they rode up to the fence. Rodolpho turned and said, "Well, this is as far as we can go, at least in this direction."

"Whose land is that across the fence, Rodolpho?"

"Well, Davy, it's mine!"

"Yours? Okay, so why the fence?"

Rodolpho dismounted and tied up. He bent down, grabbed a handful of dirt, and threw it over the fence. His face was very pensive. He no longer wore his built-in smile. His eyes looked across the fence to a place and time of long ago.

He began slowly, "Some time before I met Ireñe, there was an old man and his wife that lived there. I used to wave at him as a boy, and, one day when I grew older, we met at this fence and introduced ourselves. His name is not important right now, but we met several times. One day he invited me to his home. I had the honor to be there and meet his wife. A short year later, she passed away. He kind of lost interest and began selling the property piece by piece. One day I was riding along the fence, hoping to see him, but he wasn't where we usually met. Three or four days I rode here with the same results. A month or so later, I came home and my mother handed me a letter. The return address belonged to a lawyer from the city. It seems my old friend had followed his beloved wife and left me the house and the acreage that was left. He had no sons. I've kept the house up all these years, but I'm afraid the land has been in neglect. One day I will figure out what to do with it." Rodolpho finished his story, and they mounted the horses and continued on.

Davis' curiosity won out. "Well, Rodolpho, that's quite a story. Tell me, after he sold all that land off, how much was left?"

The broad smile returned, and he said with a slight chuckle, "Oh, not that much, Davy, maybe two thousand acres, give or take a few."

Davis looked at his friend like he'd been had. Rodolpho saw the surprise and had some fun with it. "It's not like you think, Davy. I would not kid about a thing like that."

They rode all the way home with very little conversation. It was like Davis and Willie. They could spend like what seemed forever not speaking and pick up where they left off without missing a beat.

After cooling and rubbing down their mounts, they headed to the house for a glass of wine before dinner. Ireñe heard them coming in the front door and began to uncork a nice year of red wine. She had been wondering since that night who Davis' lady friend could be. She would not normally ask, but she figured she had been patient enough. Tonight, she *would* ask.

Chapter Eighteen

Around the turn of the century in Barcelona, Spain, Armando Canaveras worked with his father who owned a shoe repair shop. He was only doing this temporarily while deciding what he wanted to do with his own life. The elder Canaveras was well-known for his expert repair work and would occasionally make special shoes for those who could afford fine quality workmanship. Armando's mind was made up for him when his father was accidentally killed on a hunting trip. The boy had to feed a rather large family, so any dream he had before would have to take a back seat indefinitely.

He took the skills passed to him and went a step further, developing an eye for knowing fine leather. When his younger brother was old enough, Armando taught him to do the basic repairs needed to keep the business going, while he concentrated on making custom boots and shoes in styles no one had ever done before nor could copy. Out of necessity, he began to fulfill his dreams.

One Sunday evening at a church social, he met Lucia Sanchez. Lucia worked for a lady's dress shop after school and on Saturdays. It was one of those wonderful things that just happened now and then, and nobody knows why.

After they were married, Armando bought the store next door to his, opened the wall and installed a door, which connected the cobbler shop with Lucia's new lady's boutique. This worked out very well, and just before the First World War, they were blessed with a new addition. They named the beautiful baby girl Ireñe Angeleña Cañaveras.

World War I came and went. Ireñe grew into a young lady who was blessed with that rare combination of beauty and brains. The young men in town were crazy about her and, many times, followed her from school. This sometimes created a problem, but the sly young miss would often end up selling them a dress for their mothers. Her parents saw that she was something special. So, although they weren't wealthy, they managed to send her to the best schools available. She finished college, which in those days was not usually the norm.

She wasn't an *all*-work-no-play gal. She found time to date a few young men but nothing serious. Her parents were a bit concerned about her staying single but didn't try to influence this bright young woman who seemed to be waiting for something. "It will happen, Mama and Papa, when the time is right. Don't worry, it will happen."

It was unusually warm that afternoon in the spring of 1934. Winter was still trying to make her last impression before giving up for the year. The citizens of Barcelona were eager to get outside and celebrate the change of seasons. Whatever the reason, business was slow.
Lucia had packed a delicious lunch as she did quite often. Ireñe fixed a plate for her father and carried it from the boutique into the shoe shop where he was just trying to keep busy. He had just torn a warm tortilla in half, but, before he could dip it in the mixture of goodies on his plate, the bell on the front door jingled. They looked up to see a handsome, broad-shouldered man in his early to mid-thirties walking toward them. He removed his hat and said with a big smile, "*Mí llama es Rodolpho Montoya.* I hear you people make boots."

In early January of the following year, two things happened that *didn't* make all the papers. Miss Ireñe Cañeveras became Mrs. Ireñe Montoya in Barcelona, Spain and Elvis Presley took his first breath in Tupelo, Mississippi.

Rodolpho Montoya was a selfish man. He had waited almost thirty-five years for his bride, Ireñe, and didn't want to share her with anyone. He was the eldest of five children brought into this world by Esteban and Linda Montoya and had had to share all of his life. One day, he woke up and was an only child, so to speak. All his younger brothers and sisters were married while he still lived at home. He had tasted the candy on several occasions but never wanted the whole bagful. He had never brought any home…until now.
Yes, he still lived at home, but it was *his* home, like it had been his father's and about four fathers before him.
Rodolpho was *indeed* a selfish man. This caused no problem with his new wife because she also had waited a long time for him to come into her life. They were so much in love that they were in no big hurry to expand their family.
It *was* his home, and it was a big house. Mrs. Montoya had no objections to sharing her new home. His parent's bedroom, in proximity to theirs, was

like being in two different towns. The only change made to the two-hundred-plus-year-old structure came when the Montoya's daughters were born later. Ireñe thought it would be nice for them to start anew. Rodolpho's parents lived there until their death. His brothers chose to find lives of their own, knowing that Rodolpho would fair well whatever circumstances should arise.

Spring, with many species in many countries, means the beginning of life. This is true in the animal *and* plant world. There is always an air of excitement whenever and wherever this magical time arrives. Things were no different north of Barcelona, Spain in the spring of 1942.

There was a high level of excitement shared by the Montoya family and many friends in the area. After all the talk and all the excuses, Ireñe was pregnant. At the end of the usual time it takes, she gave birth to their first child, a lovely baby girl. Rodolpho adored her. The saying "daddy's girl" took on a whole new meaning.

For a couple that had waited so long, one might think they were trying to make up for lost time. Within what seemed like a few weeks, Ireñe was expecting again. Praise the Lord, it was another baby girl. Ireñe knew that most men longed to have a son to keep their name alive, and Rodolpho, she figured, was no different. When she told him she was sorry and knew he was disappointed, he would fake a look of horror, grab her, and pull her to him, lovingly caressing her private parts while whispering in her ear, "We have so much fun making babies, we'll just have to try again."

They tried again and everything looked up to par until delivery time. Ireñe developed some near-fatal complications, and a C-section was required. Needless to say, a hysterectomy followed, which made Ireñe distraught. She believed that she had failed her husband miserably and went into a state of depression. This, too, would pass. Although Ireñe looked for it, she never saw a trace of disappointment from Rodolpho, not even in his eyes. This was only one of the reasons she loved him so very much.

The front entrance to the Montoya's home was very beautiful architecturally. When one left the driveway and parking area, he would encounter a four-foot-high fence made of multicolor bricks and rocks. In the center was a pair of wrought-iron gates that bore the family crest. They split when opened and became solid again once they closed. The patio was formed with individually cut stones in various shapes, sizes, and colors. It was a fairly large patio, about forty feet in length and about twenty-five feet from the iron gates to the Spanish oak front doors. The way it was structured created an echo.

Ireñe was in the foyer and heard the click of Rodolpho and Davis' heels as they hit the walkway. She smiled as she envisioned them coming home drunk one night and trying to sneak in. She greeted her men, "Hola, señors. What have you two adventurers been up to this fine afternoon?"

"We've been riding, nosey woman. I showed Davis the property east of ours but only from the fence."

"Did you tell him the story?"

"I did, my love."

"Good. You two have time to wash up and relax for a while before dinner."

This is what they did. As they were enjoying the usual tasty Spanish cuisine, Ireñe began to explore the thing that had been on her mind for a few days. She waited until she figured out a good time to casually slip in a question or two. She didn't have long to wait.

Davis helped her by saying, "Ireñe, I think I'd like to go into town tomorrow night. Would you...."

"I will leave the keys on the counter. Oh, Davis, who is this girl who caused you to become blind from the morning sun?"

Davis was caught with his mouth half-full and held up a finger so he could politely finish chewing. He looked at Rodolpho, as if asking for permission. Rodolpho only shrugged his shoulders and stuck his fork in another mound of food.

"Her name is Estrelita…"

"Estrelita Bravo?" she replied.

"Yes, that's right. Rodolpho said that you know the family. She's very nice, and I had a wonderful time."

"I'm glad you had a nice time, Davis. She's an unusual young lady, to say the least."

She gave Rodolpho one of the "why didn't you tell me" looks and took a sip of her wine.

Ireñe was a bit surprised at this and would scold her husband about holding back this bit of information a little later.

She knew of Estrelita and her family history. She tried to put herself in the young lady's situation, asking herself what Rodolpho would do if she left him to raise their daughters, and how it would influence the way the girls grew up.

She admired what Estrelita had accomplished and how she had handled the loss of her mother. Still, she was unlike any Spanish woman Ireñe had ever known. Although Ireñe did not know her all that well, she didn't particularly care for the ambitious young woman. She wondered how she and Davis could get along. Her young American friend was not pushy, very mannerly, and was very vulnerable since that letter. She just couldn't imagine them having any kind of long-term relationship.

Rodolpho may think that Davis had regained the look of eagles, but Ireñe didn't believe so. In her opinion, he had no future with Estrelita.

Estrelita was like a drug to Davis. She was captivating in every sense of the word. She was witty and extremely charming, and he loved the smell of her hair and the touch of her creamy skin. When she put her arms around him, the rest of the world disappeared. She was truly an amazing creature.

As he drove toward town and the Casa de Oro, he thought of Ireñe's reaction on hearing about Estrelita. She really didn't say anything negative about her, but there was something in her voice when Davis mentioned the young lady's name.

When he picked his date up this evening, he couldn't help but notice she was dressed a bit more casually. That, however, was okay. She could look great in just about anything. They greeted each other with a hug, a kiss, and hellos, and were off on another adventure.

As they were leaving the hotel entrance, she moved closer to him, and asked, "Davis, how would you like to see a part of our city that not all the tourists or visitors go to?"

"That would be great. Let's do it."

As they were driving, she pointed out a few places of interest. They motored down the Rambla, which is the main thoroughfare stretched from the port to the Plaza de Cataluna, the hub of the city. They turned northeast and Davis noticed the streets becoming very narrow and the buildings very old. She noticed the wonder on his face. Like any beautiful tour guide, she said, "This is called the Gothic Section. Some of these buildings go back to medieval times, but here are some of the best little restaurants in town. Most are old family businesses that have been around forever. Wait! Pull in right here."

As he brought the big car to a stop, she put a reassuring hand on his shoulder and teased, "Now, Davis, there is no maitre d' here, so we're going to save you a lot of money. Who knows, maybe enough to buy me more flowers?"

He loved this. She could always keep him up, his spirits that is. He gave her a gentle cuff on the chin, and they went inside.

There were only about eight or ten tables. The waiter was young and spoke excellent English. Davis figured that he had probably attended the university. Again, he was in for a new adventure in dining. The food was superb and the company was pretty good, too.

After dinner, instead of going dancing, they drove down the Rambla through modern Barcelona, all the way to the boulevard's seaward end. At the end was the Plaza de la Paz. As they got out of the car, she grabbed his hand and said, "Come with me. There is something I want to show you."

They walked down the concrete paths through the shrubs and flowers. The paths were fairly well lit, but, since it was nighttime, the vibrant colors were somewhat muted. When they came to a circle, she tugged on his arm, and they stopped walking. She gave his arm another slight tug, and said as she raised her hand and pointed, "Look up."

When Davis looked up, he almost fell backward. It was a two-hundred-foot-high pedestal with a statue of Christopher Columbus crowning the top. She laughed at his surprise and asked, "Do you feel like doing a little climbing?"

"Yeah, sure, where?" Davis responded.

She led him to the other side of the statue to open doors that led them through a small lobby to a flight of stairs, a *long* fight of stairs. Even being young and healthy, at the end of the climb, they were both out of breath, but it was well worth it. The view was even more breathtaking than from their booth at the "La Sierra del Brisas" on their first date. With all of Davis' education, he could only exclaim, "Wow!"

The descent was much faster, and the ride back to the hotel was much too quick. They went to the bar, had a Spanish coffee, and said goodnight. It was another near-perfect evening.

About halfway back to the ranchero, Davis was brought back to earth by a deafening crack of thunder followed by one of Mother Nature's own natural fireworks shows. Then came the rain! Not just a light sprinkle or medium downpour. This was a serious rain.

Davis got back okay. It wasn't all that late, so Rodolpho and Ireñe were waiting up for him. The storm had awakened them, and they were obviously worried. A look of relief filled their faces when he walked through the front door. From the garage Ireñe's car called home to the house, he got drenched.

Ireñe went to a cupboard in the hallway and brought him a large towel. As he was drying off he almost shouted, "Rodolpho, where in the hell did that come from?"

"It is called the beginning of our rainy season, my boy. We have been very lucky since you arrived here. The rain comes much later this year."

In this part of Spain, the climate is influenced by the Mediterranean. The month of August is usually the warmest and January is the coldest, but the combination of the sea and the protection of the mountains keeps the seasons from having a distinct difference. However, after August and for the following two months, the former principality of Catalonia receives the major amount of rain. That amount varies from twenty to twenty-two inches per year. Needless to say, it limits activity on the ranches and farms.

It rained all of Sunday and Monday with no visible sunrise. Breakfast was served a little later than usual. Instead of the gloom that sometimes accompanies rainy days, there was an almost gala atmosphere. This rather surprised Davis, so he decided to ask, "Why is everyone so happy?"

Rodolpho dabbed his tortilla in the red sauce that covered his eggs and began to explain, "You see, Davy, we have learned in our country to take what He…as he pointed upward…gives us. It only rains for a short while and that feeds the fields that put food on our tables." He took a mouthful of egg and tomato sauce, chewed it for a second, then added, "And it makes new grass grow for all my babies!"

This brought a laugh from everyone. They went on with enjoying their breakfast. When that was finished, Davis asked of Rodolpho, "There's not a whole lot we can do today is there?"

The big man chuckled and said to his friend, "Oh, I'm sure there is something we can do that will keep us out of Ireñe's way."

Rodolpho went to a large closet in the hall, took out a slicker and matching hat, and motioned to Davis to try it on. Davis did so while Rodolpho donned his. They left the house to brave the soggy walk to the main barn.

Willie Hampton had learned many things from Amos Hubbard. In turn, Willie passed all he could to Davis. Now that Davis was gone, he shared them with The Colonel. They were valuable things to know. As they sat and talked in the veterinary, Davis was again amazed by this man's knowledge. Every day he could see that there was more than he could fathom behind Rodolpho's laughing eyes and broad smile.

There were limitations on what could be accomplished inside, so they didn't always work all day. In the next few weeks, Davis started seeing Estrelita a little more often. Instead of just evenings, he would brave the weather and go into town in the early afternoons and evenings. Of course, if the weather was too severe, he didn't venture out.

He called Mississippi once in a while just to keep in touch. There were no arguments or pleas for him to come home. They had more or less accepted the fact that their prodigy would return when he was ready.

The Davis-Estrelita romance was moving along at a steady pace, or maybe heating up would be a better description. Every trip into town was followed by not wanting to return home. When they were together, it was so intense that they never felt anyone around other than themselves.

One thing, though, did matter. Estrelita was starting to call all the shots. Where they would go, what they would do when they arrived, and what time they would leave. At first, Davis didn't know his way around too well, so this was acceptable. Later on, her beauty and charm allowed her to get away with it. Little by little, it was starting to irritate him, mainly when they were apart and he had time to think. When she was in arm's reach, it didn't seem to matter nearly as much.

One Friday afternoon, Davis and his mentor finished early. As he usually did, Rodolpho gave a last check and blew a kiss to his prime "charges" in the special stalls, looked around, and turned out all but a few lights. As he locked the big doors, he looked to the heavens and said, "Well, Davy, it looks like it stopped for a while. This evening we won't have to swim to the casa."

He barely got this out of his mouth when he looked at Davis to say something and stepped in the middle of a remaining puddle. This amused Davis more than it amused his friend, but Rodolpho joined his buddy in a healthy chuckle.

"You'll never get past Ireñe with those boots!" Davis snickered.

The two men entered the foyer with boots in hand and saw Ireñe talking to the cook by the entrance to the kitchen. They sat the boots down and walked over to greet her.

"What have you planned for our dinner, my sweet?"

Davis excused himself and started for his room. He heard Ireñe say, "Are you joining us for dinner, Davis?"

"No, thank you, Ireñe. I'm going into town this evening."

Ireñe went to get her purse, came back, and put her keys on the bar, then gave her husband one of her special looks. *I'm so happy that someone tells me what is going on around here!*

Davis went to his room and called Estrelita to see where they were going tonight. He just automatically did that. Every time he promised he would stop, he'd think, *Ah, what the hell.*

"Davis, my love, I'm so glad you called. I have a little surprise for you. My girlfriend is a hostess for Air España and she is on a run to New York. She has given me the keys to her apartment and she will not be home before early next week. Would you mind if we didn't go out and spent some time alone…really alone?"

Davis didn't mind that at all. While he was getting dressed after his shower, he stopped and mused, *My God, she even asked me!*

She told Davis that he would never find the place himself, so to please pick her up at the hotel. Well, she was back to running things, but, somehow in the anticipation of the evening, he forgave her…again.

He kind of gathered this would be a good night when he met her in the lobby and she was caring a rather large-sized tote bag. As he relieved her of her burden, she tiptoed up and kissed him on the cheek, and it was off to paradise.

It was a nice little apartment in the Gothic section right at the edge of old town, about two city blocks above the Rambla. Estrelita had made up and packed a platter of cheese, meats, and fruits. She also included a couple bottles of wine from the hotel cellar. They ate, drank, played some music, and began to dance. It was like no dancing Davis had ever experienced, it would be better described as making love standing up.

He couldn't tell if she was love-starved or if this was just the way she did this naturally. She literally chewed on his lips, and, with one hand, he wasn't sure with which, she was unbuttoning his shirt. Her hair seemed to be all over the place, in his eyes, his mouth, around his neck, etc. This flurry of passion continued for several minutes, then she jumped up, wrapped her legs around his waist, threw her arms around his neck, and said with a throaty sound, "Hurry! Take me to the other room!"

She was pointing to a door at the end of the long couch. He put his arms around her back, and half-walked, half-stumbled through the door to where he saw the bed. They fell heavily on the end of the queen-sized playground, and for the next hour or so it was like a no-rules wrestling match. Davis had learned a little more Spanish every day that he'd been in Barcelona, but each time Estrelita reached her peak, he heard a lot of new words that weren't in the handbook. It wasn't until they finished and lay spent that he had a chance to gaze at her wonderful body. She was every bit of what he'd imagined when he'd stared at her fully dressed. He lost track of how many times they made love, or tried to, but they finally passed out from sheer exhaustion.

Estrelita told Davis as he was dressing that she would like to stay and wished he would also. He explained to her that he felt a need not to abuse his privilege of using Ireñe's car, so maybe he would try and make it tomorrow night.

It really felt like it was about to rain when he got to the car. It sure enough did as soon as he reached the highway going back home. That was okay, though. It gave him time to reflect on the evening…and Italy. He slowed down and turned on the wipers. The rhythmic swish, swish, swish was almost hypnotic, but he shook his head…and went back to the restaurant and bar in Lombardy.

The Benevento brothers had a lot of fun with Davis and he with them. However, they knew the language and customs, so he was definitely at a disadvantage and sometimes the brunt of their harmless pranks. More than once they went to a group of girls and, in Italian, tell them that their friend was a famous movie star and singer then leave him to face the girls, running off hysterically.

The rain had stopped temporarily, so Davis turned off the wipers. The road was wet so he maintained his slow speed. He smiled when he recalled the night the brothers ditched him and he ended up with the beauties at the hotel. One night towered above the rest however. The boys had seen this beautiful young woman at a particular bar in Napoli and tried to pull off yet another prank on their new buddy. This time Davis didn't have to combat a whole troop—it was just one on one. He was a long way from home and a little tipsy, so he decided to go for it. He thought he was doing quite well until Francina said, "I don't care who you are or who they think you are. If you want me, it's going to cost you."

Davis laughed as he drove on. He shook his head as he recalled that he was low on cash and asked the lovely Francina if she would take travelers cheques. He thought at the time about cheating on Becky and, like most southern gentlemen, justified it because there was no love involved, just money.

He thought one more time about Francina. No, as far as he was concerned, it was Estrelita. Despite the few differences that existed between him and the fiery Spanish girl, he couldn't imagine going anywhere else.

Sunday morning, no, let's tell the truth; Davis rolled over to face the window, and it was closer to noon. He wanted to see if it was raining, but some knucklehead had closed the blinds when he went to bed earlier this morning. He looked at the clock and knew he had missed breakfast, so he got up and went to the window. He tried to open the blinds from the wrong side but recovered and finally was able to see that it had stopped raining…for now, anyway. The sun had not yet persuaded the clouds to go away. There were puddles that resembled small lakes everywhere. He looked at the bathroom door, then at his bed, deciding that his bed was something he would like to spend a couple more hours in.

That little extra time proved to be perfect. He awoke again in the best mood he could ever remember being in. He only hoped that he hadn't missed lunch. He made it to the bathroom this time, showered, dressed, and went to join the rest of the family downstairs. They had started without him and explained why. "We didn't know if we would see you today or not when you missed breakfast."

Ireñe told a little lie. This was their first meal, too. They had coffee and pastry earlier, but that wasn't considered a meal on a ranch. They could see that Davis was in a good mood and they were right. He was smiling like Willie had told him their entry had just won the Kentucky Derby. However, there was something else on his mind this mid-day. In between bites, he asked Rodolpho, "I know it's impossible today but, if it clears up by tomorrow or Tuesday, could we ride over and look at that property on the other side of the fence?"

This wasn't really what the Montoyas expected to hear from their young man right off the bat. They sort of figured he would tell them about his evening. They exchanged glances for a long second, then Rodolpho spoke, "Davy, we can take a look at it any time you want. We could see the house today, but, you're right, we should wait a day or so and then if the rain permits us, we could see more of the pastures. What may I ask are your reasons?"

"I've been doing some thinking the last few days. I really like it over here. I like being around your family, and, well…I think I would like to buy it from you."

This was something to think about. After pausing for a few seconds,

Rodolpho looked at his wife and asked, "What do *you* think about this, Ireñe?"

"You know I never ask about your business, my love."

Rodolpho nodded and knew that he would certainly get her opinion on this a bit later. For now, he promised Davis they would go there the first dry day.

Rodolpho undressed and slipped into the old comfortable pajamas that his wife had given him as a birthday present many years before. She had bought several other sets since then that ended up in dresser drawers, folded and unused. She kidded him from time to time about those "old things," that even with mending were still frayed. But the soft cotton was something he loved and would not give up.

He lay in bed waiting for her to prepare for bed and looked up just before she turned the light switch off. He saw her silhouette briefly, and, in seconds, she was in his arms. They made love for the millionth time, and it was *still* as tender and fulfilling. As they lay in each other's arms, she began a conversation that was inevitable.

"Rodolpho, my love, what do you think of our young man's suggestion about the other side of the fence?"

He took his free hand and stroked her forehead and hair. She took his hand away and held it while she waited for his answer.

"I'm sure you can see that I am very fond of the boy and would love to see him be a part of us, but I'm a bit frightened. Only because I know he has many ties to his parents and his homeland. I wonder if his sudden desire to acquire this land has anything to do with his attraction to this daughter of Alejañdro?"

Ireñe was silent for a few minutes. He could not see her face, but he could feel her wheels turning. She finally spoke, "My dearest, I have a confession. I am also very taken by this fine young man. He has gone through many changes in his short stay with us. He is like the son I wish I could have given you, but never could, and I see...."

Rodolpho took his hand, found her lips in the dark and gently put two fingers on her mouth, "Shush, my love. Please don't bring up old things we cannot change or control. I love you and our daughters more than anything in this world, and, even if I could, I wouldn't change one moment of our life."

They agreed to terminate this conversation and just see what would happen in the next few days.

Tuesday morning appeared and brought with it a beautiful sunrise. The ground was still mushy, but, at breakfast, they decided to take a look at the adjacent property.

Davis didn't want to overstep his boundaries but suggested that Ireñe accompany them to explore the house that Rodolpho had kept up over the years. At first, Ireñe declined, but she saw the sincerity in Davis' eyes and agreed. They boarded the red Chevy with Ireñe sitting between them and drove up the road to the driveway leading to the old house. He observed her enthusiasm and was glad she had consented to come with them.

The furniture was covered, but the wood floors had a layer of dust that showed all their footprints. In the kitchen cupboards, the dishes were still neatly stacked as if they were waiting for a new generation to use them. Davis was hooked, but he didn't utter a word. He had finally developed something he had lacked for several years…patience. Like the Montoyas, he adopted the philosophy of "let's wait and see."

When they arrived back at the hacienda, Ireñe's maid Yolanda told her that Davis had two messages from Estrelita. The first lady of the Montoya family began to hand the young man the piece of paper. She hesitated briefly, then put it in Davis' hand. He bowed and thanked her and went to his room.

After removing his boots, he sat on the bed and unfolded the note. The contents contained pretty much what he expected:

Davis, please call me. I need to see you.

Chapter Nineteen

Davis looked at the note from the woman he'd recently spent that unforgettable night with and laid it on his nightstand. He thought about where she would be this very minute in the hotel. He knew her reasons for calling. He had told her at her friend's apartment that he would try and get back the next evening, but, of course, that never happened.

He looked at the phone, sat up, and, after a few seconds, lay down again and looked for some new and interesting figures on the ceiling. Finding nothing of interest, he closed his eyes for a short nap before dinner.

Upon awakening, he showered and began dressing, all the time glancing at the phone. He figured he had procrastinated long enough. He sat on the edge of the bed and called the Casa de Oro.

Estrelita went off on him right away. First, she was upset that he hadn't come back the next night and hadn't even bothered to call. She would, however, forgive him if he came into town tonight. When he told her that would be impossible, she let that Spanish temper explode, leaving him with trouble explaining his reasons. When she finally slowed down, he started saying, "I promise I'll see you this...."

She was no longer at the other end of the line. *This is a bit rude,* he thought, but he decided to call her toward the end of the week.

The next two days were filled with soul-searching. He wanted to see Estrelita as much as she did him. There was all the fun they had, the dinners, the walks, and the sightseeing. She introduced him to things he had not experienced in his young life, many of them very appealing. Yes, he did want to see her!

This young man who had been in such a hurry was changing a little every day. He could have used his parents during this time, but he hadn't seen them in two-and-a-half years, so the Montoyas became kind of a surrogate family. Indeed, they brought a steady influence to the table.

As much as his body yearned for Estrelita, his mind was turning on a caution light. In the future, if indeed there were to be one, would this kind of reaction occur every time she didn't get her way?

He wanted to confide in Rodolpho on this matter but figured he had gone to the well enough already. He knew that Ireñe was not crazy about her, so he decided to do whatever it took on his own.

He called her Friday, right after the mid-day meal. "Estrelita, I would like to come by tomorrow night. We could have dinner, and then I think we need to talk."

"Sure, Davis. I'd love to see you! I'm sorry about the last time we talked on the phone."

They said good-bye with the promise of seeing each other the next evening. As Estrelita slowly hung up the phone, she could sense that something was not exactly right. She had to think things over. *What could be on his mind?*

Saturday, about an hour after sunset, Davis took a sport coat off its hanger, put it on, adjusted his tie, and went downstairs. He saw Ireñe talking to Yolanda and pardoned himself, "Ireñe, could I...."

"The keys are on the bar, Davis. Have a nice time," she interrupted.

As Davis walked to the front door, Ireñe paused briefly, shook her head slightly, and then went back to the conversation with her maid.

About halfway into town, Davis turned down the radio. The music wasn't bad, but he only understood a few of the lyrics. This ride to town gave him time to think. He was rehearsing what he wanted to say, as the lights of the Casa de Oro came into full view.

From the moment they got in the car, Davis noticed something very unusual. She had no plan for their evening.

"Wherever you want to go is fine with me," she announced.

All she did was smile and squeeze his hand occasionally through cocktails and dinner. He had not seen this before and was certainly not prepared for it. By the time dinner was finished and it was time for his speech, he had only this to ask, "Estrelita, is there anything you would like to do or somewhere you'd like to go?"

She slid over a little closer and looked up into his face and whispered, "I don't care what we do as long as I'm with you."

Her girlfriend, the hostess for Air España was out of town again. They both agreed that a nightcap wasn't necessary before going there. The minute Estrelita fell into his arms, there was no need for any help...from anywhere.

An hour or so before dawn, on his return trip home, he assessed the evening and early morning. If one were to keep score, it would have read: *Heart - one, Mind - zero.* As he neared the Montoya boundaries, all he could do was yawn and utter, "Ah, what the hell?"

As he had done before after his trips into downtown Barcelona, he carefully sneaked through the front door and placed the keys to Ireñe's Cadillac on the bar where she had always left them. He had never done this at The Willows, for obvious reasons. He'd never been out all night with Rebecca, okay, once or twice, and his mother didn't have a Cadillac, only a big black car with Daniel on beck and call twenty-four hours a day. The red Chevy was the only transportation he'd ever had.

Although his room was the equivalent of a half block away, Ireñe still heard him come in. She didn't wake up her sleeping husband this time. She just looked at him lovingly, covered her head with the goose-down-stuffed pillow, and whispered softly, "The boy is home safe."

This wise lady could see what was happening with her husband and their guest, who was no longer considered a guest. She knew full well of her man's intentions regarding that property on the other side of the fence. She wanted Davis to have this land, but she was very concerned about how this would eventually happen. Rodolpho would not give this to him, but would make it very easy for Davis to own. Her biggest worry was the possibility of Estrelita being a part of it. She decided to wait a while longer and see what would happen. She had a plan that could only work if the Davis-Estrelita situation transpired the way she thought it would. She didn't have long to wait.

Davis was confused with Estrelita's sudden change of attitude. Why was she now so agreeable and not trying to run the show anymore? He had heard from the Montoyas about the history of her father, but it was very brief. He and Estrelita had many dates, but she rarely mentioned her father. The next date, she would have to answer his questions.

They agreed to have dinner at the hotel Friday evening. This was a bit unusual, but so was everything they had done up to this point.

"Davis, meet me at our private table at seven-thirty," Estrelita directed.

The Colonel and Lillian DeLongpres' son walked through the lobby and met the seating captain who led him to the reserved table. He was surprised to see his date sitting with an extremely well-dressed older man.

Estrelita saw Davis about twenty feet away and beckoned him with her hand. As he approached the table, the gray-haired man stood up and extended his hand with polished fingernails and said, "You must be Señor DeLongpre from Mississippi, U.S.A. I am Alejañdro Bravo."

Davis was a taken aback. Estrelita had not mentioned that her father would be present. He didn't really mind, although he had wanted to discuss a few things that had been put aside and replaced by passion on their last meeting. He was confused by the one-hundred-and-eighty-degree turnaround. Now she was making all the plans again.

Davis observed Señor Bravo during dinner. He was obviously a man of class who had been around elite people from his country and beyond. He was wondering from where Estrelita got her fiery disposition. Nothing that she had told him about her father—and that wasn't much—made any sense. Señor Bravo sipped on the wines that went with the courses and had very little to say. Estrelita, much to his amazement, was unusually reserved.

The two-hour meal finally came to an end. Davis watched the man take the napkin from his lap and gently dab at the corners of his mouth. A thought flashed as he recalled the dinners at home with his parents. Davis was waiting for Alejañdro to light up a cigar, but this didn't happen. The seasoned Spaniard just cleared his throat like his father always had and said, "Señor DeLongpre, that is French, isn't it? Are your parents from France originally or were they born in the United States?"

Davis gave him a brief answer and waited for the man to continue. Alejañdro liked Davis' answer and began again. "My daughter has led me to believe that you are a very special young man. I have seen a few of the silly muchacos that have tried to win her favor. She has also expressed to me how fond she is of you. How do you feel about my little girl?"

Davis glanced at Estrelita and she bowed her head slightly. Suddenly, he felt very uneasy and a bit foolish. He played with his napkin and fought the urge to play with his hair. *What the hell is going on here? What can I say or how can I answer a question of this nature honestly? Does this man know that I made love to his "little girl"? How can I answer a question like that? Why is this man putting me in a corner? Is this some scheme from Estrelita's planning mind?* He decided that honesty would be the best way to field this question.

"Mr. Bravo, I have enjoyed your daughter's company on several occasions. I am fond of her, but, with all due respect, I would like to know why you ask? Where are you going with this?"

Señor Bravo looked at his nervous daughter and back to Davis. The silence at the table was like the three people had been caught up in the eye of a storm. The distinguished Spanish gentleman broke the awkward moment with, "Please forgive me if I have spoken out of turn, but Estrelita has made me believe that she wants you for her husband."

Davis started to speak, but Señor Alejandro raised his hand and added, "I can see that you are nervous about meeting me for the first time. I understand this, but, please, let me say that I am all for this union. I am just wondering if you will like being in the hotel business?"

That did it. Davis now realized that the talk he wanted to have with Estrelita had now gone beyond necessity. All the infatuation and all the intimacies he had enjoyed with this woman now took a very opposite turn. He finally realized and understood the feeling Ireñe Montoya had shown with her looks every time the name Estrelita had come up. He looked across the table and met her gaze. What he had to do now would be extremely difficult, painful, and uncomfortable. He put down his napkin, then slowly stood up and said, "It was nice meeting you, Mr. Bravo, but I have to leave now. Estrelita, I will talk to you some other time."

He bowed and began walking away from the table, heading toward the dining room entrance. As he walked through the lobby, he heard Estrelita's voice, "Davis, wait. Please, Davis, wait!"

He turned and saw her running up behind him and his stare stopped her. He could see the tears flowing down her beautiful face and felt himself choking up. Still, he turned around and kept walking.

On his drive back to the ranchero, his countenance slipped from sad to furious. The only thing he wanted to do was get back to the place he thought of as his second home.

This time the hour was early, and he saw the lights still on. He didn't put Ireñe's Cadillac in the garage. He pulled the big car up to the entrance and burst through the front door.

Rodolpho and Ireñe were sitting at the table discussing the land on the other side of the fence. They looked to the sound of the closing door and saw the fury on Davis' face as he approached them.

Rodolpho was the first to speak. "What is wrong, my boy? You look like you have fought with the devil."

Davis sat down at the table with them and ran both hands through his short brown hair.

Ireñe softly questioned, "You look like a young man who needs to go back to his homeland. Is that what you would like to do?"

Rodolpho picked up a decanter of brandy, poured a generous portion into a snifter, and slid it in Davis' direction. Davis took a long draw of the warm liquid and said very matter-of-factly, "No, Rodolpho. No, Ireñe. I don't want to go home. There is nothing for me there!"

The Montoyas let this sit for a moment, and then Ireñe said very gently, "Davis, you are wrong, son. There is everything for you there. A woman has again upset you, and, as many young men do, you are showing a hurt that is clouding your judgment. Now that your affair with the Bravo girl seems to be at an impasse, maybe we can all sit and reason together."

Rodolpho looked at his wife and again marveled at his lady who'd said yes to him many years ago.

Ireñe continued, "My husband and I have been discussing at length the possibility of you acquiring the property next to ours. We love you as one of our family and there is no one my Rodolpho would rather give it to than you. However, we believe that your father and mother should know about this and be included in any decision. We are into the month of the holy time, a time to combine all families with celebrations of the Lord's birth. Do you think your father and mother would be interested in joining our family for this most sacred of times?"

Davis was completely surprised by this suggestion. His anger and frustration were replaced by a warm, almost luxurious feeling, making his fury turn into joy. He rose and knelt between Señor and Señora Montoya. For the first time he could remember, he sobbed openly and kissed each of them on their cheeks.

The fourth day of December, that special day, would prove to be the most significant day in his life.

Chapter Twenty

The rainy season in this part of Spain was beginning to fade, but, in Mississippi, the climate was a bit more brisk. An early cold mist covered the land a few miles north of Hattiesburg. This location happened to be the plush area known as The Willows.

Lillian DeLongpre and her staff were taking precautions to protect her award-winning rose garden. She was content that her roses were covered and wouldn't be completely exposed to the cold and flakes of snow falling about. She pulled her shawl over her shoulders and left her charges with a prayer.

Messieurs DeLongpre and Hampton had made sure that their prized imports were protected and then huddled in the office.

When The Colonel decided to get totally involved in the horse situation, he had phone extensions installed that would not allow any calls to be missed from anywhere. Davis' father and mother heard the phone ring and just happened to pick up the receivers at the same time.

"This is the overseas operator. I have a call from Barcelona, Spain. Is either Colonel or Mrs. DeLongpre there?"

"Momma, Daddy, hi, it's me!" they heard Davis say.

Davis explained how all this had come about and how the Montoyas would like to meet them. He didn't go into great detail, but let it be known how wonderful it would be if they could see their way clear to make the trip. After his parents agreed to this hastily planned adventure, Davis had one more idea, "Daddy, would you do me a favor?"

"What's that, son?"

"Would you mind asking if Willie and Darcy will come with you? Not only would I like to have the whole family together, but I would also like Willie to see the operation over here," Davis added.

The Colonel knew that his wife had a lot more to talk to her son about, so he and Willie ran across to the Hampton residence to break the good news to Darcy.

The Colonel and Willie had the operation running like clockwork. The last shipment of horses was doing fine and there were plenty of folks around to take care of the Hampton kids. It was like they say, "'nuff said."

There were preparations to be made on both sides of the Atlantic. In Spain, the mother of this idea had to prepare for the now obvious meeting of Rodolpho and Davis' father. She was a bit apprehensive of meeting the mother of this boy to whom they'd grown so attached. The last great plan she had invented, snaring Rodolpho for her own, had worked out rather well. This, however, was a touch more complicated. The first lady of the Ranchero de la Montoya was not intimidated and drew upon her many talents to make this all perfect. On the other side of the great pond was her counterpart, Lillian DeLongpre.

Lillian had accompanied her husband on many trips. Yes, there was that one trip to London, England (which she hated), but most of them had been local, or at least within the U.S.A. *Where the hell is Barcelona?* She was an educated woman and she knew full well where Spain was, but, to her, Barcelona was only a dot on the map. She had no idea of the significance of this city or that it was the second largest city in Spain. All she cared about was seeing her boy. *Should I call and share this with Rebecca?* Their communication had become less and less frequent. *No, I'll just call her when we get back home.*

Darcy Hampton had married The Colonel and Lillian's adopted son, Willie. She had come to this unique island known as The Willows and knew full well that this paradise was protected against all the wrongful prejudice that existed just a few miles outside. She didn't want anything to jeopardize this. She was worried about going through the complications of travel. Willie reminded her of The Colonel's great wealth. It was still hard for her to comprehend that her loving husband was indeed wealthy in his own right. Her fears were washed away when The Colonel called and ordered his own private plane to be gassed up and made ready for the flight to Spain. The thrill was further appreciated when the private plane was soaring over this great expanse of ocean, twenty thousand some feet free of the world. This special flight with only seven people on board, the DeLongpres, the Hamptons, and the flight crew was something that made this orphaned, beautiful black lady take her hanky from her purse and blot her happy tears.

Willie looked at this lovely lady whom he still referred to as his bride and tried to count his blessings. There were too many, so he just isolated a few. He looked to the other side of the plane, watching his "Tilly" nervously putting on her fancy little gloves and then taking them off. It reminded him of other gloves from a while back, that time in his life when he and his mother were unable to communicate when he spent many hours watching Lillian work in her garden. He was thinking about how ridiculous those ugly rubber gloves would look on Tilly's hands now.

The Colonel looked at his wife and at his other traveling companions. He was thinking about some twenty-six years ago when going to see their son in Europe would have been no more than a wish.

The Colonel was seventy years old now, and he was just as excited to see his boy as his wife was. But just how special was this? Who was this man, Rodolpho Montoya? What did this rancher have to offer his son that he couldn't? There had to be a reason for Davis not wanting to come home. He decided not to dwell on this, so he excused himself and went to the cockpit to converse with his pilot and co-pilot.

"What is our E.T.A. for Barcelona?" The Colonel requested.

"About 21:30, Colonel, and the weather forecast is favorable. Would you like to sit in, sir?"

The offer was acknowledged and politely refused. The Colonel could have done this but he had hired the best man for the job. He sat down in back of the navigator's seat and just observed. The pilot told his boss that he had connected with the Barcelona tower and had been given clearance.

The Colonel left the cockpit, headed back to the passenger area, gave his wife a big smile, and announced, "Fasten your seatbelts. We're eighteen minutes away from seeing our son."

Davis was very excited about his parents' arrival. He wanted everything to be just perfect for their visit, so he planned several outings for them.

When the day arrived, he invited the Montoyas to accompany him to the airport, but Ireñe declined, smiling at her husband. Rodolpho read his wife's glance and agreed that this should be a private reunion. There would be plenty of time later for all to get acquainted. Ireñe did add, however, "I'll ask Yolanda if her husband will follow you in one of Rodolpho's trucks."

"Follow me?" Davis replied.

"Well, yes. There are four people and with two of the party being women, there just might be some extra baggage. And does your father's private plane have a flight crew?"

Davis and Rodolpho looked at each other and all they could do was shrug and tap themselves on the noggin. They called the airport to see where the private plane would be landing. Davis was off with the red pickup in tow.

From where Davis was standing, he couldn't see the plane's passengers get off, so he asked one of the security people where they would be arriving. The gentleman pointed to a door and told Davis it would be twenty minutes or so to clear customs, but, since it was a private flight, it might not take as long.

It really didn't take all that long, but it seemed like it to the anxious young man as he stared at the door waiting to see his family's smiling faces. He saw his mom and Darcy first, then the others. As they drew closer together, he thought, *Wow! Do they look good!*

Lillian saw her boy and separated herself from the group. She made a beeline and literally jumped into his arms. She held onto him tightly and wouldn't let him go. Davis finally freed an arm to put around his father. He looked at Willie and Darcy, gave them a smile that meant he had no more arms and he would be with them in a second.

On the trip from Barcelona's airport, Davis tried to point out some of the historical places of interest, which was no more than nervous chatter. As the lights of the city faded, the conversation became more intent. His mother sat next to him like she was his date. Darcy sat next to his mother, while his father and Willie sat in the back.

The thirty-mile trip that Davis had always used for reflection and contemplation now seemed like going across the street. Before they knew it, they were within the boundaries of the Montoya spread. They parked the Cadillac, followed by the Chevy pickup in front of the hacienda. Davis asked Yolanda's husband to take care of the luggage as the five of them made their way to the front door.

Rodolpho, Ireñe, and their three daughters were waiting at the huge Spanish oak table laden with a variety of their country's food.

There was the expected amount of handshakes and hugs. Lillian couldn't keep her hands off her son, and Rodolpho was talking The Colonel and Willie to death. Ireñe and Darcy were hanging around the kitchen, while the daughters were giggling and making teenage comments about the clothes their American women guests were wearing. This party went on for several hours, and the travelers from Mississippi forgot how tired they were.

Willie was much too busy to notice the ease of how these families meshed together. Darcy, however, was worried about the black thing and was amazed that nothing was said and nobody cared. She must have been as surprised as Josephine Baker on her arrival and immediate acceptance in France some twenty-five years earlier.

The first day or two of their visit, The Colonel pulled Davis aside for a moment and whispered, "Does Mr. Montoya always talk this much? If he wasn't such a pleasant chap, it could be irritating."

This brought on a hearty laugh from the younger DeLongpre as he put his arm around his father's shoulder. "Daddy, I've been listening to him for a few months now, and he knows what he's talking about. Trust me, he will grow on you. He reminds me a lot of you in many ways."

The Colonel smiled and walked on with his son. It was nice to hear "Daddy" again.

Rodolpho did indeed grow on him. In a few days, they were both talking. The usually reticent gentleman from Mississippi was doing more than holding his own. This shocked his wife and son alike. This was a side neither had ever seen. Davis stayed a little in the background, enjoying his two heroes getting together.

This was a good thing for Ireñe, also. Her protective concerns for her husband were quickly evaporating. It was nice to see her man making new friends. She felt she could see some good things happening in the near future. She was so busy thinking about her husband's happiness that she didn't realize right away how much she was enjoying Lillian and Darcy. They all would learn a lot about each other and about their country's customs and cultures.

This was all just great for Davis and Willie. It gave the "brothers" a chance to catch up on everything from horses to the latest dirty jokes.

All those involved would unknowingly develop feelings that would last the rest of their lives. The friendship being established was not confined to their mutual love for Davis, although he was the central player. It was more like what they all seemed to have in common. It was a special magic only rivaled by being an actual large family, which for all intents and purposes, they were becoming.

The month of December was very fulfilling for all the visitors from

America. One morning, The Colonel came up with a suggestion, "Davis, I hate to break you and Willie up, but Rodolpho and I have done a lot of talking, as I'm sure you are aware. You probably would have come up with this later, but we think that Willie should spend some time with Rodolpho, also. What do you think there, Willie?"

"Well, Pop, you don't have to ask me twice. If I learn half of what Davis has, I'll be happy," he replied.

While the ladies were listening to all this, Ireñe stood up and said, "Ladies, this will give us time to see some of Barcelona's sights and restaurants…and there are plenty of shops where we can spend some of the money our husbands are going to make."

Lillian and Darcy thought this to be a fine idea, so the ladies went off to town. Willie and Rodolpho went to school, while The Colonel and his son decided to go riding together.

Davis knew every horse in Rodolpho's special stable. He knew "Black" was his mentor's pride and joy, and no one, not even he, was allowed anymore than a casual feel of the horse's forelock, or a hand across the back. But the hundreds of hours he had spent with Rodolpho told him he was allowed certain privileges.

Davis had his own mount that he had enjoyed riding since his arrival at the Montoya ranch.

There were less than a dozen prime horses in this part of the barn. As Davis looked at his seventy-year-old father, he knew that there was a big Andulsian that was perfect for him. Big and strong, yet gentle, just like The Colonel. He led the horse to the stall and tied him to the rail. "Daddy, this is yours. How does he look to you?"

"Fine, my son. Just fine," The Colonel answered.

A black leather saddle sat on a form to the right of the gate for the horse's stall. Davis walked over to pick it up and assist his father. The Colonel raised his hands, signaling to his son that he could handle the big steed. Next to the saddle was a black and white blanket that The Colonel carefully placed on the animal's back. Davis watched in awe as his father threw the saddle on and adjusted the leather straps. He saw the great man slowly run his big hands from the saddle horn up the horse's neck, talking softly all the while. Then with the smoothness and confidence of a seasoned cowboy, he put his left foot in the stirrup and smoothly threw his right leg over and into perfect position. The Colonel was seated and primed to go. He took his left hand, adjusted his Stetson, and announced to his son that he was ready.

Davis said with his teeth together and under his breath, "Why was I so worried?" He went to the stall where the horse he had been riding ever since his arrival was kept. It didn't take him long. He had obviously had plenty of practice in the last couple of months. In less than five minutes, he said to his father, "Okay, Daddy? Let's hit the trail."

The Colonel was aware of his son's apprehensions and got quite a kick from it. A lot had changed in the last three years. As they began their ride to wherever, the elder DeLongpre looked to a place known by no one but him and whispered, "Thank you once again, if you're listening."

They galloped past places that The Colonel and Rodolpho had seen in the past few days. One of the richest men in the world had finally reunited with his son and after all these years now followed *his* lead.

Davis pulled his mount to a stop near the same place he and Rodolpho had been only a week or so earlier. The Colonel saw the fence and it reminded him of The Willows' boundaries. He also saw the look in his son's eyes. There was something more to this ride than the two of them just being together. He saw the maturity that had developed during the last three years. Like all those special times at home, he decided to let his son say what was on his mind. The only thing missing was his after-dinner cigar, double brandy, and, oh, yes, his wife shoving her dessert away and pulling on her curls.

Davis sat on his mount for a few moments before deciding to speak. "Daddy, this is where the Montoya Ranch ends, but, as we look over this fence, as far as you can see is also Rodolpho's property."

"What are you trying to tell me, son?"

Davis was caught in a trap as it was. He wanted to tell his father about the conversations he'd had with the Montoyas, he just didn't know how to do it. He wanted to tell this man, whom he had just gotten to know before he left for the Army, how much he'd missed him. He had only called him "Daddy" a few times. Every boy or man in the South those days, whether five or fifty, called their fathers "Daddy" and their mothers "Momma."

As they rode back to the hacienda, The Colonel looked at his son. He was extremely proud of the gift he had given his wife so many years ago and how great this well-kept secret had turned out. His only fear was that someday Davis would find out the truth. This would probably never happen, but he could see what was going on. The boy was so much like him and had the same ambitions, and he knew that Davis wanted to do all this on his own. The Colonel owned property in the U.S.A., Europe, and parts of Africa, but because of the Spanish Civil War, had shied away from trying to do anything in this area. He knew after talking to Rodolpho that his boy was following in his footsteps. He would, however, lay back and watch the outcome.

Although a myth, it has never been questioned the world over that December 25th, or Christmas, is what most of the world believes to be Jesus' birthday. Which is actually okay, even if it's false. But it meant something else to the DeLongpres. It meant that The Colonel declined his birth celebration in deference to the baby Jesus. Lillian thought that, since witnessing this monumental change in her husband in this new environment, this would be a good time to finally celebrate her husband's birthday. She would have to overcome a certain obstacle before this could happen.

The December weather flirted with the Spanish countryside like a ripe young virgin would with her silly young pursuers. There were the later-than-usual rains and erratic changes in temperatures.

Lillian had plotted with Ireñe to surprise her husband with a birthday celebration. Ireñe didn't understand this at first but then recalled something similar with her father, the cobbler, in his later years.

Davis didn't want to do anything to disrupt this plan that his mother had conveyed to him, but one thing had to be cleared up—the letter from Becky. He had kept it in his jacket pocket since his parent's arrival.

As never before, the dining table was filled to capacity. To the right was a tree that spread out several feet wide and towered to its full height, almost touching the beams in the ceiling. It was surrounded by beautifully wrapped packages. There were gifts for everyone from both sides of the world.

Willie and Darcy wanted time together. This was their first big adventure outside of The Willows. The Montoyas decided to go up to the special hill and renew their vows. The girls had things to do also, like hiding gifts for their parents all over the hacienda.

Davis motioned to his father and took his mother's arm and walked her to the passenger side of Ireñe's Cadillac. At last, the three of them were alone.

The DeLongpres were no strangers to luxury, but when Lillian saw her son behind the wheel of the Spanish woman's Sedan Deville, she couldn't help but be proud. She had never seen her son drive before. She was fully aware of the red Chevy pick-up but had never ridden in a vehicle while her boy was driving. After all these years of enjoying her lifestyle, Lillian still had never learned to drive.

Davis drove the coffee-colored car that still smelled of Estrelita (at least to him) to a point that showed the old house and part of the land. He pulled the car to a stop and opened his door. Davis got out to open the door for his mother.

"What are we doing, Thurston?" Lillian wondered aloud.

Davis cringed at the sound of the name he hated, replying, "Momma, I've made up my mind about a few things. I want to buy this land next to the Montoya's spread."

The Colonel saw the surprise spread over his wife's face. Now he knew he was right about what he was thinking the day he and his son rode from that fence to the hacienda. The Colonel wasn't surprised. He had amassed his fortune by reading and knowing his opponents, but this young man was not his opponent, this was his son.

"Daddy, Momma, let's go for a walk. I would like to show you something."

Lillian took one step out of the car and felt the December wind blow the brim of her hat up, giving her a chill, and said, "No, Thurston, you and your father go do this foolish exercise."

Davis' heart was threatening to bounce out of his body. He'd had this letter for a couple of months. Did his mother know? Had she talked to Becky?

His father exited the passenger side as Davis froze for a second. He reached into his jacket pocket and gave the letter from Rebecca Thompson to his mother. He and his father walked up to a knoll where they could see the fence and way beyond. The Colonel took his son by the shoulders and looked directly into his son's eyes. "Is this what you want? Is this what has kept you here? Do you have any idea what you are doing?"

Davis felt his father's big hands on his shoulders. He backed away to regain his breath. The six-foot-tall son looked up at his six-foot-two-inch father and firmly said, "Yes, this is what I want! I love you and my mother, and I want our family to be strong. Can't we own land in Spain, Daddy?"

Lillian read the letter and then read it again. She was furious but now realized why her bond with Rebecca had diminished. She sat fuming in the back seat of Ireñe's car. She saw her husband and son come into view. As cold as she was, she put her light coat over her shoulders, jumped out of the car, and ran to meet them. She ran up to her son and pounded her hands on his chest.

"I told you. I've told you time and time again. You really messed up, Thurston. Now she has somebody else!"

The Colonel was amazed by this outbreak from his wife. In their years together, he had very seldom ever witnessed her temper. Lillian thrust the letter into her husband's chest. T. D. read the letter from Becky and looked at his wife. He saw his son sitting on the fender of the car, his countenance slipping from his shoulders to the soles of his French cowboy boots.

The Colonel had solved many problems in his illustrious career but nothing this close to home. A moment later he said to his wife and son, "This is a very unpleasant situation. Before we return to our hosts, I think we should do our best to resolve this."

Davis slipped off the fender, and they got back in the car. He noticed that his mother was still shivering when he started the engine. The heater kicked in, and Davis left the car running in park. He half-turned and put his right arm over the back of the front seat. He first looked at his father, then at his mother. He saw the tears coming back to her eyes, making him feel even worse. She pulled herself together and began talking, first in a whisper, and then her small voice grew stronger.

"Thurston, honey, I'm so sorry, and so embarrassed. I had no call to do what I did. I was just upset...."

"I'm sorry too, Momma, I just didn't know any other way to tell you."

No one spoke for a few seconds. The Colonel cleared his throat and untied his scarf. As it fell loosely over the lapel of his coat, he said, "I'm sorry to hear about the situation with Rebecca, but this thing with the land...I think a few more opinions need to be heard. What would you say to a meeting with the Montoyas, Willie, and Darcy?"

They both nodded their approval. After a few seconds, Davis put the car into drive and they drove back to the hacienda. He was putting the car away as Lillian stood by her husband, tugged his coat sleeve, and whispered, "What are we going to do about Thurston and Rebecca?"

The Colonel looked down at her and said softly, "I'll tell you what we are going to do and that is nothing!"

It had been an afternoon of some significance for all three couples. Many years had passed since the last time Ireñe sat on a horse. It hadn't been that long, but she made a joke about women riding sidesaddle. They took their time and eventually reached the magic place where it began many years ago. When they finally reached the bench between the two oak trees, Rodolpho took his scarf and dusted it off. There wasn't as much room on it now as there was when they were both a bit slimmer, but they managed. He took her hand and asked, "My beautiful Ireñe, would you do me the favor of being my wife?"

"Well, I don't know, this is all so sudden," she giggled.

"My lovely, remember, it is a long walk back home," Rodolpho kidded.

They embraced and said "I do!" once again.

Willie and Darcy began walking to the various buildings where Rodolpho and Willie had been the day before. Darcy could see the excitement in her husband's eyes as he pointed out all the new things he had seen. "Isn't this great, honey?"

"Yes, my dear, it's absolutely wonderful!" Darcy replied.

He knew she was having fun with him and this made him laugh and then take her in his arms. It was Mrs. Hampton's first hug and kiss…in Spain.

The DeLongpre trio entered the foyer and walked to where the family always congregated. Both of the other couples had arrived a while before. Lillian was still miffed but managed a smile. She could tell by checking her watch that it was a couple of hours before dinner. "Please don't think me rude, but I have a slight headache and I don't want it to get any worse. I think I'll rest a bit before dinner."

"I think I'll join my wife," The Colonel added. "We'll see you at dinner."

Davis sat down and joined his friends. They talked for a while about the day's events and then he asked his partner, "Willie, I need to talk to you for a few minutes, if these fine folks will allow me."

Everyone nodded and the two men rose. For some unknown reason, Davis asked Willie's wife, "Do you mind, Darcy? We'll only be a few minutes."

Darcy gave out one of her funny little chuckles and looked at the Montoyas. "After all the years with these two, I'm very used to this. Go on now, get out of here!"

They started walking out toward the barns…imagine that. Willie could see the pensive look in his friend's face and broke the silence, "Okay, pard, what's up?"

"Oh man, I shoulda' said something to you earlier or even a couple months ago. I just didn't know where I was going at the time, so I just dummied up. I know it's a lame excuse, but maybe if you would have been…."

"Davis, what?" Willie shouted.

"Well, ya see, when I first got to Spain, there was a letter waiting for me…from Becky. She wasn't exactly happy with the way I had been acting, so she, well, she broke up with me. I guess she found somebody that pays more attention to her. It really tore me up for a while and I just couldn't...."

"Aha!" Willie snickered. "That's what this has been all about. That's why you didn't want to come home."

"Yeah, but that's only part of it. I've become kind of fond of this country or at least this part of it. Rodolpho, Ireñe, and the girls are great. And, I've really learned a lot from them. The deal is, Rodolpho has a couple thousand acres adjacent to his that already has a house and other buildings on it that need very little work. I want you to look at it with me a little later. I think we should buy it."

"We?" Willie questioned.

"Of course, we. What did you think I meant?"

"Well, it sounds to me like you have plans to stay over here, and I don't think that's a real good idea. Is that what you're talking about?"

Davis let that ride as they walked a bit further and then added, "No, Willie. I want to come home after a while, but I think it would be good for us if we had a place like a branch office, so to speak. I know we're not big enough to warrant this right now, but I'm sure we will be. And another thing, I know the price will be right."

Willie digested this for a few moments. He came to a stop and turned to face Davis. "It sounds pretty good, buddy. Where is it?"

"Just down the road a couple miles. I'll tell you what. My dad, our dad, or whatever, is going to call a meeting for all of us, probably after dinner. I just wanted to sort of prepare you for it. We'll see how that comes out, then you and I can go see the place tomorrow if you want."

"Sounds good, pard." Willie was a little taken back by this sudden news flash, and, though it sounded okay, he decided to let it ride until he had heard all opinions. He hadn't spent all those years around The Colonel without listening. But, his partner had a point—it sure was nice over here. The Rebecca thing, however, was something he wanted no part of.

There were ten people at the dinner table that evening. The Colonel had asked his host if it would be possible to have a meeting following dinner. Rodolpho saw no harm in that and agreed.

As soon as the remarks were made about dessert and compliments about dinner were finished, The Colonel tapped his glass. Rodolpho excused his daughters and motioned the man to continue. The gray-haired, broad-shouldered man stood up and cleared his throat. As he had been in many parts of the world, he was an imposing figure. Let's just say he commanded attention without uttering a word. He sat his glass down and said, "First of all, I'd like to say how grateful I am for the hospitality given me and my family by our great new friends. I've never been, and I'm sure that my wife and son will concur, treated this royally while away from home. Thank you, Rodolpho and Ireñe. I know that the other part of our family, Willie and Darcy, feel the same way."

They all raised their glasses as a thank you gesture to the Montoyas.

The Colonel continued, "My wife, son, and I went for a ride today and had a couple of surprises dropped on us. One was of a personal nature, while the other pertains mainly to some recent business discussions. I'm just wondering if the two are somewhat related. My son wants to acquire some property here in Spain and that sounds like a good idea…if it is for the right reasons. This is a family meeting, and I would like to hear from all present. If you don't mind, I'll call on my wife first."

He gestured to Lillian that she had the floor. She hesitated and then declined. There was too much going on inside her to make any rational statements, or at least that's the way she felt. There were still visions of her and Rebecca having tea and biscuits or lemonade and cookies on the terrace. She wanted more time. She could buy it if she let the others talk first.

This was an informal meeting, but it still needed some kind of order. It just so happened that Ireñe was sitting next to Lillian, so then he asked if she would like to be next.

Ireñe nodded, pausing to try and translate her thoughts into English. She finally said, "When this young man first entered our home, he looked and talked like a conqueror of the world. I gave him a letter and hours later he had lost that look. My husband did not see the look. I did. After a few weeks, it began to reappear. He has brought great joy to my husband and to our home. I know that he has been through a lot and has not always thought clearly, but I believe he is on the right road. As far as this talk about land, I will, as always, defer to my husband."

The Colonel thought that his son and Rodolpho should be the last to speak, so he pointed to Willie and Darcy. Willie motioned to his wife to go first. Darcy glanced at Lillian and then looked over at the man this was all about. "I don't know too much about all of this. I do know that I love Davis and that he wouldn't do anything to hurt his family. He and my husband are closer than brothers, and I'm sure it will always be that way. And you know what? I'm just really happy to be here!"

Her refreshing point of view brought smiles and a little laughter from the group. It was Willie's turn. He thought for a moment as a smile slowly spread across his face. It was like he had taken a trip backwards. "I can't believe that a little guy who used to follow me around like some puppy is now thinking about buying part of Spain. I have watched him grow up, and, yes, he has acted a little nuts at times, but haven't we all? I know one thing for sure. Our families have many years of history. Now, we've met another family that I'm proud to call my friends. They have also been good for Davis. I've seen a difference in him in the last three years. I can't help but think that Rodolpho and Ireñe had a lot to do with it. I know other people have to talk, so I'll end with this. Davis is my friend and partner—and that, my friends, is that!"

This brought an ear-to-ear smile from Davis. Willie wasn't sure, but he thought he saw the corners of his pal's eyes moisten a bit.

The Colonel looked to his wife to see if she was ready. She thought for a quick moment, while looking at her son. After a slight tug at her ringlets, she finally spoke, "What's going on here with the land is probably a good thing. The other issue is something I'm not quite ready to discuss openly, no disrespect. I'll trust my husband and you, Rodolpho, to do the right thing for Thurston. I only want to see him home safe someday soon. I thank you."

The Colonel looked at his wife again and gave her a tender smile. He then turned to Rodolpho and asked, "Before you give us your opinions on this matter, I would like to ask you a question. You and I were together for a couple of days and you never brought this up. If you don't mind, would you tell us your reasons?"

"Colonel DeLongpre, I don't mind at all. Yes, I do have my reasons. Davis confided this to my wife and I as a man, not a boy. We had witnessed his maturity increase as the days went by. We knew something was bothering him, but we let him choose the time to tell us. I figured that this young man should be the one to tell his parents. As far as this property is concerned, I think it is a fine idea. I have grown quite fond of your son and have now developed very special feelings for his family. One thing is for sure. That land is not going anywhere. Davis has the first and only option. Let us just be patient and see."

All that The Colonel needed to say was, "That's good enough for me. Now, it's your turn, son."

Davis was a bit overwhelmed and didn't have much to add. He looked in his mother's direction and saw her fighting the urge to tug at her curls.

He began thoughtfully, "Thank you, Daddy, thank you all. And thank you for your generosity, Rodolfo. I think you are right. Let's just wait and see what happens. Let it be known, however, that I love each and every one of you with all my heart."

The Colonel had concluded one more very successful meeting. He had become quite proficient at that. Lillian decided to put all her feelings and frustrations on hold. She knew in her heart that this visit to Spain and the friendship established with the Montoyas was important in all their lives. There would be plenty of time to look into the Rebecca situation upon their return home.

After a day of soul-searching, she decided to attend midnight mass. The DeLongpres were not necessarily one-denominational, but she was a deeply religious person, having asked her Lord for advice on many occasions. One piece of advice had turned out pretty good about twenty-six years ago. Tonight she asked guidance about breaking a promise that she had made to her husband many years before. This Christmas they should celebrate The Colonel's birthday. The time and the setting were perfect.

The next morning she called her son aside. Davis' first thought was, *Oh, my God, I'm going to get it now!* But he underestimated his mother and was totally thrown off guard when she offered her idea. He thought it was wonderful because not celebrating his father's birthday had always bothered him. It also mended fences between them for now.

Lillian's next step would be to clear this with the lady of the casa. That was easy. With these two "sisters" from opposite sides of the great pond combining forces, there wasn't much chance of anything getting in their way. The most difficult part would be concealing their efforts from the man himself. But then it came to them. It was going to be Christmas Eve for goodness sakes! With all the commotion of preparations going on for this event, how hard could it possibly be to hide this from the "birthday boy"?

In some parts of the world, folks celebrate this special time on the eve, others on the day itself. The Smiths on one side of Posey Lane might do it differently than the Joneses across the street. Christmas Eve at the ranchero would be one to beat all that any of the families present could ever remember…or forget.

The Colonel and Lillian were in their sumptuous guest quarters just down the upstairs hall from the room their son had occupied since his arrival at the sprawling hacienda. They were preparing for the Christmas Eve activities when they heard a knock on the door. The Colonel opened the door to see their son dressed in a handsome red turtleneck sweater. If nothing else, it was very seasonal.

"Hello there, Daddy. Could I come in for a moment?"

The Colonel laughed at his son's politeness and made a sweeping gesture for Davis to enter. He was a bit surprised by his son's request.

"Daddy, could I speak to Momma for a few minutes? It's nothing all that important. She can tell you about it later."

Both parents gave him a questioning look but smiled their okay. The Colonel was dressed and ready, so he excused himself, saying he would meet them downstairs. He wondered what this could be about. He knew his wife was still upset about the discovery of the Rebecca situation, and just assumed it was a carry-over from earlier. He looked in the mirror by the door, made sure his collar lay perfectly over the lapels of his pale blue sport coat, and walked the half city block down to the gathering place, which was, of course, the dining room.

The festive table was covered by many exquisite Spanish offerings. The Montoya daughters were there, along with Yolanda, her husband, and several of the ranchero's employees.

The Colonel had seen most of the many animals on his new friend's spread, but, with all the farm animals he had seen, there was no sight of anything resembling a turkey. Right in the middle of all the traditional dishes sat a huge bird that The Colonel estimated to weigh about twenty-five pounds. He smiled at Rodolpho and Ireñe. They had obviously done this in respect for him and his family. Rodolpho looked around and inquired of the whereabouts of Lillian and Davis. It was unusual to see The Colonel without his wife.

Everyone began picking up plates and helping themselves to the buffet-style feast. Still no Lillian and Davis. The Colonel was about to see what was keeping them, when he stood up and all the lights went out. He thought out loud, "What the hell...?"

For a few seconds it remained dark, then he saw a flash of light out of his left eye. He saw the swinging doors to the kitchen burst open, and a huge cake with what seemed like thousands of lights on it came into the room. Pushing the cart were the two most important people in his life. It was quite a treat for the eyes and ears. He had never heard "Happy Birthday" sung with a Spanish accent.

Lillian knew her husband very well and could most of the time feel and even predict his moods and reactions to most everything. This was a subject that had only been discussed once and that was many years ago. She saw the surprise, no, that wouldn't cover it. She saw the shock on the face that had been so stolid over the years and decided that now would be the best time to make her move. She ran to him like a little girl would to her daddy, threw her arms around his neck and put her lips to his ear, "I hope you don't mind, darling."

The shock began to fade into a smile, but, before he could answer, his son made the hug a trio. Everyone in that part of Spain began congratulating him.

The party was a great hit, and, sometime during the night, they all remembered why they were all there to begin with. The Colonel's birthday went right into Jesus' without missing a beat. That should have pleased The Colonel and did.

Early Christmas morning, a few hours before daylight, the revelers all went their separate ways. The Colonel thanked all present, especially the Montoyas and his son. He would reserve the right to thank his wife properly in private.

Christmas day was as it should be. The families all went to church around 11:00 a.m. and then came home to a wonderful Christmas dinner...Spanish style. They compared this holiday and how it was spent in America, then how it had been done in Spain for hundreds of years. They all wondered about other countries. Did they celebrate in the same way? The Montoya daughters had learned in school, just recently, how Santa Claus was pronounced in several languages. Everyone got a big laugh when someone would struggle over vowels in the wrong places and sometimes the lack of vowels. After a bunch of this silliness, they settled on St. Nick. This was indeed a special Christmas, but what really happened here? It was far more than just a celebration. This December would change the lives of everyone who was at the ranchero.

Lillian and The Colonel were obviously very happy to see their son for the first time in nearly three years, but look how much more than that had happened. Lillian had never seen her husband take to anyone like he did Rodolpho. Of course, there was Ben and Willie Hampton. Ben was certainly family, and she all but raised Willie, but now T. D. had a buddy!

Lillian socialized with the women in her various clubs and a select few actually visited her famous rose garden, but she had never met anyone quite like Ireñe Montoya. She was attractive, well-educated, and the way that she and Rodolpho carried on just tickled her to death. Even with the unfortunate business with Davis and Rebecca, the mistress of The Willows would leave Spain with her heart full.

Darcy Hampton was always comfortable around Lillian and always had been since that glorious day her Willie brought her home from college. She had been well-protected against the bad things since she'd lived at The Willows, and, except for Lillian, and the ladies at the club, had not really met anyone on the outside. She was obviously a little younger than the other two women, but Ireñe took her in and treated her like an older daughter. This made the little lady from Clearfield College warm right down to her clear-polished toenails.

Willie was without a doubt happy to see his pal and partner. However, he couldn't get enough of Rodolpho. Ever since the two first rode together, he tried to steal him away from everyone if the opportunity presented itself. He marveled at the man's knowledge that seemed to flow out at beck and call. One thing was for certain. Willie didn't have to think of anything to say. Rodolpho's incessant talking filled in all the blanks quite well. In the two weeks left before returning to Hattiesburg, they would have several more rides and sessions.

Rodolpho was a little surprised with these Americans. He at first thought Davis was an exception, but after meeting The Colonel and Willie Hampton, he could put aside any prior feelings or apprehensions. They were not at all like some of the people he had dealt with before from the United States. He knew one thing for sure. He would certainly miss The Colonel when he returned home. He didn't know what Davis had in his mind, or at least not all of it. He saw how much the young man loved his parents and the Hamptons, but could sense something going on in the boy's head. He would worry about missing him a little later.

Ireñe, the woman so instrumental in putting this event together, had also made some new good friends. She thought Lillian was special and wanted to be like her in many ways. Darcy, well, she was just plain delightful with her expressive eyes and quick wit. She was most grateful for the way her husband felt at ease. She knew how he felt about Davis and it was good for Rodolpho to see where he came from and what he was about. Although Davis would not be there forever, he would always be a part of the Montoya family. She now thought it was a good idea about the land on the other side of the fence.

Davis knew he would have to leave soon, which did not make him particularly happy. What a ride these last few weeks had been. He couldn't believe how well everything had worked out. The Rebecca situation he had gone through with his mother still stuck in his heart a bit, but the rest of that wonderful time seemed to wash most of it away. The remaining few days would pressure him to make a decision that wouldn't be easy, but he was a DeLongpre, and he would handle it.

Willie didn't spend all the final days with Rodolpho. He managed a few hours with Davis at his partner's insistence. Davis wanted him to take a look at the now infamous adjacent property. Willie had been patient, as he always had, and now looked forward to seeing the land next door. Davis didn't have to ask Ireñe's permission to use the Cadillac (or Rodolpho's to use the Chevy pickup) but always did out of respect. He figured that Willie had spent enough time on Spanish saddles during the previous days, so he asked the head man at the ranchero if he could show Willie the property and take the truck instead of saddling up. Rodolpho pointed to the keys hanging on the hook by the front door. Davis nodded his thank you, and the partners made their way to the truck.

They climbed in, and Davis turned the key. This was a time to remember the work and escapades they had enjoyed back home.

"Davis, it's a Chevy, and it's red! It's almost like old times!"

They laughed at that, slapping their right hands together. As they drove the next few minutes to the entrance of the property, they reminisced on the good and not-so-good times. Davis down-shifted the V-8 powered Chevy and turned onto the road that led to the house and adjacent buildings that had not been lived in or used for several years.

They got out of the pickup and stood in front of the house for a few minutes. They could see that, at one time, in another era, the house had been a thing of beauty. Rodolpho had boarded up the windows, and they could see evidence of re-roofing and painting but sensed the absence of life.

"Do you want to go in, Willie?"

"I don't think so, pard. I'd almost feel like an intruder. Have you been in there?"

"Yeah, I have. It's a little spooky."

"Okay, good. Let's check out some of the buildings," said Willie cautiously, and they both got back in the truck.

The barns and stables were in surprisingly good condition. Again, Davis saw the evidence of Rodolpho's loyalty to his late friend. He saw the amazement on Willie's face and asked him to comment, but Willie declined and made a motion for them to move on.

They drove to the perimeters of the property and stopped several times to discuss their findings. The fields were green, plush from the seasonal Spanish rains. It was evident that no horses or cattle had been filling their bellies on this range.

Davis stopped the red Chevy in front of the house where their excursion had begun, shut off the engine, and turned to face Willie. He didn't have to say a word. Willie noticed that his pal's mannerisms had not changed since he was the little white boy that used to be his shadow. He got out of the truck, and Davis did the same. They followed the rock-lined path to the front porch on the house where two old chairs still stood. Willie used his index finger to push back his hat.

"I like it, pard. I really do. All I can do is ask you why? I'm trying to understand why a rich boy like you would feel the need to go thousands of miles from home. You could have any part of Mississippi, Georgia, or anyplace else if you wanted. For that matter, so could I. There is something else going on in that noggin of yours, and, before we talk about anything else, I want to hear it. Your folks miss you, Darcy and I miss you, and we all worry about you. I'm going to stand right here until you spit it out!"

Barcelona, the second largest city in Spain, enjoyed a fairly moderate climate. It was protected from frigid weather by the mountains that rose between it and the rest of northern Spain. When one traveled through the pass into the flatlands, the weather could change dramatically. The rainy season had subsided for the most part, but it was still December. The partners had been on their excursion for a few hours and the late afternoon was giving way to the evening. Both agreed that their conversation should be continued in the confines of the red Chevy cab.

A son or daughter should be able to discuss anything of importance with their parents. They should, but somehow it just doesn't always happen that way. Davis decided to tell Willie everything that he had done for almost three years. In the next hour, plus a few minutes, he confided in his best friend.

There wasn't a whole lot to say about his first stop in Amiens, France, because he was there less than a week. However, he did mention the golden girl and how she had acted when he was leaving. Just as he got Willie's attention, he jumped to the Beneventos in Torino, Italy.

Willie interrupted Davis for a brief moment about the extravagance of his purchase of Highlander Chief and foal and how The Colonel had fumed about it. He apologized and motioned Davis to continue.

Davis related in detail the Estrelita story. He told of how he had met her and the temptation he endured at the first sight of her. He described her height, weight, and color of her eyes and hair. He did his best to convince his pal that nothing ever happened until he got that letter from Rebecca.

Willie sat and listened to the adventures of the man he had known as a boy. During the time it took Davis to tell his story, Willie went from his mouth being agape to laughing and slapping his knee all the way to pure amazement. When Davis finally slowed down, all Willie could say was, "You little son of a bitch. I never thought you had it in you!"

It was getting dark now and the talking was just about over. Davis turned out of the driveway of the old ranch, and, as the pickup lights guided them back to the ranchero, Rebecca's name came up again. It was dropped before they pulled to a stop at the hacienda.

"Do you have anything to say, Willie?"

"Yeah, I'm hungry!"

Davis and Willie had a few more brief conversations the following days about the possibilities of acquiring the old ranch. Willie understood why Davis wanted to have something he could call his own. He also knew that Davis wanted him to be a part of it. They had plenty of sources to draw from without Davis going anywhere else. The Beneventos had hundreds of animals with famous bloodlines, Rodolpho Montoya, even more, but Davis still talked about going to Saudi Arabia.

The past few weeks had been magical, even bordering on religious. The DeLongpres and Hamptons were considered as one family and had established a bond with their new friends in Spain. The two families were unified in a way that few in this world have ever had the joy of knowing. The great span separating these two families called the Atlantic Ocean now seemed like a small lake. Their bonds would last for the rest of the lives.

Christmas Eve and Christmas had been absolutely wonderful. The Colonel's surprise could not have been scripted any better if an Oscar-winner had written it. Due to the magnitude of this celebration, New Year's Eve was no more than a formality. However, one more event would have to be celebrated. That would be Davis' twenty-sixth birthday. On his request, it was done without the usual hoopla. The time to say good-bye was now drawing near.

In Memphis, Tennessee, a few days earlier, another young man celebrated his twenty-sixth birthday. It was, however, much more of a blowout for the reigning King of Rock and Roll. Not many people can predict the future, but could it be possible that one day Elvis Aaron Presley and Thurston Davis DeLongpre, III would share their birthdays together?

On the morning of January thirteenth, The Colonel asked his flight crew of three to go to the airport and prepare the DC-4 for the trip back to Hattiesburg. He thanked Rodolfo, along with everyone else, for putting his crew up for the time they were there. His host assured him that, in a house this size, it was absolutely no problem whatsoever.

Davis and his mother spent a few moments together before the family's departure. Lillian asked her son only once if he would please return home with them. She did not beg, but it was a tearful moment as they held each other closely. He held her face in his large but gentle hands and wiped the tears from her cheeks. He told her that he had to finish his business by going to Saudi Arabia but placated her by saying, "I'll be home soon, Momma. I promise."

Davis asked Rodolpho to accompany them to the Barcelona airport. Rodolpho at first declined the request but submitted when Davis insisted. Davis drove with his mother and Darcy sitting in the front seat and with his father, Willie, and Rodolpho in the back. The conversation in the front seat was somewhat subdued. In the back, the three men were quite busy discussing future plans. The Colonel made Rodolpho promise that he and his wife would visit them at The Willows sometime soon.

Davis pulled the Cadillac to the gate at the private entrance. The Colonel rolled down the back window and showed the guard his clearance papers.

The plane with the name "*LILL*" painted under the pilot side window was already warming up as they said their final good-byes. Davis and Rodolpho stood on the tarmac while they watched the silver and blue DC-4 taxi and waited for clearance from the tower. The pilot hit the throttle full bore as the big bird lifted off the runway and disappeared into the cloud cover.

They were about halfway back to the ranchero before a word was spoken. Rodolpho looked at Davis and noticed the somber look in his eyes. He was searching for something appropriate to say but nothing would come to mind.

Deciding to go against the mood, he chuckled softly and said, "You have grown quite comfortable with my wife's car. Tell me, how does it drive?"

Davis looked at him quizzically and answered, "You mean you don't know?"

"Know? She's never let me drive it!" Rodolpho responded.

This broke Davis up. Rodolpho's attempt at humor had done the job and they shared a much-needed laugh.

For the first couple of days after the visitors from America had departed, the Montoyas felt an emptiness that was very new to them. Their lives had been enriched by this special time, and, as they lay in bed together at the end of the day, they talked about their feelings. They found it difficult to brighten the bleak air that permeated the ranchero and wondered how Davis was coping with his own feelings. They could see that he was not ready to leave them yet, noticing that he was finding excuses and things to do to avoid his eventual departure. They went along with this because, as selfish as they deemed it to be, they were not about to question his reasons. They didn't want him to leave either.

While Davis was still in the service in Germany, he had carefully researched and planned his itinerary. He had been to Amiens, France; Torino, Italy; and Barcelona, Spain, where he was now. The last stop in his plan was to Saudi Arabia, where many of the world's finest horses were from. He had only spent a few days in the first two locations. However, he had been at the Montoya Ranchero for almost half the year. It had been almost three years since he had been home, but he was finding it very difficult to leave this place he had grown to love.

Like when he was in the Army, he adjusted to Rodolpho's early rising. He acquired the habit of keeping the drapes open on the large window in his room that faced east. It had been about a week since his parents and the Hamptons had left. He was sleeping on his side and felt a warming sensation caused by the rising sun bathing his face. He got up, dressed, and went downstairs to the kitchen and dining area but didn't see Rodolpho or Ireñe like he normally did. Yolanda was there, busy with breakfast preparation. He bid her cheery "*buenos dias*" and she told him that they probably slept in. He wolfed down a sweet roll and coffee and headed toward the barns.

Rodolpho had one of the most modern operations Davis had seen in his brief travels. There was the finely equipped lab, the luxurious stables for his prime breeding stock, and the latest machinery available, but the Spanish rancher also retained many of the old traditions that he and his family before him had started. There was also an old barn that stood alone a few hundred feet from the others that wasn't used much but, like the old house on the other side of the fence, was kept up.

He opened the big barn doors and walked over to the ladder that led to the hayloft. He tested the first couple of rungs for stability and climbed to the top of the loft. He saw the bales neatly stacked against the wall, then padded his way across the carpet of hay that covered the floor. He pushed open the doors where the golden straw was pitched to the corral one story below.

As he stood looking at the ground below, he recalled Rebecca snapping a rose from Lillian's garden and the two of them taking a walk. They were in their teens and everything was wonderful. Rebecca would take one petal at a time, hold it up and let the breeze flutter it away.

"He loves me, he loves me not. He loves me, he loves me not...."

Davis didn't have a rose or even a flower but suddenly got an urge. He took the pocketknife that Rodolpho had given him and always carried, cut open a couple bales and grabbed a pitchfork. He pitched the hay from the loft to the dirt below until he had used up the two bales. He cut open another two and continued pitching until the sweat went clear through his denim shirt. He took off the shirt and pitched some more.

"She loves me, she loves me not. She loves me, she loves me not...."

He did this in rhythm and went to, "Should I leave tomorrow, should I leave the next day? Should I leave tomorrow, should I leave the next day…?"

The exhausted young man stopped and looked at the pile of winter hay that had accumulated below. He suddenly felt very foolish. He shook his head and wiped the sweat from his forehead with his forearm. His gloveless hands were sore as he chuckled, "Did I just think what I think I thought? This is getting way to deep."

He laughed, dropped the pitchfork, and dove onto the pile of hay below. There was a substantial pile of the ground, but, when he landed, it knocked the breath out of him. When he was able to breathe normally again, he said to the sky he was looking up at, "It is time for me to get back to business!"

Chapter Twenty-One

The DC-4 reached its cruising altitude by the time the visitors from Hattiesburg had settled in. They flew over Madrid, then Portugal. There was nothing under them now but the blue waters of the Atlantic. The weary travelers unfastened their seatbelts and went to the lounging area situated over the wings. To help pass the hours, they began discussing the events of the month they had just spent in Spain. This was not one of The Colonel's meetings. It was kind of like a relaxed forum of sorts, where anyone could and was expected to voice their opinions. However, someone had to initiate the proceedings, and, since no one volunteered, The Colonel began with, "Well, what do ya'll think about the month we spent in Spain? Lill, honey, do you want to share anything with us?"

She sat still for a moment and, before answering, tugged at her curls. "T. D., I had a wonderful time. It was so nice to see my boy, I mean our boy, after all this time, but he *has* changed. I don't know if it's because he's older...well, tell me, T. D., didn't he look a lot older? The Montoyas made us feel at home, and I hope they will come over and visit us, but damn it! I want him to come *home* where he belongs!"

The Colonel saw little tears starting to grow in his wife's eyes and put his arm around her. He understood, more now, what she must have endured all those times he had been traveling and left her alone.

The Colonel had listened to his wife's input and now waited for Willie or Darcy to voice *their* assessments of the trip to Spain. The Hamptons had had a wonderful time and, like Willie mentioned, most of what needed saying was said at the meeting after dinner with the Montoyas. They all agreed this was true, so after recalling some of the highlights, they just ate and had a few drinks.

Lillian and Darcy took short naps. The next thing they heard was when Captain Rex Henderson broke in from the cockpit, "Colonel, I just want to let you know that we've been fighting a headwind for about eight hundred miles, and we're going to have to set down in Miami instead of flying straight through. Refueling will put us behind about forty minutes, no longer."

"Any other problems, Rex?"

"No, sir. None other."

Davis took his time packing his bags. Every sock, every set of underwear felt like it weighed a ton. Every shirt had a memory of one day or night he'd enjoyed at the ranchero the past few months. He finally finished and placed his bags on the floor by the door. He went to the window where he first saw that imaginary movie. It seemed that nothing had changed since that first day. At least the view hadn't changed. He needed to have one last look at this picture to take with him now that the end of his stay was here. He announced to an empty room, "I know I'm going to really hate this part."

His thoughts were interrupted by a knock on the door. He recognized Yolanda's high-pitched but sweet voice as she called out, "My husband is here to take your bags downstairs…and then he can drive you to the airport."

As he descended the wide staircase to the foyer, he saw the whole Montoya family assembled to wish him *"vaya con Dios."* He gave each of the three girls a hug, then hugged and kissed the cheek of a teary-eyed Ireñe. He and Rodolpho gave each other a hug, then made it manly by slapping each other on the back. His friend pulled away and they began the walk across the hardwood floor through the big oak doors and onto the stone patio. He heard the familiar clacking of Rodolpho's hard-heeled Spanish boots hitting the inlaid rocks on the veranda. He wondered how long it would be or if he would ever hear them again. They stood silent for a moment watching the horses move across the fields.

"Davis, I am a man with many blessings. I find it impossible to put into words what the past few months have meant to us. You are like the son that Ireñe and I never had. My daughters adore you and will miss you also. We are proud to include your whole family as part of ours. It is important for you to know that our ranchero will always be your home. If your future includes your spending part of your life living in Spain, my heart would be filled with much joy. There are several matters I want to discuss with you *and* your family, so Ireñe and I intend to come to your Willows as soon as the mares give birth come spring. I wish you luck in the desert, and *vaya con Dios*."

As they drove away, the waving Montoyas began to fade from sight. Soon after, the hacienda did also. This was a sad sight for the twenty-six-year-old eyes that began to mist over. He was glad to hear they were going to visit the

Willows and wondered what kind of business, other than horses, Rodolpho was talking about. He figured it had something to do with the conversation he and his father were gabbing about on the way to the airport last week. No matter, he was glad he would see them in the next few months and couldn't wait for Rodolpho and Ireñe to see what The Colonel, Willie, and he had built.

The mind does indeed play strange games. He had tears in his eyes. Was it because he was leaving the Montoyas and Spain, or was that big hole that Becky's letter left in his soul not healed yet? As he checked his wristwatch to see how much time he had to catch his plane, he did it again. He knew of the six-hour time difference and figured that Rebecca was probably having lunch with her husband or whomever. He hated that habit he'd acquired. They had no future. No matter who was to blame, that is just the way it was. He should just leave it at that and move on.

He was thankful for one thing at least. She didn't live in Hattiesburg anymore. He knew eventually their paths would cross and seeing her would certainly be unavoidable. He half-heartedly wished her well because *he* wasn't all that happy. Yes, he had to move forward now, but how? Rebecca had been his only girl...unless you count Estrelita. His sadness turned into a low chuckle as he tried to imagine his mother serving tea to Estrelita on the east terrace. Oh, yeah, she would fit right in at The Willows...*wrong!*

As the car crested a hill in the pass leading to the city, the morning sun broke through the cloud cover and caught him full in the eyes. It was as if a flash camera had gone off. Everything was awash in a golden haze...Céleste Genevive...she had not made a big impression on him when he had been at the chateau in France, but he would be a fool if he didn't notice her sultry glances. Sultry might be the wrong description, but they were sure as hell more than casual. He rubbed his eyes until the blur from the flash of sunlight was gone and remembered that last morning when he was leaving for Italy. The sound of hooves and that golden hair flying in the breeze and how the sunlight framed her now became like the frozen frame of a movie. She was a beautiful young woman but couldn't have been more than seventeen or eighteen. He thought his mother might like her, but there it was again. Would she accept anyone other than Rebecca?

As the car pulled to a stop in front of the terminal, he was jolted back to reality. How quickly the forty-minute drive had gone by. He flagged the skycap to take his bags, checked the car for anything he might have dropped, thanked his driver, and bid him *adios*. He was finally again on track, so why did he feel so damned weird? He shook this off and got in line. There were three or four travelers in front of him, so he had a few minutes to think. When it was his turn, he began to give the desk attendant the necessary information…but then stopped.

"Could you please change that for me? I would like to book a flight through Paris to Amiens, France."

Chapter Twenty-Two

Davis had some time to kill after changing his airline ticket and used that to alert the Genevives of his sudden arrival. He had discussed the greedy Frenchman with Rodolpho and now thought he knew him a little better than when he left. He also knew that the Frenchman would like to see him at any time and, if not him, at least his money.

Hubert Genevive loved his sister, but he didn't believe that his father showed him the proper respect due an eldest son. She was the last of the four children born to Jon-Pierre and Emma. It seemed that Céleste was the center of the universe, especially where her father was concerned. He didn't care for any of the suitors that pursued his sister from time to time, and *that* part of being a big brother, he enjoyed. After Davis left, he used to tease her about being so obvious in front of him. Not to be outdone, Céleste came back with, "Obvious, my brother? At least I didn't give him a pair of my boots! However, that will be our secret, okay?"

An agreement was struck or a deal made, and no one but the two of them would ever know this. Maybe he could get her married and go to America? This thought made him chuckle, but, in truth, he was the only member of the family who cared for the American...other than the obvious.

As the months passed, Hubert was becoming more involved with helping his father run the huge ranch. This pleased Jon-Pierre, but Hubert didn't know if he really did this for real or was only trying to make his father notice him more. His father had given him some light bookkeeping to do toward the end of the month. He sat at the big antique desk and looked around the luxuriously appointed but very manly office. As he took it all in, he forced a smile that said, "one day all this will be mine." He finished basking and went back to his paperwork. The phone jolted his thoughts with its loud, penetrating ring. This startled him, but, after two bells, he picked it up. "This is Hubert

Genevive. What can I do for you?"

"Hubert, this is Davis DeLongpre. How is everything in Amiens?"

"Hello, Davis. Where are you?"

"I'm just now finishing up in Spain, and I thought I would take another look at the stock up there, if that's okay?"

"Fine, I'll tell my father. Bye the bye, how are the boots working out?"

Hubert closed the ledger and went to look for his father. He had buzzed the extension to the main barn and no one picked it up, so he decided to find Jon-Pierre and deliver the news. He didn't know what his father's reaction would be but wanted to find out what would happen if he made a decision on his own.

He spotted his father and two of his assistants at the workout corral observing a two-year-old hopeful. The boss heard his son calling, turned toward the entrance, and motioned to Hubert to join them. The eldest son went to where his father was leaning on the fence and stood beside him.

"Davis DeLongpre just called. He's leaving Spain and asked if he could return here to look at more stock."

"What did you tell him?"

"I told him to come on. We are always open for business."

Jon-Pierre gave his son a stare that made the hair on his arms stand up, but it gradually turned to a sneaky look of greed. "When will the overly eager American be arriving?"

"About an hour before sundown today. Shall I send Robey and the driver?"

"No, my conscience bears just a little twinge at the enormous amount of francs he left me in exchange for Highlander Chief. I think *I* will meet him this time."

"Okay, Papa, but, instead of the driver, let me take you into town."

The elder Genevive looked at his son again for a brief moment and then put his arm around Hubert's shoulder. They began walking to the house. "Okay, my son. Let's do that."

As they went in the back door toward the dining area, the conversation continued, "Remember, Papa, you did give him that foal, so I don't think you should concern yourself too much."

A wicked little laugh from the Frenchman stopped short.... "I wonder what he wants this time? Well, we won't have to wait very long to solve the mystery of his return. I think it would be interesting if he stays with us instead of in town. I would like to arrange to meet the pup's father. He's the prize."

Emma heard the men come in and went to see if their lunch was ready.

After seeing that it almost was, she entered the room. "Who are you talking about, my husband?"

The news of the visitor's arrival did not bring her any pleasure. She stared at the elder Genevive and said, "I'm mystified by your behavior. After all the trouble we had with Céleste when he left before, I'm shocked that you would ever allow him back!"

"Emma, first of all, it's business. Secondly, it has been many months and I believe *ma petite* has no doubt forgotten all about him."

"I'll remember your words, monsieur!"

Céleste had indeed given her parents, especially her father, quite a bit of grief after Davis' departure. She went out of her way on several occasions to bring up his name. When some of the local young men would ask her out, she would shut them down and remind her mother and father of her prediction that Davis would return for her. This had caused a good amount of friction among the family. The only relief from this was the teasing from her brother Hubert and her sarcastic comebacks to him.

Her father always delegated chores and responsibilities to her three older brothers but never to Céleste. She took full advantage of this, and, whenever she could, she would spend a few days with her girlfriends in town or at one of the surrounding ranches.

They finished their late lunch and were preparing to leave for Amiens. Minutes before their departure to pick up the young traveler from Mississippi via Spain, Emma left them with a departing comment, "Highlander Chief must have done well for him!"

The lady said a little prayer that Céleste would stay in town with her friends for the weekend, or at least until Davis had finished his business and left for home. Sometimes prayers are answered…then again, sometimes they are not.

Davis landed in Paris and made the connection for the short shuttle flight to Amiens. There were only six passengers on the two-engine plane, and the slightly nervous Mr. DeLongpre struck up a conversation with a well-groomed English-speaking French gentleman, who introduced himself as Dr. Montatari. He was the head physician for the small Amiens hospital.

The pilot expertly maneuvered the small craft through the buffeting winds from the English Channel and made a near-perfect landing.

Davis extended his hand to the doctor and told him it was nice to have made his acquaintance. Dr. Montatari returned the gesture and said, "Monsieur DeLongpre, I don't know how long you will be staying in our country, but, if you should develop any gastric discomfort from our food, please feel free to drop by, and I'll treat it for you. Or we could just share a 'dose' of our hospital coffee."

Davis had expected to see the imposing figure of Robey meeting him like the last time he landed. It was a surprise, to say the least, when he saw Jon-Pierre and the giver-of-boots standing beside the limo. *Hmmmm*....

When Davis had said good-bye to Uncle Sam and called Jon-Pierre Genevive from the ten-room hotel in Amiens, he'd been given the courtesy of a penniless drunk trying to hustle a drink at a neighborhood bar. The Frenchman made him wait two days before inviting him to the chateau. Now this same rude man was there to meet the plane. In about a half a year his stature had improved one hundredfold.

Davis was not the only man in Europe who was not fond of the greedy French rancher. Vittorio Benevento knew who he was. Rodolpho Montoya had either experienced firsthand or known someone who had dealt with this man with no conscience.

A slight young man in a tan uniform was unloading the baggage for Davis and his new friend, the doctor. He brought Davis' three bags over to the dark blue limo, got the key to the trunk from Hubert, and quickly put them in the proper place. Davis had the monetary system worked out and tipped the attendant a bit more than customary. Jon-Pierre saw this and manufactured a smile.

"Welcome back to our little part of northern France. We are flattered that you have chosen to visit us again."

"Many thanks, Mr. Genevive, and you too, Hubert."

Davis pulled his trouser leg up a few inches and displayed the now broken-in boots. This brought a nod and smile from Hubert. His father, however, had no idea what this signified but covered his curiosity by saying, "Monsieur DeLongpre, we want you to be a guest at our humble home while you are conducting business with us."

They motored through the same pass as before, but this time Davis was aware of them being on the Genevive property much sooner. He could only muster one question, "Where is the big fellow, Robey?"

Hubert was driving as his father and Davis were conversing in the back seat.

"Robey, as we call him, is attending to other tasks I have hired him to do."

"Oh, that's fine. I only asked because I was so impressed by his congenial manner."

Hubert turned the custom-made Rolls Royce off the two-lane macadam surface and began to drive the quarter mile of crushed pebble driveway that led to the chateau. About halfway to the mansion, he pressed the button on the dash that lowered the window separating the front seat from the passenger area.

"Papa, do I pull up in front or drive to the back entrance?"

"Hubert, a guest of Monsieur DeLongpre's stature will always enter our home through the front door."

Davis could only laugh inwardly about what a difference six months could make. The only thing missing was the beautiful Céleste charging up to meet them on her steed.

Emma Genevive, although not happy about the American's return, still heeded her husband's comment about this being business. "If that's the way he wants this to be…why not take this situation to the extreme." She and her staff decided to go the distance and make a special "American meal" of hamburgers and French fries. This would probably be the first time ground beef patties were served on croissants.

Davis and Jon-Pierre exited the car. No sooner had they done this than two of the chateau's employees were picking up his luggage. Hubert and Davis crossed the foyer and began the ascent up the stairs, with the people carrying his bags right behind. They went to the same room where he had spent the two nights during his first visit. Jon-Pierre watched this and was a bit puzzled by the attention being paid by his son to the returning American guest. When Hubert came back downstairs, he saw that the door to his father's office was open. He tried to sneak by, but he heard his father's voice, which said, "Hubert, come in here!"

The young man froze in his tracks and obeyed the command. He stood in front of the big desk and waited for further instructions. He sat down when ordered and again felt the stare from the man he had feared his whole life. After enduring these moments of silence, he heard his father ask, "Why are you paying so much attention to Monsieur DeLongpre?"

"Papa, the man is carrying a substantial bankroll. I just want to make sure he spends it all with us."

Jon-Pierre felt a sense of pride coming from his first born. He had sometimes doubted the young man's abilities and tenacity. Maybe, just maybe, this boy could someday take over the empire that had been handed down to him by *his* father.

It had been one hell of a day for Davis. He had made a major decision at the Barcelona airport. He picked up his heavy leather bag and heaved it on the bed. He was surprised that the man who had treated him so rudely and gaffed him on the price for Highland Chief had been there to pick him up at the tiny airport. This was, however, something he could figure out given an hour or so.

The golden flash of light on the way to the airport was something that nobody other than he could ponder and enjoy.

After Jon-Pierre was satisfied with his son's answer, he dismissed him and went to talk to his wife, who he already knew was not thrilled with the American's visit. He was pleased with her choice of food for the evening. He thought, *They are beginning to understand. The dinner should make their guest feel as if he were home, comfortable, and easy to deal with.*

Emma could see that her husband was pleased and decided to quench her curiosity.

"Tell me about your ride from town."

"Well, Emma, he says he wants to take another look at our stock, but I sense a subtle change in his demeanor."

"Like I said before, maybe Highlander Chief has done well for him."

"I'll see for myself this evening. Somehow I believe there is a little bit more involved here, but if all he wants to do is take another look at our stock, that's all I care about. Have you heard from *ma petite*?"

"No, and I hope she doesn't change her mind."

With that Emma rose and began to leave the room but said over her shoulder, "Dinner is at eight o'clock. Our other guests should be arriving around seven-thirty. I'm going to bathe and get dressed."

The evening was a success. Everyone seemed to enjoy the American bill of fare, and, after the dessert and a libation or two, the guests began departing.

Jon-Pierre thought the time was right to talk to Davis about the real reason he was here. Not that he totally disbelieved him, but the American had seen his herd only months previous, and the ranch had not produced any new foals. There had to be another reason for this unexpected visit. He asked Davis if he would like to join him for another snifter and cigar. Davis agreed and the two men went to the bar and poured a generous amount of the mellow liquid in the bell-shaped glasses. Davis had never actually enjoyed cigars but now and then relished the cognac. As he watched, Jon-Pierre tipped up his glass and took another drag from his leaf-stuffed brown tube. It reminded him of all those after dinner discussions at the table with his father and mother.

They had talked quietly for a few minutes while making plans for the next morning when someone who was not expected surprised them. They turned to the source of a tea-with-cream-and-honey voice that said, "Monsieur DeLongpre, it is so nice to see you. What an unexpected pleasure."

Davis looked at this lovely vision with her hand placed on the doorjamb and her torso and hips positioned just right. He couldn't see her face, but the glow from the chandeliers and candles in the dining room framed her perfectly. Once again, the golden sensation enveloped his being, that same sensation that made him change his plane reservations.

Both men were spellbound, but in two distinctly different ways. Davis was mesmerized, and Jon-Pierre was painfully aware of his *ma petite's* obvious beauty. They both heard her emphatic statement.

"Papa, I know you and Monsieur DeLongpre have business, but it will have to wait until we finish our morning ride."

Jon-Pierre was, for once, speechless. He wanted to reprimand his daughter for her rude behavior, but nothing would come out. How did she know the American was here? Céleste turned and said, "So, I'll see you in the morning…Davis?"

As she left the room, both men turned and looked at each other. Again, nothing came out of their surprised mouths.

The morning at the chateau was kissed with sunshine, but it was late January and quite nippy. With the fresh baked croissants and cups of hot coffee warming their insides, they took off to the stables.

A ranch hand was there, holding two horses all saddled and ready to ride. Davis saw steam coming from their mouths and kiddingly exhaled in Céleste's direction.

Céleste had selected a powerful stallion for her guest, almost as though she was testing his mettle. Davis had ridden most of his life, especially in the last few months with Rodolpho Montoya, so he looked forward to the challenge.

The ride through the still-dewy fields began very quietly, but after fifteen minutes or so, a silent competition began. Céleste goaded her mount into a full gallop and laughed back at Davis. He spurred his own horse, and the race was on. Even as small as she looked on her big mount, she handled her charge with expert hands. She rode like there was no tomorrow, completely fearless. They were neck and neck as they all but flew over a rise and scrambled down a hill to a lovely pond at the bottom of a valley. Céleste actually beat Davis to the pond and was already on the ground and leading her horse to the water's edge when he stopped his mount. She cutely cocked her head slightly and smiled up at him. "Next time, I think I will let *you* win."

After giving their winded mounts a breather, they began a slow ride back to the stables. Davis had a difficult time starting a conversation with her, but she didn't seem to mind, so he just left it at that.

Céleste gave the reins of her horse to a stable hand and went to help Davis. As they were backing the high-spirited animal into his stall, he banged against the walls. The noise startled a barn owl. The frightened bird screamed, swooping down from the rafters. The roaring sound of its flapping wings pushed the big stallion over the edge. The horse reared in panic. Davis reacted instantly.

"Céleste!"

He dove, pushing her out of the way but wasn't able to get clear himself. The big hooves came down and struck the side of his head. Davis collapsed in slow motion, and Céleste screamed, "Davis, my God!"

She saw the blood flowing from the large gaping wound. The stable personnel heard her scream, and, in minutes, a half dozen men converged on the stall. Jon-Pierre also heard his daughter's scream and ran in the direction of the stables. Her father took over in his brusque manner, giving orders that were obeyed instantly.

The men put several layers of straw in the bed of a pickup and covered it with heavy blankets for the ride to the hospital in town. Jon-Pierre got into the passenger seat and motioned his daughter to do the same. "No, Papa. I'm going to ride in back with Davis."

The ride into town was very scary for all concerned. Céleste tried to stop the bleeding by holding a heavy cloth over the wound. It was very cold in the back as the pickup sped toward the Amiens hospital. Two of the ranch hands were on either side of Davis to make sure he didn't slide and complicate his already life-threatening injury. Céleste knelt over him and tried her best but couldn't do much except pray.

The small staff at the emergency room reacted quickly and was able to stop the bleeding to the point where they could shave all the hair off one side of his head to prepare for the almost one hundred stitches that would be needed to close the wound. The doctor who performed the stitching said to one of the attending nurses, "I can't believe this. I just shook this young man's hand two days ago and invited him to come in and say hello. He sure didn't waste any time."

The staff did the necessary clean-up, dressed their patient in hospital attire, and settled him into the intensive care unit where round-the-clock nurses were assigned. Jon-Pierre gave instructions that no expense would be spared. Whatever it took, he demanded Davis got the best, even if they had to bring help in from other towns or cities. From the time the horse's hooves struck his head, to when he was being stitched up, Davis never regained consciousness.

As soon as he was put in bed, Céleste was given permission to take up a vigil beside him. The nurse took one look at the blood-covered young woman and said that, while it would be all right for her to do this, she'd have to clean up first. She showered and was lent some of the nurse's hospital clothes to wear. Once ensconced by his bed, she was determined not to move.

Finally, Jon-Pierre had time to call Emma. She had witnessed the truck hauling Davis away to town and was obviously concerned. A half an hour or so later, Hubert showed up and was mad at himself for not being there when his friend was in trouble. He was pacing back and forth when the phone rang. They both went to answer it at the same time, but Emma held up her hand before picking up the receiver.

"Jon-Pierre?"

"Yes, dear, see if you can find the DeLongpre's file, so we can call his parents when we find out more."

"Is he…?"

"We don't know yet. He is in the ICU, and your daughter won't leave his side. Please try and find that file. No, when you find it, just get Robey to drive you in."

"Okay, but we have another situation. Hubert just got home, and he wants to be there also."

"Emma, I don't know. It is quite crazy around here, and I am not sure if there should be…."

"Jon-Pierre, I don't think he is going to take no very easily!"

"Okay, just hurry!"

Robey dropped Emma and Hubert off in front of the small Amiens hospital. He asked if there were any instructions and Emma told him just to stay close and check in from time to time. Mother and son went to find the father. They found him in a hallway close to where Davis lay in the ICU. He took the file from Emma and scanned it quickly and said, "I've been trying to get an opinion from one of the doctors, but they have only shaken their heads and told me they have not made all the tests yet. I don't know *what* we are going to tell his parents."

"Maybe there is nothing to tell them yet. Maybe in a few hours he will wake up."

"I pray you are correct, Emma. This could turn into a terrible tragedy."

The Genevives tried to take their daughter to get something to eat but without success. When they returned from supper, they brought some soup and hot bread, but again she refused. Jon-Pierre and Emma took turns staying close to their daughter as she held Davis' hand and stared at his motionless body. After hours of this, they became almost as concerned about Céleste's behavior as they were about Davis' condition.

From the moment he arrived, a steady stream of doctors and technicians came in and out of Davis' room. Their tasks were not nearly as difficult as getting Céleste to move so they could work. As soon as one of them had gone, she would be right back beside him again. They complained to the admitting doctor when he came in from a nap.

Dr. Montatari checked on his patient's vital signs, and they were as good as could be expected, but he was still unconscious. He took the Genevives aside for a short conference, suggesting they now call his parents. He also asked that they please get through to their daughter and tell her he's not in favor of her being here. But, if this is the only way, please tell her to cooperate with the nurses and technicians.

"Doctor, I don't want to alarm his parents unnecessarily. Can you give me more specific information?"

"Monsieur Genevive, there is nothing to do but wait. Sometimes with an injury of this nature, a person wakes immediately, while other times, it may take days or even weeks. There is no way to predict how the body will protect itself. Something has happened to the brain, and his body has shut down to allow the healing process to begin. If there is any additional swelling, we will have to move him to surgery. So far, none of our tests indicate this to be the case. Right now, that's the situation we're in. I wish I could tell you more."

"Should my husband call the young man's parents in America now, or wait a while longer?"

"I think it would be wise to call them as soon as possible. They should be made aware of the situation. At this point, it could go either way."

The Colonel finished most of the second half of his bacon, lettuce, and tomato sandwich. While waiting for his wife to finish hers (with the crusts cut off), he toyed with the remains of his potato salad. The sign that she was through was when she daintily dabbed at the corners of her mouth with her napkin. After more than thirty years of marriage and him watching her eat, he still wondered how she never really seemed to chew anything.

"Merciful heavens, T. D., I have just too many things on my agenda for this afternoon. I wish I had never let those women vote me president of the guild."

"Honey, you always moan about it, but I know how you like to organize things and hang around with those uppity women. I'd rather you organize than gripe about them."

"I wish you wouldn't tease me about my friends. They are really good at heart. Anyway, what are your plans for the day?"

"Willie and I have a lot do with the last of the horses that came in from Spain, and…oh, I called Pasadena this morning and they assured me that your shipment of bare roots would be here this afternoon. I've got the men preparing the beds as we speak. I'll be interested to see if your new hybrids live up to their glowing reports."

"Oh, good. Please remember to tell your guys to add enough mulch and, for God's sake, not to drown them with all those concoctions they keep coming up with."

"Yes, my love. I'll watch them like they were my own. Now you have a nice day with all your…."

"Oh, there's Daniel blowing his horn. Gotta go!"

The Colonel kissed his wife good-bye, took his hat off the hook in the hallway, and stopped in Lillian's garden to see if the workers were following instructions.

"James, put a little more bark shavings in those holes before you add the fertilizer."

They nodded and began to follow his orders. He proceeded to join Willie at the office adjacent to the stables. As he walked through the massive barn doors and entered the office, he saw Willie sitting at his desk poring through the daily mail. He imagined his late friend Ben doing the same thing if he had been here.

Willie looked up when he heard the door open and said, "Good morning, Pop."

Every time Willie called him "Pop," it took the great man back to the time when Willie was a little tyke and had lost his father. "Pop" was something special that he liked the sound of. In all the years since Davis came into the picture, his son never called him that. He was always called father, and then daddy when he curtailed his travels and began spending more time at home. Willie was forty-one years old now, and "Pop" still sounded great.

The two men were discussing things pertaining to their daily business when the phone's ringing broke into their discussion. Willie had always and would always be the one to pick up the instrument.

"Good morning, Willow's Wind Stables."

"This is Jon-Pierre Genevive in Amiens, France. I'd like to speak with Colonel DeLongpre." Willie recognized the name and handed The Colonel the phone.

"This is Colonel DeLongpre. What can I do for you?"

"Monsieur, ah, Colonel DeLongpre, I am at the hospital in the town close to my ranch. I am afraid I have some bad news for you. Your son Davis has been injured."

All the color from The Colonel's face began to drain. His heartbeat increased as he took a deep breath and said, "Mr. Genevive, please continue."

Jon-Pierre went on with the horrible details. The Colonel's mind was traveling beyond the speed of sound. Willie could sense that something was terribly wrong and got up from his desk and went to The Colonel's side. He saw the anguish and frightened look in the man's eyes and waited while he hung up the phone in slow motion.

"What is it, Pop…Davis?"

"He's been hurt, Willie. A horse kicked him in the head, and he's in intensive care."

Willie felt his countenance cave in. All he could do was put his hand on the big man's shoulder.

"Willie, we've got to find Lillian! We've got to find her now!"

Willie asked The Colonel to sit down while he went to find Daniel. He didn't think either one of them should drive. He didn't find Daniel, he was with Lillian, and so they piled into The Colonel's personal car. The Colonel started the car, but Willie ordered him to stop.

"What are you doing, Willie?"

"Sorry, Pop. I'm going to get Darcy."

"Oh, okay, you're right."

Willie jumped out of the car and scrambled the one hundred plus yards to his house. He grabbed his surprised wife and half dragged her back to the waiting vehicle. The men had no idea where Lillian was at that moment, but Darcy did. It was a woman thing. The men didn't know the location, nor had they ever concerned themselves with this information. Darcy told Willie to drive to the Women's Guild headquarters.

Lillian was giving a Badge of Merit to one of the club members. They were standing on a slightly elevated stage where Lillian was giving the award. She saw her small audience turn their heads to the entrance of the hall. Lillian followed their collective stare to see her husband and two great friends standing by the door. Darcy had been there several times before, but her husband and The Colonel never had. This visit was totally out of the ordinary. She cut the speech short, stepped off the stage, and walked up the aisle to where the trio stood. "What is going on, T. D.?"

Although Colonel DeLongpre had been a part of many volatile situations all over the world and had solved most of them, the sight of his bride of thirty plus years coming toward him made his throat tighten up. He really didn't know how to deliver the news. After all the confrontations he had ever experienced with heads of companies and heads of the state, he decided to just go for it.

"Lill, our boy has been hurt up somewhere in France. Honey, before you ask, he didn't go to Saudi Arabia."

After Mr. and Mrs. DeLongpre embraced, Darcy put her arm around Lillian's shoulders. They all boarded the car and headed back to the only place of peace they all knew. The huge trees that bordered the lane now seemed to be singing a different song. They now wept as willows should.

Daniel was also concerned. He had been involved with this regal family for many years now and had always been in the background. This had not changed over time and never would. He drove the car containing his family to the parking area between the big house and the path leading to the Hamptons residence.

The limo came to a stop. Darcy still had her arm around Lillian and walked her to the back door. Doctor Scanton Lane was summoned and, in the span of a half-hour or so, was there to administer a sedative to The Willows' first lady.

Lillian and Rebecca had not been in touch the last few months. This had weighed heavily on the lady's mind and no wonder. She had picked Miss Thompson to be her boy's future wife. She found the reason for this lack of communication on the plains of northern Spain one chilly day.

This was a very traumatic time. The family doctor's sedative helped a little, and, while his wife was still in a state of semi-consciousness, The Colonel was planning for the trip to France. After giving instructions to his crew to ready the private plane again, he had to talk to Willie and Darcy. He took Mr. and Mrs. Hampton aside to ask their advice.

Willie was somewhat of a mess to start with after hearing about his brother Davis. The worst thing was not knowing what the *worst* thing could entail. He wanted to go to France, but then there was the business they had all worked so hard for. The few weeks in Spain had been wonderful, but the business at the ranch had suffered somewhat for it.

Willie took the pressure that he knew The Colonel was feeling off by saying, "Pop, I really want to go, but I choose not to. You and Tilly go. If things get to the point where you need Darcy and me, then we'll be there in a Mississippi second."

"I know that, Willie. This is something I most certainly will depend on."

This freed The Colonel's mind to do what he had to do. He went to his wife and informed her of how this emergency trip was going to be handled.

Lillian told him that she had not informed Rebecca about them going to Spain. He understood this, but asked his wife what she wanted to do now. The sedative had worn off, and she was thinking a bit clearer. "T. D., I think I should call Rebecca and let her know what's happening and invite her to join us."

"Lill, do what you think is necessary, but make it brief. We have to go immediately."

Lillian called Rebecca's number in Gulfport and left a message when it was obvious the girl was not at home. She also tried the Radio-TV station, only to find that Rebecca had taken a couple of days off. This was all Lillian could do, but at least she made an effort.

Colonel DeLongpre was a man of vision. He knew he couldn't manage his empire by car or train any longer. He had acquired holdings in many parts of the world. The advent of jet travel was still in its embryo stage in 1959 when he purchased a Douglas DC-4 transport and gutted it. He had a conference room built and made every seat first class. Next came a bar and a bed in the section just before the tail. The plane was equipped with extra fuel tanks to be able to fly great distances. Then something happened to change all this. He became involved with his son and Willie's plan to establish a first class horse ranch. He could afford to have this refurbished aircraft be at his beck and call. The trip to Spain was as important as his trips to places like South Africa and Australia. Now, he would need it again. When he called Captain Rex Henderson to prepare for this emergency flight to France, he was having a wonderful afternoon with his son and daughter. When he came home and was told by his wife that The Colonel needed him, she was disappointed, but he could only say, "Well, honey, he does pay the bills, and we are living pretty damn good." Rex returned his boss' call and listened to his request. He told The Colonel what was required.

"The airport in Amiens can't handle our plane, so we have to land in Paris and arrange a shuttle of some sort for the remaining ninety miles."

The travel arrangements were made. All that was left was a final call to the hospital in Ameins.

Jon-Pierre had not slept all that much. He even questioned himself about his concern for the American boy's well-being. Sometime during this crisis, his intentions had taken a full turn. Was he now only thinking of making himself richer, or was he really concerned? Was he worried about his *ma petite* or the young man who was injured on his property? Nevertheless, he was still staying at the hospital, waiting for the possible ramifications of Davis DeLongpre's prognosis.

One of the nurses came up to him in the hall next to the ICU and told him quietly, "Monsieur Genevive, you have an overseas call. From America, they said."

The Colonel wanted Jon-Pierre to know they were on their way. The brief conversation concluded with, "Jon-Pierre, please watch over my boy. We'll be there within twenty-four hours."

Davis' condition had not changed since he had been cleaned up and put in the ICU. The only change was to the bandages, and that had to be done a couple times a day. The nurses had to work around Céleste, moving her away from his bedside as her vigil continued.

Captain Henderson's last checkpoint was to the Raleigh, North Carolina tower, and the DeLongpres were soaring over the Atlantic en route to Paris, France. It was late evening. The Colonel looked at his wife. She looked pale and rather tired. He knew exactly how she felt. He squeezed her hand gently and suggested she try to get some rest. She fought it for a while longer, then heeded his suggestion, falling into a fitful sleep in the back. She was a little more spent than she realized.

As the minutes ticked by, The Colonel reviewed the events of the past few weeks. All the joy in Spain had now been diminished by this terrible accident. He wasn't really a drinking man, but, as the trip wore on, he got up, went to the bar, and poured himself a double Walker Black with a splash of water. He began comparing the flight they were taking now to the one in the first week in December. Their flight to Spain had been filled with joy and anticipation. He and his wife were going to see their son for the first time in almost three years. Now, they were again going to see him but for all the wrong reasons. The anticipation was there, but it was what they were afraid of finding out. They could only wait and see.

He had drifted off also when he heard someone calling to him in what seemed to be a dream.

"T. D...T. D.!" He shrugged his shoulders slightly and turned his head to one side, but there it was again, and this time familiar. "T. D...T. D.!!!"

That did it. He awoke and realized it was his wife calling him from the sleeping area. He felt the glass in his hand and noticed the remnants of a couple ice cubes. He felt a little foolish as he sat it on the table and got up to see what Lillian wanted. It was a glass of ice water. They hadn't had time to get a flight attendant this trip, so he went to the bar and poured her a glass of cold branch water.

This flight to Paris would cost The Colonel thousands. Captain Henderson and the co-pilot were just the start, the fuel being the biggest obvious expense. It would have been less expensive to fly commercial, but the difference to him would be like the average person throwing away a Bic lighter. Getting to their son as fast and as comfortably as possible was the main priority.

After adding three hours for the time change on top of the eight-hour flight, the DeLongpre plane landed in Paris early Monday morning. The Colonel had reserved a small shuttle aircraft. After waking up the airport manager and loading the plane, Captain Henderson obtained the flight maps to Amiens.

The manager was an ex-pilot and asked how long it had been since he had flown anything that small. Henderson said it had been a while, but he didn't foresee any problems. The ex-pilot gave him some final advice. "After you pass the last honing tower before your decent, you will be flying directly into the winds from the channel. Remember that, and you should have no problems."

Before take off, The Colonel took his pilot aside and let him know what he had been thinking about during the flight over.

"Rex, I know that I am paying you well, but I want you to know I really appreciate what I'm asking you and Mack to do. I don't know if we are going to be in Amiens for two days or a few weeks. I'll put you guys up at the best hotel there for a couple of days, or until we find out what is going to happen with Davis. I don't want to keep you from your families too long, so if this takes very much more time than that, then you fellas go back and take the DC-4 home. I may call you again or just go home commercial."

"Whatever you decide, Colonel. You can count on me."

The two men shook hands, but, before they could take-off, there was one thing left to do. He needed to call the hospital and try to locate Jon-Pierre so he could either meet them or have some one else be there when the plane landed. This task completed, they were airborne.

Rex Henderson took the manager/ex-pilot's advice and, even with the winds, made a smooth landing. Robey watched the red and white six-passenger aircraft taxi and come to a stop. He had no trouble spotting the travelers from America and proceeded to walk to them. He pointed to a baggage attendant who quickly moved to pick up the DeLongpres luggage. "My name is Robey. I will take you folks to the hospital."

After they were all in the car, The Colonel asked the large man who was chauffeuring them to drop his pilot and co-pilot off at the best hotel in town. Robey said he could handle that since there would be no vacancy problems this time of year. After this was done, they headed for the hospital.

"Have you heard anything about the condition of our son?" Lillian questioned.

"Well, ma'am, I would rather not comment on that because my employer has given me instructions only to take you to the hospital. We will be there in a couple of minutes."

When The Colonel talked to Jon-Pierre from Paris, they were almost ready for take-off. The Frenchman allowed for various weather conditions and knew within a few minutes what time to expect the DeLongpres. Jon-Pierre, Emma, and Hubert were sitting on a large hospital light-brown divan when they saw Robey opening the door for the expected travelers. It was obvious both parties were exhausted, but the Genevives rose to greet them. Jon-Pierre eyed The Colonel first and said inside, *So, I finally see the great man face to face. He is indeed an imposing-looking fellow!*

They exchanged greetings, but one of the DeLongpre party was not for standing around having small chitchat. Lillian made it quite clear she wanted to see her son. Jon-Pierre responded, "Doctor Montatarie has requested that you folks meet with him before you see the boy. I am only relaying his message."

Lillian protested slightly, but, after a squeeze from her husband's hand, they made their way to the doctor's office. As the two families entered, the doctor took off his silver-framed glasses and stood up. He moved around to the front of his desk and extended his hand. "I'm Doctor Georges Montatarie, Davis' doctor. It is nice to meet you in spite of these sad circumstances."

The doctor appeared to be in his late thirties or maybe forty, no more than that. He was almost as tall as The Colonel but not as wide-shouldered. His hair was medium-brown with a crooked little streak of gray just off left center. His mouth was framed by a pencil-thin moustache a la Errol Flynn. He had an air about him that seemed to make one feel confident he was in charge. He asked everyone to sit while returning to the chair behind his desk. He opened Davis' chart and ran his finger down the margin, then said, "I wanted to brief you, Colonel and Mrs. DeLongpre, on your son's injuries and condition before you see him. He has endured a severe blow to the right side of his head…that could have ended his life."

Lillian put her hand to her mouth and gave a faint cry. The doctor continued, "He has been in a coma for the entire time since we've administered this wound. I have seen situations where some patients wake in a few days, then again weeks or even months. I am sorry we will not be able to determine this now. We will take more x-rays and conduct additional tests as his healing process continues. Now, Jon-Pierre feels as horrible about this as we all do, but he has told me if Davis requires any additional or specialized treatment from outside our area, by all means to proceed. I assume this is still the case."

The doctor paused and directed his glance to Jon-Pierre who nodded his approval. The physician continued, "Now, unless you have any additional questions, you may visit your son."

The DeLongpres were still absorbing all this when a nurse appeared and led them down the hall to the ICU. With everything that was going on, the Genevives forgot to mention that Céleste would be by Davis' side. Emma realized this, but only when they and the DeLongpres were halfway into the room. She gave her husband a glance that meant, *too late now.*

The first thing that Lillian saw made her knees buckle. She knew it was her boy, but, with the tubes and the monitoring wires attached all over his body and the bandaged head, she became almost nauseous. When she regained her composure, she went to the opposite side of the bed. She grasped Davis' one hand in hers, using her other hand to wipe the tears flowing down her cheeks.

Emma Genevive took her daughter's hand away from the grip she had on Davis', firmly taking her by the shoulder and pulling her away. If this had been a few hours ago, this task would have been nearly impossible. Now, the fatigued young woman offered minimal resistance.

"Come now, *ma petite*. His parents are here from America. That is his mother by the bed and his father next to your papa. Come now, *ma petite*. We are going home now."

Lillian had other things on her mind when she saw Céleste sitting by her boy's bed, clutching his hand. The fact that this young woman did not appear to be a nurse did not sink in until later that evening. Yes, she was wearing nurse's garb but wasn't wearing a cloth cap. None of the nurses were that young or possessed long, flowing blonde hair. However, Lillian's priority was to take up the vigil Céleste had maintained for almost three days.

Before the Genevives collected Céleste and decided to return home, Jon-Pierre told The Colonel of the rooms nearby that he had arranged for them. "We are going home now for a little rest. Here is our number at the chateau. Please feel free to call us. No, I insist you call us if there are any changes in your son's condition!"

A tired and forlorn Céleste sat between her parents in the back seat of the family limo. They both tried to console her by saying, "*Ma petite*, we are proud of your stamina *and* your concern for the young man. You did all you could, but his parents are here, and it is now in their hands. We want you now to forget this for the time being and just get some rest. Okay, *ma petite*?"

The vigil had taken its toll on the beautiful girl and the strain made her angelic face look old beyond her years. She didn't acknowledge her parent's comments, just stared straight ahead. When they finally arrived home and the car had pulled to a stop, she sat there motionless. When they managed to get her out of the car and on her feet, she spoke her first words. "It is all my fault, it's all my fault. I love him, and now he may never be able to love me back."

This did not sit well with Jon-Pierre and Emma, but they managed to get her to her room and into her pajamas. Emma brought a bowl of onion soup minutes later, but she refused it and collapsed from exhaustion.

Chapter Twenty-Three

Rebecca Thompson was not in a good mood. She hadn't been since New Year's Day. Her place of employment, KJUN Radio/TV, had given her four complimentary tickets to the Sugar Bowl game. The only football games she had ever attended were the ones she was head cheerleader for—the Hattiesburg Hornets. The only reason she enjoyed the actual game was because her Davis was the team's quarterback.

She had accepted the tickets because she figured it would be a good weekend to get away from work and spend some time with her new love, Mark Lewis. She invited another couple from work, but, at the last minute, they cancelled. She told Mark about it, and, when he asked her if he could bring a friend of his from out of town, she unknowingly said yes.

The hour drive from Gulfport to New Orleans would be very enlightening, but extremely disappointing. Embarrassment would be an even stronger emotion. Mark's friend, Geoffrey, was almost as pretty as she was and had an ass nearly as nice-looking as hers. They had two rooms reserved at the Monteleone for her and Mark. She and the handsome anchorman had not slept together yet. She checked them in and then ran back out to her car. All the way home, she could only repeat between cuss words, "Boy, can I pick 'em. God damn, can I pick 'em!"

She went back to work and performed her many duties quite well. She couldn't avoid Mark Lewis in the small station, but, when he saw her in the halls or wherever, he could see those beautiful black eyes emitting serious contempt. He knew she was a professional. She had taken him step-by-step through his adjustments to the station's routines. He knew she would never blow the whistle on him, but he still moved very cautiously. Dancing on eggs might describe his approach to the matter.

However, this was a bit too trying for the young woman from Hattiesburg, so she requested some time off. The station manager realized her value, but there was no such thing as weekend leaves. Because of her perfect work record, however, they gave her off the last weekend of the month.

"Rebecca, I can see something is troubling that beautiful mind of yours. Go away! I don't want to see you 'til next Monday…or even Tuesday."

She entertained the thought of going home and spending this time with her parents but didn't want to take a chance that they might question her like they had when she was a little girl. She drove the short distance to Bay St. Louis and checked into "The Captain's Anchorage," a hotel that catered to people with above-average incomes. She spent the first night at the bar and the remaining time shelling mounds of crawfish on her bed and watching soaps. These ridiculous programs were so bad they actually made her life appear normal.

It was time to go home and get back to work. She drove home, parked her car downstairs, and felt good that the biggest responsibility she had to face was watering her plants. First, she needed to check her messages. The third message was from Lillian DeLongpre. It simply said, "Rebecca, this is Lillian. T. D. and I are leaving for France. Davis has been seriously injured. Here is the phone number for the hospital he is at in Amiens, France." Rebecca was stunned. Did she hear what she thought she heard? She checked the message again. Yes, that was Lillian. The Lillian she had not seen in a while. Yes, Lillian had said they were going to France. Why? Because Davis had been injured!

The DeLongpres would not fly to France for a broken arm, no way. She looked at her watch. It was 10:05 p.m. All of a sudden, the message hit. She dropped the sprinkler can and watched the water run over her kitchen floor. Her legs were like rubber, her stomach felt like it had been in a small boat on a stormy lake. She collapsed on the couch next to the divider separating the small kitchen from the living room. A few minutes later, she recovered and picked up her white phone.

In 1961, overseas phone calls were quite common but always time-consuming. The number she requested from the overseas operator would take a few minutes. Operator 9 called her back and said she had the Amiens Community Hospital on the line.

"Hello, this is Rebecca Thompson in Gulfport, Mississippi. I would like to speak with Lillian DeLongpre."

"I'm sorry, Mademoiselle Thompson. There is no Lillian DeLongpre here."

"Please, ma'am, her son is there at your hospital, and I need to know his condition."

"Are you a family member?"

"No, I'm not, but I...."

"Sorry, Mademoiselle. I can't give you any more information."

"Could you at least give her or her husband a message and my phone number?"

"That I will be happy to do, mademoiselle."

Rebecca sat back on her couch and relived the horrible decisions she had made in the last few months.

Colonel Thurston DeLongpre was frustrated. During the decades of his illustrious career, he had faced countless situations, and, no matter the magnitude, he had always been able to solve almost any problem presented him. This was the first time he could remember that he had come up against something he could not control…or have a say about its outcome. He needed time to think this out.

He and his wife had forced down the dinner of hospital food, and, although it was French cuisine, it was still hospital food. He watched Lillian go from the meal back to her son's bedside. He stood there watching this as long as he could, then he then realized something was missing—his after dinner cigar.

He took one more look at his wife and son and left for the room provided for them. He picked up a brown leather suitcase and threw it on the un-slept-in, still-made bed. He took the zipper in his hand, ran it all the way around, felt in the side pocket until he found the little package of Havana Tampas, and put it in his sport coat pocket. He went back to the ICU and looked in on his family, shook his head sadly, and moaned, "Nothing's changed. Nothing I can do." He walked down the hall to the lobby, and, as he was passing the admission's desk, a white clad nurse called out his name.

"Monsieur DeLongpre, I have a message." The nurse beckoned him to approach the desk, which he did.

"I'm so sorry, monsieur. The nurse I replaced this evening forgot to give this message to me. I just found it here by the phone. It is from America and marked urgent for Lillian DeLongpre. Will you accept it?"

He nodded his answer, took the folded note from the nurse, headed toward the entrance, where he pushed open the right side of the double doors and stood on the landing. The wintry air of Northern France was nippy but refreshing. He took several deep breaths before reaching into his coat pocket and pulling out a cigar. There was no brandy to go with it, but somehow that wasn't important. He clipped off the tip, lit the tobacco-packed tube, and took a satisfying puff. He paced back and forth on the landing. After a few more puffs, he realized that this cold air filling his lungs was now becoming uncomfortable. He buried his cigar in the sand-filled receptacle to the right of the entrance and again passed the admission's desk before heading toward his son's room.

He returned to see his bride still sitting by their son's bed. He put a big hand on her shoulder and said, "Lill, I have a message from home for you."

She didn't respond immediately but finally looked up to meet her husband's gaze. Her eyes were dead, and this saddened The Colonel even more. He waited for some kind of acknowledgement, but none seemed to be forthcoming, so he sad quietly, "Don't you want to read it?"

"I'm sorry, T. D. Please read it to me."

The Colonel opened the folded note and said after reading it, "It's from Rebecca, my love. She wants you to call her."

Lillian heard Rebecca's name and remembered the message she had left only minutes prior to their departure. She felt her husband's hands on her shoulders and listened to his request.

"Darling, our boy is being well looked after. We both need some sleep."

She took a final look at all the tubes and wires connected to her son's body. She saw his chest moving up and down in a weak but steady rhythm. After giving his hand a final squeeze, she stood up and fell against her husband's big chest, feeling the strength and security of his arms.

When they got to the room, he picked her up and laid her on the bed. He carefully removed her shoes and everything else she was wearing, then pulled the covers up to her neck, and began undressing himself. He crawled into bed, looked at his exhausted wife, and marveled about how beautiful she still was. It seemed like only minutes since their walk though the Fontaine gardens all those years ago.

Lillian felt her knight in shining armor lying next to her, as he had for many years. It felt just like all those precious times he had come home after his numerous travels. As she snuggled up to him, she said, "We'll call Rebecca tomorrow, T. D."

The morning of January 28, 1961, in Amiens, France.

The Colonel went to sleep with his wife in his arms. He too was exhausted and hardly moved for nearly six hours. When he awoke, he rolled on his side and reached for her with his left hand but came up empty.

Lillian had awakened about forty minutes earlier and had smiled at her mate's snoring. It wasn't the aggravating snore that keeps everybody awake within earshot, just a little excuse-me snore, probably brought on by all those hundreds of Cuban and Connecticut Valley cigars he'd enjoyed over the years.

She knew how tired he had to be and decided to let him sleep a little longer. She had showered, dressed, and made the walk to the ICU. She checked to see if anything had changed in the last few hours, but the nurse told her no. She sat for a few minutes with her boy before returning to the room. Now might be a good time to return Rebecca's phone call.

When his arm came up empty, The Colonel sat up and rubbed his eyes. He heard his wife talking to someone while trying to keep her voice down. She saw him sit up, blew him a good morning kiss, and resumed her conversation at normal voice level. He lay there for a few minutes and listened to half a conversation.

"That's about all we know, Rebecca. Uh huh…yeah…. Well, I know that Davis would appreciate your support and so would…yes, I read the letter…yes, it was very unexpected…well, we're going to stay here until we know…like I said, Rebecca, he is in a coma and doesn't even know *we* are here, so he wouldn't…okay, well, you think about it and decide. Oh, by the way, what would the new man in your life think about your coming here?"

There was an uneasy pause in the conversation and Rebecca was certainly glad Lillian couldn't see her face. A few more tidbits were exchanged before the women said good-bye.

Lillian hung the phone up, took a deep breath, and lay down on top of the blankets next to her husband.

"Well, what's the story, Lill?"

"I just don't know, T. D., Rebecca and I have drifted apart. I don't know what I can do about it. The one thing I do know is that I'm not leaving here until we're sure everything is going to be all right."

The Colonel patted her on the shoulder, slipped out of bed, put on his robe, and headed toward the bathroom. About halfway, he turned and said, "No change this morning, huh?"

Lillian sadly shook her head. The Colonel was getting in the shower, and, as he was balancing the hot and cold water, he decided to let his pilots go home. He finished bathing, and, while dressing, he suggested they have some breakfast. Until then, Lillian hadn't thought about eating, but she felt a bit hungry now that he had brought it up.

On their way down the hall to the hospital cafeteria, they heard a familiar voice. Jon-Pierre called to them. As he and The Colonel shook hands, he asked about Davis. Lillian said she had seen him and the nurse only moments ago and things were the same. They asked if the Frenchman would join them for breakfast, but he declined. "Oh, no, thank you, I had breakfast hours ago. Besides that, I have eaten *here* before. Let me take you to Lucienne's just down the street. I will have coffee with you."

As they approached the door to the small but very attractive restaurant, the smell of fresh baked bread and steamed sausage filled their nostrils. Now, Lillian realized how hungry she really was. As they sat and began to order, Jon-Pierre came up with a suggestion.

"Since no one knows when your son will regain consciousness, my wife and I would like to invite you to stay at our chateau. It is only a half an hour drive and there is plenty of room. You will be more comfortable and will not have to endure hospital food. We can keep in close contact with Doctor Montatarie and his staff."

After Lillian's few questions of concern, such as transportation to and from the hospital, were solved, they graciously accepted the invitation. They finished breakfast and returned to check on their son.

Rebecca Thompson had a decision to make. She knew that she could arrange for time off to fly to France, but what would she be facing upon her arrival? She sensed coldness in Lillian's voice. It didn't sound like the same Lillian whom she had shared all those intimate conversations with on the east terrace at The Willows when there was no Davis around. She thought, *I could be wrong about the coldness in her voice. She has been through a lot. I know how I feel right now.*

It was too far to drive to go sailing on the little private lake behind her parent's home. So, the next best thing was to fill the bathroom tub and have another conversation with its sympathetic walls. After close to an hour of this and a glass of wine, she decided to put in a call to Amiens, France. Two glasses of wine later, she decided to get some sleep and make the call in the morning.

About one-thirty in the afternoon, the nurse at the administration desk received the overseas call. "I'm so sorry, Mademoiselle Thompson, Lillian DeLongpre is not here. However, she has informed me that there might be a call from Mississippi, USA. She and her husband will be back here later on this evening."

That was enough for Rebecca to arrange her trip to Northern France. She called her place of employment and was granted a leave of absence. She packed a few clothes and female necessities before calling the airlines. Her tickets read…"Gulfport to Atlanta—Atlanta to New York—New York to Paris, France—Paris to Amiens."

Céleste Genevive had been taken from Davis' bedside by her parents upon the arrival of the DeLongpres. She had little or no recollection of this and had isolated herself in the privacy of her bedroom. Yes, she was exhausted and had slept most of the time, but she had nightmares of the horrible incident, and woke up crying every few hours or so. Even the many trays of food sent by her mother had been ignored or rejected.

Her strength came from an unexpected source, her oldest brother Hubert, who had called and informed her of Davis' arrival while she was staying in town with friends. He finally got her to eat something. Though it wasn't much, it did help a little and so did the comforting conversation. He wasn't opposed to the way she felt about the man who lay injured half an hour's ride from where they were.

Céleste and her brother had teased each other about Davis on a few occasions. Her obvious attraction to the American along with the boots Hubert had given him brought sister and brother closer than they had been in several years, maybe even closer than ever. Until then, a barrier existed that Céleste never understood. She could get to her father and enjoyed this, but wasn't aware that her three brothers couldn't. She was aware on a small scale, but was too caught up in her own little selfish feelings to really care. The crisis they were all affected by now made the little princess sit back and look at this differently. She didn't understand all of Hubert's intentions, but that would change in the following weeks.

One thing she knew for sure was that she wanted to see Davis, although she had been told by her father to stay in the background. It would be difficult to do this, especially with his parents staying at the chateau. Getting around her father would present a challenge.

It was going on six days since that horrible morning at the stalls. The two families finished breakfast and The Colonel told Jon-Pierre that he wanted to call the hospital. After doing this, he came back with the news that Davis was still in a coma, but his vital signs were improving. Jon-Pierre ordered his driver to take his guests into town.

The Air France flight from New York to Paris was about twenty minutes late. Rebecca had to go through customs and was only seconds away from missing the daily shuttle to Amiens. She was tired but kept awake by a man and woman arguing in the seats in front of her.

There was no one waiting for her when she left the plane, so she had to walk the fifty or so yards to the tiny terminal. The winds from the channel blew her dark hair straight back and blurred her eyes. She finally got inside and shook her head from side to side and smoothed her locks with her fingers. The attendant at the desk smiled at the windblown traveler asking if he could be of assistance.

"Yes, I need transportation to the hospital. Can you arrange this for me?"

The young man easily sensed that she was American and knew exactly why she was here. The news of Monsieur Genevive's special friend had spread like an avalanche throughout the little French town.

Her driver took Rebecca and her luggage to the hospital and carried her bags into the waiting room. She paid the fare and unintentionally made the man's whole week. She went directly to the front desk and made her presence and mission known. The nurse had a good idea who she was but had to deny her request to see their star patient. No employee at the town's only hospital would dare go against Doctor Montatarie or Jon-Pierre's instructions. The frustrated but exhausted Rebecca sat on the couch next to her bags.

Jon-Pierre's driver delivered the DeLongpres to the hospital and asked them if he should wait. The Colonel said that would not be necessary because they would most likely be there for a while, besides, the room where they had spent the first night was still available if they needed to rest.

The now famous couple waved to the nurse at the desk but did not see her point in the direction of the couch in the waiting room. Lillian saw Rebecca with her coat up to her neck and her head tilted back. She gestured to her husband and said, "Well, T. D., I wasn't sure, but here she is."

"Did you have any doubt of this, Lill?"

The disappointment and anger Lillian had felt on that chilly afternoon in Barcelona now subsided for a moment. There sat the beautiful young woman in whom she had placed all her dreams with for making her a grandmother. She sat down beside Rebecca and looked up at her husband.

The union they had consummated over the many precious years again came into focus. Their eyes locked for a few seconds, and then The Colonel smiled and nodded slightly. The "letter" now seemed to dissolve. All was forgiven, at least for the moment.

Lillian slipped off her gloves, gently caressed Rebecca's forehead, and ran her fingers into her hair. Rebecca stirred and slowly opened her eyes. She looked into Lillian's face and tears began to trickle down her cheeks. All she could say was, "Lillian, oh, Lillian!"

"It's okay, child. We're all here. It's okay."

She looked past this, saw The Colonel standing there stalwart as always, and simply uttered, "Hi, Colonel. It's so good to see you!"

Lillian took Rebecca's hand and helped her up from the couch. They began the walk down the hall to the ICU. The Colonel stayed a few steps behind the two women with their arms around each other and said under his breath, "I don't know about this girl's involvement with the young man mentioned in the letter, but, whatever the magnitude of the situation, I have to admire her guts. She has traveled many miles from home to be with my son."

As the trio entered the room, the nurse in attendance saw the familiar faces of the boy's parents, stood up, and excused her self. They walked closer to Davis' bed where Rebecca took her first look at her precious love. The sight of all the tubes and wires, plus the bandaged head, weakened her knees. Lillian steadied her while Rebecca regained her composure. "I'm okay, Lillian. I'm okay."

When the lovely newswoman from Gulfport, Mississippi recovered, Lillian let go of her hand. Rebecca edged a little closer to Davis' bed to put her hand on his. Lillian saw the tears forming, choked back a couple of her own, and watched.

Rebecca squeezed the hand with the tubes coming from it and tearfully said, "Davis, I love you so much. Please, come back to me."

That statement raised Lillian's eyebrows, and she shot a questioning look at her husband. This little lady seemed to want it all. Was that letter she read in Spain legitimate or just a threat? All this was forgotten for the moment when, for the first time in almost a week, Davis stirred a bit and shifted slightly. Lillian gasped and joined Rebecca bedside. But alas, that was all there was.

The two women were encouraged momentarily but then became distraught. The Colonel however, summoned the nurse and asked her to call Dr. Montatarie. The doctor was there within moments and checked his patient. "This is a good sign, Mr. and Mrs. DeLongpre, but don't get your hopes too high right now."

"Doctor, is there anything my husband and I can do, anything at all?"

The French physician thought for a moment, and then replied, "As a matter of fact there is. Your son lost a considerable amount of blood on the way in to the hospital, and we have had to give him a few transfusions. If either or both of you are up to donating blood it would certainly help us!"

Lillian started to volunteer, but her husband cut her short. He said to the doctor, "That sounds like a good idea, Dr. Montatarie, but as much as my wife wants to help our boy, she's been a little anemic of late. We will talk it over and let you know shortly."

Lillian looked at her mate with shock in her eyes as he whisked away toward their room.

Before they got there, she realized what she had almost said and suddenly felt very foolish. In her anxiety to help, she had forgotten one small thing. There was a good possibility they may have different blood types than Davis. She said meekly, "I'm sorry, T. D., I wanted so much to help him, well, I just didn't...."

"It's okay, love. It probably wouldn't matter being this far from home, but I would like to save us any embarrassment certain questions from the doctor might cause us. Besides, as thorough as Jon-Pierre is, I'm sure he included extra blood when he told the staff not to spare any expense."

The Colonel called the chateau, informed Jon-Pierre of the situation, and told him not to send the driver because they would be spending the night there. This new development did not fall on deaf ears at the chateau.

In the thousands of stories we have heard about life after death, there are tales of white lights in a tunnel when some one has experienced almost dying and coming back. People have allegedly been in a deep coma and remembered someone talking to them. None of this has been proven, but who is to say that it doesn't happen?

The Willows was a big place. Forty thousand acres is a big place, even in Africa or the outback of Australia. After Amos Hubbard had done his best to replace Ben Hampton and taught Ben's son, Willie, about the land and the plantation animals, there were still parts of this paradise that had not been completely surveyed. When Davis received the news from Uncle Sam, he panicked and rode to the outer reaches of the estate. He finally pulled the heaving stallion to a stop, dismounted, and fell face down in a foot-tall jungle of wild grasses. He lay there for some time, trying to sort everything out. He slipped into a light sleep, and when he awoke, his head was clear, but his body was crying for water. It would take several minutes of riding to find water to quench his thirst.

The DeLongpres and Miss Thompson retired for the evening but found it very hard to go to sleep. They were all anxious to see if Davis had made any more movements.

The winter sun peeked over the hills surrounding the village of Amiens. It scared away the usual mist that always hovered like a big white blanket. The always-present channel winds decided to go bother some other part of the region. Mother Nature took a few days off.

Lillian's earlier solitary visits to her son's bedside were history. Her husband and the girl who had spent many hours with her on the east terrace of The Willows mansion joined her. Again, Lillian thanked and dismissed the R.N. who had been at Davis' bedside. They both squeezed his motionless hands and began to move to the chairs close to the bed. They were halted in their tracks by a very familiar voice. It wasn't The Colonel, but sounded a little like him. The two women first looked at T. D., but saw his hands gesturing that said it wasn't his voice.

"I'm thirsty."

Lillian and Rebecca turned and rushed back to where Davis lay. They saw his blue eyes straining to focus and then looked straight at them. The Colonel joined his wife and Rebecca at the bedside, leaned between them, and said in a controlled voice, "How ya doing, son?"

Davis didn't answer. The eyes searched the three faces hovering over him and, after several seconds, finally said, "I'm thirsty. Please, can I have a drink? Where am I?"

"Davis, you've had an accident, but we're with you, son, and you're going to be all right."

Davis felt the plastic tubes in his nose and then saw the wrappings around his wrists and the wires attached to his chest. He wanted to rub his eyes, but couldn't. All he could say was, "Who are you people?"

Lillian and Rebecca were rendered motionless, not to mention dumbfounded. The Colonel was also shocked but used his common sense to realize what was transpiring. He left the women to find Doctor Montatarie and any available nurses.

The French doctor was prepared for this and immediately accompanied The Colonel back to the I.C.U. The nurses escorted his parents and the young lady from the room, asking them to wait for the doctor in his office.

The head nurse came back to Davis' bedside and took the young man's hand. She looked into the curious, almost frightened eyes of her patient, trying to calm him down as he uttered, "Who are these people? And who are you? Who am I? What's happening here? What's going on?"

The nurse had been there, alternating with the other R.N.s and attendants for the entire week. She had not seen Davis' eyes and the intensity of them until now. Again, all she could do was to try and calm him.

Dr. Montatarie met The Colonel and his wife and the new American arrival in his office. He asked them to sit down and try to relax if they could. He pulled his chair away from his desk, sat down wearily, and rubbed his fingers gently on his temples. After taking a deep breath, he began to explain Davis' situation as well as he could. "I know that you are all very concerned. This is understandable. This particular injury is very serious, and we still do not know the extent of it. We are obviously dealing with some form of amnesia. I believe what Davis is experiencing is what we call retrograde amnesia. This means that his brain is blocking everything that happened before the accident. This is hardly ever permanent, but the recovery time is impossible to estimate. Again, he has youth on his side. Other than his injury, he is in excellent health."

"Doctor Montatarie, I'm his mother, and I think we need more than this medical theory to ease our minds. Is this all you can tell us?"

The doctor nodded his head sadly, and, after a few questions from The Colonel and Rebecca about it being beneficial or harmful for them to be around Davis, they left for the ICU with the doctor's okay and blessing.

Davis saw the trio approaching his bedside. He saw the tenderness in the eyes of the women and wondered why the gray-haired gentleman stood a few feet behind them. The older woman was very attractive, and he could smell the fragrance of some kind of flowers coming from her.

The young man was in a very weakened state physically, but his mind was alert. The young lady standing next to the nice smelling older woman was extremely beautiful. He said to himself, *I don't know her, but I sure would like to!*

The Colonel placed his hand on his wife's shoulder and whispered in her ear, "I have some phone calls to make."

The time in Spain was a new and unique experience for the two families. The Colonel thought that Rodolpho and Ireñe should be informed of Davis' accident...and his condition. But wait! There were two people back home who should be the first to know how their boy was progressing. He found Doctor Montatarie and requested the use of his office and telephone.

Willie Hampton had made his decision to stay at The Willows but found he could not concentrate on the daily business. Darcy saw this in her man and tried her best to lend moral support.
Willie awoke, sat down, and picked and shoved at the breakfast Darcy had prepared for him. She finally removed his barely touched plate of eggs, grits, and bacon and took it to the sink. She sat down and turned to face Willie as he toyed with his coffee cup. He looked up and saw his wife standing there removing her apron. In a suggestion that sounded more like an order, Darcy said, "Mr. Hampton, you have the number over there. Just go to your office and get this over with."
Willie took one more sip of coffee and stood up. He went to his wife and gave her a hug, a warm kiss right on the mouth, then went to the office.
He procrastinated for a moment and messed with the pile of bills in the basket on the right side of his desk. He finally reached for the phone, and, as he did, it rang. He froze for a moment. Should he pick it up? Could it be good news or bad?
"Hello, this is the Willow Wind Stables, can I...?"
"Hi, Willie. This is your pop."

Ireñe Montoya checked the table settings that Yolanda had for many years faithfully arranged and then went to her bedroom to change her clothes. She slipped on a comfortable dress, touched up her make-up, and went back to the dining area, expecting her husband, but no Rodolpho. For one of the only times in all their years of marriage, he wasn't there at mealtime. She waited another ten minutes before deciding to go to his special place. She donned a light coat and headed for the stables.
The doors to the main barn were ajar, so she proceeded down the straw-covered walkway. As she neared the stall where Rodolpho kept his prize stallion, she heard her husband talking to El Negro Grande. She still got a kick out of the way he talked to everything that moved. She crept up to the gate and saw him caressing the big horse's neck. "Rodolpho, your dinner is ready."
The Spaniard looked up to see his wife's smiling face. He was a bit embarrassed but recovered nicely. "Oh, my love, I was just thinking."

"Yes, you were—and out loud, my husband."

" I am only wondering how our son Davis is doing in Saudi Arabia. We haven't heard from him."

"I am sure your horse was wondering the same thing. It is nice he has you to talk with. Come, my love. Put your large pet to bed, and let us join our daughters for dinner."

They walked arm and arm from the barn to the hacienda like they had done so many times before. As they thanked God for their blessings, the phone on the bar rang like it was boiling over. Rodolpho hated being bothered during dinner, but something made him slide his chair back and pick up the persistent instrument. "Hola, este es Rodolpho Montoya."

"Rodolpho, this is T. D. I have some news that you will not want to hear. I am in Northern France, and I'm afraid Davis has been in a bad accident."

The Colonel and Rodolpho talked for a few minutes, and, although the news was quite shocking and depressing, both of these great men's minds had reached a workable solution. Keep in touch were their final words.

The Colonel completed the necessary phone calls. He hung up the phone and leaned back on Dr. Montatarie's leather chair. It felt good and reminded him of the one that was waiting for him upon his return to his ranch. He didn't want to go back to the ICU and look at his son who didn't know who he was. *Life is a blessing that can turn into a curse when the wind changes.*

Davis' condition remained the same. Dr. Montatarie was always available, and, although there wasn't much he could do for his patient, he was there for his family if they needed to consult with him about anything.

The Genevives were also informed on a daily basis. Jon-Pierre and The Colonel had a few discussions about the growing medical expenses, but the Frenchman told him that he figured it was his responsibility, and did not want to get into any further arrangements until the condition of Davis had improved or at least stabilized.

Rebecca was very frustrated for a couple reasons. One was Davis' amnesia, and the other was the lie she had been living with. She wanted to have a talk with Lillian. She longed to be close with her friend, just as she had all those times when they enjoyed tea together, which now seemed so very long ago. She just didn't know how to mend the fences that had come between them.

Two more days passed and nothing had changed. On the third morning, she decided to tell Lillian and The Colonel she was going to go home. She paced around the room that was provided for her at the hospital for several minutes, and then took the only suitcase she had opened and laid it on the bed. She took the things she had hung in the closet and began folding them and placing them inside. Tears filled her dark eyes as she sat down beside it and sobbed. "That letter, that God damn letter! I would cut off the hand that wrote it if I could take it back! Goddamn Mark Lewis! God damn me! God damn everything! I've got to get out of here!"

A few miles away, another young woman was equally upset. For as long as she could remember, Céleste Genevieve had been able to cope with her teenage problems by taking long rides on her mare. But since the accident, she had not been able to even go near the stables.

She didn't remember a whole lot about the vigil at Davis' bedside, but she was very aware of her love's parents staying at the chateau. She knew one thing for sure, she had to see Davis whether he knew who she was or not. She lay in her cozy bed for a few more minutes, then slipped out and went to her closet. After selecting a pair of tan gabardine slacks, she went to her dresser and took out a dark-brown turtleneck sweater. She laid the ensemble on the bed and padded to the bathroom. She bathed and applied a little make-up. She never wore much and didn't really need to. She dressed, brushed her golden mane, and set out to find her brother Hubert.

When he didn't answer her knock on his door, she went downstairs. She peeked through the open door to her father's office. He was on the phone but looked up and saw her. He smiled and waved. She waved back. She walked to the kitchen area and saw her mother talking to one of the household employees. Perfect, now she would try to find her brother.

She looked for his truck and saw that it was where it was usually parked. Reluctantly, she headed for the stable area. As she neared the dreaded structure, she saw him exiting the big entryway and walking up the path between the corrals. He waved and they met fifty feet or so from the end of the path.

"I was checking on your mare, my sister. You haven't seen her, and, although she seems fine, she appears a bit barn sour and needs riding."

"Thank you, brother, but I just can't do that right now. I need a favor from you. It is very important to me."

He smiled and put his arm around her and they began walking toward the house. "And what would that be?"

"I want you to drive me to the hospital." They stopped walking.

Hubert turned to face her. "Céleste, I don't think this is a good idea. You know what Papa said about interfering with his family." He looked down at her flawless face and saw the intensity in her eyes. They had only recently become close, and he didn't want to do or say *anything* that would spoil this new bond they had developed. After a pause that lasted only a few seconds, he said softly, "Okay, but let's go before I have a chance to think this over."

Brother and sister Genevive talked about many things on the ride into Amiens. The reprimands they expected from their father, the situation they might encounter with the DeLongpres, and their new sibling relationship. All of this had involved Davis DeLongpre.

They arrived and went to the admission's desk in the lobby of the little hospital. Céleste asked the nurse if they could visit Davis but was politely denied her request. "My instructions are to admit family only. However, I remember you from the first day he arrived here and the time you spent with him. I will call the room and tell his parents you are here."

The woman wearing the white uniform gestured for them to have a seat while she buzzed the ICU. In a few minutes, they looked up to see the stately Mississippi colonel standing only a few feet away. He motioned them to follow. As they walked down the hall, The Colonel was recalling the last conversation he'd had with Dr. Montatarie. "Colonel DeLongpre, I'm in favor of anything that could conceivably be a catalyst to jog your son's memory. We just have to be very careful."

As they entered the room, Lillian saw them followed by her husband's gesture for her to come to him. She left her son's side and stood next to her man.

Davis looked at the two new players in this drama and forced a smile. He looked into their faces briefly and then slowly closed his eyes. His parents had seen this many times in the past few days and could only thank the Genevive brother and sister for their visit.

As they bid the DeLongpres good-bye and headed for the door, they almost ran into Rebecca Thompson. They excused themselves. Rebecca looked at Lillian and asked who they were.

"They are the Genevive's son and daughter. The young lady was with Davis when he got hurt."

"Oh, Lill...I'm going home. I don't want to, but I think I should. You know, my job and all."

"Oh, honey, I understand. We really appreciate you being here. Please thank your boss and your man for their consideration. Have a safe trip home, and we will stay in touch."

Rebecca took a last look at Davis, gave Lillian a hug, and shook The Colonel's hand before leaving the room. She walked down the hall to her room and gathered her things. It would be a long and sorrowful trip back to Mississippi. All she could think of was going back to work, seeing Mark Lewis, and wanting to find a way to make him pay his dues. No, that wasn't all. *Will I ever be able to make Davis know how much I still love him?*

Céleste and her brother Hubert had left and Rebecca was on her way home. Davis was asleep, so Lillian and The Colonel decided to return to their room. They laid down on the double bed in each other's arms and fell into a restless sleep.

It was late afternoon when Lillian awoke. She lay there motionless and reviewed the events of the earlier part of the day. She took her husband's hand from her shoulder and carefully slipped out of bed. The tired lady said softly, "Maybe this will be the day. Maybe today my boy will come back to us." She dressed and made her way to that prison that was holding her son's mind hostage. She arrived to find Davis sitting up and taking nourishment.

He smiled at the attractive lady whom he had seen quite often the past few days. "Good morning, Lillian. Thanks for stopping by."

Lillian smiled but didn't answer. They had tried everything they could imagine to bring back his memory. As she was struggling to come up with another approach, she unconsciously reached up and played with her graying, strawberry-blond locks. She was twirling them in her dainty fingers when Davis sat straight up almost yelling, "Momma!"

Lillian's hand dropped from her curls and fell to her side. She took one step toward Davis and fainted dead away. Davis sprung from his bed, disregarding the IV and the monitors ripping from his wrists and chest. He went to his knees and picked up his mother in his arms. The nurse who was waiting across the room saw this. The suction cups attached to his body were no problem, but the needles imbedded in his wrists were a different story. As Davis held his mother in his arms, he was bleeding profusely. The nurse couldn't separate them, so she went to the speaker monitor attached to the bed and let all know this was a code red.

The expert emergency staff Jon-Pierre Genevive had ordered to be there came in within seconds. They got Davis back into bed, stopped his bleeding, and revived his mother. Davis was hooked back up and calmed down.

The Colonel arrived and picked up his revived wife, and, as he held her in his arms, he said, "Welcome back, son. You gave your mother and me quite a scare."

Doctor Montatarie was right in the middle of all this. He was not surprised by Davis' recognition of his mother. When he had the situation in hand, he went back to his office, sat down and said, "I called it right, but with a blow like that, I really didn't think he would recover quite this fast." He shook his head and had to believe that the practice of medicine was no more than an educated guess.

In all the confusion the doctor forgot he had not had lunch yet, so he went to the commissary hoping he might get lucky and find a decent meal. He finished eating and began putting two ingredients in his coffee. He took a sip of the not-so-savory brew while thinking about the turn of events regarding his patient Davis DeLongpre. He knew that there was not a whole lot more the staff could do for the young man except to observe him and keep him stable. His physical condition had been improving steadily, and now they had a breakthrough on the mental side. He would let this go one more night and make his decision in the morning.

Early the following morning he made his rounds and then went to see Davis. As early as it was, Davis was a bit groggy but seemed to be very positive and even friendly. *He has every reason to feel better after yesterday.* He asked the nurse to tell the father and mother to meet him in his office when they made their appearance.

The DeLongpres sat in the two chairs facing the doctor on the other side of the desk. Lillian quizzically looked at the pensive physician, and, when he didn't begin right away, she reached over and felt for her husband's hand. She found it and their eyes met.

"Mr. and Mrs. DeLongpre, I am very, very pleased with the events of the past twenty-four hours. I have to be honest. I wasn't sure whom or what would bring him back, but I'm glad it was you. Obviously, the boy has enjoyed a sound and loving atmosphere during his formative years. I don't know how strong his memory is, but I am a bit reluctant to put too much on him right away. I want to release him today, but traveling worries me a little. Maybe you could all stay at the Genevives' chateau for a few days. I'll keep you informed of his progress." The doctor rose, extended his hand, and wished them the best.

Jon-Pierre heard the phone ringing as he entered his office. Davis' injury had put a strain on him, even more than the rest of his family. After all it did happen on his property, which made him responsible. He was beginning to genuinely like the boy, but there was still the connection with his daughter that would take some time for him to get comfortable with. He picked up the phone and what he heard made his face light up. *"Oh mon Dieu, quelles nouvelles merveillueses!* Yes, that is marvelous news! Of course you all can stay for as long as is necessary. Colonel, you did not even need to ask. I will send Robey as we speak, and, no, I insist, however long it takes you are welcome. Oh yes, I will have one of my house staff send some of his clothes."

Davis was looking forward to getting wet and scrubbing all over. Those baths the nurses gave him just didn't cut it, to say nothing about being embarrassing. All the monitoring pads and IVs had been removed...*and boy did that feel better*! Being free of all this, he stretched and went to the bathroom. He looked in the mirror for the first time in quite awhile and saw something that almost frightened him. He saw the half a haircut and gently touched the bandage, muttering, "Man, are you pretty!" He donned the plastic cap the nurse had insisted he wear when bathing and stepped into the shower. He could not imagine how anything could feel better than that.

Davis remembered the extra large Robey Monton, and, as they motored toward the chateau, the rolling hills and white fences became very soothing. He adjusted the cap his mother had bought him to cover all the doctor's handiwork and turned from the window to his folks. "Momma, I have a feeling about something. Please tell me. Becky was here, wasn't she?"

Lillian looked at her husband, saw his lips tighten, and after a long pause said, "Yes, honey, she was here for three days. We thought it was very nice of her to make the trip…considering all that has happened."

"Did she, or is she still, well, is she…." He couldn't finish.

"Honey, she didn't say she was married and didn't say she was wasn't, and I didn't want to back her in a corner. I was, well, your father and I were grateful for her just being here for you."

Davis nodded and, for the last half of the ride, looked at the countryside. Things were coming back into focus as they turned into the long driveway leading to the chateau. Before the car came to a stop, Davis broke his silence, "Have you talked to Willie?"

"All taken care of, son."

"Uh, how about Rodolpho?"

"All taken care of, son. They both want you to take it easy and hear from you when you feel up to it."

Elvis Presley was dog-tired. After his release from military service, he boarded the Army transport in Germany and headed for home. No sooner had he touched the ground of his homeland than *his* colonel was already putting him back to work. The first performance was the Frank Sinatra Special from Miami, Florida, which was a welcome home tribute to Elvis. Then it was off to the studios to make new records, followed by a trip to the West Coast for a couple of movies.

After the wrap party for *Wild in the Country*, Elvis and his entourage went to his Bel Air mansion to unwind. Following a night of partying, he was taking a shower when he slipped and banged his head on the edge of the tub. It didn't hurt all that badly until the next day, but then he developed a migraine-size headache that came and went for the next two weeks. Elvis told one of his guys, "It feels like I got kicked in the head!" One morning he woke up, and it was gone.

Davis, with his mother on his arm, ascended the stairs and entered the large doors held open by a household employee. He saw Jon-Pierre and Emma Genevive coming toward them across the marble floors. Jon-Pierre extended his hand. "Welcome back, Davis. You are looking well."

Davis took the Frenchman's hand and thanked him like the gracious southern gentleman he was. He saw the look in the man's eyes go from the handshake up to the baseball cap that covered his stitches and half-shaved head. With his free hand, he reached up to adjust the cap. This motion caused him to look up to his left and see the golden girl looking down at him from the head of the stairs on the second floor. He let go of the handshake with Jon-Pierre and walked to the base of the stairs.

For a brief second, he saw the horse's hooves and the terror in Céleste's eyes. It made his knees buckle and he grabbed the railing. When the flashback cleared, he looked back up at the beautiful young woman. "Céleste?"

"Davis!" She started down the stairs as he began to climb them to meet her.

Both parents witnessed this special moment with a torrent of mixed emotions. Shock and fear filled the foyer where they stood. No matter what any of them felt, there was no denying the drama of the moment.

They all knew how this tragedy had occurred and who the principal players were. The other members of the welcoming party were Hubert and his brothers. They stood in the background while this scene was being played out, then Céleste's oldest brother motioned his younger siblings to leave the room. Lillian had listened to her son's inquiries of Rebecca on the ride from the hospital. She was amazed at her boy's sudden change in the matter of a few moments. The Colonel put his arm around his wife's shoulder and glanced at the Genevives. Jon-Pierre followed suit, and the parents of both children left the foyer and departed for the cathedral-ceilinged dining room.

Davis and Céleste stood face to face in the middle of the plush carpeted stairway. They didn't touch, but the electricity between them could rival a spring storm on the sometimes-angry English Channel. The heir apparent of the DeLongpre fortune and the daughter of the bi-centennial Genevive family tradition had a lot to talk about. The both realized this but knew without saying that this was not the right moment. They decided to join their families in the dining room.

The decades-old mahogany table that sat beneath the high ceiling was about four feet by twelve. At each end of this magnificent table sat a tufted armchair. On the sides, there was room for any number of smaller chairs, depending on the number of people selected for any specific occasion.

It was not time for dinner, but it was indeed a special occasion. When the Genevives were informed of Davis and his parents' arrival, Emma ordered her staff to prepare a special banquet.

When Davis and Céleste entered the room, they saw Jon-Pierre sitting at the head of the table farthest from the kitchen, with Emma sitting at the opposite end. Céleste's brothers were seated on one side with one vacant place setting. The Colonel and Lillian were seated on the other side, which had another vacant setting. Davis and Céleste saw this and sat at the empty places. Céleste sat with her brothers and Davis between his father and mother.

No matter what meal, in most countries on the European continent, dining was not just eating; it was time for relations with family and friends and a celebration of the bounty. There was no such thing as a thirty-minute lunch or breakfast or a forty-minute dinner. It was a time for gathering and to enjoy the family structure.

This was acknowledged and appreciated by the visitors from Mississippi. But the guest of honor was still not at full strength, so he begged forgiveness and excused himself to take a nap.

Before his announcement, the two families picked up on the glances of their offspring across the table from one another. It made both sets of parents a bit uneasy, but, taking into consideration what had transpired, they decided this was normal and probably justified. Jon-Pierre had reason to worry though, because his little girl had made clear her feelings about the young American way before that horrible day. The Colonel and Lillian didn't know about this, and, when it came down to it, they were just grateful that their only child was even sitting there.

The following three days were uneventful but nonetheless enjoyable. Jon-Pierre and The Colonel spent time looking over the estate and also lounged in the office where they smoked cigars and swapped success stories. There was no bond established, as had been with Rodolpho Montoya and The Colonel, but to some extent a friendship was developing.

Lillian and Emma found plenty to talk about. Among other things, Emma was interested and maybe even fascinated with her American friend's description of her rose garden. This, of course, delighted Mrs. DeLongpre.

One afternoon, Davis and Céleste were talking on the landing atop the steps to the front doors of the main house. Davis was nervously fidgeting with his cap when Céleste had an idea. She grabbed his cap and ran her fingers through the longer hair that hadn't been shaved. His hair had grown a little, but not enough to hide the scar over and behind his right ear. It was all out of balance. Céleste suggested, "Davis, why don't you cut the longer hair to match the new growth? You are so handsome anyway. What would it matter?" They both laughed and decided that this was a good plan. At the end of every day, there was always a lovely dinner in the cathedral dining room.

Davis was making remarkable progress. Most of the players in his life were in focus and, every now and then, something would pop up and clear up some of the fuzziness. For some reason, he woke very early one morning and couldn't go back to sleep. It was more than an hour before anyone at the chateau would be rising. Hell, the birds weren't even celebrating the new day yet.

Davis was still using his green Army duffel bags, so he took the big one out of the closet in his room, heaved it on the bed, and began to explore. It was a little chilly, so he found his robe, put it on and sat down beside the bag. He removed and examined each article until his fingers touched something in one of the side pockets. He pulled out an envelope that was addressed to him. The returnee's name just happened to be Rebecca Thompson. He let go with a long exhale and said, "Oooohhhh yeah!"

He read the letter through, tossed it on the bed, and paused for a few moments. He sat there on the bed staring at a piece of paper that had caused his trail in life to take a notable turn. His legs were crossed in some sort of yoga position, and, from there, he reminisced. He picked it back up, read it through again, took a deep breath, and emphatically tore it in several pieces. He found a wastebasket in the bathroom, held his hand about four feet above it, and watched the pieces fall into the receptacle. He sighed with finality, stretched, and walked to the window where the sun was trying to make an appearance.

There weren't very many days in February when the sun paid a visit to this part of France. But, on this morning, it shone brightly through the beveled panes and brought much-needed warmth to Davis' body and soul. A kind of warmth that allows one to relax and, yes, reflect. He stuck his hands in his pockets and continued staring at nothing in particular. The brown winter grass and the white fences seemed to join and then blend into the horizon. As the early sun further warmed him, he began thinking of all the women he had known. This brought on a wry smile as he chuckled out loud, "Three." With another smile of the wry variety, he added, "Well, three that count, anyway."

There was the up-until-now love of his young life. The one he thought he always had but, to his knowledge, had found someone else. The same one he threw in the trashcan just minutes ago.

He thought about the Spanish beauty and the few unforgettable nights in Barcelona. She was something special, for a fact, but there was no future with her. All he could come up with was, "Damn! What a shame!"

Here, now was the golden girl. The beautiful, sassy woman-child he had come back to see. The woman that almost got him killed and yet may have saved his life. He felt the electricity between them and knew it wasn't a one-way street. He needed to talk to her before he did something he had never done in his life.

Davis had never lied to his parents and didn't want to start now. However, he couldn't come up with a reason to stay on in France. *No way* was his mother going to take no for an answer again. He had an idea, but wanted to talk to Céleste alone first. This would not be easy, but he would find a way.

Céleste wasn't in her room. Davis had a pretty fair idea where to find her, so he looked for a way he could sneak to the stables without being obvious. He made it as far as the head of the stairs and stopped. Even though he was still pleasantly warm from the time he had spent by the window, he returned to his room to get a jacket. From the side of the house he could see her standing by the railing that led to the main stable entrance. She was still having trouble going in to the place where she almost lost the man she loved.

Davis reached the corral fence and eased up behind her. "*Ma Céleste*, how ya doing?" She didn't turn around when she heard the familiar voice, just continued looking straight ahead. He joined her, rested his elbows on the top rung of the railing and said, "My folks are getting antsy. They want to leave tomorrow."

"Yes, Davis, I know. My mother told me last night after you went to bed." She felt that if she looked in his eyes she would lose it, so the lovely young woman continued to gaze at the fields. Davis knew why she wouldn't look at him and that she wouldn't until she heard what she wanted to hear.

On a few of the walks they had, she had expressed her love to him both verbally and physically, but somehow the words wouldn't come out of *his* heart. This had to be the time, if there ever was one. He followed her gaze to nowhere and back, then gently touched her shoulders. He took his right hand and gently turned her face towards his. Her eyes were beginning to mist as he said softly, "I love you, too, honey!" They embraced and, after a warm, passionate kiss, returned their elbows to the top rung of the fence to begin discussing the two major obstacles in the way of their future—their families, or to be more specific, Davis' mother and Céleste's father.

Willie Hampton finished his last forkful of scrambled eggs and washed down the last piece of bacon with orange juice. He gave Darcy a kiss and a farewell pat on the butt before heading to his favorite place in the world next to Darcy's bed; it was his beloved stables and office. He was halfway down the rock-bordered path when he heard his wife's voice over his shoulder. "Honey! Phone call! Overseas! Guess who?"

Willie hadn't talked to Davis since the accident. The Colonel had called, but that was it. He rushed back and grabbed the phone and, at the same time, motioned for Darcy to pick up the extension in the bedroom. "Hey, pard. How ya feeling?"

"I'm coming around, buddy. How's Darcy?"

"Tell him yourself...honey?"

"Hi, little brother. I'm just fine now that we know you're okay. We miss you and love you. Get better and get home!" Darcy hung up to let the partners talk business.

Willie listened patiently while Davis revealed his new plans and his reason for not returning with his parents. He wanted to stay at the chateau a few more days, then follow his original plan to check out the Arabian market.

Willie was all for this, agreeing that since Davis was over there, why not?
"Okay, pard. I'll see you in a few weeks."

Step one was completed. He still had to break the news to his folks, and that would not be easy. He could convince his dad and already had convinced his partner Willie that this was necessary, but his mother didn't give a damn for horses. Also, he figured he had damn near pushed her to the limit already. He began trying to work up a real good story *and* the nerve to approach her.

The Colonel was not overjoyed, but he was ecstatic compared to Lillian's reaction. She hadn't seen her boy for the better part of three years. True, there was that magic month in Spain with the Montoyas, however, that was all but erased by the horrible accident of a few weeks ago. It wasn't so much the extra few weeks or so that bothered her. She just wanted her boy home...and safe!

Though it was a bit frantic for a few minutes, The Colonel calmed his wife down by reminding her that Davis had always been allowed to make his decisions, if he had the right reasons. The DeLongpres said their reluctant good-byes and were off to America.

Jon-Pierre Genevive was a bit perplexed about Davis going to Saudi Arabia when there was so much to choose from right here on his own ranch. His confusion would not end there, as he would find out a little later.

Chapter Twenty-Four

The day after his folk's departure, Davis began to feel a bit remorseful about his trickery and asked Céleste for a few minutes to explain. He told her that maybe he should go to Saudi Arabia for real because he felt guilty about lying to his folks and Willie. Now, it was Céleste who was on the verge of throwing a fit. This was not even close to a good idea in her opinion. They talked a while longer or rather she did but then stopped in the middle of a sentence. Her face lit up when she said, "Davis, tell them you changed your mind!"

"Changed my mind?"

"Yes. Tell them you decided on some of my papa's stock instead."

Davis thought about this and agreed. His decision would certainly make Jon-Pierre happy...at least for a while.

The next few days were filled with looking at stock with Jon-Pierre (this time he wasn't in a hurry) and taking walks with Céleste. They would sometimes go into town for various reasons and, every evening, enjoyed dinners with the family. In other words, their life for the time being was carefree, and they did just about what they wanted. The only thing they didn't do was to go to a place both of them would rather just forget.

One afternoon, they went for a stroll down one of the many bridal paths. About an hour into the walk, the temperature decided to have some fun with them. It dropped several degrees and, in addition, began beckoning its friend, the wind. They were dressed warmly enough for the average day in the season, but now it was turning downright cold. Céleste snuggled up to her man as close as she could. She reached up, kissed him, and purred, "I could stay right here for the rest of my life."

He agreed, "Me too."

After dinner one particular evening, the couple announced their intentions to take in a movie in town. Jon-Pierre had been observing their behavior for the past few days but had said nothing or interfered in any way. When he heard of their plan this evening, he still didn't say anything but looked at his wife with raised eyebrows. They actually did go to the theater, but no movie would be seen this evening.

They met a young lady that Céleste had gone to school with—this same lady had the address of a *juge de paix* in Bethune, about an hour northeast of Amiens.

Bethune was a bit like Amiens in size and topography, but was far enough away in distance where any acquaintance of the family couldn't intercede.

French laws are similar to America's for the most part. After a drive full of anticipation, they found the address, and the *juge de paix* pronounced them man and wife.

For the moment, it seemed as though two nations that didn't particularly like each other were now getting along. The groom became a *citoyen de bourgeois* through *contrat de marriage*, and Céleste's name only became more French, Céleste Genevive DeLongpre.

The newlyweds checked into a rustic, but very nice hotel called "The Villa Aras."

After they had all their stuff in the room, Céleste said to her husband, "I'd better call my family and tell them my name has changed and that we won't be home until maybe tomorrow."

"Tomorrow?"

"Well, like I said, *maybe tomorrow*. I hope you're not going anywhere but here for right now."

Emma Genevive looked once more at the six-foot-tall grandfather's clock that stood in the corner next to the bar, as it had for generations. It had chimed once on the half-hour and now read 2:45 a.m. Céleste had visited friends in Amiens on many occasions, sometimes spending the night, but had always called home to let them know. She had also been to town with Davis but never this late.

Finally, the phone rang. They looked at each other anxiously, hopeful that nothing bad had befallen their daughter or her date. Emma was closest to the phone, so she slowly picked it up. A welcome voice greeted her.

"*Ma mère?*"

"Oh, my heavens! Yes, *ma petite*. Where are you? Your papa and I have…oh, I see…I guess we will see you soon." Emma hung up the receiver and looked at her husband. He noticed the flush on her face as she looked at his half-angry stare. She slowly uttered, "I am afraid our *ma petite* is no longer our *ma petite*."

The late night and early morning hours at the nuptial and the Villa Aras were like the seasons of the year for the newlyweds. The God of Love and Happiness touched the couple with His magic wand, providing soft breezes, gentile winds, lightening and thunder, and then the calm that covers the country after a storm.

The groom of twenty-six summers picked up his bride of only nineteen years of age and carried her over the threshold. They opened the second bottle of bubbly that had been buried in ice. She took one sip and puckered up her pretty lips. "Whew! This isn't as good as the stuff from our vineyards!"

Enough champagne though, she had been waiting for Davis a long time, or at least it seemed like it to her. She excused herself and went to the bathroom. In a few minutes she emerged with a sexy, short negligee that enhanced her hair and clung to her ample curves. She was not a large woman, but everything was in wonderful proportions. She said in a low oozing tone, "You are still dressed my dear."

It didn't take long for him to respond to her observation and do something to remedy the situation. He took her hand, led her to the large bed, and laid her down. They embraced and kissed, softly at first, then their emotions built to a boiling point. He entered her easily, and she told him not to worry. All those years of riding horses had lessened the possibility of pain on her first encounter.

They made love again and again, until they lay in the calm of each other's arms and fell into a delicious sleep.

The morning arrived gray and still but brought with it the promise of many years of happiness. They celebrated their union once again and ordered a gigantic breakfast.

The drive home, however, brought on a whole different set of emotions. Céleste had always been able to get around her father, but this would require the little actress' best performance. Davis was just plain nervous and tried to be stoic. It fooled everyone…except himself.

The sun that had paid the chateau a lovely visit a day or so before, now departed and allowed its opponent, winter, another chilly visit. The gray skies and mist enveloped the grounds as the "newest DeLongpre" and her new husband approached the front of the mansion.

The dreaded reception both had anticipated was not to be. There was definitely an awkward silence when the kids entered the dining room, followed by many questions of why they had to go away to get married, when they could have had a "million dollar" wedding right here at home. Lighter moments were provided by the kidding from her brothers about finally getting rid of her.

The disappointment from her parents was well-concealed. The women embraced and the men shook hands. There were no hostilities or threats of dissolution brought forth, only one additional question from Emma. "Davis, do your folks know?"

"Uh, no, ma'am. They don't."

The following hours consisted of many more questions, such as where they were going to live or what their plans were. Would they stay here or go to America? These questions may have sounded a little ridiculous, but, given the element of surprise and lack of time for adjustment, they were accepted and answered as well as possible.

In their hearts, Jon-Pierre and Emma wanted them to stay in France, but realistically they knew this was only a hope.

Davis told his bride to take her time. They were not on a schedule. He knew from experience how difficult it was to leave home and how painful it was for friends and loved ones. He wanted her to spend as much time as possible with her family and say good-bye to her horses.

He felt a bit silly when she started giggling at his suggestions. She knew that they were mentioned out of respect and concern for everyone's feelings. Céleste adored her parents, brothers, loved her home, but this exuberant young woman was chomping at the bit to begin her new adventure. Thursday morning she kissed her family good-bye for the *next* to last time.

Willie Hampton watched one of his cowboys work with a promising two-year-old they had acquired locally. The same postman who had delivered Davis' draft notice had gotten used to taking official-looking mail to the stable's office, especially since The Colonel had joined his boys in the business. On this day, the letter was *from* Davis. It was an overnight message that simply said:

> To my family,
> Leaving France tomorrow for New York City.

May spend a day or two there.
I will call when we arrive in Atlanta.
>Love,
>Davis

    Willie finished reading the letter and put it back in the envelope that was addressed to the DeLongpre Stables. This brought a smile to Willie. He went to get Darcy but found her in the middle of making herself a bit more beautiful with a leisurely bath. He stuck his head in the door and yelled, "Little brother is coming home. I'm going up to the big house."
    He walked by Tilly's rose garden and up the path to the mansion's back door. He couldn't remember any time when any of them had ever used the front door. He shrugged and said to himself, *All the important stuff is back here, that's why!* He went through the always-open rear door into the great hall, and yelled, "Pop, Tilly, it's me!"
    Lillian was in the kitchen going over the evening's menu and yelled back, "Kitchen, Willie!" She saw the envelope Willie waved in his hand and the smile he was wearing. She deduced this was the news they'd all been waiting for. "I'll get T. D. He's in the study."
    The Colonel came back to the kitchen with his wife, took the envelope from Willie's extended hand, opened and read it. A big smile crossed his face as he boomed, "Well, it's about time! But…what the hell would he have to do in New York? You got any idea, Willie?"
    Willie shook his head slowly and said, "Gee, Pop, I ain't got the slightest, we don't have any business up there."
    Lillian sat down to hear the news and began playing with her curls for a second. As she stood up and straightened her apron, she sighed deeply and said, "Well, at least he's coming home…at last."
    Willie told them good-bye and went back to his house. He wanted to tell Darcy more about the letter. As he was passing through the kitchen, his wife was coming out of the bathroom. She was dressed only in a pale yellow robe and wrapping a matching towel around her wet curls. After all these years, she still took his breath away. She smiled and asked, "Tell me about little brother." Willie walked to her and took her in his arms. She smelled so great! He kissed her gently at first, moved his mouth down slowly and tasted her neck. Darcy could only pant, "Honey, make sure the door is locked."

Céleste Genevive DeLongpre had been to Paris and London and had read and seen many pictures of America's best known city, but she had never been there. She had asked her husband if they could see it before going home to Hattiesburg. This sounded interesting enough, and Davis said, "That's great. Come to think of it, I've never been there either."

They took a beautiful room at the Plaza, saw a couple of plays, and did the other things that newlyweds do. The Big Apple was as exiting as it usually is for anyone who visits for the first time. The new Mrs. DeLongpre took advantage of several of the exiting stores that were there at her disposal. After a few days of this, the young couple had had just about as much fun as they could stand and left for home the following morning.

Lillian came home from one of her Guild meetings late in the afternoon and decided to take a nap before supper. She looked out the kitchen window and saw T. D. and Willie with *those horses*. She still associated them with almost losing her son. She would, however, get over that picture in time.

She took off her club dress, kicked off her shoes, donned a light robe, and reclined on her side of the bed. No sooner had she closed her eyes than the bedside phone began ringing. She let it ring a few times, remembering that T. D. had installed a phone with a new number in the stable office, so they would not have to be bothered by all the business calls. She sighed, and uttered some kind of secret little swear word known only to her, before picking up the receiver. "This is Lillian DeLongpre."

"Momma?"

She jumped like she had pricked her finger with a thorn from one of her rose bushes. "Davis, honey, where are you? Are you okay?"

He assured her that all was well and gave her the time the Atlanta to Hattiesburg shuttle would be arriving. He finished with blowing her a kiss and said, "Bye, Momma, *we'll* see you tomorrow."

She jumped up, put her slippers on, and began racing down the hall when she stopped suddenly, remembering Davis saying "we." Then as always, in her best Scarlet O'Hara said, "Oh, I'll just deal with that tomorrow." She hurried to within earshot of The Colonel and Willie and yelled, "T. D., Willie, come a-running. Our boy's coming home!"

Willie called home to get Darcy to join him and the DeLongpres at the big house. After Lillian had filled them in on the arrival stuff, she mentioned that Davis had said, "we'll" see you tomorrow.

"What does that mean, T. D.?"

The Colonel knew that the Hamptons had no idea what that meant, but he knew. He knew Lillian knew, too. "Well, my dear, it sure wouldn't be a horse now, would it?"

No matter how an offspring may try, it is damn near impossible to fool parents. But Lillian still wanted to deal with her problem tomorrow.

A few months to a year after Elvis Presley was discharged from the Army, he became lonely for a little girl he had met in Germany. He then sent for the girl who would be his future bride and brought her to Graceland.

A little under three years following Davis DeLongpre's discharge, he brought a little girl he had met in France to The Willows. Imagine that.

A voice came over the speakers in the waiting room at the small Hattiesburg airport. "Shuttle flight 77 will be landing in four minutes and will be deplaning on the green concourse." The foursome saw the door open and the stairs come to meet the ground. After half the plane had emptied, they saw a handsome man with a close crew cut and a girl with golden hair by his side. Before the hugs and kisses began, Darcy heard her husband say, "She's pretty."

She gave him a half-hearted scowl and elbowed him in the ribs. "My, my, Willie, what did you expect?"

Davis hugged the waiting foursome. As soon as that was finished, he slid his arm around Céleste's waist and said, "Momma, Daddy, you remember Céleste? Willie, Darcy, I'd like you to meet my wife."

Darcy Hampton was a beautiful, educated woman. She loved her family at home and her other family that resided a few hundred feet away. She had always been impressed by the quiet control The Colonel had exhibited in various situations. She adored Lillian and had learned a lot from her and not just woman things. She had watched Davis grow from a cute boy to a handsome young man. Most of all, she was thankful to be a part of this family her husband had known all his life. She had seen the ugly problems that sadly existed outside the fences of The Willows and each night thanked the Lord for guiding her to this place.

Darcy was also a listener and observer. Now, all her dear ones were together in this big car…and things just weren't exactly right. She remembered how frightened she had been on her first trip here. She wasn't a whole lot older than Céleste when she first arrived and had a feeling that this young lady and she would become good friends in time. She had listened to Willie for days about how great it was going to be to have his friend and partner back. They had so much to discuss and time to make up. She saw her husband bursting at the seams like a little boy waiting for Christmas all the way back to The Willows.

Lillian had talked her silly since they returned from France, and, even before that, she had been counting days for years. She had shared the bitter disappointment Lillian had felt when she thought Rebecca had married. Again, she could see the frustration on her friend's face who was acting very subdued. The Colonel was very amicable, but he too was unusually quiet. She knew that most of this behavior was due to the presence of…Céleste DeLongpre.

Darcy crossed her legs, smoothed her dress, looked out the window and said with out moving her lips, *Hang in there, little lady. You'll make it.*

Davis looked around at everyone in the car, then turned to his new bride and squeezed her hand. He glanced out the window in time to see the big arch that had framed the entrance to The Willows for a lot longer than he had been around. He felt a warm wave wash over his soul. His road to recovery was nearly complete. He asked Daniel to stop just short of the stone pillars. "I would like to get out here, please."

He took his wife's hand and led her between the pillars that he hadn't seen for over three years. At first, The Colonel was surprised by his son's move, but then it hit him. He had done the exact same thing many times over, and it always felt great. His son was really home.

He motioned for Daniel to role down the car window, and yelled, "Momma, Daddy, we're going to walk, if y'all don't mind."

Céleste was no stranger to beauty, as she had come from beautiful surroundings herself, but there was something about this long, tree-lined lane that was indeed breathtaking. She could see why her husband was proud of it and why he loved it so much.

Lillian wanted to have a welcome home party for her wandering son, but really didn't know when he would be home. She knew he would eventually, but, with that two-day notice, there just wasn't enough time. Now that he was here, she was thrown for a loop by the surprise that he had for them. What was she going to say? "This is a welcome home party—and, oh, by the way, this is his new wife!"

She talked it over with The Colonel and the Hamptons and decided to let the kids rest for a day or two before having something simple. There were many Willows employees and a few friends from town and the outlying areas that loved Davis and could make for a nice get-together. So, the first lady decided to proceed with that plan.

Lillian thought the party went rather well. She watched as Céleste handled all the questions from surprised guests. Her fine upbringing shined at every turn, and she could see that her new daughter-in-law was no stranger to entertaining. She was beautiful, and the folks seemed to enjoy her English…topped off with a helping of French vanilla.

It was difficult for Lillian, though, living with the fact that there would be no Rebecca. She reminisced about all those years she had seen her son and "the little Thompson girl" playing together and how they had grown before her eyes. There were those times on the terrace when Rebecca had kept her company in Davis' absence then her great disappointment hearing about this Mark Lewis. She was confused as to who was to blame for this disaster. At some juncture, she blamed everyone involved. She would have difficulty trusting someone with her son all over again. But Lillian DeLongpre was a lady, an exquisite lady who was taught to handle almost any situation. She may never be close to this French belle, but she would make the best of the situation…guaranteed! There would be tests, to be sure.

Unlike many families of vast wealth, the DeLongpres kept a rather low profile. Very rarely did you see their name in the news. Even when The Colonel was traveling all over the world by himself, there was never any scandal or nasty rumors with some fortune-seeking woman or reports of bar fights. Maybe The Colonel did fall to temptation a few times. He was a rich, handsome, and powerful man, but, if indeed he did, it was very discreet and properly handled.

It was pretty much the same locally. If a stranger in Hattiesburg or any of the surrounding areas would hear the name DeLongpre and asked who that was, he would probably get an answer like, "Well, they live out yonder 'bout half an hour north. Seem to be decent folks. Don't get into town much, 'cept for the Mrs. She and that ladies club seem to have something to do with a lot of things. Got lots of money, I hear. They must own near half the Mississippi by now. Hear they are mighty nice to their coloreds, too."

Davis' welcome home party was no different—very nice and low-key. As usual, the guests were treated to the finest food and drink. They were all hand-picked, and, of course, all working at The Willows were automatically invited. Like most of the parties over the years, it went extremely well.

Chapter Twenty-Five

Rebecca Thompson had outgrown K-JUN TV in Gulfport. She had been passed over a few times and had said nothing. This didn't go unnoticed by Mr. McDaniel. He saw how talented she was and knew she couldn't go much further at the local station. He came to Gulfport and asked the station manager to call her in for a meeting. "Miss Thompson, do you like working for me?"

"Yes, sir, of course I do. I've been here...."

"Yes, I'm aware of how long you've been here. Do you want to keep working for me?"

"Yes, sir, but I've worked very hard, and I think I deserve a higher position...."

"Then pack your bags. I need you to anchor the five and six o'clock news at our station in Memphis. You'll be the first woman to do this. Good luck! I know you'll make me proud!"

Howard McDaniel was a man of his word. He also must have thought a lot of Miss Thompson. Along with the obvious big jump in pay, the corporation paid for her moving expenses and the deposit on her new luxury apartment. At least it was luxurious compared to Gulfport...and there was no Mark Lewis.

There's seldom a situation that is totally perfect. Although all the components are present, there is always a price to pay. Rebecca was now even farther away from home and had to make all new friends.

The one other thing that surfaced, something that she somehow over looked, was that one of the most famous people in the world called Memphis his home. Way back when she was home from school and had unpacked that program from the Overton Park Shell, the eerie similarity between Davis and Elvis had haunted her. And now, one of those faces was everywhere she looked in her new town. *Ooohhh boy!*

The past few weeks had been rather hectic for the young soon-to-be anchorwoman. There was that confusing and hurried trip to France and the ensuing let down. Then, no sooner is she home, when she's hit with the big surprise. However, her emotional roller coaster was only halfway down the track.

Boxes were everywhere in her new apartment. She found her coffee machine and cleared a path to her breakfast nook. Some of the dishes and flatware had been put away, but everything was still pretty much in disarray. She kept ties with her hometown when she was in Gulfport by subscribing to the Hattiesburg newspaper, and that's one of the first things she did when she arrived in Memphis. She liked reading about some of her friends, and then there was always the little three-inch by three-inch square inside the front page that reminded folks there was still a Thompson's hardware.

She looked forward to this first Sunday in Memphis. It had been a frantic week getting the feel and routine of her new job. But this was her pay off, and all she wanted was to open all the boxes and put things away. But, first things first, which meant plugging in the coffee maker and finding her paper.

She sweetened her coffee and then idly stirred it while scanning the front page. The mayor had just dedicated some historical old house as a tourist attraction. That was the exciting part of the paper. She felt a little warm tingle come over her as she saw her father's ad that was a little larger on Sundays. But wait just a minute...what was this?

> Davis DeLongpre of the Willows Ranch returns home after three years....
> With a French bride.

"Jesus Christ!" Rebecca's hand knocked over the coffee cup. Part of the hot brew found its way to her paper, which is all that kept her from fainting. She sat there stunned for several minutes, then recovered and found her phone under some trash by the sink. She dialed and waited for an answer. Her heart was about to jump out of her rib cage. Finally, a familiar voice came over the wire, "Good morning. This is Lillian."

"Lillian, what's going on there?"

"Oh, child, I'm so sorry. I tried calling you in Gulfport, then at your folk's place. This is just as big a shock to T. D. and I as it must be to you."

They talked for several minutes and somehow Rebecca managed to tell her oldest friend about her new job. They ended the conversation by Lillian asking, "Things certainly have been busy haven't they? By the way, what does your Mr. Lewis think of the move?"

"Uh, he didn't come with me, Lill."

The week-and-a-half following the newlywed's arrival was very laid back. They would walk or go for rides around the estate. Davis would point out places where he had experienced some pleasant or harrowing event. He showed her some of the places he would retreat or run off to when he had to be by himself. They were quite a ways out when he pointed to one of his hideaways, making Céleste giggle.

"That's quite a long way to run. You must've been in good shape back then." They shared a good laugh, leaned in their saddles, and enjoyed a long warm, passionate kiss. Their days were filled with long walks, sometimes accented by a picnic. Their evenings were shared with the folks during and after the evening meal. Their nights were shared with *no one* in the room where Davis grew up. This would not last for long, as they would outgrow his original quarters.

Willie had been holding in his feelings from the time they picked up the couple at the airport. If nobody believed this, all they had to do was ask Darcy. About the ninth or tenth day, he was sitting at his desk muttering about almost everything. He was not aware that he had an audience. "When is that boy going to come to work?"

There was more muttering and then the pen he was using ran out of ink. He uttered a quiet curse and deposited the pen in the wastebasket. He reached for another in the leather-covered jar on the right corner of his big rustic desk. He heard a shuffle and looked up to see the silhouette of a tall stranger filling the doorway. The stranger pushed his hat forward to his eyebrows and drawled, "Let's see now. How much money are we losing, ol' pard?"

As Willie was thinking about a snappy retort to this, they were joined by the man they called "The Boss." This was indeed a new beginning. This day would renew a partnership that would not only develop into one of the most successful breeding teams in the country, it would last the rest of their lives.

The trio sat for an hour or so going over the books and discussing their progress. Davis sat down at the desk that had been waiting for him for the past few years and leaned back in the leather chair. "Well, Daddy, Willie, how far are we away from being competitive?"

The Colonel looked at Willie and then over at his son. He motioned for Willie to answer, but Willie gave way to the man. "Son, I truly believe that we are about three to three and a half years away. I hope...I live that long."

Davis and Willie said that was good but didn't want to hear any of that "I hope" talk. Davis thought his father looked fitter than he did.

He remembered having passed Highlander Chief's empty stall, so he asked, "Hey, Willie, I didn't see the Chief. Is he okay?"

"Yeah, buddy, your million dollar stud is up in the corral on the other side of the lake, hopefully earning his keep." This brought a hearty laugh from the men. It looked like things were going to be just fine.

It was a good thing for the partners to be together again. Davis was working and that was good for him. In his earlier years, his work and study ethics led him to be extremely success-oriented. Some might even say he had tunnel vision. He had lost his first love because of this. Well, at least that was part of the problem. Now, a more mature and relaxed mind guided his actions. Another thing he had in his favor was a wife who liked the horse business as much as he did.

Céleste did her best to get close to Lillian, her *belle mère*, but found the going difficult. Lillian wasn't rude, in fact she was congenial. If an outsider were observing, they might say she was acting cautiously. When Céleste asked her *belle mère* about Davis' childhood and teenage years, the answers always came in short sentences. This was very frustrating to the younger Mrs. DeLongpre.

After several attempts to communicate with Lillian, Céleste decided to stay back and just observe what was going on around this new home of hers. She didn't want to tell Davis how she felt right away for fear it might cause friction between mother and son. She could see that Lillian went to her club meetings on the average of twice a week, and, when she wasn't doing that, she was working in her rose garden, planning meals, or just being Lillian. She also noticed how close Lillian and Darcy were.

One day when Lillian was off doing one of her ladies club projects, Céleste decided to go hang with the guys where she always seemed to be welcome. On her way out, she saw Darcy with a basket in a corner of the famous garden. She turned off the path leading to the stables and cut across to where Darcy was cutting some roses. "Hi, Darcy. What're you doing?"

"Oh, hi, little lady. I'm fixing a centerpiece for my dining room table. Would you like to help?"

"Well, yeah, sure I would."

Darcy cut a couple more flowers and handed the clippers to Céleste. "Here, you do it."

When they were finished, Darcy asked if she would like to put the arrangement together in the house. Céleste was so happy to talk to someone…another woman…that she eagerly accepted. They began arranging the different colored flowers in a big glass tray with a half an inch or so of water, just enough to float the beautiful petals a tad. It was starting to look really nice! Céleste couldn't hold back any longer, so she hesitantly began, "Darcy, I can see that you and my mother-in-law are good friends. May I ask you something?"

Darcy looked at her rather quizzically and, after a slight pause, nodded.

Céleste continued, "I've tried talking to her, and I want to get to know her. I like her and I want her to like me, but it isn't working. Am I doing something wrong? I just don't think she likes me. I wish…."

Darcy held up her hand signaling Céleste to stop. "Before you go any farther, honey, you're right. Lill and I are great friends. I would do anything in the world for her. There isn't a finer lady in the entire south. I will listen to you, but I will never talk to her on your behalf or get involved in this!" Darcy paused and Céleste felt a bit embarrassed. Darcy thought she had better continue. "Honey, did Davis ever talk to you about Rebecca Thompson?"

"No, I mean, not really. I sensed there was a connection, but I didn't ask."

"Let me tell you about her. Promise this'll stay here at my table?"

"Of course."

"You see Davis and Rebecca have known each other all of their lives. Lillian became very fond of her, as we all did, but Lillian was bound and determined to make Rebecca part of this family. She and Lillian became very close over the years. I guess Davis and Rebecca had some problems. She waited a long time for him then found someone else. This crushed Lillian. She's not going to easily accept anyone else right away. The last thing I'm going to say is, don't push it. Just take it easy, honey, and I'm sure she'll come around."

Everyone who ever met Darcy Hampton liked her or loved her. Céleste was no exception. This was not the last conversation the two women would have but probably the most important. Céleste felt better after talking with Darcy, but she had an ally that she wasn't even aware of.

The Colonel was also very fond of "the little Thompson girl," but he had made his name and his fortune by being able to read a situation and either fix it or move on. He had been in enough business deals and other relationships to know if he was being soft-soaped, conned, or just plain lied to. He knew if someone was "talkin' through his hat." When Céleste would hang around the guys, he would watch and listen to her observations and say to himself,

This little lady knows about this horse business we're in. Maybe, in time, we'll learn something from her.

There was no doubt that Céleste loved her husband, but she also kind of liked those other two guys. Maybe she was just more comfortable around men. Sometimes this happens.

This wonderful island in southern Mississippi had known harmony since post-Civil War days, those days when two great men first put on the gloves (garden gloves) many years ago. The spirits of these men, Jarrod DeLongpre and Isaiah Hampton, still tread upon this special land. At night, they talk to each other via the winds in the willows and are determined to keep this almost sacred harmony in tact.

This harmony was not beyond being tested; there was the sudden and tragic death of Ben Hampton, the heir apparent almost lost his life in Amiens, France, the disappointment felt by Lillian over Rebecca, and, lastly, the new foreign addition that joined The Willows' foundation. This was more than just a piece of land with a few people living on it. This was *The Willows*, and it would heal itself when the time was right.

If it were possible for a forty-room mansion to be crowded then the big house was becoming that. Even sisters who have grown up together still have trouble with co-habitation once they reach adulthood.

Céleste continued trying her best to fit in and often offered to assist her *belle mère* with various tasks and projects. She even tried showing interest in Lillian's roses. But, even *if* the grand dame of the estate had been more in favor of the new wife's presence, it still would not have been easy. Lillian was not especially difficult to get along with. It was the structure of her life and most things in it. Even her first choice for a daughter-in-law would have required space and a period of adjustment.

Davis had made mental notes of this at the family's evening meals. Céleste was fine when she was hanging around with the guys in the office and stables, but when she and his mother were together, she was almost too polite. This bothered him, but somehow he chose not to talk about it.

The Colonel, on the other hand, thoroughly enjoyed the new addition to their family. Every day he could see more and more of the values Jon-Pierre and Emma had instilled in their little girl. Her obvious attributes were pleasant, but she was also bright and a pleasure to be around. She also provided something he never had, a daughter. He hoped that someday his wife would feel the same way.

This situation continued for several months until one evening, following one of their always-sumptuous meals, The Colonel lit up his customary cigar.

The sound of another match being lit drew the attention of all to the other end of the table. Lillian looked first at her husband, then to her son, and, with her eyes, she let it be known that one cigar was enough at this table. "Daddy, I think I'll finish mine outside."

"Fine idea, son. Use some company?"

The Colonel did his best to stifle a grin but wasn't too successful. He blew a kiss to his wife and then to Céleste. Father and son rose and departed for the outdoors. Céleste looked after them, wishing they made cigars for ladies.

The two men walked down the path to their usual place at the fence. The Colonel took a small puff, relished it, and exhaled, watching the falling ashes barely miss his boot. He began speaking as he always did, slowly and methodically. "Son, it appears we have a problem here. It is not a big one, but one that I think needs attention. You and Céleste are just as entitled to live in this house as your mother and I, but I think your bride would like her own windows to hang curtains in. What are your thoughts on this?"

Davis thought for a moment and said to himself, *I'm starting to think exactly like him. I never thought this would happen. Not bad though, I could do a lot worse.* His cigar had gone out, but he flicked it anyway. "Daddy, I wanted to bring this up for a while now, but I didn't want to hurt you and Momma. I'm sure Céleste would agree to it in a heartbeat."

The great man chuckled and put his arm around his son's shoulder. "How about you and I goin' for a ride in the morning. I've got something in mind."

"Okay, Daddy." Father and son walked, arms around shoulders back to the house.

The morning sun was Davis' alarm clock. He felt the warm rays coming through the window, caressing his face. He rubbed his eyes and rolled on his side to kiss his bride good morning. She pulled him to her and mumbled sleepily, "Where do you think you're going so early?"

"I didn't tell you last night, but my dad asked me to go riding."

She was awake now and sat up. Her nightgown slipped about halfway off and as she grabbed to pull it back up, Davis smiled, leaned over and kissed her gently. "I'll be right back."

"Wait! Can I go, too?"

He put his hands out in a calming gesture and finished pulling on his jeans and boots. With his shirt half-buttoned, he went downstairs to find his father having coffee and reading the business section of the paper. "Morning, Daddy. I was just wondering if...."

"Oh, good morning, son. Say, why don't you ask Céleste if she wants to go with us?"

Lillian had never cared too much for horses, especially the one in France, so they let her sleep in and sneaked out before breakfast.

The Colonel adjusted the saddle strap a little tighter on his big bay and then gave Céleste a foot up. As he mounted, he motioned to Davis to ride alongside. *What a wonderful day to be alive and well,* the big man thought. He looked lovingly at the future riding to his right. With his big left hand, he secured his hat and gently slapped the bay's flanks.

Many years before, he and Willie's father had begun adding more livestock to the already prosperous plantation and were working on a way to make more water accessible to the herds. A meandering stream that flowed from the hills north of The Willows' borders seemed to be the perfect solution. They decided to build a dam between two knolls and let the water fill this natural valley. It was only about one hundred and fifty feet wide at the dam, but it was a large enough lake to handle a huge amount of livestock. Over the years, it had become somewhat of a wildlife sanctuary.

They rode past the lake into a stand of cottonwood trees and up a little rise. The Colonel yelled, "Whoa," spinning his mount around. Davis and Céleste followed suit by riding over next to their father. The Colonel shoved his hat back a bit and said warmly, "Isn't this a great view?"

As the young couple looked in the direction his gloved hand was pointing, they saw a flock of ducks landing on a finger of the lake, surprising a large heron looking for breakfast.

Davis said, "Yeah, it sure is, Daddy. What's up?"

The Colonel smiled broadly, dismounted, and walked to a tree. He slapped it, and then walked across a small clearing to another tree and slapped it. The couple looked quizzically at each other then back at The Colonel. "Well...if you don't have any previous plans, I think this would be a wonderful place for your front porch!"

It was a wonderful ride back home with the anticipation of a big breakfast...and a chance to share the news with Lillian.

The following months were very busy for the entire family. The Colonel decided to oversee the construction while his boys ran the stables. Davis and Céleste had approved the blueprints, agreeing on most things. Céleste made some minor changes in the master bedroom and, of course, the kitchen, but that was to be expected. Everything else was going smoothly. The big boss would never give a gift that wasn't perfect, now would he?

At the close of the day's business at the livery, Willie and Davis would go up to the site and hammer a few nails themselves. The main structure was nearly finished. One could easily use his or her imagination on applying the finishing touches.

One morning, Céleste found Lillian sitting at the kitchen table with glasses on and pen in hand. She carefully approached her and said, "Good morning. I know you're busy, Lillian, but could I have a minute of your time when you're finished?"

Lillian looked up and saw something in her daughter-in-law's eyes that made her say, "Well, yes, child. What is it? Oh...please, sit down."

Céleste nervously pulled a chair out, sat down, and slid up to the table opposite from her *belle mère*. She looked into the eyes of this lady she admired, saying, "I'm sure you know our new home is almost done. I've noticed the way you have decorated your home so elegantly. Davis told me you did most of it yourself."

"Well, I more or less just...."

"Lillian, it would mean the world to me if you could find it in your heart to help me do ours...if you have time that is."

"Well, now, I don't know, child. I haven't done this for a long time now, and I don't know if you would like what...."

"Oh, I don't care. I love what you've done.... Please!"

Lillian just couldn't say no. Just as she was about to consent, Céleste rambled on. She had tried long enough to communicate with her mother-in-law and was not about to give up the floor just yet.

"Another thing. I want to have my folks come over when it's done. And while they are here, well, Davis and I have been thinking about renewing our wedding vows, if it's okay with you and The Colonel. Because we...."

"What did you say, child?"

"I said, Davis and I want to get...."

Lillian reached over, took her daughter in her arms, and squeezed her until she couldn't breath.

If one were standing facing the lake, the master bedroom would be on the left. The front door would separate it from the living room where a huge picture window would provide a panoramic view of the lake and beyond.

On a Saturday morning, Davis, his dad, and Willie were assisting the workers putting the glass in place. When The Colonel stood up to adjust his hat, his eyes beheld a wonderful sight. He tapped his son on the shoulder, and Davis turned to see his mother and his wife walking hand in hand with Darcy right behind them. They were headed to what would someday soon be the kitchen.

There have been celebrations of great movies and stage plays, openings of famous galleries, but this time at The Willows was truly a "Kodak moment."

It had been over a year since Davis brought his bride to The Willows. The new home had been completed, and it was indeed lovely. If one were leaving the back door of the big house, he would walk through the pathway that split Lillian's garden, then turn left before he reached the stables. The Colonel had a road built that followed the lake for a hundred yards plus, then turned up the hill to the grove of cottonwoods. Where the road ended, a path of seventy-five or eighty feet in length, bordered by foot-high grayish-green stones, led to the new house. Between the stones and the lawn was a row of Lillian's handpicked rose bushes on either side. The front of the one story house was layered with used bricks and all the windows trimmed in eggshell white. The big trees that surrounded the house and yard in a semi-circle were only partially visible from the barns below.

Lillian loved the idea of her son and daughter-in-law having a real wedding at The Willows. Truth be known, this was the ice-beaker that brought them together. The two women decided to treat this occasion like it was the real thing and the elopement had never happened.

One morning the women were filling out the invitations, a job that they could've had done for them, however this was a special occasion, and it required a personal "hands on" approach. Darcy and Willie's wedding was the last one celebrated here; it was truly wonderful, but *this* was Lillian's dream. She wanted to be right in the middle of everything. She finished addressing the envelopes and took off her glasses to rub the bridge of her nose. She looked across the table at Céleste, who appeared to be in a writing frenzy. The bride-to-be looked up and caught the older woman staring at her. She gave her a big smile and asked, "What is it, *belle mère?*"

Lillian was embarrassed, but recovered nicely, "I was just thinking…you look very happy, child."

"Oh, I am! By the way, I have the name Rodolpho and Ireñe Montoya here, but no address. Do we have one?" she asked, then recalled, "Oh, aren't they the people from Spain that Davis told me about?"

"I've got it somewhere, child. Just let me look."

With that, they took a break and decided to have tea on the terrace. It had been some time since Lillian had been there. As they sat and talked, Lillian remembered the last thing Rebecca had said to her when she asked if Mark Lewis had accompanied her to Memphis, "He didn't come with me, Lill." As much as Lillian loved Rebecca, she shook that thought off. Now, it seemed so long ago. Her dream for grandchildren was sitting right in front of her.

Jon-Pierre Genevive finished walking his daughter's horse. He turned off the walking machine, unhooked the tether from the bar, and led the cinnamon-colored mare back to her stall. While he was drying and currying, his thoughts turned to his *ma petite*. She had been gone for over a year, and he ached for her every day. He missed the way she stood up to him and defied him at times. Yes, he loved his sons and his wife, but when Céleste left for America, she left his soul feeling empty. Every now and then he would ride the cinnamon mare or at least put her on the walker. Today, it was the walker. *The next time, who knows?* He finished, patted the big mare on the neck, lovingly ran his hand from her forehead down to her to nose and said, "I miss her, too. I miss her, too." He closed the gate to her stall and walked slowly on the hard clay floor to the main doors. He secured them before beginning a lonely stroll to the house.

Every self-respected rancher has a favorite truck. They all have several vehicles for work, pleasure, or family functions, but they all have that one special truck. Amos Hubbard had a truck. Yes, he preferred to do business on horseback, but he had a truck. Willie Hampton had one, Davis had one, and Rodolpho had his old beater. All their trucks were old, like comfortable leather jackets. No one knows exactly why this is, but it's something one has to accept. That's that.

Jon-Pierre looked in the direction of his truck. It was parked as close to the back of the house as he could get it, without being on the lawn or in Emma's flowerbeds. He walked over to it and hoisted himself on the front fender. He reached into his pocket for his walking around cigar pack, which were his little cigars. The big ones were in the decanter on the bar and only used after dinner with a snifter full of cognac. His wife's piercing yell startled him to the point that he slid off the fender and fell to the ground on his derriere.

"Jon-Pierre! If you can part company with that dirty truck, you have a very important phone call!"

The rancher was not in the best of moods this day and really didn't feel like talking to any one just now. He said with a trace of irritation, "Emma, who is it?"

"Oh, just someone you haven't seen for over a year."

He put his cigar in his mouth, dusted himself off, eased around Emma's garden, and walked to the house. He'd known Emma long enough to tell by the tone of her voice whether it was good news or bad. This tone was of a teasing nature, but very warm and cheery. He started walking, which turned into half-run to the back door.

Inside, he crossed the dining room floor to the bar where his smiling wife was standing with the receiver in her ear. "That sounds wonderful, *ma petite*. We will talk later. Here is your papa."

The Genevives had been married for two and a half decades. She had never seen him cry. *What had happened to this man of concrete at this particular moment?* Céleste had briefed her mother of her intentions and repeated more or less the same request to her father. Emma watched as her husband hung up the phone, turned, and walked to her. She saw the moistness in his eyes and asked, "Does this mean we're going to this Hattiesburg, America?"

Céleste told Lillian that her parents would be coming and maybe her brother, Hubert. Lillian liked her parents, but wasn't sure if she knew which brother her daughter-in-law meant. The short time they were in France, there was quite a bit on her mind.

The Montoyas were the only ones left to call. Lillian said she would do this, but they thought it would be much nicer if Davis made the call himself. Céleste went to the stables to fetch her husband and found the trio right where she knew they would be. They looked up as the golden girl entered the room and listened as she said, "Lillian and I have been doing invitations and phone calls, but she thinks you should call Rodolpho, honey."

The Colonel looked at his son in mock horror and growled, "I'm surprised you haven't done that already!"

Davis slapped himself on the side of his head and said, "What wasn't I thinking?" They shared a chuckle; Davis looked at his watch and picked up the receiver.

Rodolpho Montoya had talked to The Colonel on a regular basis since the accident. During these conversations, these men who had bonded during that magical month in Spain had firstly been concerned with Davis' condition. There were also other matters they had discussed briefly, like the property on the other side of the fence. This, however, was put on hold until they knew more about how the more serious matter would develop.

They were obviously delighted with Davis' steady improvement, but neither man knew of or had prepared for the situation that had happened between Davis and Céleste. When the newlyweds arrived home from France, so much was going on that The Colonel just let that slip by. This was one of the only times this man ever forgot an important matter such as that. It is a fact—he was getting older, but that could not be used as an excuse. There was just too much going on.

When Céleste had followed Lillian's idea to ask Davis to call the Montoyas, The Colonel covered his embarrassment by teasing his son. This balanced out, because Davis also was embarrassed about forgetting the Montoyas. Again, there was just too much happening.

Rodolpho and Ireñe sat on the corner of the big dining room table. Their daughters were away at school and, for the first time, the Ranchero was without all the energy and life that had always been around. This did not affect them only. Yolanda and the rest of the staff were also looking for something to occupy their time. Ireñe had given most of her staff a month's paid vacation, but Yolanda and her husband would always be there no matter what.

The playful touching and grab-ass action they had always displayed was no longer taking place. There was nobody there to show off to. The phone on the bar that had always been busy with their daughters' would-be suitors was also silent. There were business calls during the day, but this evening, like most others, found the black talking instrument eerily null and void.

The Montoyas had season tickets to the theater in Barcelona. They seldom used them, except for the times when a big name play came to town. Ireñe rose and went to her desk in the office adjacent to the dining room and scanned the schedule. She returned to the table and suggested they take the cover off the Sedan Deville, which had not been driven very much since Davis left. They agreed on this and rose to dress for the play. The almost dormant telephone now began to come to life and rang like a sleeping monster emerging from hibernation. The surprised couple looked at each other in astonishment, and, after the forth or fifth ring, Ireñe jumped up and made her way to the source. She picked the receiver off of its base and gently said, "*Buenos noches, este es Ireñe Montoya. Como esta usted?*"

"Ireñe, this is Davis. I'm calling from my home in Mississippi. How are you and Rodolpho?"

"Davis! *Mi Dios*! What a wonderful surprise!"

The second Rodolpho heard Ireñe say, "Davis," he jumped up like he had been sitting on a giant spring. He rushed to his wife's side grinning like a little boy who had just found out he wasn't going to get spanked. Ireñe saw the excitement in his eyes, which was nice to see again. She had not seen this for a quite a while. She said good-bye to Davis and handed him the phone. "Davis, my boy. How are you? How are you feeling? You gave us quite a scare a few months ago!" He listened as Davis explained his desire for them to come to his wedding. Ireñe watched as he said "yes" a half dozen times. Finally, he said, "My boy, we would not miss this great occasion for anything on this earth. Of course we will be there!" He hung up the phone and gave his wife a bear hug that literally lifted her off the floor (another thing he had not done for some time). She squealed like a teenager.

"My love, you are finally going to see America!"

"That's wonderful, my husband. Now, maybe you can slow down and tell me why."

"Our boy is getting married!"

"Is it that young lady who made him lose the look of eagles?"

Rodolpho calmed down and answered sheepishly, "*Mi Dios*! I forgot to ask!"

There were a few additional phone calls to France and Spain. The Colonel was back into organizing things again. The Genevives and the Montoyas would be landing in Atlanta within an hour of each other, so The Colonel called Rex Henderson to meet them there with his private plane. As most things T. D. DeLongpre attempted, it worked out to a tee.

On the short flight from Atlanta to Hattiesburg, a twenty-three-year-old Frenchman looked out the window of the DC-4 and smiled. Two of his wishes had been fulfilled. He would now get to see part of America and his friend

Davis. He only wanted one more thing—a size six-and-three-quarter coal-black Stetson cowboy hat.

The first two days were about as perfect as anyone could wish for. Jon-Pierre would see his *ma petite,* and they would walk down the aisle for him to give her away. Rodolpho would again see the son he never had, and his "babies" that he had sold to him years earlier. Ireñe would get to see her friend Lillian and make a new friend in Emma. Davis and Céleste could hold hands and dream of a future while drinking in all this love that surrounded them. Davis gave Hubert a Stetson that he wore everywhere but to bed. The Colonel took pleasure in showing Jon-Pierre and Rodolpho what he, Davis, and Willie had accomplished in a relatively short time. The gentlemen ranchers from France and Spain weren't easily impressed by the things they'd seen all their lives...until now.

Many years before this, there was a beautiful wedding at The Willows. Darcy Williams had become Darcy Hampton next to Lillian's rose garden, but this was before Lillian had finished and remodeled the old mansion. On the eastern side of the grand old house was a ballroom that had seen many lavish parties while the South was in her heyday preceding the Civil War. This was the last room that she had tackled, and the young bride had restored it as close as possible to its original grandeur. The hardwood floors were sanded and polished, along with the hand-carved ornate walls and mosaic ceiling, right down to the bandbox. Over one hundred years later, it took everyone who saw it back to another time.

There was no doubt who would be Davis' best man, and, with the friendship Céleste had easily developed with Darcy, there could be no other choice there. The Hamptons two sons made adorable young ushers. One could say the Hamptons were well-represented this glorious morning.

The visitors from the two countries in Europe would stay a few more days after the newlyweds left for their Caribbean honeymoon. The Montoyas left to return to their ranchero in the rolling hills outside Barcelona, while the Genevives departed for their chateau in Northern France.

Actually, *most* of the Genevives left. One of them decided to stay at The Willows a while longer. This was fine with the DeLongpres and Hamptons, but met with some opposition from his French family. His promise sounded similar to what Davis had told his folks on two previous occasions. "I will be home soon, Papa, Mama. I promise," Hubert swore.

Chapter Twenty-Six

Mr. and Mrs. DeLongpre spent close to a month on several islands in the Caribbean, including an island owned by The Colonel. They walked on the pure white sand beaches, snorkeled in the pristine aqua waters, enjoyed the many culinary offerings each place had to offer, and put away their share of the drinks with fruit and umbrellas on the top. They made love in their bungalow anytime the urge came over them. Every day was a new adventure. The sun was never warmer and the stars never brighter. When this time in paradise was over, they had a wonderful home and family to return to. Things couldn't be more perfect for this young couple. This was the beginning of what they hoped would be a long, loving and beautiful life.

Davis and Céleste's wedding at The Willows was an event enjoyed by all in attendance. Granted, they were legally married in that little town not far from Amiens, France, and that was never questioned nor could be, but the renewal of the couple's vows was like the real thing as far as everyone at The Willows was concerned, especially Lillian.

But if one were to go back in history, there have always been two sides to everything. Misery to some people has meant happiness to others. Floods and fires have destroyed families and cities, but made others rich. One person a few hundred miles north of Hattiesburg, Mississippi, did not share the jubilation that enveloped The Willows.

About an hour before noon was when Ms. Rebecca Thompson's day began. She was the first anchorwoman, later "anchorperson," in the fledging TV News business. People loved her weather reports and, because of this, loved it when she graduated to prime time. Before going to work she would read the dailies at her breakfast table. When she finished with those, she would pick up the one from her hometown and relish it like some special dessert. From time to time, she would put the paper down, take a sip of coffee, and remember special things. One of them was the lingering image of Davis sitting on the floor after destroying her father's gasoline can display. This was a special day in her young life. After all, that was the day she first laid eyes on the man who still held her heart in his hand. Every time Davis crossed her mind, that image jumped right out in front. She recalled the price of those empty cans, ninety-nine cents, and would sometimes lament that her life wasn't even worth that without her first and only real love.

Rebecca's life was indeed worth much more than that. She had accomplished quite a bit in her young life and had made inroads into a tough business for a woman to get into at that time. Yes, she had gone where no woman before had, and she was just getting started. There was a hole in her life, however, that she couldn't fill. There was a dark cloud that she always seemed to be under when she was alone. Getting a roommate crossed her mind on several of these downtimes. She would eventually do that.

On this particular morning, however, more rain would fall from this little black cloud. The smile she always wore upon seeing her father's ad slowly became a frown when she read in large black print:

> Mr. and Mrs. Thurston Davis DeLongpre, III renew vows at
> The Willows.

After she caught her breath, she read on about the guest list and what a big blowout it was. The rain from that cloud continued to fall as she threw the paper in the trash. She added two cubes of sugar to her lukewarm coffee and said to herself, *Well, that's that!* Then she stirred and stirred and stirred.

Lillian looked across the table at her husband building something with his mashed potatoes. He looked fit for a man who would turn seventy-three at the end of the year. A wry smile crept over her face as she realized she wasn't that far behind. It had been a good life—a good year for that matter. She had become quite fond of Céleste, and the two women had nearly finished the new house. As she sat at the dinner table that evening, she could only wonder if he missed having the young folks around as much as she did.

Lillian and The Colonel both enjoyed helping raise Willie after Ben died and, of course, got great pleasure and satisfaction bringing up their Davis. But now everyone had grown up. Although the kids were not far away up there on the hill, Lillian had an empty feeling. There was something missing. She knew what it was, but there was only one way that her wish could come true.

It had been two years since Davis returned home from France with his bride, and almost a year since the big wedding. Céleste's brother used one of the many rooms at the big house while enjoying all that his stay in America could offer. The Colonel got some sort of kick about Hubert preferring his ranch to his father's. The way it looked, it would take an act of God to get him to go home.

Davis and Willie arrived at their office within seconds of each other this fine spring morning. They casually discussed the progress they were making toward their ultimate goal of developing future racing champions and were quite satisfied with what they had accomplished. They wanted to find a jockey who had proved himself capable in the racing circuit. He would have to be someone who would be satisfied to grow along with their long-range plans. He would not have to depend on winning every race to make a living because a team who could afford to be patient would pay him. They had a few names in mind and would do the necessary research before making some calls. Putting the mind-boggling work aside for now, they decided to go out to the paddocks and watch one of their future stars being worked out by their ace trainer.

As they assumed their favorite positions of leaning on the top rung of the fence surrounding the training area, Willie looked to his left and saw The Colonel descending the back steps of the big house. The great man still had his Stetson in his right hand. He ran his fingers through his thick crop of nearly white hair and finally got the hat in place as he reached the path that split Lillian's gardens. The Colonel was becoming more and more casual and less punctual about arriving early at the office, but this sure as hell didn't bother anyone. He had earned the right to do any damn thing he wanted.

As he adjusted his hat, the sun caught the sterling silver band, and, for a second, it flashed like a bright star. This brought a big smile from both Davis and Willie, as they waited patiently for him to join them and rest his elbows on the same top rung. He still struck an imposing figure that made them both proud, as it always had and always would. "Morning, boys. I see you're still waiting for me to get this here day started. Who are we looking at this fine morning?"

They watched for a while and departed for the office. They sat in the room that was dominated by the sight and smell of wood and leather as The Colonel listened to his boy's plan to find and hire a jockey. As always, he listened intently, pushed his chair back slightly, put his boots on the desk, and leaned back. He lit a cigar. After taking a satisfying first puff, he stroked his healthy gray moustache and thought for a moment. "I like it, boys. Any ideas of who, so far?"

This was pretty much the way things had been going for some time now. Everything was progressing like a well-oiled machine. It seemed like nothing could possibly go wrong on this land in the south of Mississippi. The only slight change was the absence of Céleste hanging around with her men. During the early days of her arrival, when she and Lillian were not what one would call "close," the golden girl spent most of her time at The Willows livery.

Ruthie Devereaux listened to her friend's request and was shocked, to put it mildly. This had never come up in the history of the Women's Guild, and Ruthie was struggling to come up with an answer.

Lillian was the president and Ruthie the vice-president, just above the secretary-treasurer. She could have had the final say in the matter, but decided to exercise the democratic process. Ruthie finally managed to spit (not literally) out her opinion. "Lill, I don't think so. I mean she is a beautiful young woman and seems to be well-educated, but, for God's sakes, she's...well, she's colored!"

"Well, Ruthie, I can see how you feel about this, and twenty years ago, I would've, too. But times are changing. If you and the ladies decide against this, I'll have no choice but to resign my office and membership!"

Lillian looked at the open-mouthed Ruthie as she struggled to reply. One week later, Darcy Hampton was accepted into "The Greater Hattiesburg Women's Association."

That was several years ago, and now Lillian wanted to sponsor someone else. There would be no objections or even discussions. Mrs. Céleste DeLongpre would become the association's newest member. The only person who was not thrilled with this event was the younger Mrs. DeLongpre herself. Although she made the dressmakers proud, the French import would always prefer Levi's and boots and, of course, spending time with the horses and her men. However, she decided to make allowances for this. It had taken her too long to get Lillian's approval. If this was one of the ways to do it, well so be it.

Lillian however, was thoroughly enjoying her daughter-in-law, something she would never have anticipated a year or so ago. All those times she and Rebecca had enjoyed together when Davis was away at school, were something she would never forget. She was so happy that she had finally given Céleste a chance and noticed that she drank tea on the terrace as good as Rebecca did.

Let's be honest about Lillian. She had many loves, especially now, but if she hadn't at least tried to get Céleste interested in her rose garden...well, it just wouldn't have been Lillian. Céleste, like everything else where her *belle mère* was concerned, tried her best to please, but Mrs. DeLongpre had little trouble seeing that all the young bride was interested in was viewing and smelling. After a few of these sessions in the garden, Lillian, one afternoon, pushed back her straw hat with her forearm and put her hands, palms side out on her hips and half-laughing, half-scolding she said, "Okay, child. Go play with your boys and those smelly horses!"

Lillian need not say another word. The little French lady put her apron, gloves, and hat in the potting shed and was off to her little part of heaven.

On one of the mornings that Céleste always looked forward to, she had gone to the office with her husband and, as usual, had a chat with The Colonel and Willie. After asking Willie what Darcy was up to, she decided to take a leisurely hour to two-hour horseback ride. Darcy, according to Willie, was busy with some project, and anyway, it would take an act of congress to get her on a horse. It didn't daunt her spirits in the least to go riding alone.

She bid the men good morning and went to the stall to prepare her horse for the ride. She led her mount from the barn, out to the side of the corral where they all began their rides. As she slipped her left foot in the stirrup and grabbed the saddle horn, she suddenly felt weary and dizzy and then fainted!

As she fell to the ground, it spooked her mare, making her stomp and whinny. The men in the office heard the commotion and ran out to find Céleste lying next to the fence. They were all shocked. Willie told Davis and The Colonel to stay and he would call a doctor, then Lillian. He didn't have to call Lillian, though. She saw the rider-less horse walking by the edge of the fence.

Twenty minutes or so later, the doctor arrived with the ambulance in time to see Céleste sitting up and Davis helping her to stand. She was more embarrassed than anything, she explained to the doctor.

He checked her out regardless, and asked, "Do you have any pain anywhere?"

"I'm sure I'll have a bruise on my butt, but that's nothing new. I did have this headache, but it seems to have gone away."

Lillian insisted that she go to the hospital for a complete check-up. Nothing would ever happen to her daughter-in-law if she had anything to say about it. Of course, Davis and his father concurred. The Colonel and Willie stayed behind while mother and son accompanied Céleste to the hospital.

The two of them were sitting in the waiting room hoping everything was all right. It seemed like forever, but no more than an hour had passed when they looked up to see a nurse pushing Céleste in a wheelchair with the doctor by her side. As they approached, the smiles on the patient, doctor, and nurse's face led the worried son and mother-in-law to believe that all was well. Céleste looked up at the doctor and gestured to the bespectacled physician to give her family the news. The tall thin man of medicine in the long white coat, smiled and said warmly, "Mr. DeLongpre, Mrs. DeLongpre, it seems that your little lady here is with child!"

The following months at The Willows were filled with joy. Davis and Céleste were obviously ecstatic, as was the entire Willows family. The anticipation of the new birth did not stop with the DeLongpres and Hamptons, it spread all the way through the fifty plus employees.

The last celebration was the arrival of Willie and Darcy's second child a few years earlier. There had been births among the Willows' employees, and while they were treated with importance, as they should be, everyone knew the order of their universe. The heirs apparent, or the "prince," as they thought of him, and his lovely wife would continue the legacy and insure, for certain, a future for themselves and their children.

No one was more pleased than Lillian. She thought back to that marvelous afternoon when The Colonel brought her from their wedding in Meridian and she met little Willie. She thanked some higher power for giving her Davis every day since it happened. She doted over Willie and Darcy's boy and girl and did her best to spoil them without getting in the way. But this was going to make her a grandma, and what a blessing this was for her, in these twilight years of her life.

Céleste was also enjoying her pregnancy. She had been very athletic all of her life, and, despite the requests from her husband and her *belle mère* to slow down, she still hung out with her men and rode her mare almost daily. The only discomfort she experienced was an unexplainable occasional headache. She never mentioned this because she wanted no one to fret, as she knew they would. Her brother Hubert would remind her from time to time to call home.

The nine months that it normally takes for this miracle to occur went by rather quickly. Davis and Céleste would sometimes have dinner at the big house, or for a change would have the folks over at the new place on the hill. The after-dinner conversations would always end by talking about the most important thing going on in their lives. Lillian and Céleste would come up with possible names for whatever the gender of the upcoming child may be, but the biggest concern was for the baby to be healthy. Just for fun, the women would choose the girl's names and the men would choose the boy's names. It was friendly and fun, but the underlying desire to keep alive the DeLongpre name always surfaced. The Colonel and Lillian would exchange knowing glances that only they knew. "You are right, T. D. We do want to keep the name alive, but I know that these young kids will have many chances to accomplish this."

That's the way it went at The Willows. The time everyone there had been waiting for was drawing closer and closer. Céleste at eight months looked as pregnant as most women did at five. Her cream-colored skin and golden hair only became more beautiful. Lillian and Darcy fussed over her like proud lionesses, to the point you would have thought it was their baby.

About two weeks before Doctor Lane had predicted, Céleste woke suddenly as if someone had kicked her in a dream. However, the sun saying hello through the bedroom window made her realize it wasn't a dream. She gasped, reached over, and solidly tapped the sleeping Davis. It was a little after 6:00 a.m. That was the time he was used to waking up, but not usually so abruptly. He responded to the tapping and, with sleep-filled eyes, asked, "What is it, honey…oh, my God!"

"I think we should head for the hospital!" she whimpered.

Davis jumped up and fetched the suitcase that had been ready to go for several days previous. He helped his wife to the bathroom and saw she was okay for the moment and then called the big house and awakened his parents. They in turn woke the chauffeur, Daniel, about the same time Davis called the Hamptons. Willie told Davis that it would take them too long to get ready and to just go ahead. "Call us as soon as you know anything!"

On the way to the hospital, they all kept asking the mother-to-be if she was all right. She patiently told them several times that she was okay, considering the obvious, except for that headache that seemed to come and go at will.

For thousands of years, the seasons have come and gone. Empires have risen and fallen, and Camelot is only a "sometimes" thing. It had been proven many times that no one, but no one, is untouchable. Everyone in the world at some level or another eventually has to pay his or her dues.

The two hours that had passed since Céleste was admitted seemed more like a full day. Davis kept looking at his watch and then at his parents, as the three of them lingered impatiently in the waiting room.

Doctor Lane took off his rubber gloves and threw them in the white trash can in the corner of the surgery room. He pulled his mask down around his neck. He pushed open the double doors and walked down the hall past the admitting desk to the waiting room. The DeLongpres looked up into his tired eyes and waited.

Willie and Darcy had been waiting by the phone since Davis' call early in the morning. Darcy had fixed breakfast, as usual, and though it filled the house with its delicious aroma, they both did little more than sip on coffee and watch the kids eat. Willie looked smilingly at them, remembering a time when all he had to worry about was getting full and how good things tasted.

The phone call they had been anticipating finally came. Willie pointed to Darcy with a "please you get it" glance. She excitedly moved to pick up the ringing instrument, "Hi, this is Darcy. Is this going to be what we have been waiting…?"

As Darcy listened Willie could see her hands shaking and hear the trembling in her voice. The last thing she could remember was The Colonel saying, "Darcy, honey, Doctor Lane said it was some sort of an aneurysm. She didn't make it through…. No, the baby didn't survive either."

Darcy looked into Willie's worried eyes and could only say, "Oh, baby. This is absolutely awful!"

Davis remained surprisingly stoic as he listened to the doctor deliver his somber message. That was, however, only on the outside. The Colonel left mother and son to their grief while he called the Hamptons. Doctor Lane waited patiently, as he watched the aging but still tall, broad-shouldered patriarch of the DeLongpre family leave them to make the call. He felt so incredibly helpless. Although he could not have actually seen this coming, a feeling of guilt filled his being.

Lillian stopped sobbing for a moment and eased back from her son's embrace. He kept his arm on his mother's shoulder and asked the doctor in a quiet, sad voice, "Doctor Lane, I would like to see her…if it is all right?" The doctor nodded and Davis took his mother's hand and began to follow the doctor to where his wife lay.

Lillian stopped and slowly took her hand from her son's grasp. She nervously fretted with her curls and said almost crying, "Not just yet, honey. You go, though, if you want to."

Davis walked side by side with the bearer of bad news without either man saying a word. They passed through the swinging double doors, as the doctor pointed to the covered bed.

Doctor Lane gently pulled back the sheet as Davis watched. With his heart and entire being dragging the ground, he inched up to her side. Her golden hair, although still wet from her final battle, spread loosely across the pillow. He swallowed hard as he remembered that was how she had looked many times after she had showered and come to join him in bed. He ran his fingers over her forehead and laid his head on her chest. Without looking up, he motioned the doctor to leave them alone.

He sat on the edge of the bed and began talking to her, as he had so many mornings before. This time though, she would not wake up smiling. He drifted back to that horrible time in France when he had been told that she stayed at his side for days while he was in a coma. "You were there for me, my golden love, and now I can't be there for you. This just isn't fair. Nothing is fair. I am so sorry. I love you so much. I hope that some way, wherever you are right now, you can hear me." He stroked her forehead and hair one more time and then pulled the sheet over her face.

He somehow made his way back to the waiting room where he found his father and mother still sitting in the colorless empty room. The Colonel beckoned him to sit down, but, instead, he turned to the patient Daniel, and said, "Please take us home now."

Hubert Genevive heard the annoying rapping on his door and yelled at whomever the intruder was to go away. The young Frenchman had a major league hangover.

Since his arrival at The Willows, he had enjoyed his new freedom and lived it to the maximum. Being away from his father had given him a whole new personality he relished. He respected his hosts and did his fair share of work alongside his friend Davis, The Colonel, and Willie. At the end of the workday, he played just as hard. He had met several of the local Hattiesburg southern belles, charming them as only a single Frenchman could.

The annoying rapping on his door continued. Finally, the person knocking became impatient and pushed the door open. "Hubert, it's Willie. Wake up!"

When the DeLongpre's arrived home from the hospital, they saw the Hamptons and Hubert sitting at the table in the large country kitchen. There were very few words exchanged in this stricken group of unbelievers. The family could only compare this sad moment to the passing of Ben Hampton many years before.

There were many things to do, as there always are in a trying time such as this. Naturally, funeral arrangements had to be made, but the most difficult task would be calling France. After much discussion, all agreed that Hubert was the man for this unenviable job. Besides, he really wanted to. This call to his father would be one of many in the next few days.

Céleste's death was obviously devastating to Hubert. His sadness was compounded by all of the regrets of what he should have done. The guilt he felt for not loving her as much as he should have for all those years was eating him up inside. From the morning Céleste was born, she was the ultimate "daddy's girl." Hubert and his two younger brothers had to take a back seat when it came to the attention heaped on her by her father. It appeared to them that, for all intents and purposes, they didn't exist.

Hubert had wanted to get away from his father for years but couldn't figure how to do it without hurting his family. If the truth were known, he was probably afraid of how he would make it on his own. When the handsome American made his first visit to the chateau, and he saw how his sister went totally crazy for Davis, the oldest Genevive son saw a window of opportunity. Davis was over twenty-one and could qualify as a guardian, and Hubert wanted to go on this horse-buying trip with him. *Now, if Davis took a fancy to his sister...*

He tried desperately to talk to Davis, but he was always getting cut off, either by his father's plan to try and screw the American out of major money, or by his sister's subtle attempts to seduce him.

The morning of Davis' departure was at hand, and Hubert knew he could forget about his desire to go with him. He thought, *Maybe he likes my sister, maybe he will return to see her.* As a last ditch effort to get Davis' attention, he gave him a parting gift. He guessed that he and Davis wore the same size shoe, so he gave him a new pair of French-style cowboy boots that he had made for himself.

He had accompanied his parents to America for his sister's wedding but went against their wishes when he decided to stay at The Willows. Now he had to do something he dreaded. He had to tell his parents they no longer had a daughter.

The young Frenchman's palms were sweaty and his hands were trembling as he picked up the phone. He took two deep breaths, finally dialed "O" and asked for the overseas operator.

Emma Genevive was going over the grocery list she made up for the cook. She heard the phone. It rang a few times too many because her husband had told her he was going to the stables for an hour or so. When she remembered, she walked over and answered it, "*Bonjour, la maison de Genevive.*"

"*Maman, c'est Hubert. J'ai peur que j'apporte des nouvelles terribles.*"
Emma's face lost all of its color, and she almost dropped the phone. She shared a few minutes of grief with her son and told him good-bye.

She walked to the window with a view of the stables. Her eyes began to water because she, better than anyone, knew how much Jon-Pierre loved his daughter. She said sadly, barely above a whisper, "This is going to kill him." It almost did.

Jon-Pierre walked through the barn doors and looked toward the house. He saw something very unusual. His wife was walking toward him less than fifty feet away, and she hadn't been near the stables in years. He didn't like the look on her face. When they came together, she put her arms around him and gave him the terrible news.

He took a step backward. Suddenly his eyes bulged, he gasped for breath, and a split second later grabbed his chest and fell forward. Somehow Emma was able to overcome two shocks in a matter of a few minutes. She asked one of the workers to call emergency, and, in less than twenty minutes, she heard the chopper overhead. It carried them to the same hospital where Davis had spent a few weeks a little over two years ago. It was touch and go, but Jon-Pierre would survive and would get to bury his *ma petite*.

Hubert had realized his dream of getting out from under his father's iron fist. But that victory was completely washed away when he suddenly lost his little sister. He didn't want to return to France with her remains, but he felt that he owed her at least that much.

All in this region of Northern France suffered the devastation of this tragedy, when he brought his sister home. The funeral services were exquisite, the best that money could buy. Davis was the only family member from the Willows who attended, per agreement from both sides of the Atlantic. On a beautiful day in the French countryside, Céleste Genevieve DeLongpre was put to rest. Davis, somehow, made it through his beloved wife's second funeral.

Hubert spent hours by her grave asking for her forgiveness. He would live with this emptiness for the rest of his life.

The Willows had celebrated many things over the generations. There had been wedding unions, like, Isaiah and Lovey, and Ben and Jenny, and although The Colonel and Lillian had not been married there, they did enjoy the reception given them by all at the plantation. Willie and Darcy's had been wonderful, and, lastly, Davis and Céleste's renewing of their vows...but never a funeral. From Jarrod DeLongpre's time until now, it was understood that The Willows itself meant victory over many obstacles, from the Depression to racism. It was for celebrating life, not death. Ben Hampton's services and now Céleste's were held in a chapel right outside the city.

From the back door of the mansion, if one were to walk a straight line through the garden, on through the stables, and then another two thousand yards over a knoll, one would come upon a small cemetery where everyone associated with The Willows had been buried since the beginning. It was still within The Willows' boundaries, but hidden from sight from everything else. This tradition was about to continue when a phone call came from across the Atlantic pond.

Jon-Pierre and Emma Genevive wanted their daughter buried in her homeland. After several minutes of discussion and about twenty-four hours of consideration, the DeLongpres and the Genevives came to an agreement. Hubert Genevive accompanied his sister on her final journey. After their absence of two years, Jon-Pierre and Emma would finally have both of their children back home.

Chapter Twenty-Seven

Céleste Genevive DeLongpre had only been at The Willows for about two years, but the hole that she left would take much longer than that to fill. It was no wonder that everything at The Willows was put on hold. No one seemed to know how to handle this great loss. She had worked so hard to be loved and accepted by everyone, especially Lillian. Everyone else had more or less liked her immediately, but again, it took a while longer for Lillian to come around. Although this finally happened, it seemed that, other than Davis, his mother was taking this loss the hardest.

One week following the morning when Céleste's body, Hubert, and Davis had boarded The Colonel's private plane for France, Davis returned to their house on the hill. He was emotionally drained and desperately needed sleep. He lay down on their bed and closed his tired eyes, but the scent of his wife's perfume was all around him. He opened his eyes and stared at the empty pillow to his left. He lay there for a moment more, then got up and began walking from room to room. It was just too much. He dressed, went to the big house, crept up to his old room and cried himself to sleep.

His sleep was filled with many dreams from the previous three years. These dreams included visions of the golden girl charging up on her horse when he was leaving the chateau in France on his way to Torino, Italy. He saw the vision of her in his arms by the lake they rode to. He saw the hooves of the horse crashing down that almost ended his life. He saw his bride in the middle of his mother's roses, as her beautiful form faded in and out amongst the vibrant colors of the beautiful garden. As his vision of pulling the sheet over her head appeared, he woke up with a start.

He once again recognized the room he had known for many years as a boy. He went to the bathroom, splashed his face with cold water, and returned to find his clothes loosely spread over the foot of his bed. He dressed in his two-day-old clothes and went downstairs in the direction of the mansion's country kitchen. As he entered the door from the great hall, he saw his father sitting alone at the table. "Good morning, Daddy."

The Colonel heard the greeting and raised his head with a startled look on his seasoned face, "Well, hello, son. I sure wasn't expecting you!"

"I know, sir. I'm sorry if I frightened you. I came over here last night very late 'cause I couldn't sleep at home. Where's Momma?"

"Still in bed, son. I'll go wake her."

"Oh, no, Daddy. Let her sleep. I just wanted to be here."

Davis sat down next to his father. He realized that this was probably the first time they had sat at this table without his mother or anyone else present. The senior DeLongpre took a sip of his coffee and asked his son if he would like a cup. Davis nodded and picked up the beverage his father had poured for him. He took one sip of the bitter brew and decided it needed whitening and sweetening. He added two spoonfuls of sugar and a generous portion of cream from the sterling silver cream decanter. Both men sipped their coffee and remained silent for several minutes.

"Are you hungry, son?"

Until his father posed this question, Davis didn't realize that he had not really eaten anything for the last couple of days. The Colonel called the rotund woman who had been in Lillian's employ for several years. As the smiling cook approached the table, Davis smiled and thought again how much she reminded him of Hatie McDaniel from *Gone with the Wind*.

Before father and son had finished their second cup of coffee, the smiling lady returned with ample portions of soft scrambled eggs, country pork sausage, and fried grits covered with honey. The Colonel smiled as he watched his son clean the plate.

Davis had his fill of the country breakfast and leaned back in the chair. He looked in the eyes that had always stared right through him and uttered softly, "Daddy, this has been a very terrible few days, hasn't it?"

"Yes, it has, son, for all of us. I have tried to talk to your mother, but she seems to be in another place. I recall those first months when you brought Céleste here…" His words were muffled as he found them choked with tears.

Davis put his hand on his father's arm and responded with, "I know, Daddy. I know."

The Colonel regained his composure and came up with a suggestion, "My boy, I have an idea or, if you will, a suggestion. I think you should get away from here for a few days or even weeks. Why don't I call Captain Rex and have him fly you somewhere?"

Davis saw what his father was trying to do and this brought a tear to his eyes. He thought for a moment while trying to formulate his response. The Colonel could see the wheels turning in his son's head and waited for his answer. The answer was plain and very simple.

"Daddy, I appreciate what you're trying to do, and I love you for it, but right now, I just need to be with my family. This where I draw my strength from."

Davis drew strength from his whole family, especially Willie Hampton. Willie would talk to Davis about almost anything. He had a quick wit and wonderful sense of humor and could get a laugh out of Davis at almost anytime…and under the worst of circumstances. *This* trying period was no different. It was a sad occasion and too much levity would not be proper, but somehow Willie knew when the time was right and when Davis would need a lift the most. But none of this was more important than his just being "Willie." That is what Davis needed and counted on.

Lillian, however, had lost a daughter and been robbed of being a grandmother. For the first few weeks following Céleste's passing, she would rarely leave her room. This concerned everyone. She not only grieved the loss of Céleste, she hated herself for taking so long to accept the bubbly little lady from France. "All that time wasted, all that time wasted!" she would say this out loud, whether anyone else was in the room or not.

One afternoon, The Colonel and Davis came up to house for lunch. Again Lillian did not join them. This wasn't unusual, especially lately. The Colonel asked their cook, Loretta, if she had talked to his wife this morning.

"Yes, sir, Colonel. She went out the back door about an hour ago. Said she had to take care of her roses."

The two men had to pass through the middle of the garden to get from the back door to the stables. There was no Lillian working among the fragrant blossoms.

"Why would she tell Loretta she was going to the rose garden if she wasn't?"

"Daddy…the flowers up at my place!"

They asked Loretta to hold lunch for a while longer. They both went out back and got in the Chevy pickup to make the quarter mile drive to the house on the hill. *Lillian had never walked that far in her life,* they both thought at the same time.

Sure enough, they arrived to find her broad-rimmed straw hat, gloves, shovel, and clippers on the front porch with the front door wide open. They walked through the big oak door and saw wife and mother placing cuts of roses in water all around the house, talking to Céleste as though she was right beside her. Both men looked at each other, sensing the worst.

Lillian wasn't going nuts. When they caught her talking out loud, she was more embarrassed than anything. Nevertheless, that was enough for Davis. In the next couple of days, he took all of Céleste's clothes and belongings, including her horse, and donated everything to some local charity. He moved all his clothes to the big house and locked up the place on the hill for some time to come.

Since the day Jarrod DeLongpre and Isaiah Hampton shook hands so many years before, The Willows had remained a constant. Even before it was named The Willows, this magical part of Mississippi had possessed powers that seemed to weather all storms and heal most of the problems presented to its inhabitants. There were many trials that could have possibly broken the spell this wonderful place seemed to offer, but alas, all of these tests had never proved too awesome to overcome.

The tragic death of Ben Hampton, as difficult as it had been to accept, had only made all concerned a little bit stronger. Dealing with the passing of Céleste was equally as trying, but this too would, in time, fade into another part of The Willows' history. Nothing it seemed could destroy the feeling all felt when they passed through the stone pillars and wrought-iron sign that opened to the willow-lined driveway leading to the mansion.

In the two years following the loss of Céleste, Davis and Willie spent their energies continuing to develop and realize their dream. The Colonel was in his mid-seventies and seemed to be made of iron. True, the shoulders stooped slightly and the hair was now completely white, but the mind that put most of this great land together remained sharp as ever. He liked to refer to his present status as "semi-retired." What that meant was that he would travel maybe twice a year and now and then, he would say, "Come on, Lill. Let's go for a plane ride!"

"Now, T. D., you know I've got this thing with the Guild to do, and then there's...."

"Lill! Let Ruthie handle it!"

"Okay, T. D. Okay! Okay!" She really did enjoy going with him, but she also enjoyed seeing him a little riled...to a point. That was one of the things that probably kept their marriage of one third of a century still full of sparks. That and throw in a whole lot of good love.

This "semi-retirement" was good for the horse business, also. When The Colonel wasn't out of town, it freed up Davis and Willie to take their horses out of Mississippi to other tracks, like in California. On their second trip to the golden state, they were quite successful.

The Colonel sat at his desk going through some transportation bills. He thought to himself that shipping these horses around the country was getting a bit pricey. He was thinking about what he could do to change this, when the phone exploded, breaking the silence. He caught it on the second ring and answered importantly, "Willow Wind Livery, this is T. D. DeLongpre."

"Hi, Daddy. How ya doin'? Well, we finally broke through. We placed at Del Mar and showed at...."

"Yeah, I know, at Pomona Downs and you're on your way to Golden Gate Park."

"Wait a minute, how did you know that already?"

"Son, your old man isn't too feeble to read the papers, not yet."

Davis laughed then smacked himself upside the head for asking such an obvious, okay, *stupid* question. Father and son talked for a few minutes more.

"Yeah, your mom's just fine. Say hi to Willie. I love you, son."

"I love you, Daddy."

That was the end of it. As "the boss" hung up the phone, he leaned back and placed his silver-tipped boots on the desk. First, he looked at Willie's empty desk, then to the right at Davis' chair. He lit up a cigar and bellowed to an empty office, "God damn it, next time I'm going with those pups!"

Chapter Twenty-Eight

A few hundred miles north of Hattiesburg, a young woman sat at her desk, half-heartedly going over the five o'clock news report. It had been over two years since she had heard or read the news of Céleste's sudden passing. As she had done thousands of times, her thoughts would drift, and there was Davis right in front of her. Sometimes it was so real, she felt like she could reach out and touch his handsome face. She was too proud to call or write him, so she just hoped that some day she would cross his mind and he would pick up the phone. Until then, well, that's the way it would have to be.

Her co-worker Susie Ames interrupted her thoughts suddenly; she looked up to hear, "Rebecca, he's here! Are you coming or not?"

"He, who? What?"

Then she remembered that Elvis was scheduled to do a promo at the station for a children's cancer benefit. He would highlight the show in which several local entertainers would be donating their time to help the kids. That Davis-Elvis thing on an evening of long ago still spooked her. She muttered as she straightened her desk and stood up, "Oh, shit! That's just wonderful. That's all I need right now."

Now let's be honest. As she and Susie neared the booth where all this was to take place, the anticipation took over and she became a little excited. They walked to the end of the hall and took a right into the room with the glass-enclosed booth, where the entertainment director was interviewing "The King of Rock and Roll." The two women, as well as most of the station's employees, were looking through the booth window as the five-minute promo was being taped.

When the taping came to an end, Elvis turned to smile and wave at his admirers. As his blue eyes scanned the group, they met Rebecca's and stopped right there. When their eyes met, Rebecca felt a quivering sensation in every part of her body. There were some differences, such as the black hair and crazy clothes, and enough gold and diamonds to support the whole city, but that face, well, it was just a little too much.

Rebecca turned and fled for the security of her office, but before she could get through the crowd and the door, she heard behind her, "Wait a minute! Ma'am, wait a minute!"

She stopped and turned to see Elvis extending his hand. "Hi, I'm Elvis Presley, and you are?"

"Uh, I'm ah, ah, oh, I'm Rebecca, Rebecca Thompson. I'm part of the news team at 5:00 and 6:00 p.m."

"Oh, yeah, that's where I've seen you. You are a beautiful lady!"

"Well, thank you, Davis, I mean Elvis. I really have to go now!"

As Rebecca bolted down the hall, Elvis turned to Susie Ames and asked with disbelief in his voice, "Did I do something wrong here?"

Susie couldn't even speak. She only shook her head.

Elvis threw up his hands and said to his guys, "Jesus! I don't believe it. Let's get the hell out of here!"

For the next few days, Miss Thompson was a wreck. She would forget things, run into objects and people, and even forget why she walked into a room. Her work didn't suffer however, as she was always a consummate professional. She came so close, so many times, to picking up the phone, but just couldn't bring herself to go through with it. Finally, she traded airtime with another member of the news team and went to Hattiesburg.

Both of her parents were still alive and healthy for their ages, and her father still owned the hardware and nursery, but now had a manager and didn't work nine days a week anymore. Rebecca spent the next four days going out on the boat. The water still seemed to be some kind of tonic for her soul.

The lake where the Thompson's sailboat was moored was not a big one. It was oval-shaped and covered about eleven acres. This was adequate for the five estates that shared it. None of the homes on the two-acre plus lots were what one would call mansions, but, when her father purchased their parcel so many years ago, they were considered upper-middle class. There had been many attempts from developers to buy out all of the families that resided in this valuable expanse of real estate, but a strong bond existed. They had all stuck together and defeated those big shots. All of the original owners had only passed on their titles to immediate family when some died.

On the afternoon of Rebecca's last day before returning to Memphis, she walked down to the pier and untied the lines. She felt a good breeze at her back and set out for the middle of the lake. It was not a deep lake, and as she threw the anchor over the port side, she could feel the tug as it hit bottom. From her vantage point, she could see all of the five homes. After several moments of taking this all in, she removed the cushions from the two bench seats and piled them in a comfortable fashion against the starboard side. She lay back with her head slightly elevated and stared into the Mississippi sky. The gentle rocking of the boat caused her to close her eyes and fall into an easy warm sleep.

Visions of moonlit rides with Davis to "make-out mountain" and sharing cherry fizzes with two straws filled her daydreams. As she relived all those wonderful youthful days, something woke her from this delicious special sleep. Her hand twitched as she imagined she felt the pen that had written Davis that ill-timed Dear John letter. She sat up with a start, and, while putting the cushions back, she realized what she had to do.

Mary Louise Thompson's nose twitched slightly as she smelled the pork roast baking in the oven. She opened the door and pulled the rack out so she could baste the five-pound entrée one last time. As she went to the sink to wash the potatoes, she looked out the kitchen window that overlooked the fifty-yard spans of lawn divided by the path leading to the pier. Rebecca was about halfway up the walk to the house. Mary Louise could see that her daughter had something on her mind other than enjoying the lawn and flowers. When she entered the kitchen, Mrs. Thompson said cheerfully, "Dinner is almost ready, honey. By the way, how was your sail?"

Rebecca took a sliver of raw celery that was intended to accompany the roast and, in between chews, shocked her mother with, "Momma, I have to be the only thirty-year-old virgin in the state of Mississippi! At least I feel like one!" Rebecca left the kitchen and her wide-open mouthed mother and went to her room. She glanced quickly at the picture of her and Davis at the prom and picked up the phone.

Lillian DeLongpre was nearing seventy, but had enjoyed a good life. Her strawberry-blonde curls that she had tugged at over the years were now mostly gray. The Colonel and she had discussed the idea of her going to the beauty parlor and having the gray removed. The conversation always ended up the same.

"Lill," her man would say, "I've been lookin' at that purty head for a long time, and I don't think it needs a thing, but you go on along and do whatcha want."

She still possessed the same Donna Reed figure that had kept her husband and others' attention over the years. By the way, she never did make it to the beauty parlor.

She took off her gloves and put her little green shovel with the tan rubber grip in the potting shed. Her routine to meet with "Hattie McDaniel" was interrupted by the resounding echo of the phone ringing in the great hall. She sighed and picked up the instrument from the three-legged desk. "Hello. This is Lillian DeLongpre. Can I help you?"

"Lill, this is Rebecca. How are you?"

"Merciful heavens! Is that you, child?"

"Yes, it is, Lill, and I *am* sorry it has been so long. Is it possible we could have tea on the terrace one more time?"

The women talked for a few moments and caught up on several years, but it was agreed that a phone conversation was not nearly enough. Before they hung up, Lillian informed the girl she had always wanted for Davis, that her boy was out of town. Somehow, this made no difference.

Lillian was not a deceitful woman. She had been incredibly honest all her life…with the exception of a couple times. The secret that had given her and her husband that wonderful gift thirty years ago was one of only two blemishes on her entire ledger. This was something she had worried about but had never felt an ounce of remorse. It was meant to be and that was all there was to it.

It felt wonderful to Lillian seeing Rebecca again. It had been some time since these women had sat under the big white umbrella and shared tea with exquisite varieties of pastries. There was a ton of catching up to do, and they did their best to cover most of the years. Rebecca related her recent meeting with Elvis at the T.V. station. That was the only topic that didn't bring a smile to the older woman's face. She was not trying to upset her hostess, but she had noticed in the past that every time the comparison came up, Lillian showed signs of irritation and withdrew from the conversation. She would often say, "I just don't like my boy being compared to that, that…I don't like it, that's all." It was no different that afternoon. Rebecca finally gave it up, after all, it was their first time together in a long while, and she didn't want to spoil it. That doesn't mean the T.V. news lady dismissed it from her mind entirely.

Rebecca had asked Lillian not to tell Davis that she had met with her on the terrace or even called. Lillian promised her that would not happen, but after several hours of soul-searching, she had to break the promise.

The Colonel was so busy in the stable's office that he wasn't aware of his wife and Rebecca's meeting. There was a lot of work to do during Davis and Willie's absence, so he spent most of every day making plans for his boy's future. Lillian was always up front with everything but decided to not break this news to him right away. Instead, she called on Mrs. Hampton.

Darcy was a bit hesitant at first but saw the reason for Lillian's need to test the waters. Realizing this, she gave Lillian the phone and room number of the hotel where her husband and Davis were staying at in San Francisco.

Davis and Willie were on their way to dinner, when the desk clerk in the hotel lobby saw them walking to the dining room. "Mr. DeLongpre, you have a long-distance phone call."

Davis turned to Willie and said, "Might be the boss. I'd better take it."

Davis picked up the beige house phone and said, "Hi. This is Davis DeLongpre."

"Thurston, how are you doing, son?"

"Momma?"

"Honey, I hope I'm not bothering you, but I just had a wonderful conversation with someone from our past...."

Davis hung up the phone and looked at Willie. This man, who always seemed to be around when Davis needed him, had only one thing to say, "Well, it looks like we're about ready to go home."

Willie was ready to go home also. The forty-five-year-old, who had only known one woman his entire life, longed to be with her and his kids. Somehow, he knew that Davis was ready to find love again in *his* life. It had been long enough since he lost Céleste.

The aging-but-always-there Daniel picked up Davis and Willie at the airport. During the twenty-five minute drive to The Willows, the two men talked of the success they had enjoyed on their trip to the West Coast and how it would be another step toward realizing their dream.

As the pillars came into view, they again felt the joy and security of being home. It was *really* nice to be back. Davis put his luggage in his room and, after unpacking, took a long shower. No matter how much he and Willie had paid for hotels during their stay in California, the showers were always lousy. The one in his bathroom had enough pressure to pound out all his tight muscles and blast off all the soap.

As was the custom at The Willows, a welcome home dinner was planned for the returning travelers. Lillian and her cook again made sure that it was very special. The DeLongpres and the entire Hampton family enjoyed the wonderful meal topped off by some puffy-crusted rhubarb pie.

During the two-hour feast, Davis and his mother exchanged glances several times. No one saw this, but, if they did, they wouldn't understand anyway. It was just always so wonderful having the families together. Willie and Darcy needed to get their youngest child home and make up for the time they had been apart. Davis wanted to talk to his mother. He told his father that he needed to do this, if indeed it was okay. The Colonel was a bit curious but gestured his permission. After all, there would be plenty of time during the next few days to talk business.

Davis moved from the seat he was in and sat down where his father always had. He put his hand on his mother's and spoke softly, "Momma, I would like to hear about the person you spoke with from our past." They both knew, so no name was needed, but Davis wanted to hear everything in detail.

Lillian took her son's hand, smiled broadly, and began her story. "Thurston, you know how much I wanted you and Rebecca to be together. I was so upset when we came to Spain and read that horrible letter. Honey, I blamed you for all that happened, and I'm so sorry. So much has happened since then that it now seems so silly. I hated Céleste when you brought her home, and I know that it hurt you. Honey, but I grew to love her, and I miss her terribly, as I know you do."

Lillian began tearing up and had trouble speaking. Davis slid his chair closer to her and put his arms around his mother. She waited a few beats and continued, "Honey, I have never told you what to do since you've grown up, but I would like you to do something for me. Please call Rebecca and just talk to her. She still loves you very much, you know."

"Momma, what about that guy she...." Lillian raised her hand but didn't speak, only shook her head slowly.

Davis sat quietly for a few moments. He promised his mother he would comply with her wish. He kissed her goodnight and sat by himself for close to a half an hour. Just before going to his room, he said out loud, "Maybe it's time. Yeah, maybe it's time."

Chapter Twenty-Nine

There is an old saying that has been around for many years, "Be careful what you wish for because it just might come true."

Rebecca had wished for a call from Davis for a long time. She had resigned herself to the possibility of this never happening. As she had done for hundreds of mornings, she picked up the papers from the mat at her front door and sat at her table in the breakfast nook. She was looking for her dad's ad inside the front page of the Hattiesburg newspaper. It wasn't where it had always been. While she was looking to see if it was somewhere else, the phone began to ring. *It's probably work.* She let it continue to ring. Something made her get up to answer the persistent machine. She picked it up and said impatiently, "Hi, Susie. I'll be there in a few minutes." The voice on the other end was way too deep to be Susie's.

"Becky, this is Davis. How're ya doin', darlin'?"

It had been twenty years since Davis had rearranged Harley Thompson's display at the hardware store but hearing his voice still sent a tingle through Rebecca's being. She tried to speak but this veteran newswoman who talked to thousands of viewers five nights a week felt like a babbling idiot. To say the spark was still there would be a gross understatement. The only thing that wasn't certain was: what would they do with those feelings?

They tried talking for a while, but it was too difficult to really feel what the other was thinking. There had been too much in their history and too much was left of their future to discuss over the phone. They had to meet face-to-face and heart-to-heart. They agreed that Davis would come to Memphis the following weekend. This would work out perfectly because Rebecca's roommate Susie Ames was going out of town with her boyfriend.

Susie had just recently moved in, not that Rebecca needed a roommate to share expenses; it was just convenient since they both worked for the TV-Radio station. And, truthfully, from time to time, she was just plain lonely.

Rebecca hung up slowly like she was waking from a dream and really wanted to stay there. It was almost too much for her mind to assimilate. It had been so long. She was also still so caught up in the Elvis thing from a few weeks ago that the call just confused the picture she had of the face matching the voice, only seconds before. She whispered in her kitchen, "God, it's been what, five years…six? I wonder if he has changed any?"

She had noticed that his voice was a little different. The *attitude*, that's what it was, he sounded like he was in such a hurry before. Now, he spoke with an air of self-assurance. She mulled this over for a few minutes until her emotions got the better of her. She sat at the breakfast table and had herself a good happy cry.

Elvis' father, Vernon, was gray before he was thirty and made no effort to hide it. His son, however, was in show business and tried everything to beat Mother Nature. This included dying his hair jet black to look good in the movies and still appear young to his legions of fans. If he went too long without touching up the dye jobs, the gray was certainly there.

When Uncle Sam gave Davis his induction hair cut, it wasn't especially as traumatic as it was for others. When he had fulfilled his obligation, he didn't let it grow as long as before. It was just left close and neat, and kind of a sandy brown with touches of gray here and there. That's probably why he didn't get mistaken for the other guy more often than he did. Another thing that probably minimized his looks from Elvis was the way Davis dressed.

Around the ranch, one would find Davis, Willie, and The Colonel in Levi's, boots, and some sort of a western shirt. Willie and The Colonel always wore their Stetson cowboy hats. Davis had to wear a hat for two years in the Army and was not all that fond of having something on his head. He did have one of those "ten-gallon jobs," as he jokingly referred to them, but he only wore it when they went to town or someplace where he was supposed to look like a horse person.

As far as dressing up was concerned, he owned three suits, black, gray, and tan. Most of his shirts were white, but sometimes he would really venture out and wear yellow or blue. Unlike that guy in Memphis, he didn't dress to impress.

At seven o'clock Friday evening, Rebecca said, "goodnight," to her TV audience and went to her office to do some light paperwork. She finished, straightened up her desk, put all the loose things in the center drawer, and picked up her purse. After saying goodnight to some of her staff in the hall, she began walking to the private parking area.

It was balmy in Memphis this time of the year. She put the top down on her baby blue mustang convertible and began the two-and-a-half mile drive to her apartment. The breeze felt so good, she took out her hairpins and let her long dark-brown locks fly free. She turned on the radio, and, as fate would have it, "I want you, I need you, I love you…" came floating over the airways. As she turned up the volume, she said out loud, "He had better be there. He'd just better be!"

She pulled into her parking place, put the top up, and locked the car. She scanned the lot for Davis' car but didn't see it. As she began walking up the sidewalk to the front doors, she heard a voice out of the shadows, "I had to park on the street!"

A smiling face neared her as if it was coming from a dream. The face had a body, and arms reached out from the body, and then, the face said, "Hi ya, Becky!" As far back as Rebecca could remember, not her parents, close friends, or even Lillian, had ever called her Becky. This was a wonderful thing to hear after all these years.

Davis looked into her intense black eyes that he had only dreamed about for many years and searched for something to say. She wasn't doing much better, so they said to hell with it and fell into each other's arms. For a few moments nothing else in the world mattered.

Many things in life make no sense. One though, seems to span time and heal all wounds. This unexplainable thing that can start wars and end wars is still nothing more than a four-letter word…LOVE.

They separated slightly and just stared at each other. Both were looking for changes made by Mother Nature, but the only thing evident was that Davis was beginning to gray. Rebecca smiled warmly; her eyes were a little damp as she gently touched his graying temples. It was as if she wanted to see if they were real. "I like the look," she said softly.

He put his arm around her waist and they began walking slowly, closely, up the concrete path to the six steps leading to the wood with stained-glass double doors to her home. Davis had made dinner reservations at a restaurant Rebecca had suggested when they spoke earlier in the week. They were still holding hands as they entered the living room, when she reached up and locked her hands around his neck. She looked into his blue eyes, slightly framed by laugh lines and said softly, "You know, Davis, I hope you don't mind, but it has been such a long time, and I feel very selfish. I'd rather not share this moment with anyone. Could we stay here? I know I can find us something to eat and maybe we could have a drink or two?"

He looked down, and, as the laugh lines grew bigger with his smile, he answered, "You won't get any argument from me. What do you have?"

"You mean to eat or drink?"

"Drink!"

"Oh! Uh, I think there might be something left from a birthday party we had a few weeks ago." She led Davis to the kitchen and asked him to sit as she went to the cupboard. She pulled out two bottles, one half-full of Smirnoff Vodka, the other a barely touched quart of Jack Daniels. Davis pointed to the second.

"I guess I'll go for the Jack Daniels. We are in Tennessee, aren't we?"

"Yes, we are. How would you like it?"

"Oh, just a little water and a lot of ice."

"Hmm…I've never tried it that way. Oh, what the hell, why not?"

This special evening, this wonderful evening, this long-overdue evening would see this couple try several of these offerings from Mr. Jack. It was not a "get drunk and let's party" kind of evening, it was a "let's sip a little, talk a whole lot, and whatever happens, happens" evening. There were several years to cover, and, at last, it seemed they had time.

The first hour or two was mainly warm recollections of their childhood and teenage years. There were the school activities, dances, football games, the moonlight drives, and starlit walks. But, they didn't forget, and talked about at length, those first time encounters by their private lake. They laughed about all those things, but eventually the past five or six years had to be visited.

It took a lot for Rebecca to explain the reason for "the letter." Davis had many questions as she related the story. At times, he wanted to interrupt but decided to let her finish. At first, he couldn't understand why she did it, and then make up that awful story about being in love with Mark Lewis.

As she continued, the reason she had to say good-bye to him while he was overseas became clear. She just plain got tired of waiting. Davis let her finish and thought for a moment. He took a small sip from his drink, cleared his throat and asked, "Then, you didn't get married or even engaged? Well…did you two ever go to…you know?"

"No, Davis. We did not! Toward the end…I found out he was gay. And another thing, there hasn't been anyone else either!"

Davis stifled a laugh, smiled, and took her hand. He gave it a gentle squeeze as he moved to lean over and gently kiss her.

She kissed him back but then stiffened slightly. "Oh, no! Wait a minute. I know you've been married, now you tell *me* something!"

Davis was a bit surprised by this, but he knew she was right, so he leaned back on the sofa. He asked her softly, but firmly, "Well, what do you want me to tell you? What exactly do you want to know?"

Rebecca stuck her polished index finger into her glass and massaged the three remaining ice cubes. Over their tinkling, she said, "Everything, I want to hear *everything*!"

Before he could answer, she held up a damp finger and said, "Davis, first I gotta know. Did you really *love* her?"

"Yes, Becky, I did. I loved her a whole lot, but…well, what I want to say is…this is the first night since she died, I *haven't* thought about her."

This made Rebecca tear up. She took a tiny sip then sat the glass down on the coaster. She moved into Davis' arms and started weeping. It was a happy weep and it spread to the man who was holding her in his arms. He gently took her head from his shoulder and blotted her tears. He chuckled as he dried his own, then held her head in his large hands and kissed her again and again.

This was something they had waited for all their lives. From a pile of empty gas cans to half-empty glasses of bourbon, it had taken almost twenty years. Was there any possible way they could make up for all this precious lost time? Maybe not, but sometime after midnight until the sun said goodbye to the stars, they would certainly try.

There on the floor were two pair of shoes, one with three-inch heels and another with still-tied laces. Davis' shirt was lying on the back of the sofa as he picked her up in his arms. He stood there, felt her head on his shoulder, and saw her left arm rise and her finger point in the direction of her bedroom. It had been a long time since those wonderful days of young love making on the sand in the secluded corners of The Willows.

As he looked at her in the early morning light, he was thrilled to see that she was still beautiful without the manmade things, such as clothes, and just as God created her. It seemed like in the following hours that they had never been apart.

Davis had been with two women since he received the letter. Well, there was the professional in Italy when he was romping with the Benevento boys, but that didn't count, besides that, Francina was before the letter. The torrid affair with Estrelita was exciting and the romance and marriage to Céleste had been very special, but on this night, he was with his Becky—the same Becky he had loved since he could remember. The following few hours of passion...no, love...would overshadow and wipe from his memory anything that had happened before. They would be together for the rest of their lives. They *would* be together forever, but, as they would discover, Camelot was still a ways away....

It was nearing 10:00 p.m. Sunday evening when Davis and Rebecca shared a last kiss and hug. As he walked to his car, he heard a distant, "I love you." He turned and blew her a kiss. After starting his car's engine, he switched on the air. It was still very warm and humid, even at the late hour.

He drove away from Rebecca's apartment in South Haven, a suburb of Memphis, and made his way to the interstate that would lead him to Jackson. He had plenty of time to reflect during the three hundred and ten mile drive back to The Willows.

It had been a wonderful weekend. Once they had managed to get out of bed, they did indeed go out to dinner. It was a very intimate, small restaurant catering to those who enjoyed quality service and privacy, but other parts of that way-too-short weekend were on his mind. He also considered how the events of the last two days would change theirs lives.

A little after 3:00 a.m., he turned down the paved two-lane road that ran the entire length of the ranch's western boundary. As he came to the huge stone and wrought-iron entrance, he stopped as he and everyone else had, going back to Great Uncle Jarrod. There was something about this structure that made all at The Willows feel a sense of pride and security. As he sat in the dark just inside the arch, he thought out loud, "Will Becky ever be a part of this?"

Davis turned off his headlights about fifty yards from the mansion and crept in the back door. He took two steps on the hardwood floor, which, at that time of morning, sounded more like someone hammering. Quickly, he slipped off his boots and eased his way upstairs to his room. He crawled into bed and looked at his watch. He knew Willie would be in the office in a couple of hours. It didn't matter, though.

In a few minutes, he was floating somewhere above a football field and seeing Rebecca in her cheerleading outfit as he was throwing footballs. In the next part of the dream, they were dancing to the closing song at the senior prom.

Willie Hampton was finishing his second or third cup of coffee, he wasn't sure, at his desk in the office. He had been there the better part of an hour when The Colonel trudged in and said while he was yawing, "Saw the boy's car outside…but don't see him. You talk to him yet?"

"No, Pop," Willie said with a knowing smile, "I went to bed about 11:00 p.m., and he wasn't back yet. You know, he hasn't seen Rebecca in five or six years. If I know him, he won't be worth a damn for a day or two. You remember how it was when Céleste first got…."

The mention of Céleste made both men quiet for a few minutes. She had been gone for quite a while now, yet sometimes Willie swore he could still smell her perfume. The Colonel broke the silence, "Well, I wonder what this trip to Memphis is going to do to change things."

Davis rolled over on his right side and, though still asleep, began feeling a warm sensation on his face. He smiled and woke to find the sun kissing him good morning. He squinted through sleepy eyes at his clock on the nightstand, which read one o'clock. He yawned, "Guess I sure as hell know it's not one o'clock in the morning." He lay there for a few minutes, reliving the wonderful weekend. He smiled, threw back the covers, and hit the floor.

After showering, he donned his Levi's, shirt, and boots, before foraging. As he entered the kitchen, his mother was sitting at the table where she had been for several hours waiting to hear about what went on "up in Memphis."

"Morning, Momma. How ya doin'? Boy, I'm starved. Any food left from lunch?" He walked over and kissed her cheek.

"There's some cobb salad and pork loin you can make a sandwich with."

Davis scooped some salad out of the big bowl onto his plate where he had put together some meat slices on potato bread before settling at the table. He forgot his milk and went back for it. His mother stared at him while he was eating. When he finally realized that, he stopped chewing and took a swig of the ice-cold milk.

Lillian could not keep quiet any longer. "Well?"

"Well? Well, what?"

"You know exactly what I mean. How did things go in Memphis?"

"Oh, you mean with Becky?"

"Thurston, you *know* I mean with Rebecca! Now tell me, or I'll take your food away!"

Davis began eating more slowly now. In between bites and chews, he related most of what went on. If he even hinted at any of the intimate details, his mother would fake being shocked and suppress a giggle.

Lillian had not forgotten Rebecca. That would've been literally impossible, but, during the short time she had with Céleste as her daughter-in-law, she had put Rebecca on the shelf, so to speak. As she listened to her son talk for a good part of an hour, half of her brain was listening to the present and the other half to the past. She had certainly had some pleasant times with Rebecca, but there were those terrible years when she just didn't know what was going on, and it frustrated her. She could see that Davis was almost out of things to tell her, so she interrupted, "Well, honey, do you think anything is going to come of this reunion? Or let me put it another way, do you want anything to come of it?"

"Momma! We just got back together. Yeah, I think I want something to come of it, but there's a lot to consider. Becky's been working hard to establish herself in the communications business, and she's done a hell of a job. I don't know how it would work out with me here, and her in Memphis. I know one thing for sure. I'm going to be seeing a lot of her in the near future. You can bet on that!"

The last thing he said brought a smile to the face that was beginning to show signs of the length of her stay on earth. She rose, straightened her apron, and said in a demanding tone, "Thurston, I want grandbabies!"

She left Davis with his mouth open. He sat for a moment while his food and his mother's words were digesting. He had known her all his life and although her demand was said partly in fun, he could tell the undertone was quite serious. He put his dishes on the sink and went out to the stables where he was certain to get some good-natured razzing from his father and Willie. His anticipations were correct.

The next few months saw Davis' life fall into a pattern. He would work with Willie and his father until about 1:00 p.m. or lunchtime on Friday, then make the five-hour plus drive to Memphis, getting there around the time Rebecca finished her last newscast. His father suggested he fly, but he liked the drive because it gave him time to himself and allowed him to plan things, solve problems, or work through whatever else he had on his mind. Besides that, he enjoyed driving his new Pontiac Grand Prix.

The many weekends the reunited lovers spent together were about as good as anything could get. They talked, went for rides, and did everything they could to make up for all the lost years. They weren't wasted years per say, just lost, but there was one thing for sure, it wasn't too late. They could now look forward to many *more* great years together.

All this was going through Davis' mind as he saw the green and white sign telling him he had fifty-nine miles to complete before he would arrive in Memphis. He reached for the red bag with the gold laces that sat in the passenger seat.

Three days earlier he had gone to the jewelry shop in Hattiesburg to see if the order he had placed with the owner of the establishment had been filled. The non-descript, balding little man had indeed found a perfect three-carat, oval-shaped diamond.

He pulled off the interstate and looked at the ring once again. He held it up and saw the large stone surrounded by twenty smaller diamonds. The light from the setting sun gave the arrangement set in eighteen-carat gold the appearance of a sunset in a mythical land of yore. He put it back in the dark red velvet box and said out loud, "One hour to my Becky."

Davis again exited the interstate and drove through downtown Memphis to Rebecca's apartment in South Haven. He still had to park on the street but didn't have to wait outside for her to come home, because he now had a key.

He put the key in the lock, entered the hallway, and went to the door with the gold-plated numbers that read 212. By this time, he felt very much at home, so he sat on the brown leather easy chair and took off his boots. It was 7:25 p.m., but he wasn't worried. He knew that his "Becky" would be home soon.

In the previous months, her arrival at home varied from a few minutes up to an hour.

He went to the kitchen and put a bottle of Moët Chandon on ice. The champagne *was* necessary, but first things first. The Jack Daniels was just a little tradition they had established that first magical night. Davis went to the cupboard and discovered, to his delight, that an inch and a half at the bottle's bottom contained a sip or two of Len Mertlow's twice-filtered brew. This would take the edge off of his drive and hold him until Rebecca arrived.

He took a glass from the cupboard and went to the refrigerator to get some ice. As he tipped the bottle and watched the contents join the waiting ice cubes, he was startled by an unfamiliar voice. He turned and saw the source of the voice go from inquiry to total surprise. It was not the first time he had seen someone in shock, but Susie Ames could barely spout out her words.

"You're Davis? Oh, my God! Now I know what Rebecca was telling me! You look so much like…I just can't…." Susie's inability to speak or even finish a sentence was saved by Rebecca's arrival. Rebecca put her purse on the table and laid her jacket over the chair.

"Davis, I think Susie needs to go to her room and rest. What do you think, honey?"

Susie left without really recovering. Rebecca and Davis were alone, and what a better time for the accused Elvis look-alike to present his plan.

"Becky, please sit down. I have something to ask you."

Rebecca sat down and looked her lifelong love in his blue eyes. At this time in her life and in their relationship, she would probably accept damn near anything he had to say, but even going back to their childhood and the years that followed, she had never seen the seriousness in those expressive eyes as she did at this moment.

"Becky, I want to apologize for all the insensitive, one-track-minded things I've put you through. I understand about the Mark Lewis thing. I can understand why you decided to keep it all a secret. I want you to know I love you, Becky, and I know I always have."

Davis took her soft left hand, looked admiringly at her perfect bright red fingernails and held it for a brief moment. He took his free hand and dipped it into the pocket of his sports jacket. His heart was beating out of rhythm and his throat was dryer than the Sahara Desert. He was finally able to get the package in his hand, her eyes were full of anticipation as he fumbled with the ornate wrappings. She gasped with delight as he placed the small velvet box in her out-stretched hand. She opened the box and was nearly blinded by its contents. She understandably had difficulty speaking, so she slowly removed the ring and handed it to the guy sitting next to her.

He felt the ring pass her knuckle and slip into place on her delicate third finger. Rebecca overlooked his clumsy attempt at trying to be romantic. His throat was so dry that no water or sip of Jack Daniels could aid or come to his rescue. Like thousands of suitors before him, the message somehow got through. Before he could actually say the words, he was saved by a high-pitched squeal….

"Yes! I will!"

After a long passionate kiss and hug, Davis went to the kitchen and brought back the chilled Moët Chandon. There were things to be discussed, but tonight would be no more than a celebration of two people finally getting what they had longed for all their lives.

Halfway into the bottle of bubbly, Rebecca had an idea and stood up. Davis was a bit surprised by this, asking her with a giggle, "What's up, honey? Whatcha' doin'?"

"Just stay there. I'll be right back."

She went to the kitchen and returned with two large candles, placing them on the coffee table next to the ice bucket holding the champagne. She lit them, and reached for the lamp on the end table. She turned it off and motioned her fiancé to do the same with the one at his end of the sofa. She leaned back and said, "Perfect!"

Davis nodded his agreement and saw the reflection of the dancing flames in her eyes. She picked up the bottle and refilled their glasses. They toasted and kissed for the millionth time. Rebecca gazed at the magnificent ring again and thought she noticed something. She held it close to the candle's flame. After staring at the center stone, she began counting the smaller solitaires that surrounded it. "Fifteen, sixteen, seventeen, eighteen, nineteen…Davis, there's twenty!"

She looked at him for a moment and realized what it meant. There was one diamond for each year. This was too much. She looked at the huge grin that enveloped his entire face and dove into his arms. "You are truly amazing. It took you a long time, but, darling, this, this is simply incredible! I love you so much!"

They stayed in each other's arms for several minutes, then separated and finished their glasses. She took the bottle from the ice bucket, refilling the empty vessels, Davis' first. Drip, drip, drip and that's all that was left. "I guess that's it. Do you want to go to bed now?"

Davis didn't answer only shrugged his shoulders slightly. She realized she was still in her work clothes and cooed, "Neither do I, and I don't want this evening to end. Maybe we could just lounge around and talk a while? I'd really like to get out of these clothes. Stay there and I'll be right back."

Davis waited until she disappeared into the hall, then jumped up and went to the fridge, where he had another Moët Chandon stashed behind the gallon milk bottle and plastic container of orange juice. He popped the cork and quickly returned to the living room, burying the new bottle in the ice.

Rebecca came back in a lavender negligee and had taken her hair down from the bun she always wore at work. Her professional look now changed to that of a seductress. In the flickering light from the candles, she was as beautiful as any movie star he had ever seen. She sat down, flipped her hair in Rita Hayworth fashion, crossed her legs, and arched her back. This was very sexy, but made them both break up laughing. When the giggles subsided, Davis said, "Try the champagne again."

She looked at him quizzically and slowly obeyed. When she picked up the bottle this time, it was much heavier. She dropped it back in the ice bucket. After smacking him on the shoulder, she slightly slurred, "You shit-head! You got any more surprises tonight?"

Chapter Thirty

Davis had been making these weekend trips to Memphis for several weeks, and, in his absence on a few Friday or Saturday nights, Lillian had invited Willie and Darcy to join The Colonel and her for dinner.

The dinners sometimes lasted quite late, if one could call 9:00 p.m. late. On this particular night, she and her husband bid the Hamptons good evening and retired. As she grew older, she had difficulty getting to sleep right away, so she would read. Though novels bored her, she enjoyed reading books about roses from different parts of the world. Imagine that.

Some folks who have trouble getting to sleep use prescription pills, but The Colonel's alternative to this had been for years, a double snifter of fine cognac. Lillian very rarely drank except for various wines that went with the evening's entrée. At The Colonel's advanced age, this still seemed to work. Lillian envied him for this, wishing she could enjoy that nasty-tasting stuff.

She finally closed her eyes with the lamp on the nightstand still burning, and the book lying open on her chest. The phone next to the lamp rang several times before it woke her. She came to and looked at the clock that told her it was 3:20 a.m. She knew that her son was in Memphis. Her first thought was something dreadful. The Colonel finally heard the insistent ringing and turned to see his wife sitting straight up. In a gravely and irritated voice he said, "Lill, what's the matter? Lill, pick it up!"

"T. D., I'm afraid something has happened to our boy!"

The Colonel raised himself up on his elbow, reached over his wife's rigid shoulders, and picked up the receiver on the eleventh or twelfth ring. "T. D. DeLongpre here. Who is this?"

"Hi, Daddy. How ya doin'?"

"Davis, are you hurt? Are you okay?"

"Couldn't be better, Daddy, I know it's really late. Is Momma awake?"

"Son, we are both awake. What's going on?"

Davis was doing his champagne giggling and almost yelled, "Tell Momma that Becky and I are engaged! Ain't that great?"

The Colonel gulped a sigh of relief and handed the phone to his wife.

Davis and Rebecca ran out of champagne once more, and this time there was no stash in the fridge. They went to bed, too exhausted to make love, too full of celebrating, and passed out in each other's arms. They spent the following day in bed and ordered pizza. That evening they enjoyed a quiet dinner and went to sleep early. Instead of staying all day Sunday, Davis left for home.

It was late afternoon when he guided his new Pontiac through the stone pillars and down the lane to the parking area. Willie was halfway into the path that led from his house to the stables when he saw the car coming to a stop. He chuckled as he saw several species of bugs ending their lives on the vehicle's windshield and grill.

Davis looked like one of their horses that had been through a heavy workout. Willie looked at his friend and teased, "Well, she finally got ya, huh? Darcy said a day or two ago that you had little or no chance getting away from Rebecca this time." Willie extended his large right hand and said, "Congratulations, pard!" Before he could let go, he cuffed Davis on the shoulder with his free hand and continued, "Now, maybe we can get some work done around here!"

Davis gave him a sarcastic smile as he jaunted off to see his folks. If he thought Willie was tough…well, his day had just begun. After an exhausting hour or two with his mother grabbing and hugging him and listening to her cry and laugh at the same time, he patiently told her, "Momma, I'm beat. I need a nice long nap. Daddy, I need to talk to you about something very important! How about waking me up about an hour before supper?"

The Colonel nodded, then looked at his wife and shrugged. Most of the time he could almost finish Davis' sentences for him, but this…this sounded different. What could this possibly be about?

The colonel didn't know what his son needed to talk to him about. He did mention that it was important, and that peaked the great man's curiosity. He had a feeling that it might have something to do with Rebecca since he had just returned from another weekend with her. Anything that had involved her before, Davis usually went to his mother about. As he watched his son disappear through the door into the hallway, he said slightly above a whisper, "Oh, well, no need to fret. I'll know in a few hours."

One of the many reasons for The Colonel's success was his ability to find a problem before it developed, instead of trying to fix it while it grew. This had obviously worked rather well over the years. He had tried to instill this in his son, and he had seen it work to the young man's advantage on a few occasions. He felt confident that Davis would make the right decision, but, let's face it, he was anxious to know what was on the boy's mind.

Davis slept soundly for a couple of hours before waking and looking at the clock. It was around 5:00 p.m. He knew he had plenty of time to shower and speak with his father before supper. He propped up his pillow while lying back with his wrist on his forehead to keep away the last of the fading sunlight from his still sleep-filled eyes. He began to go over his presentation to his father. He soon decided he had it together enough to be successful.

He showered, dressed, and went to the livery office. Willie and The Colonel were not always working on Sunday, but it was hard to keep either one away from there. Lillian and Darcy had witnessed this sometimes irritating habit of their men more than a *few* times.

They were on their feet ready to leave when Davis arrived. The Colonel called to his son as he came through the door, "Hi, son. It looks like you're ready to have that talk. Am I right?"

"Yes, you are, Daddy. Let's have a seat. Willie, you can stay if you want to."

"No, pard. It's Sunday and Darcy's not too happy with me being here, as usual. I better go tell her how beautiful she still is." Willie bid his partner good evening, leaving father and son alone.

Davis pulled his chair from his desk to the front of his father's and began, "As you know, Daddy, a lot happened this weekend. Sorry about waking you and Momma up the other night. We were over celebrating a little."

The Colonel took off his hat as though trying to be serious but couldn't hold back a big grin, "Gee, I really couldn't tell, son. Go on."

"Becky has worked really hard to get where she is in the communications business, probably a lot harder than she should have but being a woman and all…well, you know. Anyway, I can see that we are going to have a problem when we get married. I really can't ask her to give up all she has worked for and move down here, and I sure as hell can't live in Memphis. So, I've been doing some thinking. You know Rusty Russell that has that morning show and owns the country station just this side of town?"

"Yeah, I know Rusty—not very well, but I know him. He's pretty popular."

"Well, I've heard that he might be thinking of selling and going to a bigger market in Georgia. If I remember correctly, you know Michael Everson who has a high position in the FCC."

"Yeah, know him, too. So what are you…you can't be thinking about buying the…?"

"Yes, I am. I want to get it for Becky. That way she can continue her career, be partners with us, and live here. And if she's the boss, she can do whatever she wants—even go to work pregnant! Now, Daddy, I haven't mentioned this to her or Momma and I won't until I hear your decision. Lastly, I can't do this without you."

The Colonel's expression didn't change for almost a minute. Davis did a private squirm in his chair and waited. The Colonel shook his head from side to side and said, "Son, I don't know what to say other than I'm really proud of you. You must have listened to me a little over the years. I don't think I could have come up with a better plan. You go tell Rebecca whatever you want to, and then you and I will go see Mr. Russell mid-week. I want to put together some figures."

"Thank you, Daddy. This'll knock their socks off! I'm not going to say anything to Becky until after we see Russell. What about Momma, though?"

"Son, I don't know. I'm thinking we will bring her in a little later."

Rusty Russell was a pleasant-looking fellow in his mid-forties. His reddish-brown hair seemed to blend in with his ten-gallon hat that was always pushed back on his head. It was hard to tell where his hair stopped and his hat started, at least from a few feet away. His drawl was so heavy one could swear that he worked overtime to develop it. When he talked, his Adam's apple moved like a bobber on a fishing line. The only audience the station had was because of *his* show. The rest of the station's jocks were not drawing much of an audience, which was why the station was rumored to be in the red.

At ten o'clock Wednesday morning, Mr. Russell stood up from his desk and shook the hands of T. D. and Davis DeLongpre. "What's on your mind, fellas? Y'all look mighty serious for this time in the mornin'?"

The Colonel smiled down on the shorter man and, while still shaking his hand, said, "We are serious, Mr. Russell. My son and I want to buy your station. We know you're in a financial bind and we are prepared to make you a good and honest offer."

"Well, I don't know, Mr. De-Long-pre, we ain't doin' all that bad."

The Colonel released his hand while asking if they could sit. He took his briefcase and laid it on the somewhat messy desk. As he unsnapped the latches, he began speaking. "Mr. Russell, we have all the figures and we've heard of your offer in Georgia. We have cash, if that's how you want to handle it. Make it easy on yourself."

In a matter of twenty minutes, and no more than that, the little cowboy saw the light. Davis watched his father, who was up in years, still perform with the power he always had. He was so proud he almost burst.

"Well, fellas, I need some time to think 'bout this here."

"Good, take a day or two and give us a call." Davis and his father shook his hand again and bid the cowboy good morning.

As they approached the car, The Colonel smiled at his son while saying, "Son, if you want to call Rebecca, go right ahead. It's a done deal."

Rebecca had been looking for the end of the day a short time after it started. There was more than the usual amount of bad news to report, which sometimes happened. Although they were trained for it and learned to expect it, robberies, murder, and the likes were never pleasant. Seven o'clock could not have come soon enough but finally did.

As she was driving home, she thought about Davis and wished it were Friday night instead of Wednesday. How nice it would be to have him hold her and maybe even cuddle up in bed together.

She opened the door to her apartment and saw the light on. She knew that Susie had gone for cocktails with some of the kids from the station, and she never left the lights on when leaving for work. She heard a noise in the kitchen. She froze temporarily, then quietly inched her way toward the kitchen and the source of the noise. Suddenly, she heard the noise again. She clamored, "Who's there?"

"Who were you expecting, darlin'?"

"Davis, what in the world? I don't understand. What're you doing? I know it's not Friday!" Davis began laughing, but Rebecca wasn't quite ready to join him yet. She sat down at the kitchen table still trembling a little bit.

"I'm sorry, honey. I should've called, but I didn't want to bother you at work. I have something I wanted to talk to you about. I think we should set a date to be married. Whadda' ya think?"

"Well, yeah, I would love to do that, but there are quite a few things we have to work out…like my job. I'm not ready to give up my career, even as much as I love you and want to be your wife…."

Davis asked if she was finished. She confirmed she was for the moment; they still had to talk this out.

He sat in the chair next to hers and took her hand. "What if you could have a career in Hattiesburg?"

"What in the world would I do in Hattiesburg?"

Davis went on to tell her about buying the station from Rusty Russell, and, although it was just radio now, they could turn it into a TV/radio set-up with a little work, a lot of cash and, well...a few strings being pulled. He further pointed out how she would be the boss and how much she could do to further the cause for women in the business.

"Davis, that sounds good, but...it also sounds pretty expensive!"

"So?"

"Hmmm. KBEC, K...I kinda like it!" she mumbled. As the shock started to wear off, she yelled, "I love it!" and jumped into his arms, kissing every inch of his face.

The only major move left seemed to be setting the time they would make known their intentions to the world...that they had become one. Davis and Rebecca spent the following few hours discussing the date for their wedding. They considered several days and months including Thanksgiving, Christmas and New Year's, but nothing came up that felt "really special."

The evening moved on toward the midnight hour. As they realized that she still had to report for work the next morning, Rebecca suddenly flashed on a date that *would* be very significant, October fifteenth. Almost twenty years ago to the day was the first time she laid eyes on the ten-year-old boy in her father's hardware store. This seemed perfect, so that's what they settled on. It was too late to call their parents now. They'd wait until morning.

Rebecca was not on the clock, so to speak, as far as her job was concerned, but she was always the professional and usually at the station early. A little after 8:30 a.m. Thursday morning, she made the call to the house by the lake.

Harley Thompson was seventy-four years old and his wife Mary Louise, a mere child of seventy-one. Mr. Thompson had turned over the day-to-day operations of the hardware store to a young man who had been in his employ for many years.

As so often happens with people who retire, they find themselves with nothing to do. When they tire out of traveling, fishing, or whatever they enjoy doing, their minds and bodies don't know how to function.

Harley Thompson was no different. He would just sit around the house and look for things to complain about. No matter what his wife of forty years did to comfort him, it was never enough. His health began to deteriorate. Mary Louise was three years his junior and was lost as far as helping him with this problem. Something had to happen to revive this man she had pledged to grow old with.

He woke this Thursday morning and walked unsteadily to his rocking chair on the porch overlooking the lake. She took the robe he had discarded and put it around his legs. She shed a tear and went to the kitchen to prepare a light breakfast.

As Mrs. Thompson was soft boiling one egg and frying the grits, the phone on the kitchen wall began ringing. Mary Louise was a bit perturbed by this interruption because she figured it was some problem at the store. She took the pan of grits off the burner and picked up the phone. The voice on the other end was very familiar.

"Hi, Momma, this is your daughter. I have some wonderful news! Davis and I are getting married on the fifteenth of October, and I want my daddy to give me away."

"Oh, honey! Congratulations!" The mother of the bride-to-be said teasingly to her daughter, "I'm so happy to hear this, finally!" As she turned toward the soon-to-be father-of-the-bride, she stopped. Mary Louise at first was hesitant to tell her daughter about her father's condition, then thought, *Maybe this might be the potion to revive him.* She asked her daughter to please hold on for a minute. She went out to the porch and said excitedly, "Harley, it's our Rebecca calling from Memphis. She wants to talk to you." Mary Louise handed her husband the phone and went back to cooking.

The eyes that had been dead for the past few months took on a glow. The legs that had not felt like walking, felt a surge of life and strength. He rose from the rocking chair and walked into the kitchen where the phone lay on the counter. "Is this really you, my daughter?"

"Yes, it's me, Daddy. I love you very much, and I would like for you to give me away at Davis' and my wedding at The Willows. Daddy, will you please do this for me?"

Harley promised his daughter that he would and hung up the receiver. "Mary Louise, our baby is getting married! Isn't that wonderful?"

Mrs. Thompson was just as thrilled as another mother was at The Willows. She had also wished that her daughter and Lillian's son would someday become one. *Why* has *this taken so long?* Mary Louise said gleefully, "Yes, it *is* wonderful Harley, dear!"

Harley was still standing by the phone on the wall. Mary Louise saw the tears flowing from her husband's eyes while she walked to him. As she eased into his embrace, she felt the arms that hadn't *really* held her in years.

It was as if the proverbial fountain of youth began flowing through his aging body. His arms became stronger and very loving. Harley Thompson was back! Harley Thompson felt a new reason to continue. He devoured three eggs, two helpings of grits and honey, plus the four strips of bacon his wife had cooked for herself.

Chapter Thirty-One

Rebecca appreciated the opportunity originally given her by the McDaniel's TV/radio network. They gave but also took away. When she was up for a promotion on many occasions, she was passed over by a man. It simply wasn't right. The one that really hurt her the worst was the *talking head faggot,* Mark Lewis. Not only did he get her job, he was instrumental in her decision to write Davis that fateful "Dear John" letter.

No, the position she held now was not in any way handed to her on a fifty thousand-watt platter. She hated to have come this far and now quit, but she loved Davis and wanted to be his wife, and nothing would stop her. However, there was more than a little compensation on the other end, in the form of KBEC. She threw caution to the wind, and gave the Memphis station three months' notice.

The ninety days passed rather quickly, as it was expected. There were wedding plans to make and trips both ways from Hattiesburg to Memphis and back. During her final days at the network, there was talk about the prospect of KBEC becoming the new woman's station. Every female employee in the Memphis operation made sure that Rebecca had her business card or telephone number.

The first lady station owner in history set out for Hattiesburg shortly after the last truck was loaded and left with her furniture and belongings. She spent a few lovely days with her parents. Then she joined her fiancé and future father-in-law in planning the remodeling and construction at the TV/radio station that would soon bear her name. It would become a fine structure, all the way from new fully air-conditioned booths and the men and women's dressing rooms, to the finely manicured lawns that stretched to the eighty-foot-high red and white towers.

Lillian took a bite of a homemade almond crisp cookie, a sip of tea, and looked across the white wrought-iron table into the face of her future daughter-in-law. All those years she hadn't seen Rebecca had been very difficult because she missed seeing the girl turn into a woman. Rebecca smiled back at her and all those sun-splashed, rose-scented days returned and made their hearts float like spring butterflies. They both felt the glorious rush and began speaking at the same time. Lillian gave way to Rebecca as she begin by saying, "Lill, I hope you don't mind me asking, but since I wasn't here, could you tell me a little about Davis and...well, Céleste's wedding?"

"Of course, child, if that's what you want, but I don't quite understand why...." Lillian tried to paint a complete picture but chose not to elaborate too much. She watched Rebecca's facial reactions when she hit on an intimate thought, and then backed off to relate a less important recall. The whole thing took about fifteen minutes. After freshening both cups of tea, Lillian asked, "Is that more or less what you wanted to know, child?"

Rebecca took a sip of the delicious apple-flavored tea followed by a healthy drink of ice water. "Lill, I hope this comes out right, because I want you to be happy, and, of course, Davis...and we can't forget The Colonel. I want this to be special, but from what you have told me about the other wedding.... Well, I don't want anything that in any way appears to be a competition; like, 'this or that is going to be bigger or better.' I want it to be so full of love that it makes me forget how way overdue it truly is. What do you think about my feelings on this, my dear Lill?"

"Child, I think you are right where you should be. I don't believe I could say anything better or feel it any differently. We have all waited a long time for this most precious event, but I will tell you just like I told my boy...." Lillian held a hand to her mouth, like she was telling a big secret. There was no one even close to earshot, but she still leaned in close and whispered, "Rebecca, I am old, and I want grandbabies!" Both women stood at the same time, laughing while they hugged.

This was how the wedding was planned—and that's the way it happened, give or take a curtsy or two.

Davis awoke and rolled to his left to give his fiancée a good morning hug before leaving for the office. His arm came up empty, and now he was really awake! Even with the drapes drawn, the room was too light for 6:00 a.m. There was a good reason for this. He finally looked at the clock on the nightstand, which informed him that it was really 8:00 a.m. He shook his head. *Now, how in the hell did that happen?*

He pulled on his blue jeans, went to the bathroom, brushed his teeth, doused his face with cold water, and ran downstairs. As he was hurrying down the great hall, he heard two familiar voices. He stuck his head in the kitchen door and said sarcastically, "Good afternoon, honey, Momma. Becky, why did you turn off the alarm clock?"

"So you could get some extra sack time. The way you've been going lately, I figured...."

"Becky, it's almost 8:30! Dad and Willie are going to shoot me! By the way what are you doing up and around this early?"

"I took the morning to help Mom here with the last of the invitations. You know, I have all this free time since I'm in between jobs."

"Oh." He fumbled with the change in his pocket and said, "Well, I gotta get going, see ya'll."

"Thurston! Sit down and have some breakfast!" his mother ordered.

Davis shoveled down some fried eggs, toast, and coffee. He stood, leaned over and kissed the ladies good morning, and headed for the office. The word "invitations" was sticking in his mind for some reason, and then it hit him. He turned around, went back to the kitchen, and asked, "Did we send an invitation to the Montoyas?"

Lillian looked at him with surprise. "Well, no dear, I thought you wanted to do that."

"Ah jeez, Momma, I forgot again. Give me one of those, and I'll do it at the office."

"And you wondered why I let you sleep in," Rebecca teased.

Davis went to the office, and, after taking some good-natured razzing from Willie and his father, he began composing:

Dear Rodolpho and Irene,

This is to let you know that I am getting married again and
I would like for you all to be here. The same girl who took
the "look of eagles" from me years ago, has given them
back, and is going to be my wife.
I hope to see you then.

                              Much love,
                              Davis

On the Indian summer afternoon of the fifteenth day in the month of

October, Davis and Willie stood anxiously on the stand built at the end of the rose garden path. The band began playing the wedding march. The flower girls were about halfway down the walk when the back door to the mansion opened. Harley Thompson, in a beautifully tailored light-blue tuxedo, walked down the steps. On his arm, was the most beautiful bride in the world, at least in the eyes of everyone at The Willows.

Willie felt the ring in his pocket and, in a few minutes, would hand it to his best friend. His best friend would put it on the finger of the girl who would wear it forever.

The wedding was not what people of wealth would call spectacular, but it *was* very elegant. "It was done in good taste," the two women that planned it would later say. Lillian and Rebecca saw to every detail personally from the wedding march to the last bite of cake and cup of punch. In attendance were a few friends and relatives of the Thompsons, some of the ladies from Lillian's Ladies Club and their families, and, of course, everyone that worked at The Willows. The only downside for Davis was the absence of The Montoya family, especially Rodolpho and Irene. They were unable to attend because their youngest daughter was expecting and experiencing a very difficult pregnancy. Irene signed the R.S.V.P. and added a short note:

> Our Dearest Davis and Rebecca,
>
> Due to a complication in our daughter Carmenita's
> pregnancy we will be unable to share your joyous day.
> We are so very happy you are re-united with your first and
> true love. She must be very special. We are also happy
> about the eagles returning home.
>
> *Te Amor Mucho,*
> Irene and Rodolpho Montoya

The bride and groom had talked it over and decided against a honeymoon. Most of this had to do with Rebecca's excitement of getting their new venture going and putting together the grand opening. There would be plenty of time later down the road.

However, one person didn't see it that way. Upon hearing of the newlywed's plans, Lillian took Rebecca aside, "Now, child, I told you I wanted to have grandbabies. If you want to make an old woman happy, the two of you need to get away from here for at least a week or so and get started. I know that son of mine; he's just like his daddy. Once y'all start working at that station of yours, they will work you to death. So, why don't y'all go down to T. D.'s hotel and have a good time!"

When Rebecca told Davis this, it brought a sad laugh because it reminded him of a couple of years ago when his mother found out Céleste was with child. All the excitement, all the anticipation and planning had been destroyed by the events of one afternoon and evening. He decided not to say anything out loud to his new bride. Everything looked wonderful now, and he didn't want to take a chance and risk spoiling the moment. Instead, he responded, "Well, honey, if it is okay with you, then I'm for it. I would have to think really hard about where I would rather be than somewhere on a beach with my new wife, so you tell me."

This is all Mrs. DeLongpre needed to make up her mind, so she smiled sweetly, and said, "Well...let's go!"

Once the newlyweds arrived at The Colonel's island and unpacked their bags in the luxurious hotel suite, they were glad they had taken Lillian's advice. Davis and Céleste had been there two years before, but, when Céleste died, The all-knowing Colonel ordered the top floor rooms to be remodeled. Davis was uncomfortable about returning there, but, when he saw the changes that had been made, he mellowed a bit. Rebecca never asked him anything about Céleste.

The hotel was booked to capacity with notables from the movie and political industries. With the exception of a few curious glances, the couple was never bothered. The only people who knew them were the hotel's handpicked staff. Actually, they were the employees hired under The Colonel's top gun, John Hubbard's, watchful eye.

The Colonel purchased the island shortly following World War II. There was nothing on the three-mile-wide, thirteen-mile-long piece of real estate in the Caribbean. His plan was to have a place he could use as an incentive to offer his clients. The construction of the hotel and small airstrip took almost two years to complete. After it was finished and one had made a good deal with The Colonel, it was a wonderful place to spend a week or so with one's family. This, of course, was gratis, but it was also a resort for the well-to-do. They began flocking there and, for the most part, left many shillings.

Once the newlyweds had put KBEC temporarily aside, they relaxed and really began to enjoy the hotel and its lush surroundings. They made love several times during the day and enjoyed the decadent food and impeccable service. When all this pampering was too much to bear, they would walk on the pristine beaches or swim in the aqua crystal-clear water. Rebecca had a glorious time learning how to net-fish. It beat the hell out of trying to put some squiggly worm on a hook like she and her daddy once did back home.

After a week, the longing to get her new project under way started to surface once again. They were sitting on the balcony of their suite on the seventh or eighth day about halfway through breakfast. The new Mrs. DeLongpre spread some butter on a breakfast roll and took a bite. It was delectable, and her satisfaction took over her lovely face. She savored the moment, washing it down with a big swig of fresh-squeezed fruit juice. She looked across the table at her smiling husband and finally spoke, "Davis, my love, this is wonderful, and I could probably do this forever. I'm sure we can come here anytime we want. Please don't get upset, but I really would like to get back and work at my new station. What do you think?" She waited uneasily for a few seconds before a big grin took over his face.

He reached over and brushed her cheek, saying softly, "Becky, I've had a great time, and I love this place, but I am ready to go too. I was just waiting for you to say it."

Later that evening, the DC-4 touched down at the Hattiesburg airport. Davis thanked Captain Henderson and told him to go home to his wife and play with his kids.

Chapter Thirty-Two

Rebecca spent the following two weeks putting the final touches on the station and hiring her staff. She hired her ex-roommate, Susie Ames, and another young woman who was with her in Memphis, known only as "Dar Lynn." She, of course, had a last name, but it was either too tough to pronounce or too hard to remember. On TV, it was just "Dar Lynn." (The guys cut it short to Darlin'.)

Rebecca was indeed a pioneer in women's broadcasting and in a great position to further the cause, but she took great care to balance her staff with both men and women. In a short time, they were ready for the grand opening, which turned out to be a smashing success.

After the dust had settled, Mrs. DeLongpre went to work. She arrived shortly after 10:00 a.m. and smiled as she saw a still steaming cup of coffee sitting on the mat that covered part of her custom-made rosewood desk. She was not particularly crazy about coffee and only began drinking it at work in Gulfport and Memphis. It was more of a social thing at first, but then she later just fell into it. Still, she could only drink it loaded with cream and sugar.

After going through her messages and mail, she leaned back and looked around her beautiful office. "Things couldn't be better," she mused. She finally had almost everything she wanted. She was married to the man she had loved for two-thirds of her life and would never have to worry about her future—and she was financially independent. That meant that she could also take care of her parents if necessary. What a wonderful gift, was her TV / radio station. It was something many people have hoped for, but hope was all they would ever get. Surprisingly, there is one thing about gifts—one never knows when they are coming or in what form.

About halfway through her second cup of coffee, she took a swallow and the hot liquid hit her stomach like a dead weight. She felt her damp face and became nauseous. She moved as quickly as she could to the restroom closest to her office.

Susie Ames knocked on Rebecca's door. Without waiting for a reply or looking up, she charged in and said loudly, "Becca! I think we should look at the next month's...." Rebecca wasn't at her desk, so Susie turned around to go find her. She saw her boss exiting the door to the lady's room and noticed that she looked quite pale. She walked to her friend and said, "Whoa, girl, you better sit down! What's the matter with you?"

"Just a little sick to my stomach. I gotta cut down on the coffee."

Susie helped her to her desk. She went to the small refrigerator in the corner and got her some ice water. Rebecca took a couple of sips, smiling to signal that she was better.

"Coffee, huh? Let me ask you boss, were you on time this month?"

Rebecca looked at her friend, mouth open, and said, "My God, I've been so busy. I plain forgot! Maybe I'd better make an appointment with the doc...."

"Maybe you should take the afternoon off and just go see him!"

The doctor took her without an appointment and she had a very short wait. While she was waiting, though, she had apprehensions about all this. If she were pregnant, would this affect her work or take away from her dream for any length of time? Seconds later, a faint smile crossed her face, and she said aloud, "I am the boss."

Susie was right. The coffee wasn't the problem. She listened to the doctor's advice and some of his rules, and scheduled a future appointment.

She went back to work and told Susie the news was positive. They both agreed that this topped *all* the news that had come into the station today. The mother-to-be asked her friend not to say anything just yet, so she could surprise the man who was responsible for this. Now she could face the woman she'd made the promise to between sips of apple iced tea and bites of almond crisps. One thing for sure, she would certainly have something to contribute at dinner that evening.

Rebecca sat for a few minutes and tried to concentrate on work, but it just wouldn't happen. She tapped her pen on the desk in some uneven and annoying rhythm, then caught herself and ceased. She picked up her phone, only to put it back down. She was trying to formulate a plan but just didn't have it altogether yet. On her third or fourth attempt, she managed to keep the phone in her hand and dial the number.

Lillian was sitting at the kitchen table poring through some flower catalogs. She could have gone to the little office that she had built many years ago or to Jarrod's place. Still, there was something with her and that table. Her husband had teased her many times, but that didn't change anything. She was just plain comfortable there, and, besides, it gave her a view. All she had to do was turn her head to the left and look out the window at her roses.

It was an hour or so after lunch. The Colonel had already eaten and gone back to the office with his boys. He would only be gone for a couple hours before coming back to take a nap before dinner. He had slowed down considerably as of late but still wanted to keep active. He could still kick ass when he wanted to, like he proved in acquiring the station for Rebecca. In his family's eyes, *he* was the king, and the king could do about whatever he wanted.

The wall phone announced that someone outside The Willows wanted to speak with someone inside, so Lillian rose and picked it up. "This is Lillian. Who might this be? Oh! Hello, child."

"Lill, I have a big favor to ask of you. I know this is terribly short notice, but I was wondering if I could ask my parents over for dinner this evening. It doesn't have to be anything spectacular, it's just that I haven't seen them since we got back, and I'm in such a wonderful mood today. I'd just like...."

"Say no more, honey. I can have Loretta make up some salads, and we can pick out some steaks—just a nice country dinner. Okay?"

"Oh, thanks, Mom. I love you. I'll call my folks and tell them to come over about 8:00 p.m. tonight. Oh, while you're getting things together, why don't you invite Willie and Darcy? Thanks, bye now."

Lillian slowly hung up the phone. This was the first time Rebecca had ever called her "Mom" and although that sounded wonderful, there was something else. *Willie and Darcy were, of course, always welcome, but Rebecca saw them all the time. Why was tonight special all of a sudden? What was going on here?* Lillian walked a few feet to the refrigerator to get some ice water, and, as she grabbed its handle, she gasped, "Oh, my God! You don't suppose that girl is...?"

With that, she opened the door, carried the heavy pitcher to the sink, and poured a tall glass full. She returned to the table and began to analyze things. She mulled over her thoughts for a few minutes, called the office, told the men about dinner, and called Darcy, who volunteered her help if needed. Once she contacted Loretta, her last job was done. She didn't tell anyone of her suspicions, however.

Rebecca decided to pick her folks up, instead of them having to drive home late. They arrived at The Willows about 7:45 p.m., about the same time as Willie and Darcy.

When Rebecca and her parents arrived, Lillian noticed a change in her daughter-in-law's demeanor. Those usually fiery dark eyes that flashed when she talked, no matter what her mood, were now almost serene. She talked a little slower and a little softer, but there was still something smoldering underneath dying to come out. She gave Rebecca a long pleasant smile before they seated themselves at the table. The salads were served and eaten. Before the steaks were brought out, Lillian tapped her glass lightly with her butter knife, "I know we usually discuss things of importance after our meal, but tonight I would like to make an exception. I believe that our Rebecca has something she wants to share with us."

Everyone at The Willows wanted Davis and Rebecca to have children. Willie and Darcy had done their job and raised two fine boys. It was their prince's turn. Two years earlier, their hopes had risen and fallen with the sudden death of Céleste and her baby. Now they would hold their collective breaths and do everything to insure that Rebecca had a safe and comfortable pregnancy. This was their future, their children's future, and the future of The Willows.

The immediate family, needless to say, was overjoyed. Everyone seemed happy, as well they should but deep in the souls of all, with the exception of Rebecca, remained a dark presence of fear.

After dinner, Rebecca took her folks back to the house by the lake. The two DeLongpre men decided to go sit on the veranda and have a snifter and a smoke. The Colonel took a satisfying draw on his Havana and let it out, "This is a great day, son. I know there is a feeling in all of us that we can't let go, but I believe, with all my heart, that this time God will smile on us."

Davis said nothing but acknowledged his father with a nod. The elder DeLongpre stood, and, after putting out the stub of his cigar, stretched, and bid his son goodnight. Davis decided to sit and wait for his wife to return.

The Colonel went to join his wife in their bedroom. As he was brushing his teeth, he heard sobbing through the half-opened door. He rinsed and walked out to see Lillian on her knees, pouring her heart out to the Big Man in the sky. He stood silently as he heard her ask for His guidance and protection for her daughter-in-law. This man with the gruff exterior felt a tear as it made its journey down his rugged face and ended on his pajama lapel.

Davis poured himself a short drink and returned to the veranda. He took a sip and leaned his head back on the stuffed Naugahyde pillow. He wondered what was taking his wife so long, but the question was answered when he saw her headlights shine on the trees as she turned off the lane into the parking area. He breathed a sigh, "She's home."

Rebecca was loved by all of her employees at the station. Everything was brand new and it was a pleasure to know that their diligent efforts didn't go unseen or unappreciated. The only thing that made the boss-lady uncomfortable was all the attention she was now getting because of her "condition." She could not bat an eyelid or even sneeze without someone there with a tissue. After about a week or so of this, she couldn't take anymore. She issued an interoffice memo:

> I love you all, and I appreciate all the attention, but my baby won't be arriving for at least seven months.
>
> Let's get some work done!
>
> Thank you,
> R. T. D.

During the few months following Rebecca's announcement, there were a variety of emotions to contend with at The Willows, depending on whom you talked to or what day it was. Of course, expectations were high, but memories have a habit of not going away so easily. Rebecca could sense this lukewarm atmosphere, and it bothered her to a point. She tried her best to understand. She *was* aware of the fact that she wasn't present during the brief two years Céleste lived at The Willows but, with all her heart, believed that *she* should have been there in the first place.

During Rebecca and Davis' honeymoon, she had promised herself that she would never again ask her husband or her new in-laws anything about Céleste again. She kept that promise up until now, but the underlying tension was too much for her to endure. It not only affected the newlywed's home life, it interfered with the running of KBEC. She decided to ask for a family meeting.

Rebecca left work early and went home to rest and get her thoughts together. It wasn't so much *what* she wanted to say but *how* she would say it.

She slipped out of her work clothes and admired herself in the dressing mirror on the outside of her closet door. She had gained a little weight but carried it well. She figured there were at least several of her dresses and various ensembles that still looked good on her. She laid out a very pale orange skirt and coordinating blouse that flattered her complexion and dark hair. She picked it up and held it in front of her while she posed once more in front of the mirror. Satisfied, she laid it back down and looked at the clock. Davis would not be home for at least another two hours, so a luxurious, lengthy bath was in order.

Davis came home a few minutes after 6:00 p.m. and pulled off his boots. He could tell by the scent of the perfume that his wife was home. He sat his boots by the dresser next to the closet door and called out, "Honey, are you here?"

"Yes, I'm here dressing. Don't come in!"

"Fine! I'll just go take a shower." Davis shrugged his shoulders at his wife's remark about not coming in, and just wrote it off as the changing moods of a pregnant woman. He had been there once before and knew all the signs. He finished his shower, went to the still-closed closet door and called out again, "Hey, you, I need some clothes! How much longer?"

"I'll be right out, calm down!"

"Be right out," took another five minutes, but it was worth the wait. She looked absolutely stunning. Davis took a deep breath and managed an energetic, "Wow!" Rebecca, with a hand swoop, gestured that the walk-in closet/dressing room was now all his. He kissed her on the cheek as he passed where she was standing at the mirrored door.

He was back from the dressing room inside of ten minutes and saw his wife looking out the bedroom window. He walked over, slipped his hands through her arms and placed them gently on her tummy. As he nuzzled his mouth close to her ear, he questioned her softly, "Now are you going to tell me what this is all about?"

She tilted her head back and leaned on his shoulder. She liked the touch of his hands on her stomach. After enjoying this for a few seconds, she let know him know, "I don't want to have to tell my story twice. Besides, it's not anything earth-shattering. I just need to make my feelings known, that's all."

The Hamptons were already in the kitchen talking to Lillian, and The Colonel was sipping on a glass of wine when Davis and Rebecca walked in and joined them. Willie gave Davis a secret "what's up?" gesture, but his friend could not help him. A few minutes later, Lillian announced dinner was served.

After enjoying rhubarb pie and vanilla ice cream, Rebecca placed her left hand over her husband's right. As the candlelight flickered on her diamond, she gave his hand a firm squeeze and said to all, "I am so much in love with my husband, and I love everyone here. Being Mrs. Davis DeLongpre is all I have wanted to be for as long as I can remember. I am excited about this new life we are beginning, and, the new life that is in my body. I want all of you to be happy for me and with me. I know that each of you were disappointed and heartbroken about the event two years ago. I wish that it could be changed, but it can't. I've been seeing my doctor on a regular basis, and he says I'm in perfect health. I know how much this baby means to my husband, my mother-in-law, and everyone here at The Willows." She looked across at Lillian and smiled. "I know that God is going to be good to us. The reason I feel this is because I know I wouldn't want to be in his shoes, especially if anything were to go wrong. Because then he would have to face Lillian DeLongpre!"

This caught everyone off guard for a split second. When her little joke finally sunk in, the room filled with laughter and a newfound joy. The gray cloud disappeared and drifted off into the sunset. The new feelings spread outwardly from the family to the other folks at The Willows and throughout KBEC.

Six months and a few days later, a smiling mother and father held up a healthy seven-pound little boy and presented him to the world as "Tyler Denton DeLongpre."

Chapter Thirty-Three

Lillian DeLongpre's life had pretty much come full circle. It had been, with a few exceptions, an almost perfect life. To begin with, she grew up in a well-to-do home, which meant good breeding and a good education. She unexpectedly met her perfect man and, with some finagling, had been blessed with a fine young boy. Her health was excellent, she was still very attractive and being wealthy didn't hurt any. Now, she had little Tyler to fawn over and spoil, as only a grandmother can. In a couple of years, Davis and Rebecca would again make her happy with a little girl.

The only big heartache she had experienced was losing Céleste and her baby that sad day several years ago. That void could never be filled, but she did have the daughter-in-law she had wanted from the beginning, plus she finally became a grandma. She would only have one more sorrow to contend with. The grand lady of The Willows would live to be almost ninety.

Nineteen seventy was a year for several celebrations. The Willows would be in existence for one hundred years. The plantation had been there much longer, but we are only counting from that great day when Jarrod and Isaiah first shook hands. That's when it became "The Willows." Davis and Rebecca would be married four years, and Tyler Denton would have his third birthday party. Last, but certainly *not* least, The Colonel would turn eighty.

Time does indeed march on and shows no favors to anyone. It's a commodity that can't be purchased, even by the wealthiest. The wealthy could rent it or prolong the inevitable with their ability to have the best diets and medical assistance available, but only for a limited time.

In the case of the DeLongpres and the Hamptons, they had the best of everything, but aging is a formidable opponent that will always come out the victor. The Colonel and his wife couldn't have asked for better health, and were no doubt an exception to the norm.

It was a beautiful late summer evening about thirty minutes west of Barcelona. The Montoyas usually had their evening meal in the dining room, but, since the girls married and moved away, things became a bit more casual. It was just the two of them now, so they did pretty much what they wanted. The faithful Yolanda served them this evening on the patio. It was a beautiful setting with the multi-colored rock floor and the white wrought-iron tables and chairs. The burgundy umbrellas trimmed in white gave the patio the look and feel of a small, but exclusive resort.

They had finished dinner and a snifter of cognac each when Rodolpho suggested they walk off their meal. Ireñe loved her husband dearly but knew what going for a walk really meant. Sure they would walk, but inevitably, they would end up at the special stalls and she would have to listen to him talk to "those damn horses." She was glad that he derived so much enjoyment from this, but he had been doing this all of his life! *She* was only good for three or four of these visits per year. She kissed him on the cheek, squeezed his arm and said, "I think I will call the daughters and send our love. I haven't spoken with them in weeks. You go ahead and see your babies. Maybe I'll join you in a few minutes."

Rodolpho nodded and walked toward the entrance to the large patio. Ireñe heard his boots clicking and the gate close as she was going through the patio door to the kitchen. She looked quickly at the clock on the kitchen stove, then went to the bar and dialed her first daughter's number.

She had three calls to make. As mothers and daughters do when they haven't talked or seen each other for a while, they tend to go on forever. She finished talking to her third daughter, stood up, stretched, yawned, and looked again at the kitchen clock. She had been on the phone for close to forty minutes.

She looked casually in the general direction of the stables. Her eyebrows rose slightly. She decided not to join him because he would be home any minute now, and she would probably meet him on his way back. Many times over the years, he would only intend to be with his babies for a few minutes, then somehow forget to look at his watch. Anyway, she wasn't worried. She took a book from the case in the library and settled into a big brown leather chair.

After reading seven or eight pages, she laid her head back and closed her eyes. An hour later the book slipped out of her hand and fell heavily on the oak floor. The noise woke her and she sat up with a start. She looked at her watch that read eleven-thirty. "This can't be," she whispered bemused. She rose and went to the kitchen and looked at that clock, same thing. It had been over two and a half hours. She put on a shawl and headed for the stables.

The right half of the huge barn door was slightly ajar and let an eerie spear of light cut into the darkness. Ireñe followed it and eased through the open space. She walked about ten paces and yelled, "Rodolpho! *Donde esta usted*?" There was no answer.

The horses stirred as they heard her passing by on her way to the end stall. "Rodolpho…Rodolpho?" She finally reached the specially built stall at the end of the walkway. She saw the "Big Black" with his head bent down…nuzzling her motionless husband.

"*Rodolpho? Oh mi Dios!*"

The Colonel finished his second after-breakfast cup of coffee, found his hat, and headed for the office. He saw his wife on the northwest corner of her rose garden and was glad to see she had listened to him about having an assistant to do most of the work. He didn't mind her out there with her gloves and bonnet on, as long as she acted mostly in a supervisor capacity. He waved, blew her a kiss, and then began strolling down the path by the corral.

Davis and Willie had been at Rio Doso Downs in New Mexico, where their entry was a two-time victor. The Colonel figured they would be back home later that afternoon. He went through the balance of yesterday's mail and began reading the new issue of *Equestrian Today* when the phone rang. He wondered who could be calling at this hour. Most of the business calls came in the afternoon, except for those from overseas. He picked it up on the forth ring. "Good morning, Willows Wind Livery."

"Hello, is this Davis DeLongpre?" He noticed the Spanish accent.

" No, it isn't. This is his father."

"Oh, Colonel, this is Ireñe Montoya."

"Ireñe, how wonderful to hear from you. I trust all is well in Barcelona?"

"I'm afraid it is not, Colonel. Rodolpho is dead! He had a heart attack yesterday…."

The big man was almost knocked unconscious with shock. His head was spinning as he tried to listen to the details. Ireñe's accent and the shakiness in her voice made it very difficult to absorb everything. He finally pulled himself together enough to get most of her conversation…that included a request.

"Colonel, if it is at all possible, I need Davis to come here as soon as he can. If you could come also, that would be very nice, I would feel better if friends were with me. Also, I found Rodolpho's final will, and, although we have a family lawyer, I would be grateful if you would look at it too. Rodolpho and you became like brothers for the short time you were here, and I know he trusted you. From what I can determine, however, my husband has left half of everything to Davis. This is fine with me, but I would still like him to come here."

"We'll be there within two days, Ireñe."

The Colonel was still almost in shock. He had trouble catching his breath for a few minutes, but then stabilized. Rodolpho was one of the only men, other than Ben Hampton, that he had called his "friend." Now, he was gone and the great man was suddenly feeling old…and very mortal. After steadying himself for a few minutes, he rose and went to give Lillian the terrible news.

Lillian was equally as destroyed as her husband. She dismissed her assistant and they walked home and sat heavily on the chairs at the kitchen table. They sat silently for several minutes and then began to stir up memories about the wonderful Christmas and The Colonel's birthday. That, now, seemed so long ago. After an hour or so of reminiscence, The Colonel shocked his wife by saying, "Lill, I feel like getting drunk!"

Lillian had known this man for a very long time and had *never* heard him make such a statement, *ever!* She had seen him have a cognac or two after dinner but had honestly never seen him "drunk." She looked back at him with her mouth agape and finally said, "Why, you old fool. At your age it would more than likely kill you." She thought immediately about what she had just said and how, at this time, the subject was a little to close to what they were grieving about. "I'm sorry, T. D., I guess it's okay if you have a couple."

Davis and Willie arrived little after 3:00 p.m. and went straight to the office. They were surprised to find that their "Dad" wasn't there. Davis turned to Willie and said, "Guess he ran out of things to do and went to the house. You want to go with me and see what's happening?"

"Naw, pard. We've been gone all this week and most of the last one, so I'd better go home and give Darcy some love. I'll check you later."

Little Tyler had awakened from his nap and was sitting on his grandma's lap asking why his grandpa and grandma were so sad. Lillian was doing her best to explain why when Tyler heard his dad coming through the back door yelling, "Where is everyone? Hey, I'm home!"

Everything ceased to exist when Tyler heard his daddy's greeting. He slid off his grandma's lap and ran into Davis' arms. His father picked him up and went to the kitchen. He could tell immediately that all was not well. He looked first at his mother whose head was slightly bowed and watched his unsteady father take another sip of cognac. He gently lowered Tyler to the floor and asked, "Okay, Momma and Daddy, what's going on here?"

The Colonel slowly sat his snifter down and motioned Davis to sit. He raised his eyes to look directly into his son's and said softly, "We just received some very unpleasant news from Spain. I'm afraid Rodolpho is dead."

Davis looked at his father in disbelief and turned to his mother, whose eyes were wet. All the color seemed to drain from his face. When he was finally able to speak, he could only manage, "What happened?"

The Colonel placed a comforting hand on his son's shoulder while taking a deep breath. "Ireñe said it was a heart attack, and, according to their doctor, death was instantaneous. That's only part of it, son. Rodolpho has left half of all his property to you, and she would like both of us to go over there as soon as possible."

Davis again was speechless for a few seconds. When he recovered, he shook his head slowly and all he could say was, "Jesus, Daddy, I can't believe it…. He can't be gone. He just can't!" Davis became downright silent, as if lost in another world. After a few moments he came to and realized he should say something, "Well, I guess we should get ready and go tomorrow. Is that okay with you?" He looked at his mother and said, "Momma, do me a favor. Call Becky at the station. I better go tell Willie."

The following evening, Davis and his father walked across the stone patio and knocked on Ireñe Montoya's door. A few seconds passed as father and son glanced at each other questionably, but then the door opened and Yolanda greeted them. She smiled and said, "It is so nice to see you both, señors. Ireñe is in the kitchen. Please follow me."

Davis was slightly amused by this. He had been everywhere in this house and certainly would have had no problem finding the kitchen, but he knew she was just being courteous.

They went to the kitchen area where Davis could remember many good times. Ireñe was sitting at the table with a diminutive man in a black suit. His coat was buttoned all the way to the collar, and the frameless glasses made his small face seem even frailer. Ireñe looked up and saw them standing there, then stood and ran to them. This was the first time she had smiled since she found Rodolpho. Half-crying, half-speaking, she said, "Thank you so much for coming. I know it is a long distance. It would have meant a great deal to…."

Davis gently put his fingers on the widow's lips and said softly but firmly, "Shush, Ireñe. You knew we would be here. Is this man a minister?"

"Yes, I have asked him to speak at the funeral services tomorrow."

Ireñe asked if they were hungry. They didn't want to put her out, so they declined. That did no good, because she asked Yolanda to prepare them a light meal. The food brought back more memories…and was, of course, delicious.

They finished dinner and sat with Ireñe for an hour or so. They reminisced about the wonderful times during the several months Davis was with Rodolpho, her, and the noisy teenage girls—and who could forget that magical Christmas? Not one word was mentioned about the will. This was a relief to Davis, but he knew it would have to be discussed in the next couple of days.

Ireñe hadn't seen Davis or his father for that matter since they attended the wedding, and *that* had been close to seven years. She noticed that although he was still undeniably handsome, there was quite a bit of gray hair showing. She looked at The Colonel quickly and then commented, "Davis, you look great and, if I may say so, are looking more like your handsome father!"

Davis thanked her and her comment brought a big smile to The Colonel's face. The trio talked for a few minutes more. The Colonel tried to stifle a yawn but was unable to do so. Ireñe laughed for the second time since that sorrowful night and said, "It is late, and both of you must be very tired. Davis, you know where your old room is, and, Colonel, yours is at the head of the stairs. *Buenos noches*. We will talk at breakfast."

Davis bid this father goodnight in front of his door, turned and walked down the corridor to his old room at the end. He went to the picture window that he had stared through for many hours, but it was dark. Even at this sad time, it would be something to enjoy in the morning. He was tired, but, when he lay down, his eyes just wouldn't close. After several moments of this, he turned the light over the nightstand on and found a tablet and pen.

He loved Rodolpho and Ireñe only second to his own parents. Davis really wasn't comfortable with Rodolpho's request. Maybe comfortable wasn't the right word. He, just plainly, didn't think he deserved it. As he sat there doodling, another idea came to him. He tore up the doodling page, started working with figures and making some notes. A half an hour later, he yawned, laid the tablet and pen on the nightstand, and turned out the light.

Ireñe woke early from a tossing and turning, almost sleepless night. She lay in bed for another fifteen minutes, looked again to the empty half of the large bed, and felt the tears starting to swell up. Suddenly, she sat up and said, "No! I am not going to let this happen! Rodolpho would be ashamed if he could see me!" She stopped and looked skyward. "Maybe, he can?"

She bathed, dressed, and went downstairs to prepare for her daughters and their families to arrive. She asked Yolanda to let the DeLongpres sleep for a while longer given the time change.

Later that morning, Davis heard the rapping on his door. He rolled on his back, squinted at his watch, which read four o'clock. *Was that possible?*

"You forgot to change the time, stupid!" he said under his breath. "Who is it?"

"It's Yolanda, Señor Davis. Ireñe said to call you for breakfast."

"Okay, is my father awake yet?"

"Yes, I woke him on the way here."

He opened his suitcase, found his bath stuff, went to the familiar bathroom, and began to shower.

While he was drying off, he walked around the bed and looked out the window at the beautiful view. It still looked like a wide-screen western…but the star was no longer with them. He dressed and went down the hall to meet his father.

He started to knock on the door when he saw The Colonel standing with his hands on the railing at the top of the stairs, looking at something. He walked over to his father's side and saw the same scene. It was something they were not quite prepared for.

There must have been a dozen people, all talking at the same time. It sure didn't look like the day of any funeral that *they* had ever seen. They saw in attendance, not only the Montoyas' daughters with their husbands and children, they saw members of Yolanda's immediate family, and "their" immediate family, along with what seemed the environs of Spain! They looked at each other and decided to join the, *festivities?*

Ireñe saw and beckoned them to join everyone. She showed them the two places especially reserved for them at the head table. The DeLongpres only knew the daughters from before, so Ireñe had them introduce as "The Americans" to their husbands and children.

After breakfast, they had to prepare for the hard part.

About two o'clock that afternoon, the cars began pulling into the big space between the hacienda and the old stables. Rodolpho had requested he be buried next to the new stables where he kept his prize horses. Since this is how he wanted it, Ireñe decided to have the funeral outside in a beautiful green meadow that hadn't been used for planting or grazing.

There were a lot of people, but the DeLongpres knew almost no one. There were some in attendance that Davis certainly did recognize. One especially.

She had to be in her early thirties by now. She still had the technicolor red hair and great figure, but a couple of things were new. A little boy was holding her hand and a much bigger boy was holding the car door open for her. About fifty feet separated them as their eyes locked briefly. She recognized Davis, although he had gained a little weight and sported graying hair. They stared at each other for a few seconds before Estrelita, her husband, and little boy drove away.

The Widow Montoya asked the DeLongpres to join her at the legendary dining room table for lunch the following day. Before the meeting, Davis gave his father the notes he had made the night they arrived.

The Colonel looked them over and asked, "Are you sure this is the way you want it, son?"

"Yeah, Daddy, and I want you to be my counsel. It won't go that far, but in case the attorney has any crazy ideas, I want you in charge."

The attorney at the table was one that Rodolpho had used over the years. After lunch, The Colonel mentioned to the lawyer that he didn't see any need for his presence. He politely suggested, "Unless you object, Ireñe? My son's intentions are quite simple. I will read to you what he wishes."

The Colonel cleared his throat and read the one page statement:

Davis appreciates Mr. Montoya's gift and the love that influenced his decision, but he also has great feelings for Mrs. Montoya and her daughters. He doesn't care to deprive them of any properties that are rightfully theirs. He does not believe he deserves the gift, however, there was talk, many years ago, about property adjacent to this that Mr. Montoya also owned. That my son still has interest in buying. He would accept this property and leave the original property in whole to Mrs. Montoya, her daughters, and their families.

The Colonel looked up and handed the paper to the attorney, who glanced at it before passing it to Ireñe. She read it and put it down in front of her. She looked steadily at Davis for at least thirty seconds before saying, "I have always been very fond of you, Davis. Maybe not to the degree that my husband felt, but, more and more, I can see the reasons for his actions in the will. I appreciate your thoughtfulness in regards to only wanting the property on the other side of the fence, but half of the worth of this property is more than enough for this old lady *and* her daughters. I, also, have never questioned or gone against my husband in any decision he made concerning the business of running this ranch. This is *his* decision, and I am going to abide by it. Those are my final words on this subject.

"Oh! Many pardons. I will also request that you and your father make the arrangements to run the day-to-day operations here. Now, if it needs to be, what do you call it? Legalized? You two and Attorney Carbon here can sign the papers. I am going to go play with my grandchildren."

The DeLongpres stayed one more day and looked the place over. They had a couple nice meals with Ireñe and several pleasant chats. It was time now to go home and figure out what they were going to do with yet another acquisition.

Chapter Thirty-Four

It had been an exhausting three days for Davis. He had made some important decisions involving the acquisition of their new property. He reclined on one of the airliner's plush seats and closed his eyes. There was a lot to think about, and it wasn't all business.

Seeing Estrelita was totally unexpected, but then he remembered that the Montoyas and the Bravos did have some connections over the years. The feeling he felt when their eyes met caused a twinge to travel all through his body. He had previously compared Rebecca to the Spanish spitfire he met when he first arrived in Spain. He did this again, but now that he *had* Rebecca, no one alive could ever compare to his wife and mother of his son.... He smiled and drifted off.

The Colonel watched his son sleep for a few minutes. He was thinking how quickly the thirty-five years had passed since they picked him up in Tupelo that cold, drizzling morning. He looked out the window, watching the huge propellers whirling in sync, and realized how noisy they really were. He decided to go to the cockpit and asked the pilot a question, "Captain Rex, do you know anything about those new business planes? I think they're called Lear Jets, or something like that."

"What would you like to know, Colonel?" The veteran pilot knew that his employer was well-read on what he asked him, but he enjoyed the courtesy all the same.

"Well...." The Colonel continued, "Captain, have you flown one? Are they faster than this old DC-4? How about fuel efficiency?"

"I can answer yes to all those questions, Colonel. This old girl has been great for a lot of years but has her limitations. We could cut the time on this trip by about two hours and also save money."

The tall Mississippi horse rancher raised his heavy eyebrows. "Rex, do me a favor when we get home. No rush, but check into one of those babies for me and we'll get back together on this. I think my boy is going to need one now that he's got holdings in Spain."

Father and son returned to The Willows, and, as always, it was good to be home. They had been gone less than a week and it seemed that a lot had happened in their absence. Well, things *had* changed a bit.

Willie and Darcy were now new grandparents from their oldest son, Darryl, and his wife. Willie wouldn't have to worry about the Hampton name continuing anymore. The lady newscaster also had a surprise for her husband. She was going to give the family another child sometime next summer.

This was all wonderful news and would need to be celebrated, but, after a couple days of celebrating, the DeLongpre/Hampton team would need to fill some positions to run their new Spanish properties. They would need someone to manage the already successful "Montoya Ranch," and then hire a team of local Spaniards to rebuild the dormant land on the other side of the fence. The buildings, including the main house, had been kept up fairly well by Rodolpho, but the land had not been worked for many years.

The Colonel called his boys together to have a "little talk over" about how things stood at the present time at home. As they were going over the books, they realized that they had spent a lot of money since day one. However, everything had been done first class. Everything from the grade of building materials to the quality of equipment, and even the types of grass planted had been carefully thought out before implementation. Yes, they had spent a lot, but they spent well, and the results were now beginning to show.

T. D. DeLongpre removed his glasses with the bone-colored rims and put them in his shirt pocket. He closed the last ledger and stacked it on top of the others. He looked at Willie and asked, "What time does the accountant come in?"

"About three o'clock in the afternoon, Pop. I'll make sure I am here."

Now that this was out of the way, the business in Spain needed to be discussed. Willie Hampton's twenty-five percent of The Willows' operations had been passed on to him from his grandfather, Isaiah and from his father, Ben.

When Davis and Willie started the project of developing racing stock, they had agreed to be equal partners. They had generated a profitable business on their own, but when The Colonel semi-retired and decided to invest "new" money and make it a first class operation, the partnership changed a bit.

They worked this out very easily. Willie would still have his twenty-five percent of *ALL* of The Willows operations but, additionally, would have thirty-three and a third percent of the horse business. This meant, that although the Spanish property was one hundred percent Davis', and he had the final say so, yet all the profits from the horse business, including Spain, would be split evenly three ways.

At the close of World War I, T. D. DeLongpre, II was an extremely wealthy man. At the end of the Second World War to present day, he was one of the ten wealthiest men in the world. This was indeed impressive because it was before the advent of the computer age. He invested heavily in his "boy's" project, but from the beginning had never taken a penny for himself.

Later, when his will was read, he requested that his split of the profits be given to his grandchildren. This meant Davis and his son, as well as Willie and Darcy and their children.

The Colonel patted the stack of ledgers on the upper left corner of his desk and pointed to Willie. He put his big hands together in the form of a church steeple and said, "Willie, you've been a wonderful son to me. You have lived up to all the expectations that your father and my great friend, Ben, hoped for. Amos Hubbard assured me that upon his departure you would use all he taught you and would no doubt excel way beyond that. He was so right. We are all very proud of you, my boy."

Willie wasn't fond of the "boy" thing but knew that coming from his "pop," it was meant in the highest loving regard. He nodded and gestured for The Colonel to proceed.

"Now, my sons, I would like to get your input on the Montoya situation. I am only suggesting that we organize and decide what...."

The phone that sat on the right corner of his desk interrupted his speech. He threw his hands up and said in an irritated tone, "This is T. D. DeLongpre. Can I help you?" His annoyed expression changed to a big smile, "Okay! Good job, Captain Rex. Just do it and sign my name."

Davis and Willie looked at him with faces that asked, "What was that all about?"

The Colonel was grinning like a boy who had just bought his first bicycle. He leaned forward in his chair and said excitedly, "Boys, we just bought one of those Lear Jets!"

Davis and Willie sat there speechless.

The Colonel continued, "Well, what do you think? Talk to me!"

Neither man could ever remember seeing him this expressive, for this man who had seen almost everything and could afford whatever he wanted, *this* was rather unexpected. Coming from him, it was like an outburst.

Davis, finally able to put a few words together, said, "Sounds great, Daddy, but when did all this come about? I kinda like the DC-4."

The Colonel didn't answer him right away. Instead, he chose to reminisce. For a few minutes, they talked about the progression they had witnessed. They spoke and laughed about the train rides and the old cars, while the older man told them once more about the first buggy ride from Hattiesburg to The Willows.

The Colonel gave his desktop a resounding slap, which brought all of this history back to the present. He said very matter-of-factly, "I decided on the new plane when we were coming back from Spain. The engines were loud, and our plane was slow and drank a lot of gas. We can afford the fuel, but I have a feeling there is about to be a change as far as fuel prices are concerned. Those boys in the Arab countries have something up their collective sleeves. Anyway, I can see you boys making several trips to Spain. The new plane will be more comfortable, faster, and, yes, more fuel-efficient. Besides that, you might want to take your families with you now and then."

All Davis and Willie were able to do was marvel. They were also proud. This unique man that they both called "father" may have slowed down a bit as he neared eighty-two, but that *mind* was just as sharp as it had ever been. It was a good thing because this mind would be tested yet another time before all was said and done.

Dr. Leland Fisher was having a bad year. In fact, the last three or four had not been all that great. He had made some foolish investments over the years, and they were now coming back to haunt him. Some of the people who knew him well said, "He was gettin' his comeuppance." Whatever the reasons were, he was broke...broke and old.

He decided to call on an old acquaintance to try and remedy the situation. He obviously knew of the DeLongpre's immense wealth, and he had done them a favor, right? If Lillian had agreed to continue the affair, he might have held off doing what he was planning, but she didn't. He was a country doctor who "shoulda' stuck to doctorin'," because he was a lousy businessman.

The Colonel arrived at the office around 10:00 a.m. and bid his partners a "good morning."

"Morning to you too, Pop. You got a phone call earlier from Dr. Fisher. He wants you to call him. The number is on the desk."

The Colonel stroked his moustache, picked up the paper, and half above a mutter said, "What the hell could Leland want? The last time we talked he'd lost his butt when that Tidewater Project went sour, of which I had *nothing* to do with."

He took off his hat and promised himself he would return the call later on in the morning. The doctor, however, wouldn't let him wait. He hadn't even been there an hour before the pesky physician called him again, "Hey, Colonel, I think we should get together and have a little talk. I have a deal for you. How soon can you come in?"

He sure didn't want the doctor anywhere close to his home or his wife, so he said to the little conniver, "Okay, Leland, I'll have Daniel bring me in this afternoon. This had better be good!"

Daniel delivered his boss to the doctor's office a little after lunch. The doctor told his nurse/receptionist not to disturb them and asked The Colonel to have a seat. He didn't waste any time getting to his devious plot, "Colonel, I've experienced some financial difficulties of late. You're a rich man, I'm not, and I need some money! As you know, I was one of the folks that brokered the acquisition of your 'son' many years ago. I know you wouldn't want that to get out. And, for a lousy quarter of a million, I would throw everything away and pretend it never happened. I know you can afford it."

The Colonel's eyes narrowed and took on that stare that had been giving people the sweats for closer to one hundred years. He sat straight up in his chair and boomed, "What in the blue perfect hell are you talking about?"

"Well, lets start with that 'son' of yours, a fine young man I hear. Now, it's too late for anyone else to care what happened way back then, but I'll bet that he and some of your friends and associates wouldn't find the situation very amusing. I'll tell you what else I'll do…for no more money. There are a few things about your wife you don't know, and that she wouldn't want to get around to all her fancy friends, that I can tell also."

The big man's first impulse was to crush the *sleazy little bastard*, but he realized that he was in his eighties, and, although he could probably turn the little man's lights out, he might hurt himself trying. He'd already been responsible for one of the doctor's investments going sour, so he decided to calm down and think this through.

He told the doctor that he'd have to think it over and let him know in a day or two. Dr. Fisher said, "okay," but warned him not to take too long. The Colonel turned his back, chuckled, and walked out. For some strange reason the doctor wasn't afraid of the powerful man. He thought he had him right where he wanted him. Silly man.

The Colonel didn't have much to say on the drive home or when he got back to the livery office. This was a matter he could not share with any of his family at The Willows. He would think this problem through. He had to figure how to deal with the greedy M.D. in a way to protect what was his. The last thing he would let happen would be to bring any level of shame to his family.

Two days later The Colonel walked into the doctor's office and said very pleasantly, "Leland, I'm going to take your deal. There's only one small problem. I have to fix it so the money I'm putting together doesn't show anywhere. As you may know, I have a resort island in the Caribbean. Why don't you go down there for a week on me? All expenses paid, including unlimited gambling and maybe a nice woman thrown in? Now, here's fifty grand, and I'll have the rest for you when you get back. How does that sound?"

The doctor was taken aback by the very calmness displayed by the man, who only two days ago looked like he wanted to kill him. He looked quizzically at his adversary and said, "Why are you being so nice about this whole thing? I figured you would be totally pissed!"

"Well, Leland, you know, I had time to think about it. You did us a favor one time, and you're right, I am rich. Now, give your nurse some time off and go enjoy yourself. But if you tell a soul anything, the deal is off! Okay?"

The men shook hands and one went home to his family. The other packed his bags and was off for a Caribbean vacation. The vacationer had a wonderful time, but the last time any one could remember seeing him, he was on the beach, drunk, trying to talk an island girl into accompanying him to his room. He never returned to his practice in Hattiesburg, and no one in Southern Mississippi was ever questioned.

Chapter Thirty-Five

Nineteen seventy-one turned into 1972, but, just before its final bow, The Colonel was blessed with another birthday. As many men do when they are reaching the end of their journey, he would say things that his family really didn't want to hear. When Lillian would ask him why he did a certain thing, he would reply, "Well, my love, I want to make sure this is done because when I'm gone...." Or he would say to Davis or Willie, "You boys do it right the first time, 'cause I may not be around to help you...." His family would cut him off when he rambled at times by telling him he would probably outlive them.

Springtime was only two months away when Davis returned home from his second trip to Barcelona. Things were taking shape over there and he was especially happy with the progress being made on the property across the fence. Ireñe was still in good health and was enjoying spoiling her grandchildren that her daughters allowed many visits from. She did look forward to Davis' trips because, each time she saw him, the memory of Rodolpho still lived on. However, when Davis came home *this* time, he had a surprise waiting for him.

A few days before his arrival, his wife and mother were having a late breakfast. Rebecca was about four months into her pregnancy and wasn't putting in as many hours at KBEC. This had a lot to do with her mother-in-law's wishes. She must have said a hundred times, "Now, child, I have waited long enough to be a grandma, and you have made me one once, but I would still like one more, so you take care of yourself, hear?"

Rebecca would laugh and tease her and tell her not to worry. She could have as many grandbabies as she wanted. Well, if that was okay with her husband. This led to something Rebecca had wanted to ask Davis for for some time but didn't know exactly how she should approach him. The name Céleste had not come up since their honeymoon. She decided to take a chance and ask Lillian her opinion. She took a deep breath and exhaled. "Lill, does Davis ever talk to you about the house up on the hill?"

This caught Lillian a little off guard, but, as usual, she recovered quickly and said, "Well, not really, honey. Ah, no, I don't believe he ever has. Why do you ask, pray tell?"

"Don't get me wrong, Lill. I really love the big house, and I know there is plenty of room, but I've been up to that place. It's very beautiful on the outside and I love the view overlooking the lake. It kinda reminds me of when I was a little girl and my daddy and I went fishing and he taught me to sail. Do you think Davis would get upset if I brought it up to him?"

Lillian thought for a moment and smiled. She took Rebecca's hand and helped her stand up. She could do it herself, but it was becoming a little more difficult every day. "Come, child, let's go take a look. I think the keys are still on that hook board in the hall by the kitchen door."

The Colonel had bought his wife a golf cart a year or so previously. She never learned to drive a car, but, after running into a few things here and there, she became somewhat proficient at operating the little battery-powered runabout. The mother-in-law and the mother-to-be climbed in and began the short trip along the lake and up the hill. Lillian had not been up there for a while. Her rose garden helper usually looked after the flowers she had planted along the pathway several years earlier.

They parked the cart and walked up the path and onto the porch. Rebecca turned and looked at the lake. She stood there with Lillian at her side but slightly behind her. It was truly a beautiful view, and she really wanted to live there. She wondered how difficult it would be to sell her husband on the idea. The place had been locked since Céleste's death.

Lillian put the key in the lock and turned it slowly. She gently pushed the big door open. The women walked in about eight feet and stopped to look around. Of course, Rebecca couldn't, but Lillian felt Céleste's presence as they explored. It brought back ghostly images to Lillian as she remembered each room that she and Céleste had decorated together. There wasn't a whole lot of conversation between them. When they had seen everything, Lillian asked, "What do you think, child? Do you like it?"

"Yes, Lill, it's a beautiful home. You certainly did a nice job."

Lillian noticed that her daughter-in-law only mentioned *her* as the decorator, which gave the elder Mrs. DeLongpre the idea that the younger woman was open to suggestions. She added, "Well, depending on what you and my son decide, I think we should tear it apart and start over."

Rebecca smiled and nodded in agreement.

Davis had just put the last bite of cherry pie in his mouth when he heard his wife's idea. He swallowed and shook his head emphatically.

"But, Davis, won't you even talk about it? You haven't even listened to your mother's and my ideas!"

"Becky, now that's it!" He turned to his mother with his voice slightly raised. "Momma, you know how I feel about that!"

He put his napkin on his plate, rose, and stormed outside to the veranda. Rebecca started to follow him, but Lillian held up her hands. She stood and took her shawl off the back of her chair, draped it around her shoulders, and went to find her son. Rebecca and The Colonel looked at each other almost hopelessly as Lillian made her exit.

She found her son standing by the railing looking in the general direction of the house just mentioned. She put her hand on his shoulder and turned him around. She said in a low but serious tone, "Look here, young man. I've never seen you react like this before, and I don't want to see it again. I don't care if you live to be a hundred years old. As long as I'm still around, you don't ever leave my table like that again…ever! I think you owe your wife and father an apology!"

The grand lady snapped a hundred-and-eighty-degree turn like someone half her age and walked briskly back to the dining room, leaving a speechless Davis in her wake. After digesting this for several minutes, he walked humbly back to the dining room and saw that his wife had already left. He walked over to where his father and mother were sitting and said sheepishly, "I'm sorry, Momma, Daddy. I guess I was a foot or two out of line. I'm sorry."

His father gave him one of those stares he had seen all those years and uttered gruffly, "We accept your apology, son, but there is someone else who needs one even more than we do."

Davis bid his parents goodnight and walked slowly to his room. Rebecca had already tucked Tyler in for the night and was lying on their bed with her back turned as he walked in. He sat heavily on his side and was silent for a few minutes. He began to speak slowly and quietly, "Becky, honey, I know that 'I'm sorry' isn't nearly enough, but if you will allow me to explain, I would appreciate it. You don't have to say anything if you don't want to."

He waited for an answer and when none was forthcoming, he continued, "I guess I've been stupid a lot of the time and maybe an asshole some of the time. Becky, I've loved you for as long as I can remember. I don't want to go into that thing with the letter again, but, when I thought I had lost you, well,

Céleste was just there. It seemed that she was going to have me no matter what. I was infatuated with her beauty at first, but that was about it. I honestly have to say that I grew to love her and, when she died, it left a big hole in my heart. I closed that house up because I wanted the hurt and everything to go away. I'm sorry for the way I acted and I know now how wrong I was. 'Cause, you see, Becky, you've filled that hole and you are here now, and I want you to be with me forever. I love you more now than I ever have. If you still want to remodel that house, you have my blessing. If you think you can trust me, then hand me a paint brush." He placed his hand gently on her left shoulder and pulled her over. He laid his head on her tummy and once more said, "I love you."

The next evening at supper she handed him a brightly wrapped package. He untied the ribbon and lifted the lid. Davis had his own paintbrush.

The makeover didn't take as long as expected. Rebecca's day, while this was going on, began with her spending a few hours at KBEC. This was just to make sure everything was being taken care of. Susie Ames and Dar Lynn were very capable of following their boss' orders, so Rebecca was usually out of there by lunchtime. She would come home and take a short nap before joining Lillian at the house on the hill.

Rebecca didn't do a whole lot of the work, nor did Lillian. It's safe to say Davis didn't really wear out that new paintbrush either, but they all made excellent supervisors. Although The Colonel didn't spend a lot of time on the job, when he did decide to leave the stable office and make an appearance, the work somehow speeded up.

By the time Stacey Lynn DeLongpre was born, the job had been completed and the new baby had a new home. Davis and Rebecca's family was as big as they wanted it to get, and Lillian had another reason to get out of bed in the morning.

The births of Tyler Denton and Stacey Lynn began a new cycle of life at The Willows. Mother Nature or God, or whomever one chooses to believe in, has been doing this since the beginning of time. This may not always seem fair to some, and, at times, almost appears cruel. This is, however, just the way it happens. Someone you want to live forever dies young, and someone who doesn't deserve to live, goes on forever. No matter how one views this, it seems that in order for new life to begin, another life has to end.

Chapter Thirty-Six

The summer of 1973 began turning into autumn in Southern Mississippi. The oppressive humid heat began to mellow. The days were growing shorter and the nights were becoming cooler. It was a welcome change for man and beast alike.

The Willows was going through these changes, and, if possible, becoming even more beautiful. The groves were bountiful and the horse business was growing at a gallop. Nothing, it seemed, could get any better.

On one fine fall morning, Lillian opened her eyes and looked at the clock on her nightstand. She said quietly, "My, can that be right?"

She sat up, grabbed her rose-colored negligee, and wiggled into her slippers. She padded her way to the window overlooking the willow-lined driveway and opened the blinds. The sun made her squint, and she turned away. As it was most of the time, the clock *was* right. She sat on the edge of the huge four-poster bed, turned, and patted her husband on the shoulder. The velvety drawl she possessed as a young lady in the garden that special evening of long ago still sounded the same. "T. D., I'm going down for coffee. Do you want to join me? T. D.!"

The Colonel finally responded and rolled over. His big hand found hers and squeezed it gently.

"Lill, darlin, I didn't sleep all that well last night. You go ahead and let me catch a few more winks."

"Would you like anything special for breakfast?"

"Surprise me."

Lillian went to the kitchenette and found her coffeepot on the warmer and the morning paper that Loretta had placed beside it. She gave the lady a "thank you" smile while picking up her glasses she always left there.

After about an hour of reading all the parts of the paper that interested her, she asked Loretta to make two orders of soft-boiled eggs, toast, and half a grapefruit. She rose to go wake her husband. At the same time, the phone rang. It was from the stables' office. "Morning, Momma, are you letting Daddy sleep in?"

"Yes, honey. He didn't sleep that entirely well. I'm going to go get him up now for breakfast."

She went upstairs and, as she entered the bedroom, heard him snoring softly. She sat down on his side of the bed and began gently caressing his forehead. This woke him, and he grumbled good-naturedly, "Okay, woman. I'm up! I don't know how I put up with you all these years."

"Oh, and you're a real stroll through the park, aren't you?"

The Colonel stood up and they gave each other a good morning hug before going downstairs to breakfast. Lillian watched her husband of close to a half a century, as he sipped his coffee and took a few bites of food. He more or less just moved it around on his plate. She wanted to say something, but, after all these years, she had learned that most of the time he would eventually come out with what was bothering him, or was on his mind. He finally looked up at her and said, "Honey, I'm really not that hungry, but I am tired. I think I'll go up and lay down for a while. Call and tell the boys I'll be out later."

He leaned over, kissed her, stood up, and headed back up to the bedroom. She noticed something different. His skin was a bit clammy and his lips were cold. This was the first time she could remember his kiss being like that.

She busied herself with various things, like she routinely did most mornings, for the better part of two hours. *He's slept long enough.* So, she took off her glasses, put them at their customary place on the table, and went upstairs.

This time when she went through the door, there was no snoring. This time when she called his name, there was no reply. She sat on the bed next to him and shook him gently. Her heart was in her throat as she clasped his wrist, looking for a pulse…nothing. She sat there staring at him for several minutes. After kissing him on the forehead, she walked around the bed and picked up the phone on the nightstand. Three rings later, she heard a familiar voice. "Yeah, Momma, what's going on over there? Is Daddy still sleeping?"

The program director at KBEC-TV looked at his monitor, which read:

> The following is a special announcement from the management of KBEC-TV in Hattiesburg.

Ladies and gentlemen...

Rebecca Thompson-DeLongpre.

The camera rolled into place for a close-up of the station's newscaster and owner. There was no radiant smile that most of Mississippi was used to seeing. A beautiful but somber face began to speak.
"Good evening, Hattiesburg and Southern Mississippi. This day, America has lost a friend. Industrialist, entrepreneur, and philanthropist Colonel Thurston DeLongpre, II has died at age eighty-three.
"The Colonel first became known as the supplier of cotton to uniform our soldiers in World War I. He then became a respected international businessman who earned the credibility of always giving his clients a fair and honest deal. In recent years, he had semi-retired and, as many of you know, built a reputable thoroughbred horse ranch, along with his sons.
"He is survived by his wife, Lillian, his sons, Davis and Willie, by his grandchildren, Tyler and Stacey...and me.
"This is Rebecca Thompson-DeLongpre...No, this is Rebecca DeLongpre, who can only say, we're going to miss you, Dad."

Everyone who worked and lived at The Willows was in a state of complete shock. This was something that just couldn't happen and could not be accepted by his immediate family or anyone else. In a matter of hours following Rebecca's broadcast, telegrams, phone calls, and flowers were arriving from all over the world. Davis finally asked his wife to use her medium and ask everyone not to send any more flowers, but if they would like to in his honor, send donations to the various charities The Colonel had established. It was difficult in this time of grief, but they managed to put together a list of the charities and air it. Once this had been accomplished, they went to comfort their mother and share her grief.

Willie told Davis he would take care of business while the funeral arrangements were being tended to. But, as hard as Willie tried, he could not function as far as business matters were concerned. He put his head in his big dark hands, sobbing profusely. T. D. was *his* dad, too and had been since Ben Hampton died in that car wreck. He leaned back and blew his nose. He sat in silence while making his decision. He closed down the entire operation until after the services. The only people that worked during this time were those whose job was to mind the stock. He took a long look at The Colonel's desk, straightened some papers, and shoved the chair in close. "Good-bye, Pop," he whispered.

He locked the door to the office and went to the front to close the big barn doors. He glanced in the direction of the main house and took a few steps. He stopped and stared at the back door for a few seconds, but then turned around and headed for his home. Right now, the only place for him was in his loving wife, Darcy's, arms.

There was no way that The Colonel could be replaced. There was no way one could fill those "size one hundred" shoes. His sons were no dummies, but the two of them, plus John Hubbard had a next-to-impossible task ahead of them. They would in time conquer, but it would take quite a while.

Unless they were invited, no one ever ventured into "Jarrod's Place." It was not because this wasn't allowed. It just plain wasn't done. It was a room that bordered on sacred to The Colonel; everyone knew that and respected it. Many meetings had been held there but always with the great man presiding. A few days after he was buried in the little valley past the lake, Davis and his mother went into the office for the first time without him. It was a very eerie feeling at first. It was as if they expected his voice to boom out, "You're all probably wondering why I've called you all here!"

Of course, this was not going to happen, but mother and son glanced at each other and continued in slow, sure steps. Davis pushed the button on the base of the chrome-plated lamp and waited for the florescent bulbs to flicker on. In the middle of the desk was an envelope with a key taped to it. The envelope was addressed "Lillian." Davis picked up the key and handed the parcel to his mother. She began to open it, but then took a deep breath and stopped. Davis gestured for her to continue.

Inside the large outer container were three smaller sealed envelopes. One contained instructions on what to do in the event of his death. Both mother and son recognized the name of The Colonel's corporate attorney on the first one they picked up. The second was a note that simply sent love to all and said good-bye. The last was marked "Lillian—PERSONAL." She held it up and stared at it for a few seconds and started to hand it to her son. Davis held up his hands and shook his head slowly from side to side.

"Momma, it says personal"

Lillian began twirling her lock of hair and fretted, "I know, honey, but...."

"Momma!"

Lillian reluctantly slipped the envelope in her jacket pocket along with the key Davis had just handed to her. They sat down and decided to call Dawson Bridger, one of The Colonel's top attorneys. After a few minutes talking with him, they set up a date for reading the will.

Lillian could not bring herself to sleep in the big four-poster bed they shared for those many wonderful years. She took some of her everyday personal stuff to one of the many guest bedrooms and settled in there for a few nights.

She made herself as comfortable as possible and picked up a book to read. She tried reading, but the words seemed to all run together. Her stare to nowhere was suddenly interrupted as she remembered the envelope and key in her jacket pocket. After retrieving these items, she crawled back in bed and broke the seal on the envelope marked "Lillian—PERSONAL."

The beginning of the note explained the key. It belonged to a safe in the back wall of The Colonel's closet. She went to the master bedroom to find it. As she separated the neatly hanging suits with both hands to get to the safe, the smell of cigar smoke still lingered, giving her goose bumps.

She had to go to the light to read the combination, returned and opened the safe on the second try. The key fit a flat metal box. She picked it up and carried it to the desk under the south bedroom window. Upon opening it, she found a stack of papers held together by two red rubber bands. The first paper on top was a note from her late husband. It simply read:

My Darling Lillian,

I hope this day finds you well. The enclosed papers are copies or duplicates of the procedure that led to the acquisition of our son.
All of the people who were involved in this have passed on. I don't why I've kept them all these years, but I did. I am leaving it up to you to either keep or destroy them.
But, if you ever decide to tell him, you will have proof. Again, do what you think is best. Everything else has been taken care of. I am sorry I had to leave you, but I know we will be together again someday.

Love for eternity,
T. D.

She sat motionless at the desk for several moments. Hazy visions of moonlit gardens, picnics by lakes, and a little boy in a yellow and white bassinet paraded in front of her sad eyes. She finally put the papers back in the box, walked back to the closet, and, for a second time, waded through the cigar-scented suits to put it away. Once again, in her best Scarlet O'Hara, she said out loud, "I'll just deal with this tomorrow."

John Hubbard had never been to The Willows. He had been running the show since The Colonel's semi-retirement and was second in command. When he learned of his boss' death, it greatly saddened him, and not just because of his affection and admiration for his father and The Colonel's friend. After receiving the telegram from Dawson Bridger requesting his presence at the will reading, he began packing. He would finally see The Willows.

The reading and all the details pertaining to "who gets what" really didn't surprise anyone. Most in attendance thought it a waste of time. It was just one of those things that had to be done.

Davis and Willie went out to the office afterwards to hash things over and see how they felt about all the details of The Colonel's last wishes. As it should be, Lillian received the major portion of her husband's wealth, but Davis was totally in charge.

Willie grinned at his friend, "Well, now, what do I call you, Head Honcho, Colonel, Jr., or what?"

Davis took an eraser off a pencil and flipped it at his pal. He leaned back and said, "You know, Willie, nothing has really changed at all. Hubbard's still running things out there, and Momma is still running the show here." This brought out a laugh from both. "I liked the trusts that were established for your and my kids and grandchildren. He left his third of the horses to be divided up between you and me, but it's been that way more or less all along. By the way, I forgot to tell you what a great eulogy you did for Dad. That was really nice."

"Thanks, man. I almost blew it a couple of times. It was all I could do to hold back the water works. Remember?"

Jennie Hampton sat at Lillian's right side at the funeral. Davis sat at her left. As she looked around the chapel, she saw a few people she knew outside The Willows but *only* a few. Mostly she just sat and dabbed at the corner of her eyes and squeezed her friend's hand every few minutes. In the back of her mind, she was reviewing all the great years her husband and Ben had known each other. She felt a gush of pride coming over her when the minister announced that "Mr. William Hampton" would be delivering the eulogy. He looked so handsome up there in his suit and tie. It reminded her of how Ben was dressed that night for their anniversary…the last night of his life.

It had been a little over a month since the funeral and business was pretty much back to normal. It was again time for Davis to go to Barcelona. He told Willie and his family Friday night that he would be leaving Sunday evening for Spain. No one seemed to mind, with the exception of Tyler and Stacey. He promised them that as soon as the top of their heads reached his belt, he would take them with him. That seemed fair to both.

When he arrived at the *Rancho de Montoya*, everything was going rather smoothly. The old property had not lost a beat and the property development across the fence was actually ahead of schedule. Irene was still in good health and, as always, was glad to see him. The daughters and grandchildren were not there this trip, so he and Irene had some extra time to discuss things old and new.

It hadn't been long since his father died and, for some reason, he missed Rodolpho even more than before. The people dearest to him were leaving, and this was creating an empty feeling inside. He was scheduled to return home the next day, but, after lunch, he decided to call Vittorio Benevento.

This was a wonderful surprise for Vittorio and Sophia. "Davis, how lovely to hear from you! What's that…of course you can visit us! We would love to see you again!"

Neither Gianni nor Angelo met him at the airport this time. Ernesto was trying to explain where his older brothers were, but his English was not as good as his brother's, so they decided to wait until they got to the ranch.

Vittorio and Sophia looked great after close to thirteen years, and this made Davis feel very happy that he had made the trip. Neither of them looked like they were going anywhere soon. He finally got around, at the much quieter dinner table, to asking where Gianni and Angelo had gone and what they were doing. Angelo had married and moved south to take over his wife's family's import-export business. Gianni had changed his major and decided to become a doctor. He was running a rehab hospital for the famous and the very wealthy that had abused themselves and needed to straighten out. This very private sanitarium was located in Switzerland and, from what Vittorio related, was doing quite well. Davis sat back and said, as if for verification, "Dr. Gianni Benevento, hmm…."

No business was done on this trip, but it really wasn't about that. The two families had done a goodly amount over the years. The main thing that it did for Davis was that he was able to "touch bases" with the people who were dear to him before it was too late. He stayed at the Beneventos' for a few more days before returning home feeling much better…about a few things anyway.

Chapter Thirty-Seven

In 1957, Elvis Presley fell in love with Graceland and purchased the estate for one hundred thousand dollars. Some say he stole it at that price, but how he acquired it is not important. The facts are that a beautiful southern-style mansion sat on thirteen acres of prime Memphis real estate.

The first eighteen years of his life were spent in poverty until he become famous. That brought riches and suddenly the young man who had gone without had more than he knew what to do with. First, he bought a half-a-dozen cars (mostly Cadillacs), then all kinds of toys, like dune buggies, sports equipment, etc. He had all kinds of fireworks and just about anything to amuse the twenty-year-old boy.

Another hobby he became interested in was horses. He naturally had to have the best. He purchased Arabians, Palominos, Tennessee Walkers, Appaloosas, and whatever he liked. He even bought a Palomino called "Rising Sun" and built a special home for it. He took the title from a hit song sang by the band The Animals, calling the barn, "House of the Rising Sun." Most of this was in the boring decade of the sixties. When we speak of boring, it means that Elvis was bored with all the stupid travel log movies and putting out mediocre soundtracks.

In the early to middle seventies, he was touring a lot, ultimately putting on a lot of weight, and depending more and more on prescription drugs. This curtailed much of his riding horses and other raucous activities. But he still loved horses and liked having them around just to enjoy and say they were his.

When he and Pricilla divorced in 1973, she retained custody of their daughter, Lisa Marie. It was a fair settlement that included having her visit him almost anytime he desired. The King would go through different stages and moods. When he wanted something special or unusual and didn't feel like putting forth the effort to go get it, he would send one or more of his "guys" out on a search. This could be almost anywhere in the country.

One day he decided that his little girl needed a horse. Not a pony, mind you, but a horse small enough for her to handle and feel comfortable riding. The guys drove and flew all over and would return with pictures and papers of horses from various farms. When Elvis viewed the photos, one by one he turned them down…all except one.

It was from The Willows ranch in southern Mississippi. One of his guys, when asked where this great-looking horse was from, said, "It's from down Hattiesburg way. The owner's name is DeLongpre, kind of a French soundin' name. But that's not all E, this guy that owns it—except for his gray hair, looks a lot like you when you were in good…."

Those famous eyes stared coldly back at the young man. He erupted, "When I was in good what, damn it!"

"Ah, well, younger I, I guess."

"Oh!" Elvis' mood changed suddenly as he paced back and forth. He stopped pacing and barked out, "Well, what the hell we doin' hangin' round here? Let's get down to Hattiesburg!"

Three years had gone by since The Colonel had passed away. The kids, Tyler and Stacey, were growing faster than the corn in the fields. Davis and Rebecca had celebrated their fortieth birthdays. Willie and Darcy were in good health and, every so often, were blessed with visits from their grandchildren. Lillian was nearing her late seventies and holding up rather well. She survived her husband's passing quite admirably but, as expected, never was quite the same since.

One morning Davis came to the office and found Willie in a mood…a little different than he had seen in a long time. It reminded him of when he was in his teens and his pal would set him up with some kind of practical joke. He looked at his friend, took off his hat, and sat down. He looked once more at Willie's grinning face and asked, "Okay, what's going on? You're up to something. Come on!"

"When you left after lunch yesterday, I thought you would be right back, but you weren't. We had some interesting buyers from Memphis. You know that little red mare that was defective at birth and we almost put to sleep? Well, she never became normal size but, as you know, was as healthy as hell. She'll never be any good to us, but these guys took pictures of her and said they may be back. That's not all."

"Not all?"

"Nope, they said they worked for Elvis Presley and would return in a few days…maybe with him!"

Suddenly Davis recalled those conversations with Rebecca when they were sipping sodas and gulping down cheeseburgers. That stuff about the resemblance flashed back all at once. He broke the pencil he was holding in half and uttered, "Good God! Wait 'till Becky hears about this!"

Rebecca *would* hear about "this," but that was only a fraction of what the following few days would do to change the lives of two men in particular…and those around them.

It didn't take long for the news of Elvis Presley's possible visit to The Willows to make the rounds. It affected everyone who lived there a little bit differently. Willie and Darcy thought it was wonderful. They had always liked his music. Most black people usually did. They identified with his treatment and feelings of certain songs. Elvis' roots did come from gospel and rhythm and blues. Darcy had made comments to her husband over the years, like, "He sings so good, and he's so handsome…kinda like our Davis."

"Yeah, honey, but have you ever heard *our* boy sing?" That would usually end most conversations.

The same afternoon that Willie broke the news to his partner, Rebecca was going over some notes for the five and six o'clock evening news. The intercom buzzer interrupted her thoughts. No matter what time of day it was or how good a mood the boss-lady was in, that tedious buzzer always irritated her. It was just one of the necessary evils one had to endure when running a business. Without looking up from her work, she said impatiently, "I'm here. What is it?"

Dar Lynn's sweet little drawl answered back, "There's a man on the phone for you!"

"Tell whoever it is that I'm very busy."

"It's your handsome husband."

"Maybe I'm not all that busy!"

Davis could tell by the sound of his bride's voice that she was indeed shocked. What he couldn't tell was if she were smiling or not. They talked for a few moments then blew invisible kisses good-bye.

She sat for a few minutes—more like a half an hour—wondering how she would tell her husband about the time she and Elvis met at the Memphis station. She hadn't thought it necessary at the time because she recalled the conversations they had many years ago about "him," and how disinterested Davis was then. Then a weird sensation came over her and gave her goose bumps. She said out loud to no one, "What if he remembers me? Naw! As many women as he's seen in his life? Naw, forget it." But she couldn't. She decided to tell Davis when she got home from work.

Davis and Rebecca didn't live at the big house any longer, and, although Jennie Hampton was still there, they worried about the two little women alone in the sprawling mansion. They made it a habit to go see them every day. If they couldn't, Darcy certainly did. After he informed Rebecca of the possibility of the visit from Elvis, Davis told Willie that he needed to go break the news to his mother.

Davis went through the back door like he had done since he was able to walk and still yelled for his mother. He heard Loretta's familiar voice answering, "She's not here, Mr. Davis."

He entered the kitchen to find Loretta cutting up vegetables for the evening meal. There weren't as many to prepare for these days, just the two women. "Do you know where she is, Loretta?"

"She said she needed to get out for a while. That uppity white lady picked her up earlier."

"You mean Ruthie?"

Loretta nodded and went back to her cutting.

Davis was surprised to hear about his mother going to her club. She had not been there or just about anywhere, for that matter, since The Colonel had been gone. He was surprised, but still happy to see her back in circulation. Yes, his mother was older and sometimes her mind wandered a little bit, but she was still a strong woman and, for her age, very full of life. However, he would have to wait until later that evening to inform her of their possible visitor.

Davis went back to the office to talk with Willie. Since he had a few hours to think about meeting Elvis, he was experiencing some strange anticipation coming from deep inside. At first, he cast it off as Elvis being such a big star and all, but, for some reason, it kept popping up as more than that. He asked Willie what he thought it was.

Willie listened like he always did and tried to come up with an explanation. All he could muster was what Davis had already been considering. "He *is* a big star, pard. Hell! I'm an old man and I'm excited! You ought to hear my wife go on about it!"

Davis grinned when he heard the "old man" stuff. Willie was only fifty-five. They hashed it over for close to an hour, then both agreed to let it lie and try to get some work done. Davis looked at his watch and figured his mother would be home soon.

Ruthie dropped her friend off and reminded her of their meeting scheduled for later that week. Lillian went right to the kitchen to see how Loretta was doing with dinner. There wasn't any real reason for this. It had just become a habit after all the years of having to feed her family. Loretta told her that Davis had been inquiring of her whereabouts and would be at the office until he had heard from her. She went to the wall phone and pressed the buttons. "Thurston, I'm home. Why don't you call Rebecca and tell her not to worry about dinner. Loretta over-cooked again."

"Sounds good, Momma. I came over earlier to tell you about a visitor that I think we're going to have tomorrow. You're not going to believe this, Momma. Elvis Presley might be here tomorrow to buy a horse!"

Lillian felt the color leaving her face and tried to answer but couldn't make any words come out.

An uncommonly dead silence was the only answer that came. "Are you there, Momma?" asked Davis.

It wasn't really that long until she recovered, but it seemed like it. She finally managed to say, "Well...that is really something.... Honey, I've got to go...see you tonight."

Lillian, after hanging up the phone, told Loretta to set four additional plates for dinner and hurried to the bedroom. She was about to make her way through The Colonel's suits to the safe once more, but, when she got as far as the bed, her legs became weak and she sat down on the edge. She took several short breaths then went to the bathroom to splash cold water on her face. The water felt good, so she repeated the splashing. She ran her left hand along the towel rack and, upon finding one, blotted her face, opened her eyes, then returned to the bed. After sitting there several minutes, she looked skyward and said pleadingly, "T. D., what do I do now?"

When Rebecca got home from work, she had her story pretty much together as to how she would tell her husband about meeting Elvis a few years before. She didn't think he would be really upset and knew he would probably ask her several times why it was never mentioned before. This train of thought was interrupted by two children who had seen their mother's car pull up and were charging down the steps from the back door of the big house. "Momma! Momma! We're having dinner with grandma tonight!"

While they did have dinner with grandma, grandma wasn't acting like her usual self. She seemed preoccupied. Davis asked her if she was excited about the possibility of seeing Elvis tomorrow. She put her wine glass down, fooled with her curls and said, "That's really nice, Thurston, but you know, truth be told, I never was that crazy about him. He sings okay, but all that jumping around and those silly looking clothes...."

They let the Elvis topic slip away and more or less made small talk for the remainder of dinner. When they finally got to their home at the top of the hill, Rebecca had some more news about the subject touched lightly upon at dinner earlier.

She was right about Davis' reaction to the Memphis meeting. He did ask a time or two why she had taken so long to bring it up, but then let it ride. Tomorrow would be another day...and indeed it was.

When Willie talked to Elvis' men a few days before, they hadn't actually said their boss *would* come back with them. He didn't miss much and never had. They left The Willows with a parting statement, "We'll be back in a couple days, but it'll be in the afternoon. We all wake up when Elvis does, and that's hardly ever early."

Willie started putting all the information together. The horse was for Elvis' little girl, making this special. He knew that if it were for either one of *his* children, he would definitely want to be there to give his approval. That's all he had to go on, but, when he explained this to Davis, his partner agreed that it made sense. Rebecca followed their line of thinking. The next morning she went to the station but came home for lunch.

It was difficult to keep a secret at The Willows. Even the least-important employees had always been treated like family and were always included in various festivities from time to time. That morning, most of the work was being done, but it seemed like everyone would look toward the entrance to the estate more often than they usually did.

About two-thirty in the afternoon, the partners were working in the office when they heard a sharp rapping on the door. Willie looked at Davis and yelled, "Come on in!"

One of the stable hands stuck his head halfway through the door and simply said, "There's a truck and trailer comin' down the drive, y'all."

The two men put down their work, grabbed their hats, and headed for the parking area. When Davis first saw the truck and horse trailer, he told Willie to go ahead because he wanted to go back to the office and buzz Rebecca up at the house on the hill. He returned as the vehicle came to a stop.

Willie recognized the same guys that were there from the first trip, but they were the only two that exited the truck. Davis and Willie looked at each other with a "no Elvis" expression and went to meet the men. Just as Willie was about to introduce them to Davis, they heard the sound of another vehicle approaching. They looked up to see a white Cadillac Deville turn into the parking area and pull to a stop. A young man in his twenties jumped out of the driver's side, went to the back and opened the right rear door, stood, and waited.

From Davis and Willie's vantage point, they saw what appeared to be a black walking stick with a silver tip followed by a black boot and pant leg. The driver extended his hand; it was taken by another hand that was heavily jeweled. Then, from behind the car door, emerged the passenger...and there he was.

Darcy had seen the truck and trailer pull up through her kitchen window and saw the two men get out. When she didn't see Elvis, she sighed slightly and looked down at the teapot she was filling. When she looked up again, she saw what everyone else did. She dried her hands then went out to join the others. As she was leaving her white rock-lined pathway to the parking lot, she saw Rebecca walking toward her about fifty feet away, so she waited for her friend. They watched while Davis, Willie, and Elvis closed the gap between them.

Elvis took Willie's hand in greeting, and Willie was the first to speak. "Elvis, I'm Willie Hampton and this is...."

"Jesse Garon!" Elvis gasped.

Willie, although interrupted, continued, "No, Elvis. This is Davis DeLongpre."

Elvis caught himself and, to avoid further embarrassment, took Davis' hand, shook it with fervor, and said, "I'm sorry, Mr. DeLongpre, for a moment you just...."

Rebecca and Darcy saw this and waited where they stood while the three men walked their way. Darcy whispered, "Rebecca, what happened? From all the magazine pictures and movies, I thought Davis and 'him' looked a lot alike, but now...."

Rebecca looked at the black hair, the bloated and considerably overweight King of Rock and Roll and said quietly back to Darcy, "Wow! You're right. Last time I saw him, he looked so much like my Davis that it made my tummy flip-flop. There's still a little resemblance, but Jesus. Elvis is still good-looking, but, boy, he sure looks different!"

As the gap closed and they were almost at arm's length, Davis began introductions. He pointed to Darcy and said, "Elvis, I'd like you to meet Darcy, Willie's wife, and this is my wife, Rebecca. These two wide-eyed kids are our children, Tyler and Stacey."

Elvis nodded to the kids and then looked back at Rebecca. He said in an almost practiced southern gentlemanly drawl, "Rebecca, ma'am, I could be wrong, and forgive me if I'm rude, but haven't we met a while back?"

"Yes, Elvis. We did. You were doing a promo tape at the radio/TV station I was working at in Memphis, and it *was* a long time...."

"Oh, yeah, you were the news lady. You know I was telling Joe the other day, I wonder what ever happened to Miss Thompson. Oh...I guess it's not Miss Thompson anymore, is it?"

The next few moments were filled with little bits and pieces of polite conversation among all present. After Elvis had gone out of his way to kneel down and shake Tyler and Stacey's hands, Rebecca said to the kids, "Why don't you two go tell your grandma that Elvis Presley is here, okay? Hurry up!"

All the grownups had decided to go look at the horse that was to be Lisa Marie's. As they neared the entrance to the barn, Tyler ran up behind them and said breathlessly, "Daddy, Loretta said, 'Grandma isn't home! She left before lunch with Miss Ruthie!'"

Davis and Rebecca exchanged curious glances. Davis glanced at Elvis to see him looking back...they would repeat this over the course of the next few hours. There was some kind of electricity that they both felt, but neither said a word or would for sometime.

Davis and Rebecca, along with Willie and Darcy, gave Elvis and his "guys" a tour of their operation. The King seemed to enjoy himself and was very attentive to what they were showing him. He also asked several questions about the different mixes of horses. He said several times, "I've got a pretty nice little ol' set-up at Graceland, but it sure ain't anything compared to this!"

His guys had been with him several years and mentioned to each other, when the rest of the group were out of earshot, that they hadn't seen their boss interested in anything this much in a long time.

Rebecca asked him to stay and join them for supper, but Elvis declined, saying he wanted to get the horse to Graceland because Lisa Marie was coming in from California the next morning. Before they said good-bye, Elvis took Davis aside and said, "Ah, Davis, I want to thank you for everything, your hospitality and the fine little horse. Could I ask you another favor? I'd like to come back again. Do you think that would be all right?"

Davis looked him straight in the eyes, paused for a few seconds, and said,

"I think I'd like that...Elvis."

The group stood and watched the truck, trailer, and white Cadillac move down the driveway, turn left and fade into the coming twilight. It had been a big day, a day no one at The Willows would soon forget.

The DeLongpres said "goodnight" to the Hamptons who headed for their home. Davis and Rebecca decided to go ask Loretta if she'd heard from Lillian. The roundish lady was about to go to her part of the house for the evening but paused when she saw them coming in the back door. When they asked if Lillian had called, the answer was "Yes. She had decided to have dinner at the club with the ladies and would be home around eight-thirty or nine."

Lillian's behavior was a bit puzzling to her son and daughter-in-law. She never acted like this. True, she had mentioned the fact that she never cared for Elvis, but this lady had been a gracious hostess all her life, plus she had always shown a big interest in the family's business and social activities. They agreed as they lay in bed later that there was something really strange here, but that wasn't *all*. Something else was strange. Davis felt something inside that he couldn't explain to Rebecca...or even himself.

Rebecca interrupted his thoughts as she kidded him, "Do you remember, honey, a long time ago, when I told you I thought you and he looked a lot alike?"

Davis looked at her a few seconds before he could answer. He then said uneasily, "Well, maybe a little back then, but not now I hope! I think he's really let himself go!"

Rebecca smiled back at him but didn't answer. She just kissed him on the ear and snuggled up before drifting off into a sound sleep. Davis wasn't quite so lucky but soon lost out to tiredness.

Lillian had missed Elvis by a few hours. After Ruthie dropped her off, she went to her kitchen for a cup of tea. She smiled as she saw the silver tea decanter and the two raisin-oatmeal cookies on a plate beside it. As she was warming the tea, she recalled all the years the sweet lady had been working for her. She was now more of a friend than an employee. She finished the tea and snack and went up to bed. She, too, would have trouble getting to sleep.

As her eyes slowly opened and closed during that mystical time between awake and sleeping, she thought she heard a voice. For a brief instant, she saw her departed husband standing at the foot of the bed saying, "He has to keep us alive, Lill. Do the right thing."

She opened her eyes wide and sat up, but T. D. was gone. She slowly lie back down and felt her heart doing double time. She began to calm down, but she heard the words, "Do the right thing...." echoing over, and over, and over. She slept on and off until after sun up, and suddenly realized what T. D. had been trying to tell her from somewhere out yonder. If she told her son what was in that box in the safe, it would ruin everything The Colonel had strived for, all his life. She didn't want that to happen. The DeLongpre name and legacy must and *would* go on. She went to the safe, took out the papers, and placed them on the logs in the fireplace. With one simple turn of the gas handle, the DeLongpre legacy would live on.

Elvis' closest friends from his entourage were starting to get concerned for him. True, they had been concerned for some time about his drug intake, but now they couldn't seem to get through to him. They couldn't and most of the doctors didn't care. It was almost impossible to say, "No!" to Elvis. This latest thing, however, was even more tedious. Ever since that trip to The Willows, it had been, "Jesse this, Jesse that, and I know that's Jesse!" The guys didn't know if it was the boss or the drugs talking. They would try consoling him by saying, "Now E, we know there's a resemblance, but you've been to Jesse's grave a thousand times. Hell! You've even taken us up there! It's impossible, E, try to calm down!"

Sometimes it would work, and other times it had no effect at all. In the past few years, he had been reading a lot of heavy mystic religious material, and, when they tried to steady him, he would say, "I know it's Jesse. He may have gone somewhere else. He may be dead, but I think God has sent me someone in his place!"

Elvis fought the urge to call and discuss this with Davis; something made him hold off on that. He wanted to, but he also didn't want to lose him...or scare him away. He was sure of one thing, he had to go back to The Willows, and soon.

Nineteen seventy-six was a busy year for Davis. He and Willie had won several major races and were about ready for the "Big Three." The Derby, the Preakness, and the Belmont were not that far from reality. He would make four trips to Spain, and then there was his new "friend," Elvis. His new friend *first* came to visit about two months after buying the horse for his daughter.

The next few times, he would come late at night when everything was more or less shut down at The Willows. At first Davis wasn't sure he cared for those late calls and visits, only because he wasn't used to being up late. However, it *was* Elvis, and it didn't happen all that often. He didn't know exactly why, but he did sense urgency in the man's demeanor. Another thing he observed was Elvis' health. It seemed to be getting worse.

On one visit, Elvis had to talk about where they all came from. The Presleys originally came from Scotland and he wanted to know where the DeLongpres originated. Davis could only tell him that it was a town not far from Philadelphia, Pennsylvania. This really didn't satisfy Elvis, so he asked, "But where were you actually born?"

"Well, my momma and daddy told me that they were on their honeymoon in the Caribbean when I was starting to make my momma show big time. They finished the cruise and were on their way home when, according to them, I wouldn't wait. Anyway, my birth certificate says I was born south of here in Poplarville. How about you?"

Elvis had mulled this over for a few seconds when he realized Davis had asked *him* a question. He cleared his throat and said, "Uh, I was born in Tupelo, up north, January 8th, in '35."

"Wow! I was born on the twelfth, same month and year!"

They talked about many things that had occurred during their younger years and found out that as much as they seemed alike, there was at least that many things that were different. Elvis had known poverty, Davis never had. Elvis' mother died young, Davis' mother was still alive. Elvis' father was still alive, and Davis had recently lost his.

One night as Elvis was getting ready to leave, he asked, "I know your daddy is gone, but you still have your mother. I'd like to meet her. Do you think I could?"

Davis of course didn't know why, but knew from a couple of statements his mother had made, and the fact that she'd made herself scarce the first time Elvis came to visit, that she didn't care to meet him. He covered up by saying, "Well, Elvis, she'd probably like to meet you too, but she goes to bed early and you hardly ever get here 'til midnight. Maybe if you...."

"Okay, I see what you mean. Maybe someday."

Davis walked Elvis to the door, and they shook hands. They bid each other so long. Elvis took about three steps, turned around suddenly, and asked, "Davis, I don't want to sound weird or nothin', but let me ask you, do you feel a little strange when we're together?"

"Yeah, I do, a little, but I thought it was just me," said Davis a little uneasily.

Elvis continued, "A couple of my guys said that you look a bit like me when I was younger. That pissed me off a little!"

This made Davis laugh, and, in a minute, it did Elvis also. It was Davis' turn to wonder as he said, "Well, you know that old story about everybody having a double."

"Yeah, I guess you're right," Elvis agreed. "I'll se ya later on."

Chapter Thirty-Eight

The summer of '76 had almost taken its final bow. The trees were changing color and *warm* days were fewer and shorter. One would wear a jacket in the morning and, by noon, wished they'd left it at home, or just the opposite in the evening, when one would wish one brought it. The nights were still clear and cool, and even a visitor to these parts could tell by the local's state of mind that the holidays were approaching.

It had been several weeks since Davis had been awake after midnight. This meant he hadn't heard from Elvis for a while. He wondered if he was well. *Damn it, I miss him!* This went on until after Thanksgiving, when one afternoon a stable employee notified the partners in the office that there was a delivery. Davis asked Willie, "Are we expecting anything?"

Willie shrugged his shoulders and stood up. After all the years together, this meant, "Let's go see!"

They walked out to the parking area and saw a young man standing in front of a non-descript van with his foot propped up on the bumper. Davis thought he looked familiar from that distance, and he was right. It was the same fellow who opened the door for Elvis on his first visit. Willie walked closer and asked, "What do you have for us, young man?"

The driver smiled, shuffled to the side-doors of the vehicle, and slid them open. Both men stood there with open mouths as they observed the entire van packed with all different sizes and colors of Christmas presents. They looked at each other, then to the driver, who said, "Mr. Presley said to wish all of you, 'Merry Christmas!'"

There were gifts for the DeLongpres and their children, the Hamptons, and their grandchildren, and for everyone else that Elvis had shaken hands with on his first trip to The Willows. The young man unloaded all the packages and then said he had to get back to Graceland. He left Davis and Willie standing by a pile of packages they could barely see over. Willie commented dryly, "I've heard he does that!"

The so-called "Memphis Mafia," was not all that thrilled with this latest habit their boss had acquired. Ever since his Army days, they had gone with him everywhere. They protected him, coddled him, and were on the spot every time he snapped his fingers. Now, he was making these trips without them. The only one who went with him was this new kid, Eddie, who'd only been with the group less than a year. He was some sort of cousin of one of the guys Elvis had met in Germany. It was hard to tell if they were worried for his safety, or possibly just upset because they weren't invited. But they all kept their mouths shut because of Elvis' mood swings in the last year or two. One could get fired just looking at him wrong.

The holiday season was as wonderful as it always seemed to be in paradise. It had its empty spots, the obvious being the big hole left by The Colonel's passing, but overall, it was very nice. There were plates of cookies and other holiday treats that delighted the DeLongpre kids and Hampton grandchildren. When darkness appeared, all the Christmas lights on the buildings and trees came on with one magic pull of a switch. It looked like a place that Santa would like to enjoy a glass of eggnog or two after his rounds.

In the middle of the week following New Year's Day, Davis and his family were just finishing the evening meal. Davis, as his father before him, liked to take this time to see how his loved ones had spent their day. He had just asked Tyler a question about one of his classes when the phone rang. Davis looked at his watch and said jokingly, "Well, I know it's not Elvis."

This drew a slight chuckle from Rebecca as he got up to answer the persistent ringing. *Well, he was wrong this time.*

"Hi, Davis. Looks like two old men are going to turn forty-two next week."

Davis got over the surprise and answered, "I guess there's nothing we can do about that, Elvis."

"Well, I think we can. I don't want to take you away from your family, but what would you say if I came down a few days after? I need to talk…it's important!"

"I don't see how that would be a problem. Talk to you when you get here."

It was around the fifteenth when the man from Memphis called and said he was on his way. Again, it was after 10:00 p.m. when he and his driver arrived. It saddened Davis to see that he looked even worse. Rebecca and the kids had gone to bed, so they would be able to talk as long as they wanted.

Davis went out the back door of the den and returned with two medium-sized logs and stoked the fireplace. He asked his guest if he was comfortable, then sat down and asked, "Okay, my friend. What's on your mind?"

Elvis went on for close to an hour and Davis listened as well as he could. Sometimes he rambled a little and his listener would have to stop him when he wasn't connecting a few of his thoughts. He wasn't drunk, but Davis could tell he was on something. It wasn't bad, but his speech sometimes slurred around the edges every few minutes. His eyes would water and his voice would choke up slightly, but he managed to finally get through it. He stopped and looked around the room, as if searching for an ending. A minute or so later, he said with exhaustion in his voice, "Davis, I'm so tired. I'm not well, and The God-damned Colonel keeps booking me solid. My performances are very poor quality and my doctor said if I didn't take a rest, 'I'm going to die.' I don't want to die. And I'm tired, so very, very tired…I'm just plain tired of being 'Elvis'…of *having* to be Elvis. I don't want to be him anymore. Can you understand that?"

Davis had to absorb this for a few moments before he could comment. He bought some time by saying he was thirsty. Elvis said he was, too. Davis excused himself and in minutes returned with a pitcher of ice water. This tasted great to both men. He then asked his guest, "I know there's a reason for you telling me all this, and I'm trying to understand what you're going through. The outside world has no idea what it costs to be a star, do they?"

All Elvis could mutter was, "Whew!"

Davis continued, "Do you want me to do anything? Is there anything I *can* do? If I can, I will. You know that!"

They talked for another hour, and then Elvis began nodding off. Davis was very tired also, for it had been a heavy and taxing conversation. Davis suggested they spend the night, but Eddie said he'd better get his boss home, as it was it would be after dawn before they got back to Graceland.

The Colonel and Lillian had brought up their son in a "Christian" atmosphere. They tried to instill in him that "Christian" did not necessarily apply to any particular religion. You could be a "Good Christian" and never set foot inside a church. However, he was taught that there was some kind of divine guidance out there somewhere, and he believed this. He thought maybe there could be something in what Elvis said about, "God sending you to me." He started believing that just maybe there was a reason they had met. The resemblance between the two men was indeed curious, but, like he had told

Rebecca years earlier, "Everyone has a double somewhere on the planet." That's as far as he wanted to pursue it at this time.

He did feel compelled to answer his friend's cry for help. He told Elvis, as he was leaving, to keep in touch every week or so. Elvis gave him a private phone number he had just installed that was known only to he and Eddie.

In the following weeks, Davis began thinking like his father. He spent hours on the phone talking to people he could trust and who he knew his father had helped. It was difficult for him not to discuss this with his wife or Willie. If he could do what he wanted to do, what his heart was telling him to do, there were only a few people that could know. No one at The Willows could, at least for now.

Just as The Colonel had done for over fifty years, Davis planned every move with the precision of a fine Swiss watch. It took months of testing and planning and many impatient calls from Elvis, but around the first of August, Davis felt that everything was ready. He dialed Elvis' private number, "I'm sorry it took so long, but now we're ready. You need to come down here once more, and let me go through everything with you. Be even more careful this time!"

Elvis and Eddie came at the usual time the following night.

Chapter Thirty-Nine

Dr. Gianni Benevento had made it through another long day. The profession he had chosen for his life's work over ten years ago was indeed very lucrative but also very time consuming. At times, it pushed his tolerance envelope right to the edge. Through the doors to his exclusive rehab center, passed many rich and famous people. Their various problems included almost everything from drug and alcohol abuse to overeating and nervous breakdowns.

Once whoever it was became a patient, they were not promised cures. That could only happen if that is what they really wanted. One thing he could promise was complete and guaranteed privacy…at a price, of course.

He took off his glasses and rubbed his tired eyes, then spun his swivel chair around and watched the golden glow the sun made as it disappeared over the snowy mountain peaks. His window framed the view like a beautiful painting. His trance-like stare was interrupted by the phone ringing on his desk. His receptionist, who was on her way out, said, "Dr. Benevento, I know you said, 'No calls,' but this gentleman says he is an old friend from America."

The doctor said sarcastically, "Hell, almost everybody I know is an old friend from America these days. Oh, hell, put him on."

"Dr. Benevento? Dr. Gianni Benevento?"

"Yes…. This is he."

"I was just thinking, you should call Angelo, and let's go on a romp through Italy for a few weeks?"

The doctor was caught speechless, but for only a few seconds…then, his whole face lit up, "This can't be who I think it is! Davis DeLongpre?"

"The same. How's everything in Zurich?"

"Busy, very busy! Davis, my father told me you came to see them. I've been wondering if I'd hear from you! To what do I attribute my good fortune for this call?"

"Gianni, I need you to do something very special for me. Something very special for a very unique person—who, I have to say, is in a bad way!"

Dr. Benevento began to explain all the various services available at his hospital, and all the discretion that was practiced, when Davis cut him off, "Gianni, I know about all that. That's why I called you. Now let me tell you who and what I need for you to do for him."

The doctor listened to his friend and when it got to the part where the patient's identity was mentioned, he was rendered speechless. He was finally able to gasp, "Incredible! My friend, you sure know how to pick them!"

Elvis had been waiting a long time while Davis was working out his plan. He did a few concerts, but his heart wasn't in them. Most of the time, he just stayed in his room and tried to get high. When asked, "why?" several times by various people around him, he would reply, "I'd rather feel nothing, than be in pain." That was how most of the conversations ended.

When he found out that Davis wanted to meet with him, he made the effort to stay straight and did. As he sat with Davis in the den, the fire warmed him and made him feel at ease. It seemed like every time he visited, he attained a certain degree of serenity.

Davis gave him a few minutes to settle in and began to unfold his plan. He stoked the fire, then walked by Elvis, gave him a pat on the shoulder, and said, "I hope you're dead serious about me wanting to help you. If you have any doubts, we'd better stop right here. Everything has to be done exactly as I say, and I mean right to the letter, or it won't work. Do you really want to stop being Elvis?"

Elvis hung his head for a few seconds, sighed, and wrung his big hands. He looked up at Davis and simply said, "Yes!"

"Okay, first we're going to need an inside man. Someone you can trust. Is there anyone you have in mind?"

"That would be Eddie. He'll do anything I ask, and, if he doesn't, he's dead!"

"Okay, everyone on this earth, with the exception of the people I've chosen to carry this out, is going to have to believe you've died."

Elvis gasped, then exhaled and let Davis continue.

"Now, Elvis, this means no one can know what we are up to. Myself, well this is something I would, except for you, never, ever do. It really goes against everything I believe in, but something is telling me to take the chance. For some reason, I think I *owe* you. Don't ask me why, let's just do it!" Davis continued to explain his plan for close to an hour, then paused and asked if there were any questions.

"I've got one or two. I hate doing this to my fans and friends, but it's gone too far now. It's my turn. I just want to see what it would feel like to be somewhat of an ordinary human being. You say *nobody* can know.... How about my daughter?"

"I'm sorry, not even her." Seeing Elvis' countenance fall, Davis continued, "Maybe after a year or so, when everything cools down, I can work something out. Yeah, I can do that. We'll just have to see when." The two men shook hands and the adventure was on.

Ten days later, a little after 3:00 a.m., the DeLongpres' private jet made its last contact with the Raleigh, North Carolina tower, banked and climbed to its cruising altitude of twenty-eight thousand feet, then set course for Zurich, Switzerland.

About fifteen hundred miles west of the Zurich airport, Davis looked at a worn out Elvis who was sound asleep. He saw his chest rise and fall, and the slight snoring that came forth, and mused, "He sure doesn't look much like a 'king' now." Minutes later he walked up to the cockpit and sat behind the navigator's seat.

Captain Henderson saw him and gave him a sly grin. "Things are sure a mess in Memphis. I just heard over the radio that Elvis Presley died. How about that?"

Davis shook his head slowly from side to side and whispered, "Yeah, how about that?"

Davis introduced Elvis to Dr. Gianni Benevento and again was promised the ultimate in secrecy. The hospital had an excellent reputation for this, so Davis wasn't really too worried. The only worried one was Elvis. This was the first time in his forty-two years that his parents or close friends weren't with him. He begged Davis to stay for a few days, but that was against the rules. The doctor advised, "It's better to get this program started immediately. It has worked all these years, and I won't deter from the formula."

Elvis didn't like this, but he'd made Davis a promise and decided for once to listen to someone. Davis and the doctor went to dinner that evening and relived that wonderful romp through Italy seventeen years ago. The next morning, he was on his way back home to his family, who thought he was just "on another trip to Spain."

The hot item at The Willows and for most of the world was the passing of the King of Rock and Roll. The minute Davis returned home, everyone from his family, including the Hamptons, to all who worked there were bombarding him with questions and comments.... "He was just here a short time ago! I can't believe he's gone! When was the last time you saw him, Davis?"

This went on for days, and he expected it would be that way, but eventually it tapered off. It would remain a shock to everyone there for some time. However, "The biggest star the world had ever known," had been there, right there at their Willows! For that, you couldn't blame them. It *was* a big deal. As it had following The Colonel's death, The Willows would eventually return to normal, as, "The Willows always had and always would."

The rest of 1977 passed without any additional earthshaking events. Nineteen seventy-eight said, "hello" in a cold and damp way. It rained on Davis' forty-third birthday. He had called Elvis four days before and wished him happiness on his. Dr. Benevento informed him that his star patient was doing better than he expected at this point. "A little rough at first, but everything is under control," he would say proudly.

Davis had been making the trip to Barcelona about four times a year since Rodolpho died. He didn't really have to, but he felt better about things if he did. Anyway, it was time to go again. He went through the usual pleadings from Tyler and Stacey to take them along. This time they were a bit more persistent, so he gave them his most excellent promise, "Y'all are in school now. As soon as summer vacation comes, I promise we'll go!"

Davis found Ireñe in reasonably good health. It seemed that no matter how she was feeling before, when Davis came over, he was like a tonic for her. It kept a piece of Rodolpho alive in her mind, and that felt wonderful.

At breakfast the second day, Ireñe asked many questions about Lillian. She always *did* ask, but not to this extent. She took a bite from her rolled-up tortilla and washed it down with some fresh-squeezed orange juice. She waited while Davis swallowed his mouthful of coffee and said, "I sure miss Lillian. I haven't seen her since your first wedding. It really would be nice to walk in her rose garden once more."

Davis mulled this over while he took another sip of after-breakfast coffee. He shoved his cup away, dabbed his mouth with his napkin, and refolded it. He looked at Ireñe with a bit of mischief in his eyes, "Ireñe, how do you feel? Do you feel strong?"

"Yes, I feel pretty good for an old lady (she admitted to being seventy-five). Why do you ask, my boy?"

Davis reached over and covered her hand with his. With a big smile he said, "Come back home with me! Momma would love to see you, and it would be good for you, too!"

This was a bit more than Ireñe could handle this early in the day. She half-cried and half-laughed. "Davis! So extravagant! Just like my Rodolpho. No, my boy, that is just too...."

"Ireñe!"

Somewhere over the Atlantic and about halfway to their destination, Ireñe finished her light lunch. She wasn't much of a traveler but marveled about how food tasted differently at thirty thousand feet. She took her bonnet off, placed her shoes next to the plush leather seat, and leaned her head back. She looked over at Davis and smiled happily, "This is *muy, muy* wonderful. How can this old lady ever repay you?"

Davis laughed, leaned forward, and looked straight into her beautiful but seasoned Spanish eyes. "Ireñe, you and Rodolpho have meant so much in my life. I would need two lifetimes and still couldn't repay y'all."

Ireñe smiled, took her hanky from her little pocket-sized purse and dried a tear. Davis leaned back and closed his eyes. A few minutes later he opened them and saw Ireñe looking out the window. He said, "Ireñe, there is one thing you could do for me, if you'd like to."

She sat up and smoothed her dress, folded her hands on her lap, and said, "Oh! There is? All you have to do is name it, and if an old lady can...."

"Ireñe, get rid of that old lady stuff. You and my momma are still beautiful!" He began again, "You see, I have a friend who is in trouble and he needs a place to...."

Ireñe put up her hands. "Now, Davis, I said anything, but if your friend is in trouble with the *Federales*, Rodolpho would never...."

Davis laughed at the starch still coming from this grand lady who was on her way to visit his mother. "No, no, no, Ireñe. It's nothing like that. He is not well, *physically*. He's in the hospital recovering and will be there for a while longer. Anyway, when he's released from the doctor's care, I want him to be somewhere peaceful and away from the crowds. You see, he's kind of famous and needs to get away. I was thinking he could do that on twenty thousand acres, thirty miles from the city. I wouldn't ask, but he's kinda...like a 'brother' to me."

Ireñe didn't reply immediately. She may have been an "old lady" as she referred to herself as, but those eyes, even that third eye, were clear and bright. They caused him to shiver slightly as they looked right into his soul.

He sat uncomfortably for several seconds, and then saw the woman's face break into a smile. As she chuckled, she said, "Famous, huh? If I didn't know he had passed away, I'd think it was Elvis Presley."

This froze Davis in his seat with his mouth wide open and no words coming out. Ireñe saw this and could only say, *"Oh mi Dios!"*

No more discussion was needed for both to understand that this conversation would not go beyond the inner shell of the plane. The request was granted and that was the end of it.

Daniel Brown pulled the black Cadillac up to the gate and showed his pass to the guard. It was merely a formality, after all the times he'd met the DeLongpre's private plane, but it was still procedure. He drove to the deplaning area and shut off the engine. He pushed his hat back and took the lid off his coffee. As the DeLongpres' driver of some twenty-five years opened the paper to the sports page, he heard the squeal of tires as the jet made yet another safe landing. Daniel noticed an extra passenger walking down the ramp with his boss.

Davis waved and they walked to meet him. "Daniel, this is my friend, Ireñe Montoya."

"Yes, sir, I remember her from your first wedding."

"Oh, yes."

This was the second time Davis had heard "first wedding" in as many days. The image flashed in his mind again, and again he brushed it off.

There is something inside a man that never grows up for some reason. It has always been that way; little boys thrive on giving their mothers a hard time or at least surprising them. On the way home from the airport, Davis picked up the car phone and dialed the kitchen phone number.

When Davis was in Spain or out of town with Willie, Lillian insisted that Rebecca and the kids had supper at the big house. She didn't know exactly when to expect him home, so she always made sure there was plenty of southern home cooking just in case. The phone on the wall began ringing just as Loretta was serving the salads. Lillian threw up her hands in a "who could this be?" gesture and picked it up. "This is Mrs. DeLongpre.... Oh, hi, honey. I was hoping it was you!"

"Momma, I hope Loretta cooked a lot. I'm bringing someone home for dinner."

"Now, Thurston, you know I hate surprises!" she lied. "Who is it?"

"Oh, just somebody I met in Spain."

He didn't give her a chance to reply and hung up the phone, giggling like some little imp. Ireñe laughed and gave him a "shame on you" with the shaking of her index finger.

Lillian walked back to the table and called Loretta to have her put the salads in the fridge. She looked at Rebecca and, in a curious tone said, "Your husband is bringing a guest to dinner. From Spain, no less!"

They wouldn't have long to wait. Tyler saw the headlights through the kitchen window and jumped up yelling, "Daddy's home. He's home!" He ran out of the kitchen to the big hall with Stacey right behind. Davis gave them both a hug then pointed to the strange lady, placed his finger over Tyler's lips and said, "Shush!"

With the kids staring at her, Ireñe walked in front of them through the kitchen door and simply said, "*Hola*, Lillian. Nice to see you."

Seeing these two old friends hugging in the middle of Lillian's kitchen was just another in a long line of DeLongpre Kodak moments. It probably added five years to both of their lives.

Dr. Gianni Benevento had just spent an hour with Elvis. It had been eighteen months since his arrival at the Zurich Mountain Hospital. Except for a few tirades by the super star, it had gone rather smoothly. Elvis had lost about sixty-five pounds and was about as healthy as he would ever get. He had gone close to two years without a dye job and his hair was completely gray. He looked older than his forty-four years, but, with everything he had put his body through, it was no wonder.

The doctor told him during their final session, "I have done everything possible to make you better, and I must commend you for the effort you have put forth. I know it hasn't been easy, but I'm proud of you. I cannot promise you a long life. You have beaten yourself up quite a bit. But, if you stay clean and watch your diet, I'm sure you'll have another ten or twelve years of good life, probably more."

Elvis had worked harder at this than he had trying to make himself a star. He looked at the smiling doctor and said as innocently as a little boy, "Okay, Doc. Now what?"

"Well, I have instructions for you to call your 'friend' Davis DeLongpre. How does that sound?"

"Sounds damn good to me!"

When Davis saw Elvis with the gray hair and minus sixty-five pounds, he now realized what people had been saying, his wife in particular. Elvis looked quite a bit older, but it still gave him goose bumps. It was something he just didn't want to get any farther into, maybe someday, but not now.

Davis and Elvis thanked and bid good-bye to Dr. Benevento, then boarded the white jet. As the plane attained the necessary altitude to clear the snowy mountain peaks, it made a one hundred and eighty degree turn, and set a course southwest. When they leveled off, Elvis loosened his belt and asked the obvious question, "Where are we headed?"

"Elvis, you like horses, don't you?"

"Yeah. You know I do. Why?"

"We just happen to be going someplace that has one hell of a lot of them!" Davis left him hanging, then leaned back in the chair and closed his eyes. Elvis had learned during the last year and a half that he was no longer in charge, so, after a few minutes, he did the same thing.

Davis wasn't really sleeping. He had just put himself in sort of a hypnotic state and was reviewing what he had just done. He didn't feel especially bad about it. He knew that he had followed his heart and had quite possibly saved a precious life. Still, he wondered if his father would have done anything like this. Would his father approve of what he'd done? He then tried to fathom the mind-boggling wealth The Colonel had left and what a big responsibility went along with it. For one of the first times, he not only missed his father terribly, but he would've given anything if he could be with him right now for counsel. As he was almost asleep, he thought he heard a deep voice saying, "You did good, my son." He opened his eyes briefly, shook his head as if to clear it, and then drifted off. He didn't know how long he slept on the short flight, but the next thing he heard was the cabin speaker.

"Davis, we're sixteen minutes from Barcelona International."

Elvis had also heard this and could only manage to ask, "Barcelona, like in Spain? Oh, well."

Ireñe's driver had been waiting for them. The thin-mustached Spaniard asked why the flight was late and if there had been any problems. In Davis' steadily improving Spanish, he assured the man all was well.

"A little choppy air," Captain Henderson chimed in.

As they were loading the car, Davis told Rex that he would be a few days. He added jokingly, "You guys bring your golf clubs?"

"Sure did, boss!"

"Well, it's up to you. If you'd like to check into the hotel Casa de Oro and sign my name, you shouldn't have any trouble. Just tell the owner to call me at the ranchero if she has a problem."

Ireñe had thoroughly enjoyed herself during the couple of weeks spent with Lillian at The Willows. It was like an intravenous youth injection to both ladies. However, the whole time she was there, and, ever since her return home, she remembered the conversation she and Davis had on the plane on the way to Mississippi. She had looked up several times, asking, "Rodolpho, why am I forever cursed with the third eye?"

This morning she woke up, and the first thing on her mind was how she was going to handle her promise to Davis. She knew that in a matter of hours, the man her Rodolpho had thought of as his son would soon be arriving with…"Him." She had mixed emotions, to put it mildly. As much as she tried to prepare herself for when the moment arrived, when it did, she knew she hadn't prepared nearly enough.

When she opened the door and saw the two men standing there, she didn't know which to hug first. She had seen Davis recently, and the "other" man did look a few years older. Still, it took a few more seconds before "welcome!" finally came out, but it did.

Davis gave most of the ranch employees the next three days off. His reason, as he told Ireñe, was to get the "new guy" comfortable with his new environment without too much interference. He went over the workings of the ranchero for two full days. They drove around and Davis pointed out all the main areas that were part of the day-to-day operations. He told Elvis repeatedly that there was no pressure on him, and there would be no major decisions for him to make.

"I've set it up to where it almost runs itself. The main thing needed here is a figurehead and a presence the people can identify with. Remember there is a hotline from here to our office at The Willows. All I have left to say is, you've come a long way in a year-and-a-half. You now have what you told me you wanted. You are no longer Elvis."

The two men embraced, followed by Davis and Ireñe enjoying a long hug. Davis picked up his coat and, as he opened the front door, turned and said, "I'll see ya'll in a couple months."

At breakfast the following morning, a sharp knocking on the door interrupted Ireñe and Elvis. Elvis looked at Ireñe as she motioned him to go open it. One of the workers began to blurt out, "Señor Davis, the big mare is about to…." The man looked at Elvis and confusion spread over his face. He finally said, "Señor Davis, are you feeling okay?"

"Ah…yeah. I'm fine."

"Señor, you told me to tell you when she was ready…do you still want to…."

Elvis turned to Ireñe and she gave him a reassuring nod. He turned and answered the excited young man….

"You bet I would. I always enjoy the beginning of a new life."